# Eros and Ethics

SUNY series, Insinuations: Philosophy, Psychoanalysis, Literature

Charles Shepherdson, editor

# Eros and Ethics

*Reading Jacques Lacan's Seminar VII*

MARC DE KESEL

Translated by
SIGI JÖTTKANDT

First published in Dutch by Acco Publishing Company, Brusselsestraat 153, 3000 Louvain, Belgium, in 2001.

The translation is funded by NWO, the state institute funding scientific research in The Netherlands.

Published by
State University of New York Press, Albany

For information, contact State University of New York Press, Albany, NY
www.sunypress.edu

Production by Eileen Meehan
Marketing by Michael Campochiaro

**Library of Congress Cataloging-in-Publication Data**

Kesel, Marc De.
    [Eros & ethiek. English]
    Eros and ethics : reading Jacques Lacan's Seminar VII / Marc De Kesel ; translated by Sigi Jottkandt.
        p. cm. — (SUNY series, insinuations: philosophy, psychoanalysis, literature)
    Includes bibliographical references and index.
    ISBN 978-1-4384-2609-9 (hbk. : alk. paper)
    ISBN 978-1-4384-2610-5 (pbk. : alk. paper)
    1. Lacan, Jacques, 1901–1981. Ethique de la psychanalyse, 1959–1960.
2. Psychoanalysis—Moral and ethical aspects.   3. Psychoanalysis—Philosophy.
I. Jöttkandt, Sigi, 1965–   II. Title.

    BF173.L1463K4713 2009
    150.19'5—dc22                                                    2009005425

10 9 8 7 6 5 4 3 2 1

# Contents

# Introduction

A psychoanalytic cure is a strange business. Several times a week for a number of years, two people share a room where one, lying on a sofa and deliberately not looking at the other, freely blurts out whatever springs to mind while the other pays close attention to every pause in his narrative, seemingly with the sole aim of making him even more confused. The fact that this ritual generally takes many years and elicits a great deal of emotional strain from both parties doesn't prevent either of them—the analysand and the analyst—from regarding it as right, good, and wholesome.

Indeed, despite its somewhat "idiotic" appearance, the cure is undertaken in the name of the Good. The analysand goes into analysis because things haven't been going well; she feels unhappy in herself and therefore goes to someone whom she imagines will be able to give her help, support, and understanding. The analyst takes her on because he is supposed to be—and supposes himself to be—an expert in providing support to people in psychological difficulty. One party hopes that she will soon feel better, the other that all of his expertise will assist toward that end. In this respect they both do not differ from the vast majority of patients and care professionals with which our society has become so well-endowed. They, too, do their utmost to accommodate our shared drive for mental health, happiness, and well-being.

But why, then, does psychoanalysis insist on staging such a strange scene? Why doesn't it let both parties simply sit together and talk face to face, man to man? This certainly does not happen in a psychoanalytic cure. Rarely or never does the analyst answer the analysand's questions directly, and even rarer are the moments when the patient feels completely understood. Here, the spontaneous empathy between patient and therapist—the starting point of other, "normal" therapies—is resisted as much as possible.

A psychoanalytic cure is definitely not a matter of direct therapeutic communication. The analyst may have his own idea of what the analysand's problems are, but he will never put it to her in so many words. And yet, this is precisely what the analysand demands: someone who will finally tell her what's wrong with her, why she feels so rotten, so unhappy, why the "good life" for which she yearns must so bitterly escape her.

It goes without saying of course that the "good life" the analysand hankers after is something ethical—as ethical as the reasons why the analyst wants to help the analysand. Both analyst and analysand aim for the good, in the highest moral sense of the word. Even the analyst's refusal to reproach his analysand—that he should be less selfish, less fixated on his own personal happiness—is a moral choice. The analyst recognizes the patient's right to be happy in her own way and he recognizes her right to demand that. To this extent, the analyst is a typically modern professional care-giver. Even if the "good" the analysand hankers after is a "good" she intends to reserve solely for herself, it would never be *for this reason* that the analyst opposes or frustrates her.

But why, then, does he oppose and frustrate her? Why won't he sit face to face with her and let her go on asking her questions? Why, out of professionalism and quality-assured know-how, does he refuse to respond directly to the patient's demands? Why leave the analysand trapped in her self-made web with its dead-end stories? Why continually throw the patient's demands back at her, without ever trying to solve them?

Simply because they are "demands." This is Lacan's both short and mysterious answer on the first page of his seminar devoted to the "Ethics of Psychoanalysis." Mysterious and short it sounds at least *to us*. For Lacan's audience on that Wednesday, November 18, 1959, it was a different story. When he talked about "demand," they recognized this word as the theoretical concept Lacan had elaborated in the previous seminars. The larger part of the audience had already attended his seminar for six years and had become quite used to Lacan's typically long, laboriously constructed sentences where, in this case, he talked about the way

> in which we have to respond in experience to what I have taught you to articulate as a demand, a patient's demand, to which our response gives an exact meaning. And in our response itself we must maintain the strictest discipline, so as not to let its deepest unconscious meaning be adulterated by that demand. (S7E: 1; S7F: 9)[1]

In fact, in the previous years, Lacan had repeatedly explained how there is always something wrong (or not wrong enough, so to speak) about the analysand's demand as such. That demand is less innocent than it seems because it is in itself already a cunning solution to the problem. On a purely formal (i.e., unconscious) level, it ascribes a specific position to both analyst and analysand in a way that in fact avoids the whole problem—at least for the time being. Simply by turning to him with a demand, the analysand implicitly makes the analyst into someone who possesses the answer to *her* problem. This implies, at least in the mind of the patient, that in principle the problem has been solved since it has been "discharged" onto the analyst.

And this is precisely the issue. The analyst, in any event, is convinced that the analysand neither can nor wants to be rid of her problems. The difficulties she wrestles with, and which we, for the sake of convenience, call "psychological problems," involve the patient "herself," in the most literal sense. There is something the matter *with her* rather than with her problems; she is messed up with herself. And this "herself," psychoanalysis has discovered, is not so much a thing whose defective parts can be replaced or individually repaired. A person *is* not so much him- or herself, but rather a *desire for* him- or herself. *Being* desire, man can never be done with desire because, should he succeed, he would also be finished off. He lives, thus, according to a permanently *unsatisfied* desire, a desire that is for this reason inevitably a little painful and awkward, and which continually reminds him of the fundamental lack that lies at the heart of his being.

It is this desire that, through the formal structure of the demand for help, will be suppressed and thrust onto an other (a health-care worker, an analyst). The analysand's demand is in fact a means of getting rid of this desire. Unconsciously, she wants to stop being unsatisfied and turns to a therapist in the hope that he will be able to heal her pain and remove the lack that torments her. The problem, however, is that in the long term this solution will not work. The analyst will never be able to give the analysand what she desires; all he can give her is desire as such. In other words, the analyst will only be able to help her to the extent that he leaves the analysand's demand painfully unanswered. This is what Lacan, addressing himself directly to an audience of psychoanalysts, says elsewhere in his *Ethics Seminar*:

> The desire of the man of good will is to do good, to do the right thing, and he who comes to seek you out, does so in order to feel good, to be in agreement with himself, to identify with or be in conformity with some norm. Now you all know what we nevertheless find in the margin, but also perhaps at the limit of that which occurs on the level of the dialectic and progress of the knowledge of the unconscious. In the irreducible margin as well as the limit of his own good, the subject reveals

himself to the never entirely resolved mystery of the nature of
his desire. (S7E: 237; S7F: 277–78)[2]

Put into Lacanian terminology, this passage says that the *imaginary*
relation hidden in the analysand's demand must be changed into a *symbolic* relation. The analysand must overcome the dual mirror-relationship
that makes her cling to the analyst and imagine that the lack from which
she suffers will be staunched by the analyst's care. She must change her
demand into an acknowledged desire: she must reconcile herself to the
fact that it is only by reference to a third, perpetually receding factor
that her desire will be sustained.[3] Only a *symbolic* universe guarantees
this triangulation. It is a universe made up of "signifiers" referring perpetually to other signifiers, thus providing a favorable environment for
desire. It should come as no surprise, then, that the analyst returns the
patient's demand to the materiality of the signifiers. Only in this way does
a misrecognized desire (misrecognized by the very "demand") allow itself
to be caught. It is thus a matter of unmasking the imaginary demand
behind which the symbolic desire has been concealed. The more explicitly
the analysand demands something, the clearer it becomes that she denies
the desire operative in her demand. Anyway, if only for methodological
reasons, it is better for the analyst—and, by the same token, any care
professional—to start with the denial that is already at work at the level
of the demand itself. Lacan turns this form of denial or "miscognition"
into a fully fledged concept that describes a phenomenon belonging to
the structural heart of the psychoanalytic cure.

This strange therapeutic starting point of psychoanalysis has far-reaching implications for ethics. The "good" the analysand demands
henceforth means a satisfaction of her desire. But since we *are* nothing
other than our desire, since desire is our very being, our demand in fact
aims at extinguishing desire, which is to say that it aims at our death. This
is what Freud's concept of the "death drive" already had its sights on.
What we desire, whether we call it "well-being," "good," or the "highest
good" is in fact, in the final analysis, nothing other than death, Lacan
concludes. What an age-old and still valid tradition names the "good"—that
is, something humankind is made for and at which our desire naturally
aims—would really, were it to be realized, kill us. It would be pure evil.
What one unconsciously demands in the psychoanalytic cure is in fact
an "evil" that would destroy us, Lacan says, and one lives only by grace
of the fact that one's demand never gets fully answered. It is just as well
that the "good" the analysand demandingly and desiringly searches for
is an illusion.[4] Complete satisfaction would simply be fatal.

If it is the analyst's intention never to give the analysand the "good"
she asks for, then, it is because of the highest moral reasons. Precisely

because he means well for the analysand, he must not give her the "good" she desires. The sole thing to be given here is purely and simply her desire. As Lacan puts it in a previous quote, this calls for a "strict discipline" from the analyst. After all, he is constantly tempted to give her the "good" she asks for, if only because his client will then award him a positive evaluation and thus confirm him in his professional honor. But, if he gives in to his own professional demand, he destroys precisely the framework that the analysand needs in order to confront her desire. This would obstruct him in his real task: to unmask the unconscious tricks hidden in the analysand's demand and to bring it back to the desire concealed within it. Both participants in an analytic session, the analysand and the analyst, are involved in a confrontation with desire, as Lacan kept emphasizing in his six previous seminars (1953–1959), and continued to repeat throughout the whole of the seventh seminar. Here, for example, in one of the last lessons of this seminar he says unambiguously:

> To have carried an analysis through to its end is no more nor less than to have encountered that limit in which the problematic of desire is raised. (S7E: 300; S7F: 347)

This is what the entire "ethics of psychoanalysis" is about: instead of giving us the "good" we desire, it must give desire *as such*.

This conclusion completely shakes up all the accepted ways of thinking about good and evil and forces an entire revision of traditional ethical thought. At least, this is the intuition that must have spurred Lacan to devote a whole seminar exclusively to an investigation of the problem of morality in psychoanalysis and of its consequences for ethics in general. In his *Ethics Seminar* he tries to think this through as rigorously as possible and to sound out its moral implications, both at the microlevel of the psychoanalytic cure and at the macrolevel of ethics as such. The least you can say is that he will hold off from endorsing any religious or humanist-inspired foundation for ethics. For him, ethics can no longer be thought from a position of belief in the inherent goodness of mankind, regardless of whether one takes an immanent-humanist or transcendental-religious approach.

It may already be clear, however, that Lacan does not turn against ethics as such. On the contrary, the idea that there is no inherent natural goodness is, in his eyes, the only possible starting point for any truly modern ethics. It is precisely because the analyst no longer preaches "good" or other humanist "tidings" to his analysand that he can help her at the point where the entire tradition has sabotaged her, namely, in her desire. It is precisely our lack of trust in the natural "goodness" of man and our suspicion about the possibility of giving someone the good he demands that put us, according to Lacan, on the path to a genuine moral engagement. They keep us from speaking and acting *in the name of* "goodness." The ethical task of a psychoanalyst is no longer that of a moral authority. It no longer lies in telling someone what he must and must not do. All psychoanalysis can do is confront the analysand with what, in a way, he already knows but cannot accept because he is unable recognize his desire. This is why the one who confronts his desire does not necessarily discover new rules to live by. He can just as well continue to live by the rules he has always had. But now, he will do so a little more freely and with more feeling for the desire operative in those rules.

For Lacan, this search for desire in ethics indicates that our relation to morality is above all fundamentally *libidinal*. In that sense, our relation to the moral law is profoundly "erotic," and it is back to this erotic relation that psychoanalysis traces the analysand's essentially ethical problems.[5] In his *Ethics Seminar*, Lacan will even explore whether a cultivated eroticism makes it possible to extend the individual's unconscious and libidinal relation to the law into the domain of conscious and public culture. Although, for Lacan, all the different kinds of sublimation do so, one cannot help but notice his preference for one particular kind of sublimation that is explicitly centered on the erotic, namely, Courtly Love. This is why the principal theme of the seminar can be summed up as a reflection on the inherent relation between "eros and ethics."

Yet, this is not to say that Lacan succeeds in totally clarifying this relation. Even while the main trajectory of the seminar heads in this direction, this is the very theme that most clearly confronts Lacan with the aporias of his own discourse. Not only will he be forced to recognize that psychoanalysis is not remotely capable of establishing a more general new "eroticism," its project of a specifically psychoanalytic ethics is itself scarcely able to escape the impasses it calls up. This will have repercussions for the way Lacan is forced to think concerning the relation between the imaginary and the symbolic. An important train of thought from his *Ethics Seminar* will force him to rethink this relation in a way that is radically at odds with the schema invoked in the preceding discussion regarding the constitution of the demand. Whereas Lacan claims that desire comes to light only after the unmasking of the imaginary, he will be forced to conclude that it maintains its place in culture only thanks to the imaginary. And, as it will become clear, this kind of aporia itself will touch the very heart of Lacan's conceptualization of psychoanalysis.

This book offers a reading of Lacan's 1959–1960 seminar, the "Ethics of Psychoanalysis." It is the seventh in a series of twenty-seven, held between 1953 and 1979. What began as an informal initiative in his home in 1951 received the official nature of a seminar in 1953 and formed the central event in what became Lacan's own psychoanalytic school in 1967.

Despite the abundance of publications in Lacanian theory, academic research into Lacan's seminar project is still in its infancy. For this reason, the reading proposed in this book is not yet able to trace the major themes from this one seminar in light of the whole train of thought developed throughout the entire trajectory of the other seminars. Hence my reading is limited strictly to the lines of thought developed in this one seminar.

It is well known that the seminars have a bad reputation in terms of accessibility and readability. This is partly a direct repercussion of an oral teaching practice where one's line of reasoning is frequently interrupted by various digressions and inspirations of the moment. The most significant cause of the relative inaccessibility of the seminars nevertheless lies with Lacan himself, who rarely manages to put things in a crystal-clear manner. He evidently preferred to place several lines of thought alongside one another, often without fully elaborating them, with the result that the reader frequently has to do his or her best just to follow the general basic argument. Add to this Lacan's preference for uncivilly long, baroque sentences and you have an apt impression of how his audience (admittedly, always more numerous) was forced to listen to him in those days. A final, yet not unimportant reason for his seminars being so difficult is the inexcusably substandard editions in which they have been published by Lacan's son-in-law, Jacques-Alain Miller. He intervenes literally in every single paragraph: shortening and rearranging sentences, changing the order of passages, adding words or leaving them out. The titles and subtitles he adds to each seminar session, as well as a division in three or four parts, are perhaps the least of the abuses that mark his editions. But it is unforgivable that he has also deliberately refrained from providing any sort of textual and editorial notes to his editions. A seminar such as the "Ethics of Psychoanalysis," for example, is full of reflections on the most diverse philosophical problems but there is not a single footnote to direct the reader to the relevant passages in Aristotle, Kant, Bentham, Heidegger, Freud, and others, although these passages are indispensable for providing Lacan's text with a primary readability. This is also true for Lacan's references to the numerous psychoanalytic essays he often comments on at the level of the letter of the text, but which the reader has to cope with without the slightest reference to the texts. Moreover, in the "official edition," Miller simply left out the contributions of guest speakers whom Lacan had invited in order to clarify some topics or even to develop seminar-long issues (see for instance S7E: 38; 156; 204; 287; S7F: 49; 186; 240; 332). The pages where Lacan goes into those contributions are therefore well-nigh incomprehensible in the "official" edition.

This is not to say, however, that the text of Lacan's seminar is completely unreadable. The shortcomings itemized here make the text's accessibility more difficult but not impossible, as I hope to prove in this reading of Lacan's *Ethics Seminar*. My intention, then, is in the first place "archeological": I will excavate Lacan's trains of thought and bring them out into the open. This is the only way that Lacan's often provocative claims can be put into their proper context. It will also help to illuminate the tensions and problematic knots in his theory. The latter indicates the second aim of my study, which is simply to make an initial attempt at clarifying the impasses and aporias of Lacan's thought in this seminar. For a truly exhaustive account, another volume would be needed.

One cannot begin tracing out the lines of thought in the seventh seminar without somehow taking those of the previous seminars into account. This is particularly true of the seminar immediately preceding the seventh seminar. Lacan regarded this seminar, "Desire and Its Interpretation" (1958–1959), as unfinished. Several times in his *Ethics Seminar*, he explicitly says that he is simply taking his previous seminar further and following up the threads he began there. You can already hear this in the opening sentence of the first lesson:

> I announced that the title of my seminar this year is *The Ethics of Psychoanalysis*. I do not think that this is a subject whose choice is in any way surprising in itself, although it does leave open for some of you the question of what I might have in mind. It was certainly not without some hesitation and even trepidation that I decided to tackle it. I, in fact, decided to do so because the subject follows directly from my seminar of last year, if it is true that we can consider that word as completely finished. (S7E: 1; S7F: 9)

And Lacan comes back to this idea a number of times during this seminar as, for example, in his lesson of May 4, 1960:

> I don't claim to do anything more this year than I have done in years past in the form of a progressive development—from the first reference to speech and to language up to the attempt last year to define the function of desire in the economy of our experience—that is guided by Freudian thought. (S7E: 206; S7F: 244)

The first chapter of this study provides a brief account of the path Lacan traveled before his seminar on ethics. The general tenor of Lacan's distinctive conceptualization of psychoanalysis is sketched out and situated in the context of what was in those days the extremely popular "object relations theory." He severely critiques this latter, although in his own theory, the "object" also takes center stage. The notion of *das Ding*, which Lacan highlights as a new concept in the *Ethics Seminar*, is really only the latest version of the same emphasis that he had always placed on the "object." In that sense, it might well be useful to begin a reading of Lacan's seventh seminar with a short overview of his theory up till then, understood as a peculiar kind of that very object relations theory. At the end of this first chapter, I focus specifically on Lacan's sixth seminar, "Desire and Its Interpretation" (1958–1959). There, Lacan deals explicitly with the problem of the ultimate object of desire. This seminar ends in a theoretical impasse that acquires a clearer focus and preliminary solution in the next seminar, the one on *ethics*. Neither the stakes nor the themes of this seminar are comprehensible if they are not read specifically in terms of the problematic developed over the course of the sixth seminar.

Following a second chapter that briefly sets out some of the main problems in Lacan's *Ethics Seminar*, the third chapter goes more deeply into Lacan's readings of Aristotle and Bentham. By way of an earlier "metapsychological" text of Freud's, the *Entwurf* of 1895, Lacan opens up a train of thought that enables him to throw new critical light on both the Aristotelian morality of happiness and the utilitarian ethics of Jeremy Bentham.

It is from this earlier Freudian text that he extracts the notion of *das Ding*, which becomes the central concept of the *Ethics of Psychoanalysis*. A thorough discussion of this "thing" will comprise the fourth chapter. Because *das Ding* is not only Freudian but also a Kantian reference, the fifth chapter brings us to Lacan's interpretation of Kant. Although Lacan fully endorses the "Copernican revolution" that Kant effects on ethics, he is convinced that we must take a further, decisive step. He will discover that the basic difference between the "ethics of psychoanalysis" and Kant's moral obligation is to be located in the notion of enjoyment (*jouissance*).

Enjoyment will be the topic of the sixth chapter where we will pursue Lacan's provocative claim that the truth of the Kantian ethics is to be found in the fantasies of Marquis de Sade. There we will note how Lacan's attempt to rigorously conceive an ethics based on enjoyment leads him to an "ethics of the singular": an ethics that is centered not on general, universally valid rules, but on a singular enjoyment that, by definition, withdraws from all forms of generality or universality.

How such an ethics of the singular can nevertheless perform a role in the wider culture Lacan will try to explain in his theory of sublimation, the topic of the seventh chapter. There, the problematic status of the imaginary becomes clearest. The *ethical* function that Lacan attributes to the *aesthetic* reveals the contours of his conceptualization of psychoanalysis. At the same time, this confronts us once again—and more sharply—with the aporias of Lacan's thought. Lacan himself discusses these in his commentary on Sophocles's *Antigone*, which is the topic of the eighth chapter.

In the final, ninth chapter, I will draw out the prospective conclusions resulting from Lacan's investigation into the "ethics of psychoanalysis." Although Lacan's general conclusion only offers a number of observations, these will nevertheless give us the opportunity to recap the fundamental arguments from the entire seminar.

# Chapter 1

# A Theory of the Subject

Psychoanalysis is not a *Weltanschauung*, nor a philosophy pretending to deliver the key to the universe. It is supported by a particular intuition that is historically defined by the elaboration of the notion of subject.[1]

The introduction of "das Ding" in the *Ethics Seminar* marks a change at the very core of Lacanian theory. Such, at least, is the consensus of practically every commentary on Lacan. Prior to his seventh seminar, so the story goes, Lacan conceived the subject as entirely determined by the signifier. Since signifiers continually refer to other signifiers, the subject that emerged was thought to be exceptionally agile, slippery, and flexible—an insight that does justice to the paradoxical and devious paths the subject is forced onto by its capricious drive-life. Yet with his seventh seminar, the commentaries continue, Lacan introduced an important correction into his theory. Despite its agility within the realm of signifiers, the subject is now presumed to remain simultaneously "attached" to something that is not a signifier: something that is beyond all signifiers and which Lacan, with Freud, names *das Ding, the "thing."* It is this "thing" that gives the subject's slippery libidinal economy its ultimate consistency. Henceforth Lacan no longer considers the subject solely as the bearer of an unconscious chain of signifiers (as in the previous six seminars), but also, and more fundamentally, as *attached* to a "thing": this is the new insight offered in Lacan's *Ethics Seminar*. According to these commentators, the idea of attachment is the key to understanding Lacan's difficult expositions in this seminar.[2]

However, although the emphasis on *"the thing"* is unquestionably there, readers will seek the word 'attachment' in vain. Nowhere is the relation between the subject and its 'thing' described in these terms, nor does it appear in any other contexts. The term "attachment," which has meanwhile been developed into a concept, seems to have been an invention of Lacan's interpreters rather than of Lacan himself. Nevertheless, this term rightly turns our attention to the "object" that the subject is related to. It presumes an emphasis on the "thing" at which the subject aims, an emphasis one can indeed find on practically every page of Lacan's *Ethics Seminar*.

Yet to define the relation between the subject and "the thing" as an "attachment" is to say more than this. It names the *nature* of that relation. It presumes this relation to be close, "attached," and involving a strong bond or "attraction." As I will show, such an interpretation is in fact far less easy—if not impossible—to extract from the text. At any rate, the "tie" between subject and object will be so much more complex that one must ask whether a notion like "attachment" is capable of doing it justice at all.

What is more, these commentaries that refer to the idea of 'attachment' seem to imply that the attention to the object pole in desire is something new in Lacanian theory, something that is only introduced in his *Ethics Seminar*. This too, however, is not substantiated, neither in the text of the seminar, nor in the wider development of his theory. It is in flagrant contradiction with the fact that Lacan had *always* put the emphasis on the object pole of desire. This was evident from the opening steps of his oeuvre, that is, his theory of the mirror stage. Many of the turns of his oeuvre are motivated by further, ongoing corrections and refinements of this first "object relations theory."

In this respect, his entire theory could be regarded as an "object relations theory," at least if we understand this term in a wider sense than that assigned by Ronald Fairbairn, the analyst who made the first breakthrough of this theory. Fairbairn defined the *object relation* as the opposite of a *libido relation*: in his eyes, object relations theory contests the primacy of the libido as the basic principle of the drive-life.[3] Lacan's preference, on the other hand, for approaching things from an *object relations* perspective is always accompanied with an even greater emphasis on the libidinal aspect of the problem.[4] If we thus understand the term "object relation" in the widest sense of the word, that is, as a psychoanalytic theory that centers on the problem of the object in the libidinal economy, Lacan's thought has always been an object relations theory. Although he has long been one of its most formidable critics, he has always moved *within* the same paradigm of the diverse object relations theories of his time.

If one tries to conceive of the relation between the drive and its object (the "thing" in the *Ethics Seminar*) as an "attachment," one must do so at least against the background of the object relations theory persisting and developed in the course of his oeuvre. And, what is more, one must conceive of that object relations theory as a theory of the *subject*. For the libidinal economy cannot solely be regarded as an "object relation." It is crucial to recall how the object relation requires a "bearer," a "*subjectum*," an instance giving support and ground to the entire slippery libidinal economy. This is why Lacan's "object relations theory" is first of all a theory of the subject. In this chapter I will cover the basic principles of Lacan's theory of the subject. Solely this perspective offers the background necessary for understanding the subject's complex relation to the ultimate object of its desire, that is, the "object" which is central in Lacan's seminar on the "Ethics of Psychoanalysis" and whose implications have far-reaching consequences for the ethical condition of the modern subject in general.

## 1. The Object Relations Theory and Its Moral Premises

In the period preceding his seventh seminar, Lacan was firmly opposed to the object relations theories that were popular in the fifties. Already in the forties—in part under the influence of the violent controversies swirling around Melanie Klein—the argument was that libidinal life is best approached from one of the four components Freud attributed to the drive, namely the drive's "object."[5] This argument emerged from an article by Karl Abraham in 1924 where he distinguishes a number of stages in "object love" that parallel the stages of the libidinal development. Already prior to attaining a "true" object love (and this is only true of the *genital* phase, the phase during which the Oedipus conflict is settled), the child displays "partial love," as Abraham called it: a pregenital relation toward (oral, anal and other "partial") objects. His study explains how the phases of the evolution of the pregenital, still incomplete "object relation" perfectly replicate the libido's evolution.[6] Following in the line of Abraham's discoveries, Melanie Klein showed, on the basis of often very convincing case studies,[7] how already in the child's earliest months there is a relation with objects that are of primordial interest for the formation of identity. From its first experiences (hence, long before the Oedipal phase) the child identifies with objects—"partial objects," such as the mother's breast, the feces, or the phallus—that are all localized in the maternal body. According to Klein, this identification is the determining factor for the subsequent course of the child's libidinal development.

Along the same lines, an entire current of both theoretical and practical psychoanalysis in the fifties focused on the intimate relation between the drive and the object. Freud had previously described the relation as free,[8] although other theorists at that time regarded this relation as more static.

The idea gained ground that the drive is more or less *naturally* attuned to its object.[9] The translation of the German word "Trieb" as "instinct" (in English as well as in many other languages) supported this interpretation. Regarding it in terms of a developmental process of *instincts* affords the idea of a natural physiological process, and object relations are then spontaneously conceived of in the same way. Psychoanalytic practice, too, doesn't escape this tendency: the cure enables the analysand to arrive at a renewed relation to the object that his entire drive life naturally aims at but with which he had become at odds. This same *object* relations theory is then able to bring the importance of the *pregenital* objects back into view, although the main emphasis remains the *genital* object. After some ambivalent (because) oral and anal adventures during the period of pregenital object relations, the drive, in the natural order of things, should turn around and evolve into a stable (because) genital object choice that is both a sign of and condition of possibility for a mature libidinal life. That such a "mature" object relation fits with the acceptable *ethical* ideal of a monogamous sexual culture simultaneously grants the latter an underlying scientific legitimacy. This type of psychoanalysis implicitly declares that the heterosexual, genital and monogamous object choice is the *normal* and *natural* one. If Lacan turns against this kind of object relations theory, it is primarily because of its unarticulated ethical pretensions. In their so-called psychoanalytic logic, the ambivalences and conflicts characteristic of our libido are supposed to find a "natural" answer in what culture postulates as normal and good.[10]

However, this is not what psychoanalysis is about, according to Lacan. For him, Freud's intuition points in exactly the opposite direction. Does analytic practice not notice every day how difficult it is for people to enjoy the so-called natural and normal objects offered to their desire by culture? Freud would never have invented a new theory had he not seen how stubborn and incurable human discontent is. In one way or another, people also "love" the discontent they hate. This is the Oedipal structure Freud discovered in human desire. And this is what he observed with the hysterics on his couch as well as with the remarkably persistent discontent in human civilization. Remarks to this effect can be found long before his famous 1930 essay, *Civilization and Its Discontents*.[11] People may love the rigid limits culture forces them into, but their relation to culture is never "natural." They relate to it from a *polymorphous-perverse* drive, that is, from a drive that "perverts" nature.

Here "perversion" refers to the way an organism does not live its biological functions for their own sake, that is, for the sake of what they are for, but for the *pleasure* they give. If life is a reaction to stimuli (as the biological definition of life claims), then this reaction, according to Freud, must be considered 'perverse,' that is, as turning around on itself, detached from the aim and the proper orientation of its function.[12] That is why its *principle* of reaction—and, thus of drive and of life—is not self-preservation, but pleasure—pleasure being a purely "formal" principle to be defined as a "perversion" of reaction/drive/life. Life, as a reaction to stimuli, is guided by pleasure, not by self-preservation: this is the axiom of psychoanalytic theory. The drive "driving" the organism may indeed be biological, but the principle driving that drive is not to be found in the biological self-preservation of the organism but in the *pleasure* accompanying the biological functioning. What "drives" an infant to suck at its mother's breast may have been caused by its biological feeding function, that is, its hunger, but the drive's reaction to the hunger stimulus starts with the *pleasure* the infant obtains from this sucking activity. At the most basic level, the child sucks not in order to live but from the sheer pleasure of slurping and sucking itself.[13] We find the same thing in adults: the sucking reflex can be "perverted" in smoking, defying the risks of cancer, or in overeating (bulimia) or in eating the "nothing" preferred above all (anorexia nervosa). Hence, it is the pleasure principle that makes life *polymorphous*. Because pleasure is not linked to the proper aim of a biological function, one can live that function for all kinds of other purposes, as these examples clearly illustrate. At the most fundamental level, it is not a self-preservation principle (i.e., the axiom of modern biology, including all Darwinist theories) but a pleasure principle that governs our drives: this is the founding axiom of Freudian psychoanalysis.

Note that the idea that life is governed by drives is not restricted to psychoanalysis. This is, more or less, what the entire philosophical and scientific tradition says, albeit each proceeding from its own paradigm. What is distinctive about Freudian psychoanalysis is its new concept of the *principle* driving the drives. At the most fundamental level, the drive attends not to the self-preservation of the organism, but to the *pleasure* that it can gain. Pleasure may be found in self-preservation, but it isn't necessarily the case. The organism can just as easily experience pleasure from what is not in the interests of self-preservation.

Moreover, Freud does not attribute the polymorphous-perverse pleasure principle to a self-conscious subject, but to a completely unconsciously functioning *libido* that, if only for that reason, carries all of the old connotations of "sin." In Augustine's Latin, "libido" stands for a bodily or psychological movement released by a will that escapes conscious, rational control. The Church Father interpreted the involuntary "rebellion" of the male genital in erection as an unmistakable expression of *libido*. This erectile "insurrection" that, by definition, escapes conscious control was, in Augustine's eyes, an exquisite sign of man's insurrection against God and his Creation.[14] This negative, Augustinian connotation is undeniably present in Freud's concept of the unconscious, polymorphous-perverse libido. Unlike Augustine, however, he does not believe in the possibility of redeeming the libido from its negative "sinful" nature. For Augustine, man's sinful, libidinal condition will be reconciled at the end of time and regain the perfection it knew in Paradise before the Fall. For Freud, in contrast, human life is basically—and will remain—a matter of a "sinful" and "disturbing" libido, which is also true for our most self-conscious rationality and morality. The libido, by definition, has no natural destination or "object" where it will ultimately come to rest. It functions only insofar it can polymorphously "pervert" everything natural.

This "infamous" insight, Lacan repeats over and again, is the core of Freudian psychoanalysis. And it is precisely this "scandalon" that many critics and even many psychoanalytic theorists try to repress or deny by, for instance, ascribing the drive (or the libido) a "natural" object. This was the main presupposition supporting the different "object relations theories" of the fifties. According to Lacan, it was their way of denying the "scandalon"—and, thus, the core—of psychoanalysis. Against these, Lacan reaffirmed Freud's basic intuition: there is simply no object that corresponds to the drive in a *natural* way. The drive relates to its object in a polymorphous-perverse way[15] and it perverts the natural logic we have always used to think about human life and its condition. This is why it demands a new logic, that is, a psychoanalytic logic.

## 2. Lacan's Target: Maurice Bouvet

In the name of his rereading of Freud—his famous "return to Freud"—Lacan fiercely attacks any form of object relations theory that fails to keep this in mind. Although he pits himself against a number of big names, for many years Lacan focuses his attention primarily on a single figure, Maurice Bouvet.[16] In this younger contemporary, he finds all the evils from which, in his eyes, the most successful of object relations theorists suffer. Bouvet, like no other, formulated the phases of the object relation as steps in a spontaneous and natural process. In that sense, he elevated the genital object relation into a "normal, ideal and natural" thing.

This already gives us one of Bouvet's central conceptual pairs. As opposed to the "pregenital type," a catchall for anything that can go wrong with the drive, Bouvet outlines the positively valorized "genital type": the type of person who, because of his or her genitalized object relation is capable of having a "normal," "objective" relation to reality, the result of which is a "strong ego." In one of his essays[17] he writes that "pregenitals" ("les prégénitaux") are characterized by a "weak ego." Their ego is still too closely modeled on the oral and anal object relation, where the various partial drives are not yet in possession of the right relation to the object. At this level, the ego so "cathects" the object that it tries to overcome the distance holding the object at bay. It tries to negate this distance and take the object as a whole. It thereby undermines precisely the object *relation* that it lives by, and it therefore continually threatens to destroy itself. The problematic identity of the "pregenitals" stems from the shaky structure of the earlier (oral and anal) ego. With the "genitals," things are quite different says Bouvet. These persons are able to acquire a more stable distance in relation to the object because their egos are less directly dependent on the object relation.[18] Later in the same essay, he characterizes the transition from the pre-genital to the genital phase in the following way:

> Once the drives that kindle the ego have been genitalized, once they have been through the maturing process that forms the transition from the pre-genital to the genital formation, they are no longer controlled by an unmanageable, unremitting, unconditional and partially destructive possessive impulse. They are instead tender, amiable and even if the subject is not willing to make sacrifices here (i.e., to act disinterestedly), even if it treats its objects as narcissistically as before, yet, it is capable of understanding and adapting to the situation of others. (Bouvet 1972; 178–179)

It is easy for Lacan to expose the unquestioned moral presuppositions in passages such as this. Here, the drive relates purely to a spontaneous, natural growth process which, moreover, coincides with the moral achievement of man as a social, comprehending being capable of making sacrifices. According to Bouvet, ethics seems to be rooted in a natural libido. It is not surprising that Lacan cannot resist taking pot shots at such a naturalizing and moralizing distortion of psychoanalysis.

Let us, however, permit Bouvet to speak first, for, from a certain perspective, his position doesn't seem to differ so radically from Lacan's after all. Like all object relations theorists, Bouvet starts out from the primacy of the object relation: the organism is *primarily* a cluster of (among others, oral and anal) object relations, and *only later*—as an effect of their mutual conflicts—does it form a more or less stable ego, rooted in a central relation to a privileged object. The ego is the agent that channels the organism's inexorable drive tensions in a good—that is, pleasurable—way. Rather than a point of departure, the ego must be conceived as an *effect* of these primordial object relations. For Bouvet, the success of the ego's formation depends on the organism's ability to identify and maintain the correct distance in relation to its central object. In the pregenital phase, however, this object relation has not yet transcended its internal contradictions and tensions. The organism can only maintain itself through an identificatory clinging to the object. In this way, it tries to negate the distance that separates it from the object. In fact, it wants to *be* its object. Both oral and anal-sadistic aggression stem from this. By the same token, when the object is another person (the mother, family members, other children), the young child tries to annihilate the distance between itself and the other and *become* that other. Because of the aggressive and destructive nature of such a relation, the other/alike elicits the greatest anxiety in the child. For the other/alike, too, is driven to (orally or anally sadistically) eat up and destroy the object. This is why, in the pregenital object relation, the child is subject to such erratically ambivalent feelings. It is unable to assume a fixed position, either in relation to the outside world or to itself.

Accordingly, the ego resulting from the pregenital object relation is particularly weak, Bouvet concludes. In this phase, the "*optimal distance*" between the organism and its object has not yet been guaranteed (Bouvet, 1972: 268). This only occurs in the genital phase. There, a "differentiated and nuanced" relation with the object predominates, enabling the ego to maintain its distance in relation to that object. It is this persistent distance that guarantees a more or less successful satisfaction of the drive ("*satisfaction instinctuelle*").[19] The subject no longer destructively cathects the object (i.e., its double) but assumes a self-sacrificial relation to it, arriving at an "understanding" and an "adaptation to the other's situation." Here, Bouvet concludes, "objective reality is perceived as such" (Bouvet, 1972: 268).

In the analytic cure, too, where the analyst takes on the role of the drive object in the transference, what is at stake is the "distance towards the object," Bouvet continues. Following the phases of libido development, the analyst will continually reduce the distance between the analysand and this object, right up until his own disintegration. The analyst's interventions are designed to help the analysand resist the ambivalences brought about by this process. This reduction to zero of the distance between the subject and the object is strongest at the moment when the transferential relationship reaches its peak. As soon as the analysand (or, more accurately, his ego) has "introjected" these aggressive and conflicting drives, he must be able to take and maintain his distance from the object again. In Bouvet's eyes, the analysand revisits the conflictual Oedipal transition from the pregenital to the genital phase in analysis, and reinstalls an Oedipal (and therefore stronger) ego (Bouvet 1972; 267).

According to Maurice Bouvet, the psychoanalytic cure essentially concerns the *distance* between the ego/subject and the object. From Lacan's early writings onward, this distance is a major topic that comes into play from the subject's earliest beginnings because it constitutes itself by identifying with the drive object—which is the foundational axiom of every object relations theory. According to Bouvet, this is a radical and, in a sense, ontological identification: the organism only exists through its drive to merge with the object or, in other words, its drive to "become" its object. *Object relations* theory must posit that the libidinal being, at the most fundamental level, *is* its own drive object. Or, as Freud formulated it elsewhere in a collection of separate notes titled "On having and being in a child":

> The child happily expresses the object relation by means of an identification: I am the object. Having it comes only later [. . .]. Mother: breast. The breast is a piece of myself, I am the breast. Only later: I have it, that is, I am not it.[20]

At the same time, the infantile libidinal being can only maintain itself insofar as it fails in this radical identificatory movement, and thus keeps itself at distance from—in relation to—this object. It can only exist as an ego precisely insofar as it does not merge with the object. It has to constitute itself as the *subject* (in the literal meaning of "bearer") of a *relation to* that object—that is, the subject of an object *relation*. In short, here we run across the basic paradox to which all object relations theories—Lacan's included—must return: on the one hand, the libidinal being finds its ultimate ground in its object (or, so to speak, it *is* its object), but, on the other, it only exists by grace of the distance it takes from this object. In this sense, it "is" both its object *and* its relation to it.

This *distance* between itself and its object is what supports the libidinal being. Note however, this "itself" (i.e., its subject or ego) is not given in advance but is entirely the result of the installation and the maintenance of this distance. For Bouvet, the regression from which all "pathologies" stem entails a loss of this distance, causing the subject to fall back into a conflictual and in extreme cases self-destructive identification with the object. Arduous, protracted analytic work is often needed before this distance can be repaired.

Bouvet's psychoanalytic theory is certainly not the most subtle of its kind, but it would be an injustice to turn him, following Lacan's lead, into a caricature. One cannot, for instance, impute a crude naturalism to his theory. In the final analysis, his characterization of the drive object has not so much to do with content (the "true" object is the genital object) as with *form*: the "true" *relation* is genital, not because the object has a genital nature but because, in the genital phase, the subject is in a position to assume the *right distance* ("distance optima") in relation to any object at all (Bouvet 1972; 195; 268). The genitalizing of the object is not so much a question of reaching the natural end of the drive's development but of maintaining a safe distance from it. It is true that Lacan shows how, intentionally or not, Bouvet's conceptualization of psychoanalysis is full of "physical," "natural," and, hence, ethical presuppositions. But if one considers Lacan's own statements in his seventh seminar, it is hard not to see how close he is to Bouvet's theoretical starting points. In his own way Lacan, too, will place the emphasis on a similar kind of "distance." For Lacan as well, the truth of the good—or, in psychoanalytic terms, the ultimate object of desire—is found in a correct "distance" from the subject. The subject's ethical attitude depends on the way he or she keeps that object at a distance. Or, to coin a phrase: not unlike Bouvet's, can Lacanian ethics be defined as an "ethics of distance"?

But before going into Lacan's *Ethics Seminar*, it is worth sketching the contours of his theory of the subject in more detail. In a different, more nuanced way than Bouvet, Lacan will try to provide an answer to the basic paradox on which all object relations theories are founded, namely, that the libidinal being "is" both its object *and* the distance it takes in relation to it.

## 3. Lacanian Object Relations Theory: A Theory of the Subject

> . . . but above all he *is* these objects . . .
>
> (Lacan, 2002: 240)

### 3.1. An Imaginary Subject Theory

As he rants about Maurice Bouvet in the fifties, Lacan is in fact revisiting his own previous theoretical position. At the end of the forties, he similarly approached the basic structure of libidinal life as an explicitly *dualistic* conflict between two antithetical parties, the *ego* and the *object*. And he, too, claims that man can neither avoid nor tolerate the strained *distance* between these two poles. The only difference in those days was that, unlike Bouvet, Lacan paid special attention to the *status* of the participants in this conflict. Bouvet paid little attention to this, beginning from the position that one can approach both the ego and the object as ordinary, *real* qualities. Lacan's starting point, in contrast, was that one must approach them both as strictly imaginary forms. In this way, he succeeds in clarifying the most basic paradox that all theories holding to the primacy of the object relation must face. For how can such a theory plausibly make the ego both its object *and* the relation to that object? How can it adequately explain why the ego wants to merge with its object (which is why it can be so aggressive and even destructive in relation to the object) while acknowledging that this same ego only exists thanks to the distance it keeps from that object?

Lacan's conceptualization of the mirror stage[21] gave an adequate formulation of this logical contradiction. There, he explains that identification plays out between purely *imaginary* antagonists. The ego's identification with the object—and, consequently, the "destruction" of the distance between them—is purely imaginary, not real. The entire explosive drama of (oral) devouring and (anal-sadistic) destroying the object remains caught in the imaginary status of this scene and, in this way, keeps the (object) relational nature of the ego in place. This imaginary scene lends a supporting surface to the entire event and, in this way, enables the libidinal being, despite those tensions, to exist at all.

The "aha-experience" the children undergo at the moment that they first recognize themselves in the mirror makes it easy to see how the ego does indeed first find itself in an outside object, that is, in its shape in the mirror. And it is also clear why that same ego, therefore, cannot "really" merge with that object. This imaginary relation permits a radical identification with the object while simultaneously keeping the distance between the libidinal being and its object intact. So, considering the entire object relation as imaginary one does full justice to the *relation as such*. Regardless of how self-destructive its dynamic is (wanting to *merge* with its object), the object relation remains a *relational* tension; it remains a *distance* toward that object.

Henceforth the ego is not only one of the two relating terms; it is at the same time the very "bearer"—the "subject"—of that (object) *relation*. The ego is capable of this because it miscognizes[22] the inner structure of the whole scene, believing to be the cause of its mirror image, while, in reality it is only an *effect* of that image. *Unconsciously*, it behaves as if it had always possessed its own identity, which is only afterward reflected in the mirror. It miscognizes the primacy of the image. Precisely this miscognition enables the ego to be the "subject," the "bearer" of its relation to its image and, thus, of the organism's entire libidinal scene, that is, of its "self."[23]

Lacan's hard-hitting critique of object relations theories in the fifties does not imply he turns against this kind of theory per se. On the contrary, like Maurice Bouvet and Melanie Klein (and not without being heavily influenced by the latter), Lacan's thought is deeply steeped in the object relations problematic. Without question, he is himself an object relations theorist, albeit in a contrary and rebellious way.[24] His first contribution to psychoanalytic theory—the mirror stage as a reformulation of narcissism—can easily be described as an object relations theory. There, the ego's narcissistic function is founded on an entirely imaginary object relation. Precisely by thinking the whole problematic as imaginary, Lacan enables us to understand how the ego is not only one of the participants in the libidinal drama (between ego and object), but how the ego is at the same time the *bearer—the subject—*of that drama. Lacanian object relations theory of the thirties and forties is therefore, in the fullest sense of the word, also a *subject* theory, a theory about the "site," the "surface," the "platform," the "stage," the "scene," the "*subjectum,*" or the "*hypokei-menon*" on which the entire libidinal economy, a fundamentally relational economy, takes place.[25] More specifically, his central argument is that *the stage on which the drive life takes place or the point from which it operates is, paradoxically, also an effect, a construction of the drive itself.* This recalls the famous story of Baron Munchausen who saves himself from drowning by pulling himself up by his own wig.[26] The "place" of the event (its "ground," its "platform," its "*subjectum*")—the supporting point from where one pulls oneself up out of the mud—is in fact a purely imaginary *effect* of that event. As the bearer of libidinal activities, the subject is at the same time the fictional result of its cunning logic.

The Freudian unconscious, which already by this time Lacan is trying to reconceptualize, concerns first and foremost the subject. That which carries one, the surface on which the mirror effect one "is" takes place, the point from[27] where that one maneuvers: this is a place where the subject can never (consciously) be. This kind of "*andere Schauplatz*" (other scene) remains unconscious, yet it is from this scene that our libidinal life is driven.[28] This "other scene" is the virtual mirror surface on which man discovers himself as the object he will never have access to—impeded precisely by the very mirror that is supposed to grant his access. For Hegel, one of Lacan's main sources of that time,[29] the subject resides at the point where the "speculative" relation is "sublated" (in the sense he gives to the word "*Aufhebung*"). For Lacan, in contrast, the subject of the object relation is located in the place where such an "*Aufhebung*" is impossible. It is located in the place—the scene, the "*andere Schauplatz*"—which escapes the dialectic of consciousness and which Freud defined as the unconscious.

Already in the thirties and forties, then, Lacan had developed a proper object relations theory. Without neglecting the conflictual, indeed self-destructive nature of the pregenital object, he succeeded in explaining precisely how this kind of relation provides the libidinal organism with a "ground." Its imaginary character and the subject's unconscious condition prevents this relation from ever being reconciled or sublated. This is why, despite its self-destructive conflictual structure, it is able to maintain itself *as a relation.* Hence in his own way, and before Bouvet, Lacan conceives of the "distance from the object" as constitutive of the subject.

However, Lacan gradually realizes a crucial shortcoming in his subject theory. It is still left unexplained why, as merely the bearer (subject) of this imaginary (object) relation, man is nevertheless able to lead a relatively peaceful existence. The very logic of such an imaginary relation means that such peace ought to be impossible. The same goes for the relational tension between the ego and its object, which is no less conflictual. If the ego is to merge seamlessly with the other in the mirror, it will not only miscognize the other; it will also want to destroy him if possible, because only then can it really *be* the other. Not only is this specular other the mirror image of my identity, he is also the image to be demolished so that I can *really* be who I suppose I am. In the logic of the imaginary, nothing can lessen this conflictual tension, certainly not the ego itself. It would thus only be logical if, in the long run, the ego (the bearer of the tensional relationship) also effectively gave way under the tension and succumbed to the aggression that such an imaginary relation inevitably brings with it. That the ego evidently doesn't and, in the midst of incessant libidinal conflict, generally conducts itself surprisingly well implies that there is something wrong with Lacan's theory. His ego-theory from those days (which is his purely *imaginary* theory of the subject) was to undergo a thorough correction.

Confronted with the object relations theory of Maurice Bouvet in the fifties, Lacan set himself primarily against Bouvet's neglect of this kind of imaginary aggression. However, it is now clear that he was at that moment primarily turning against the views he had himself held for many years. Lacan only ran across this kind of aggression at the end of the forties,[30] and it is this discovery that forced him to thoroughly revise the premises of his purely imaginary subject theory.

### 3.2. A Theory of the Symbolic Subject

Lacan's solution to this problem is well known. Until the end of his days, it will remain his most fundamental thesis. Under Lévi-Strauss's influence[31] (and, beyond, the general influence of the then upcoming structural linguistics), he conceives the entire problematic no longer in terms of the imaginary but of the *symbolic*. Identification, which is to provide a support (a ground, a subject) to the cluster of (real) drives, no longer solely refers to an imaginary figure in a mirror but now also to a linguistic "figure." This figure is not to be approached as a mirror image but as a discursive narrative, as a story carrying a name. This name, and the narrative that weaves itself around it, operates inside a largely automatically functioning field of signifiers that linguistics baptized "the symbolic order." From now on, the subject must be sought not only in an imaginary *other* (with a small o) but first and foremost in a symbolic *Other* (with a capital "O"). Lacan reserves, more precisely, the term "ego" for the imaginary other the libidinal being thinks he is.[32] The term "subject" is henceforth reserved for the "bearer" of the symbolic Other, or, more precisely, for the bearer of a set of signifiers plucked from the Other that makes up my concrete identity.

Lacan's variation on Rimbaud's "I is another" (S2E: 7; S2F: 16) is that the human being—who is, according to Lacan, first of all a *speaking* being, a "*parlêtre*"—is the subject (i.e., the bearer) of a narrative that fundamentally and irrevocably comes from an Other. The subject can only exist in an element that never really gives it *presence* but only *re*presents it (symbolically). Only in language does the human libidinal being find an element in which its alienation coincides with its realization, without immediately falling short as is the case in imaginary ego formation. In this endlessly sliding field of signifiers, it is able to be (symbolically) *present* as that which remains *absent* (in the real). For Lacan, this absence is the heart of what Freud called the unconscious, what the famous "other scene" is all about. In order to trace this insistent absence, one must continually encircle it with signifiers which hide it. This is why the psychoanalytic cure is indeed a *talking cure* (as one of the first analysands, Anna O, made clear to her analyst, Joseph Breuer).

For Lacan, this insight throws a surprising new light on Freud's entire discovery. Mankind's struggle with the unconscious is played out in one exclusive element, that is, language; therefore, the truth of the unconscious must be sought not *behind* but *in* language. This does not imply that language and the unconscious are one and the same. But since mankind is trapped in language and since each of us is its 'subject' (bearer), language is the only thing that enables us to track down something of the unconscious—and therefore something of the *subject* that bears us. Although there are many passages in Freud that contradict Lacan's emphasis on language, his thesis nevertheless revalorizes the foundational praxis of psychoanalysis, that is, the analysis of dreams, slips of the tongue, jokes, daydreams, associations—in short, the analysis of linguistic phenomena.[33] It strikes Lacan now, more than ever before, how Freud was not so much seeking the meaning behind the words, as exploring their purely linguistic interrelations. Only by closely pursuing the interrelated (metonymic) displacements and (metaphoric) condensations between the signifiers can one find traces of the unconscious. The latter does not lie *behind* the words the analysand has given himself over to. It is only *in* the word-stream itself that it can be found. This is where, hidden among the signifiers and concealed within the linguistic caprioles, the analysand must look for his "self" as being the "object relation" that, in the last resort, he "is." He must look for himself not only in the virtual image in the mirror surface but also, and primarily, in the even more slippery slope of the linguistic symbolic order in which he slides from one signifier to another.

The new premises of the symbolic put the entire object relation in a new light. The heart of the problem—the aporia that the libido "is" simultaneously its object and its distance from it—seems insufficiently explained if one regards each party solely as an imaginary entity. In such a case, they remain ravaged by an unbearable aggression that makes any kind of stable subject formation—or, what was then for Lacan the same thing, any ego formation—unthinkable. By locating the entire process in an autonomously functioning symbolic system, Lacan can keep the unbearable tension typical of the distance between the ego and its object *away from the ego*. Of course, the libidinal being remains an object relation and coincides with the strained distance in relation to the object. But the symbolic status of this object means that the entire tension is already situated at the level of the object, which makes the unbearable pressure of the ego fall away. Moreover, that object is taken up in an autonomous symbolic system where it resides neither as a *real* thing, nor as an enchanted *imaginary* figure but simply as a sliding *signifier*. By definition, this signifier exists only as a reference to another signifier, which in itself provides an appropriate platform for the object relation and its unbearable tension.

The ego too, for that matter, is taken up on that same "platform." Although it remains an imaginary entity, it functions as a signifier and not as a "subject" (bearer) of signifiers. It is, then, no longer the (imaginary) ego that must regulate the distance in relation to the object (in what Bouvet called "le réglage de la distance").[34] This is now done by the *symbolic* subject, except that this subject must not actively take this task upon itself. This task henceforth belongs to the autonomously functioning symbolic order; and the libidinal being only has to be the passive bearer (the subject) of this self-functioning strained relation. Here, *subject* and *ego* are definitively to be distinguished from one another. They are to be located on different levels—symbolic and imaginary, respectively. The aim of the analytic cure will also, in this sense, be reformulated. Freud's famous "*wo Es war soll Ich werden*" henceforth becomes Lacan's "there where the *imaginary* ego was, the *symbolic* subject must come to be." In the cure, the imaginary ego must be "de-centered" and confronted with its true bearer, the symbolic subject.[35]

In contrast with Lacan's earlier position where the ego and the object were *imaginarily* opposed to one another, as symbolic entities they are now in solidarity together. Both the ego and its object relation are part of a universe in which the tension that governs them can at any moment be discharged. The tension will by no means be lessened, but because neither the ego nor the object is the subject of the relationship, this tension will even benefit the (object) relation. It will remain "fluid," thereby advancing its relational character, with the result that the subject will also become more stable. Because this tension has more or less unlimited possibilities for discharge in the virtually unlimited universe of signifiers, it will rarely turn directly against the subject itself. This explains the relative stability the symbolic order gives to the subject permanently plagued by tension.

Lacan's major turn at the beginning of the fifties, when he introduces the *symbolic, imaginary,* and *real* triad,[36] also meant a new step in his conceptualization of object relations of which, despite his claims to the contrary, he has always been an adherent. Better than its imaginary precursor, his new symbolic concept of the subject clarifies how the strained relation between the ego and its object can maintain itself and how, nevertheless, under these circumstances a stable subject—bearing and guaranteeing the relation—is possible. Throughout the rest of his oeuvre, Lacan will never lose sight of the decisive impact of the symbolic on the human libidinal being.

Yet, this "primacy of the symbolic" will not enable Lacan's theory to definitively master the problematic tension that he finds right from the outset in the object relation. Precisely in his seventh seminar, the "Ethics of psychoanalysis," all of the problems he encountered in his conceptualization of the object relation will pile up again, and more massively than ever. In what Lacan calls *"das Ding,"* the subject will once again find itself opposite something it stands in a tensile relation to that is no less pernicious and ambiguous than the dual imaginary relation between the ego and its object. In reading this seminar, we will retrace this turn in detail and see how it brings far-reaching implications along with it.

But let us first look more closely at Lacan's object relations theory which, as I suggested, either cannot be fully explained simply by referring to the primacy of the symbolic. One cannot lose sight of the fact that, before his seventh seminar, Lacan had already forged two important concepts that brought the whole object relations problematic into very nuanced focus, namely, the *phallus* and the *phantasm (fantasy)*. The first concept enabled him to approach the object as a lack, more specifically, as a lack at the level of the signifier. This enabled Lacan to clearly show how desire advanced toward a perpetually retreating object. In this way, the sliding—and, thus, *relational*—aspect of the object relation is properly articulated conceptually (see below 3.3). The second concept, the *phantasm*, enabled him to explain the consistency and stability of this same object relation (see 3.4). Thanks to these two concepts, the phallus and the phantasm, Lacan was able to neutralize the most fundamental impasse that lurks in all object relations theory: man is *both* his relation to the phallic lack *and* that lack as such, albeit in a fantasmatic way.

In the period Lacan was putting the finishing touches on his theory of the phallus, the question arose as to whether one can think of this lack as purely "phallic"—that is, symbolic (see 5). The negative answer with which he reluctantly concluded his sixth seminar led him, at the beginning of his next seminar, to introduce a new concept. This new concept is "*das Ding*," whose status is no longer imaginary or symbolic, but *real*.

From this perspective, it is worth first looking more closely at Lacan's purely symbolic—or as he called it "phallic"—approach to the human being as an object relation. In the following section we will once more take up his sketch of subject formation but now specifically from that "phallic" departure point where the object as a pure lack or, if you like, as lack "itself" will be conceived. Only in this light will the stakes of Lacan's later definition of the object of desire as "real" become clear, as was introduced for the first time in his seminar on "the ethics of psychoanalysis."

### 3.3. Phallus . . .

It is well known that Lacan's major turn in 1953 coincides with his discovery of the primacy of the signifier in the operation of both the unconscious and in subject formation. He begins from the point that for the infantile libidinal being the very fact that it must settle down in a universe of signifiers is already a trauma but, to the extent that it is a libidinal being for whom attaining pleasure equals life, it simply has no other choice. Having no way of satisfying its life-sustaining need for pleasure *by itself*, the infant must rely on others from the outset and, because these others direct themselves to the infant through speech, it is completely at the mercy of their linguistic world. In expressing her needs, the infant encounters the other, not as someone who satisfies these needs *immediately*, but as someone who *asks* what she wants—as someone, that is, who never stops shooting signifiers in her direction.

If only because of this, the infant is traumatized. For what she is asking for is not a question in return, nor even an answer to that (linguistic) question. She asks for an immediate satisfaction of pleasure at the level of the drive. She is not asking for (distancing) words or signs; she wants actions that *immediately* turn the unpleasurable sensations into pleasure. The infant is entirely at the mercy of the other for her pleasure—and thus for her life—and the trauma of the whole event lies in this: all the other can offer is something as insufficient as signifiers. The other is thus primarily a stream of signifiers that descends on the child unasked. This is what Lacan means when he writes "the Other" with a capital "O" (*Autre*). It is via the (linguistic) Other that the child has to satisfy its life-sustaining pleasure needs, just as it is also through the Other that she must form her own identity and her own subject.

The ruses of the imaginary provide the libidinal being with an initial strategy for saving itself from the traumatic situation in which, instead of immediate pleasurable pacification, it receives alienating signifiers that require processing. It will constitute itself precisely out of the lack proper to these signifiers. Signifiers are characterized by a constitutive lack in the sense that they are structurally cut off from their meaning, their *signifié*. They do not first refer to that *"signifié"* (as taught by classical theories of language), but to other signifiers (as de Saussure has shown). They always need another signifier to say what they mean, and this lack is constitutive for how they operate. Precisely because of that lack, the signifier can constitute the solution to the infantile libidinal being's traumatic problem. It enables the infant to identify her own drive-induced lack[37] with the signifier's lack so as to be able to miscognize, at this imaginary level, all lack. More specifically, the infant will constitute her "self" as an *answer* to the Other's demand. Or, in linguistic terms, the subject will maintain itself as the signified (*signifié*) of the signifiers (*signifiants*) it receives from the Other's demand.

The infant may coincide with her demand for the Other's love; her imaginary ruse, however, lies in acting as if it is *precisely the Other who made the demand*. This enables the infant to feel that she is herself *the exclusive answer to the supposed demand of the Other*. The object to which she "is" a relation can then be situated in the Other; the infant simply acts as if she were the object that the Other demands. She thus constitutes herself as "the Other's *demand*" (*"Demande* de l'Autre") in the double sense of the genitive. On the one hand, she is a bundle of demands directed at the Other; on the other, however, she can remain blind to that traumatic fact by taking herself as the answer to the demand *of* the Other (a demand the Other makes on her). In order to "create" a self, she takes herself as the "signified of the Other"[38] and in this (imaginary) way miscognizes both her own lack and that of the Other.

To explain what is at stake where the signifier and its bearer (here, the imaginary "subject"[39]) encounter one another, Lacan uses the concept of the "phallus." The term "phallus" stands primarily for that which can be "castrated," that is, for what can be missing or lacking. In the imaginary strategy outlined here, the libidinal being occupies the point in the Other where the Other is purely a signifier and, thus, pure lack. It does so in order to deny that lack and to act as if it is itself the signified of the signifier, the filling in of the lack. In other words, it positions itself in the place where the Other is "castrated" in order to act (in an imaginary way) as if it *is* itself the Other's "phallus." It thus acts as if it corresponds with what fills in the Other's lack. In this way, the libidinal being avoids confronting the fact that the Other is irrevocably "castrated." The Other, on whom the libidinal being must rely for help with its drive-related lack, is also marked by an irreconcilable lack. It can do nothing other than miscognize the Other's "castration" (in what Lacan technically calls *"méconaissance"*), and it does this by imagining that it is itself the adequate answer to the Other's lack, that is, that it is the Other's phallus.

This kind of imaginary strategy is doomed to fail. For the Other has more than just "his majesty the baby's" pleasure needs at heart; his desires go beyond the child. This is, again, a moment of shock and trauma for the infant: its entire imaginary ego-constitution begins to totter. Now the lack characterizing the Other can no longer be miscognized. The infant can no longer act as if she herself is what was missing, that is, the *signified*, the imaginary phallus. The lack in the Other now appears to be located somewhere else than where she is. Hence, the Other can no longer be regarded as a *complete* Other (complete, because the child fills up its lack), but is now undeniably seen to be lacking. It has become a *desiring* Other. This fact—that the Other *desires*—is again a genuine trauma for the infant. Imagining herself to be the answer to the Other's lack, suddenly, at a certain moment, she nonetheless hears the Other ask, "What do you want? (*"Che vuoi?"*).[40] That "answer" destroys her entire ego-construction and pulls the ground out from under her feet. If the Other must still ask for something, what else could that mean for the child than that it is *not* the answer to the demand of the Other, and that the latter is not the complete Other the infant imagined it was? Now, she must face the lack in the Other without the comforting illusion she is that lack's answer.

The child that up till then could constitute herself as the object of the Other's *demand* must now do so as the object of the Other's *desire*. She will no longer be able to act as if she coincides (imaginarily) with that object. The Other's object now lies "beyond" the child, and, just like the Other, the child can only *desire* it. Henceforth, she can only exist insofar as she identifies with this desire, and in this sense, becomes "the *subject* of the Other's desire."[41]

Here, too, the subject occupies the position of the Other's phallus. However, it can no longer maintain that it indubitably "is" this phallus, thereby denying the Other's lack. Now it must refer to a *castrated* Other and thus to a phallus that the Other is also unmistakably lacking. The subject must now constitute itself as a libidinal being that *desires* the phallus without ever being able to have access to it. The phallus becomes a *symbolic* object par excellence that the subject can no longer identify with imaginarily. For here the phallus stands precisely for what escapes its mirror image—because it escapes the Other. It becomes exclusively that which the Other *doesn't* have and thus desires.[42] And as the subject (the bearer) of a castrated Other, the libidinal being also becomes a subject of desire.

This confrontation with the castrated Other is crucial, among other things, for the sexuation of the young child's genital zone. Initially, the genitals are invested with the same pleasure as all the other parts of the body and have no further special libidinal meaning. Now, however, they become invested with a higher pleasure because they are the place on the child's body where the lack (by which it is libidinally menaced) literally inscribes itself, as it were. The genital zone becomes the place on the body where the boy can *lose* something. Henceforth, his entire relation to his penis is affected by the fear that it is not the "real" phallus. He imagines that the Other has it, an Other he has become afraid of because it can deprive him of his "precious thing." In the same way, the girl's genital zone also becomes the place on her body where there becomes a possibility of something missing, something that could be filled in by a "phallus." With her, just as with the boy, the phallus (i.e., sexuation's point of reference) lies exclusively with the Other. However, since this Other is castrated and cannot give them the phallus they wish to have, henceforth, they can only *desire* it. Only with the sexualization of the genital zone is the child able to break through its purely imaginary relation with the Other and, therefore acquire an independent identity as a subject of symbolic desire. For Lacan, the sexualization of the genital zone and the installation of a desiring subject thus go hand in hand.

It is striking how Lacan again comes close to Bouvet's object relations theory here. Just as with the latter, the Lacanian subject can only hold its ground when, after the Oedipus complex, the drive object is *phallically genitalized*. With both, a phallic sexuation goes hand in hand with the completion of subject formation. Just as with Bouvet, sexuation in Lacan will depend on the installation of a *distance* in relation to the object.[43] This is what the concept of "symbolic castration" amounts to. Only a phallically sexuated subject can control the distance between itself and the object and is therefore in a position to relate to reality in a more or less "normal" or "objective" way.

Here, once more, the entire difference lies in the status that Lacan gives the terms. Only as *symbolic* entities, as signifiers, Lacan claims again, do they decide the sexuation of human genitality and in this way decide the accompanying "distant" attitude toward the object. The phallus holds as a matrix for sexuation not insofar as it refers first and foremost ("really") to male sexuality, but only insofar as the phallus is *just* a signifier. This is how the desired object (the child's own genital included) is structurally—here meaning symbolically—maintained at a distance.[44] This symbolic castration gives the object relation its definitive structure. It installs both the lack and the object *at the correct—symbolic—distance.*

### 3.4. . . . and Phantasm

But the subject is not only the bearer of a relation toward an endlessly receding object; it *is* also this object. This was how we formulated the founding paradox of all object relations theory. Lacan will elaborate this paradox by means of a precise concept, the phantasm. "Phantasm" refers specifically to a brief scene that repeatedly haunts the mind of the analysand during the analytic cure but at first sight has no relation to the complaints he originally went into analysis for. Besides the emotional line of the analysand's discourse, there is at first sight an indifferent but persistent little story that often appears in his stream of consciousness: this is what Lacan calls "le fantasme," "phantasm." He defines it as a more or less fixed scenario of signifiers thanks to which the subject, sliding from one signifier to another, gains a certain consistency. It provides that subject with an anchoring point, not in the form of an imaginary "figure" ("*Gestalt*") as in the mirror stage, but in the form of a fixed series of signifiers.[45] This series invariably tells how the subject in one way or another disappears *under* the signifier (because that is what it must do in order to become the "bearer" of signifiers). "A child is being beaten," a well-known phantasm that Freud analyzed with a number of his patients, reveals not only how they fantasize that their "father" beats another child, but also how they themselves would like to be beaten by the "father."[46] In other words, it reveals how they would like to disappear in (and *under*) the symbolic order, hence Lacan's interpretation. In his conceptualization, the phantasm stands for a linguistic "image" that shows in a hidden way how the libidinal being has disappeared in the Other so as, in this way, to become its subject.

At the level of the symbolic, then, the subject finds its consistency no longer in a visual (imaginary) figure (the ego), but in a phantasm in which it can disappear as a *subject* of desire without also undoing the *object relation* it originally stems from.[47] The center of gravity of the object relation now lies entirely in the object pole. The libidinal being realizes itself as the subject of desire, a subject that has its ultimate support in a small set of signifiers, the "phantasm," in which the entire weight is now placed on the object.[48] Here, the object relations paradox gains adequate expression, showing how the entire drive economy "coincides" with its object, without ceasing to be a desire for that object. In other words, the being of the drive "is" indeed both its object *and* its relation to that object.

In the sixth seminar, *Desire and Its Interpretation*, where Lacan specifically addresses this topic, he focuses on the phantasm of the miser. It is brought to his attention through a passage from Simone Weil's, *Gravity and Grace*, a compilation of aphorisms. There, the famous Christian mystic refers to the mystery of the "miser," a passage to which Lacan returns four times in the course of his seminar. Weil writes,

> To ascertain exactly what the miser whose treasure was stolen lost: thus we should learn much.[49]

The idea that a miser would miss his treasure most if it were lost is indeed not that certain. In fact, he *already* misses it. This is precisely why he is a miser: he not only denies everyone else the enjoyment of his treasure, but also himself. No matter how attached to it he is, he leaves it untouched. And if deprived of it, even he himself would not be able to say what precisely he is missing. In this sense, the miser's treasure strikingly illustrates what Lacan defines as the "object of phantasm." The treasure makes up the center of a scenario to which, at the most fundamental level, the miser owes his identity as miser. It indicates the level at which he no longer seems able to maintain himself as the subject (the bearer) of his narrative. For as soon as he is confronted, either consciously or unconsciously, with the fact that he does not know who he is and precisely what he seeks in his riches, he slides away into his phantasm. He sinks down into a scenario of signifiers in which he (as subject) completely forgets himself and "merges" with his beloved treasure. However, he doesn't "really" merge with his treasure; he only merges with the *scenario* crystallized around that object. He merges with a signifying scenario from which the treasure remains *at distance*. As object of desire, the treasure is not to be reduced to one of the signifiers that constitute the miser's life. Rather, it is located where the signifiers always fall short and, in this way, maintain the miser's desire (or, what amounts to the same thing, the object *relation* he "is"). The object is to be sought at the place of the "phallus," that is, the place where that pure (phallic, symbolic) lack is covered up by the scenario of the phantasm. Keeping everyone (including himself) from his treasure, the only experience he has of it is that of a *lack*. In the final analysis, his treasure coincides with that very "lack," which is the ultimate reason why he keeps it above all away from himself.

What happens, then, when someone no longer manages to hide that object (and, hence, that lack) from others as well as from himself? Just after Lacan cites Weil's aphorism for the first time, he refers to a scene from a film by Jean Renoir that offers a striking illustration of this. In a remarkable scene from *La règle du jeu* (1939), at a party, an amateur collector of barrel organs desires to reveal his most beautiful and precious acquisition. When the moment arrives however, the man is overcome by an intolerable sense of embarrassment and creeps away in shame.

> Recall if you have a memory of it, this film [*La règle du jeu*] at the moment when Dalio discovers before a numerous audience his last finding: a very beautiful music box. At that moment, the person literally is in the position that can and must be described exactly as shame: he becomes red in the face, he fades away, he disappears, he is very embarrassed . . .[50]

For Lacan, it is clear: the man suddenly fears that by showing his newest acquisition, he will in fact reveal only an ontological lack. That toward which his entire existence—his desire and his identity included—was aimed seems to be "a thing of nothing." All of a sudden, the "lack of being" on which as a libidinal being he rests, threatens to rise up without protection to the surface. Here, there is no single signifier to deflect attention, while the presence of the audience prevents him from dreaming himself away (i.e., of fading away into his phantasm). A direct, unmediated confrontation with this lack can no longer be avoided. Should his object undergo such a "sacrilege," the subject—that is, the object relation—can only creep away in shame and anxiety, unwilling to succumb to this confrontation. In his collection, a collector discovers precisely the *phantasm* so as to be spared this confrontation and this shame. This is similar to the unconscious motive behind the miser's phantasm as well. The latter keeps his riches away from everyone's desire primarily out of the anxiety that, if someone asked for it, he would have to admit that his most precious possession is "a thing of nothing," a pure lack.

Each in their own way, the robbed miser and the surprised collector demonstrate how in the object relation from which we stem, it is all a matter of a lack. It is thanks to this persistent lack that desire maintains itself *as* desire. And it is only to this extent that we are able to be the bearers of desire. Yet, as subject of that desire, one is nonetheless able for a moment to "fade away" and to transfer the task of "bearer" over to the object. This is what happens in the phantasm. As the libidinal being threatens no longer to be able to maintain itself as the bearer of signifiers, its entire drive economy is borne through a scenario that still relies exclusively on the object. The fantasies of the miser or the collector demonstrate this clearly.

Lacan's subject theory thus supposes the human being to coincide with a libidinal orientation toward an unreachable and, in the final analysis, purely phantasmatic object. The question that it raises here is whether one can found an ethics on such a theory? Can morality be grounded at all if, in the final analysis, man comes down to a polymorphous-perverse, unsatisfiable desire? Does the good, as object of our desire, have a sufficiently firm basis, if fantasies such as those of the miser and the collector must serve as a model for it? These are the kinds of questions that Lacan's seminar on "the ethics of psychoanalysis" addresses. This is not to say, however, that he wasn't concerned with the problem of ethics before he began this seminar. On the contrary, the train of thought pursued in his earlier seminars contains plenty of indications in this direction. The daring novelty of his *Ethics Seminar* is only rendered fully visible in the context of this background which is why the following section provides a short summary of the implicit ethics contained in Lacan's first seminars.

### 4. Ethics and Phantasm

Thus psychoanalysis maintains that the image, far from abstracting
us and causing us to live in the mode of gratuitous fantasy, seems to
deliver us profoundly to ourselves.

(Maurice Blanchot)[51]

Ethics can be defined as the human attempt to realize "the good." In that
sense, in the years preceding his seventh seminar as well, Lacan never
doubted that ethics can—and must—express its foundations by calling on
notions like desire and lack. According to Lacan, the ethical law does not
rest upon the good "in itself" but on desire (for the good or for whatever). And even if desire is rightly to be defined as based in an amoral,
polymorphous-perverse drive, it nevertheless provides a solid base for ethics,
so Lacan had argued from the very beginning of his oeuvre. Because of its
original helplessness, the polymorphous-perverse libidinal being is entirely
reliant on the Other (on other people, on the "symbolic" universe). And
because it never can totally appropriate the Other, the latter is inevitably
perceived as a law. The Other appears to the infant as an imperative, as
a law without which it is unable to become a subject. That is why ethics
is a solid, indispensable factor in subject formation. In this sense, all
"goods" and all ideals (including the Freudian ego-ideal) are to be interpreted as objects of desire. And even if they refer, in the final analysis, to
a phantasm, they support the subject in its ethical stability. In this sense,
psychoanalysis's ethical task is primarily to bring the analysand in touch
with his (unconscious) desire, rather than with moral values.

The question, of course, is what it means for someone to get in
touch with his (unconscious) desire. Of course it means that, through
the story she spins about herself, the analysand tracks down a number
of unknown, unconscious desires and is finally able to comply with them
in a less inhibited manner. Nevertheless, such a cure doesn't solve all
frustrations, nor does it definitively bring the unconscious to the surface.
Anyone who expects this kind of "good" from a psychoanalytic cure cannot but be disappointed. For that kind of cure starts from the idea that
both the unconscious and desire are the foundational structures of human
existence. This is why, after the cure as well, the analysand cannot but
remain a desiring subject. To come to terms with one's desire—which is
the fundamental task of analysis—means reconciling someone with the
fact that his or her desire will never be anything but "frustrated" and
unsatisfied.

Or, even more strongly: a Lacanian perspective implies taking comfort
in the fact that desire is unquestionably never one's "own." "Desire is the
desire of the Other" Lacan again and again tells us. Man is the subject of

the desire *of* (and *for*) the Other. He is the "bearer" of a *desiring* Other, an Other who, just like the subject, will never *be* its own "self" (in the full sense of the word), but will only *desire* it. The Other, too, in the final analysis, comes down to a "lack of self" or, what amounts to the same thing, to a mere lack. *And it is of this lack that man is forced to become the subject, its bearer.* To bring someone into contact with his desire thus equals confronting him with a radical lack that is not even his own, but which he nevertheless coincides with as with his most intimate "self." He must put up with the fact that he both stems from a radical lack and that the remedy for it succeeds only because it also radically falls short. Confrontation with the truth, however liberating, must therefore also necessarily be painful. For what comes to light could only have been tolerated insofar as it was kept repressed.

It is not a mere coincidence that in his sixth seminar, where he protractedly and thoroughly sounds out these lines of thought, Lacan comes up against Simone Weil's *Gravity and Grace*. This Christian mystic, too, starts from the same premise—the primacy of desire—to conclude that in his most intimate kernel, a human being is pure desire and therefore "nothing," "lacking" and "empty." For Weil, man must confront this emptiness. This is what she writes in her chapter "Detachment," in typically meditative style:

> Always, beyond the particular object whatever it may be, we have to fix our will on the void—to will the void. [Et tout, par delà l'objet particulier quel qu'il soit, vouloir à vide, vouloir le vide.] For the good which we can neither picture nor define is a void for us. But a void fuller than all fullness. [. . .] The good seems to us as a nothingness [néant], since there is no *thing* that is good. But this nothingness is not unreal. Compared with it, everything in existence is unreal. (Weil, 1987: 13; 1948: 15)

By freeing oneself from all attachment, by emptying oneself and accepting one's own emptiness, man comes to terms with what desire actually wants, which is "nothingness," Weil argues. For her, like for Lacan, such a confrontation with emptiness also demands a victory over the imaginary. Moreover, the "imagination," which immediately wants to fill anything that is empty, blocks the way to anyone who wants to face desire and, hence, the emptiness he basically *is*. In the first aphorism of the following chapter we find:

> The imagination is continuously at work filling up all the fissures through which grace might pass. (Weil 1987: 16; 1948: 19)

For Lacan, too, the path to such a confrontation cannot be an imaginary one; for, as he teaches, the imaginary way of dealing with a lack consists in denying that lack (i.e., miscognition). Only a symbolic approach—an approach that expressly operates on the slippery surface of signifiers—opens up the possibility, at least for a moment, of seeing beyond repression and, thus, of getting in touch with the lack upon which desire is founded. A confrontation with the lack at the level of the signifier—the lack in the Other—can bring me to the point of accepting the lack that I *am*, that is, of accepting that I *am* desire. So far, it is rather hard to see where Lacan and Weil disagree.

But they do disagree concerning Lacan's thesis that the lack of the symbolic order—the emptiness that for Weil too desire is based on—is radically *un*sublatable. "The void is the complete fullness," we read in Weil (on the same page, note, as that of her aphorism on the miser Lacan cited; Weil 1987: 21; 1948; 26).[52] Weil's "full emptiness" conceives of desire from a teleological as well as theological perspective. It functions as a "Supreme Good" or as a God-given "state of grace," a situation in which desire as such is fully satisfied. The emptiness Lacan has in mind, however, is and remains empty once and for all. For him, desire never ceases desiring, precisely because every "object" through which it obtains satisfaction is a phantasm—even the "objectless object" of Weil's emptiness.

Yet the question arises whether this is really so different from Weil's "theory of desire"? She may indeed define her "emptiness" as "full," and clothe it in deep theological prerogatives, but this does not prevent her from continually stressing how this fullness must be experienced as an emptiness all the same. Precisely *believing* in the emptiness as 'fullness itself' is the evil she argues against. Similarly, she argues against any belief that fixes itself on the *existence* and ultimate *meaning* of God. In her eyes, this is precisely what the miser does. He makes his treasure from the "emptiness" his desire longs for, which is why, according to Weil, God "withdraws himself in order not to be loved like the treasure is by the miser."[53] So, apparently, the emptiness and the lack Simone Weil talks about never operates simply as a massive fullness.

On the other side, Lacan's symbolic lack seems not to be as empty as he pretends. His concept of the "symbolic Other" is meant to be an alternative to Weil's God as the place where desire can meet "itself" and make full circle. Lacan, in turn, stresses how the point where desire is supposed to make full circle is itself lacking. The symbolic universe in which desire operates by means of that lack rests on a point of pure lack, a point where any (ontological) ground is absent. Yet one can still ask whether this symbolic order operating by means of its own lack does not, in the final analysis, end up lacking *nowhere* and lacking *nothing* at all, and whether it does not, in its own but nonetheless similar way to what Weil says, function as fullness, as completeness. On the one hand, we have the full emptiness to which Weil's God is reduced. On the other, there is Lacan's symbolic "order of lack" making full circle in that very lack. What precise difference does this make here?

After all, doesn't Lacan cite Weil precisely because he feels such a kinship with her? Is he really in disagreement with the answer that she gives to her riddle of the miser? For both Lacan and Weil, the robbed miser is missing a "lack," and his miserliness is an imaginary attachment to that ("miscognized") lack.[54] For both, he must overcome this imaginary fixation on his riches in order to be liberated from his suffocating avarice and, finally, to rediscover the real condition of his desire. However, for Lacan, overcoming that fixation does not equal annihilating it. In its quality of phantasm, this fixation remains constitutive for the subject and his desire (in this case, the miser's). Only, the miser will have to rediscover that phantasm *as such* within his symbolically functioning desire. He will have to face it as what offers his subject an unconscious support so that it can move "fluidly" from one signifier to another.

But does the Lacanian phantasm, as the point of "nothing" where the symbolic order makes full circle, differ that much from the nothing named God, that is, the pure absence and emptiness Simone Weil places in the centre of the universe? Do both God and the phantasm not function as a final veil for the finitude and the (in Lacanese, phallic) lack our human (i.e., symbolic) world rests on? And is not Lacan's phantasm, quite like Weil's empty God, not primarily meant to reconcile our desire with the unconditional imperative of the (symbolic) law whose ground definitely escapes us? In other words, is Lacan's psychoanalytic "theory of lack" really so different from the mystical Christian doctrine? Christianity too, for that matter, offers a theory of lack, that is, a theory of sin. And, similar to Lacanian theory, this Christian theory locates the way out of sin in the paradoxical confession that the greatest sin lies in wanting to be without sin.[55] Just as for Lacan, it is all a matter of admitting that we are based on an irremovable, unsublatable lack.

It is far from implausible that these kinds of questions were also in Lacan's mind in the weeks and months following his introduction of Simone Weil's aphorism concerning the miser in his seminar on December 10, 1958. Although he never explicitly utters these questions, it is nonetheless striking that he did *not* draw the same conclusions as Weil on these issues. Anyway, this is what one must deduce from what he says later in the same seminar (the lessons of April 8 and 15, and May 13, 1959). It is not impossible that it was precisely from the Christian nature of Weil's conclusions that he recoiled, that is, from a conclusion that makes a full circle of desire's problematic primacy. This might be why he staked everything on thinking Weil's aphorism of the miser in a new way. It seems as though he was initially fascinated by that aphorism as he worked on a theory of the phantasm, but that, through closer examination, he had to come to a conclusion that differs radically from Weil's.

Lacan's reading of *Hamlet* in the sixth seminar was crucial for this turn. Where the object of the phantasm was previously conceived exclusively as a signifier, after his *Hamlet* seminar, he increasingly emphasizes the *real* status of that object. This new accent will make it impossible to lock up the phantasm entirely within the limits of the symbolic. The phantasm will henceforth refer to a *real* remainder that radically escapes the symbolic (i.e., the realm of signifiers) and prevents that order from "closing" in on itself, from making full circle. The point where the order ought to make full circle will turn out to be that of an object that falls radically outside its domain and keeps it permanently open. This will make Lacan draw very different conclusions from Weil's aphorism of the miser and will force him to a radically different characterization of ethics.

## 5. Introducing a Real Object

### 5.1. A "Phallophanie" . . .

When Lacan cites Simone Weil for the first time, he is on the point of completing a theory of the phantasm by way of an extensive commentary on *Hamlet*, illustrating through it a "theory of desire" that is not at all incompatible with the one we saw in Weil. In Shakespeare's tragedy, Lacan reads how, in the final analysis, all desire is oriented toward—and based in—a phantasmatic object[56] and how the subject has to learn to assume this *imaginary* object as a *symbolic* lack. It is only as a lack at the level of the signifier (i.e., as symbolic phallus) that the object supports and maintains desire. While desire might be based in a mere lack, it is nevertheless able to find "itself" in that very lack *as such* or, what amounts to the same thing, in the signifier as such. So, Lacan's claim is very close to Simone Weil for whom everything goes back to a "lack" or an "emptiness" that equals "fullness" or "totality itself."

Lacan reads *Hamlet* as an explicit "tragedy of desire."[57] The main character gives a perfect illustration of someone who can no longer position himself as a subject of desire. Although desire might be the desire of the Other, as Lacan never tires of telling us, Hamlet's paradigmatic figures for that Other have suffered a significant dent. His mother has all too quickly—and, in his eyes, not unsuspiciously—exchanged her dead husband (Hamlet's father) for a new, living one. And his father has appeared to him, not as an Other in whom he can "bury" (i.e., repress) his lack, but, precisely the reverse, as an Other whose own lack Hamlet must now repair (by revenging his father's murder).

In contrast to Oedipus who is confronted with a "father" (the Other) he cannot escape and in relation to whom he falls short, Hamlet is confronted with a "father" who himself falls short and who demands that Hamlet repair his "paternal" lack.[58] Such a direct confrontation with the Other's lack—and thus with desire—traumatizes Hamlet to such an extent that he sees only one libidinal way out: to *miscognize* this lack in the Other and act as if he is himself its fulfillment (i.e. its "phallus"). This is to say that Hamlet falls back into an *imaginary* relation to the Other's desire. This is why he focuses on his mother. His relation to her has the structural format of a "Demand," and the position he takes in this is the answer to that Demand. In other words, he positions himself as the fulfillment (*signifié*) of the Other's lack. He is apparently no longer able to fully constitute himself within the desire of the *symbolic* Other, that which would enable him to remain a "subject" of desire; the only thing he is capable of is to (imaginarily) miscognize everything that is desire.

It is this *miscognition* that hides behind Hamlet's famous doubt, according to Lacan. His famous question whether it is better "to be or not to be" is not so much an abstract, metaphysical or existential question as a means of expressing his position within the Other's (in this case: the mother's) domain in which he must constitute himself. This is why he reads that famous question as "to be or not to be *the phallus*": *am* I or *am* I not the Other's phallus? Am I or am I not the object that fulfills the Other's desire, that satisfies and annihilates desire, and thus resolves all the lacks in the world that plague us?

This is why Hamlet is neither able to miss nor to tolerate the Other's desire.[59] On the one hand, he frontally attacks desire and characterizes it as sin and vice and damns it to hell. This is why he rejects both his mother's and Ophelia's love. On the other hand, he remains entirely preoccupied with it, given the fact that only in the realm of the Other's desire is he able to realize himself as a libidinal being. This ambiguity—that is, his inability to remain the subject of desire—makes Hamlet fall back into the libidinal format of "Demand," which makes him lose the support the phantasm normally offers. He now (imaginarily) has to act as if he *were himself* the object of the Other's desire. The phantasm would have prevented him from wanting to *be* that object, only allowing him to act through *desire* for it. This comfort Hamlet must now do without.

If the phantasm could be reinstalled, Hamlet would be given a chance to realize himself again as the subject of desire (of the Other). This is effectively what takes place in the Shakespearean tragedy, more precisely, at the moment when Hamlet "rediscovers" Ophelia, his former phantasmatic object, and remembers how he never had stopped loving her—which, however, did not happen without first having reviled, humiliated, and neglected her. For, like his mother, she was marked by desire and lack, things he despised throughout his crisis. He imaginarily denied (miscognized) the lack—or, what amounts to the same thing, the phallus—that she was to him. Until, suddenly—in what Lacan calls a "phallophanie"[60]—Hamlet recognizes the lack again, that is, recognizes the phallus that she is, acknowledging this at the level of the symbolic.

Let us focus on this famous "phallophanic" scene. Just returned from his trip to England, Hamlet is unexpectedly witness to the funeral of Ophelia who has meanwhile committed suicide. From his concealed position behind the graveyard's bushes, he watches how overwhelmed by grief, his best friend Laertes, Ophelia's brother, leaps into the grave to embrace his sister one last time. There he lashes out again at the one who has been responsible for all this, Hamlet. Precisely at that moment, the latter comes into view. He, too, leaps into the grave and there the old friends come to blows. Nobody loved Ophelia more than I, Hamlet shouts:

> I lov'd Ophelia: forty thousand brothers
> Could not, with all their quantity of love,
> Make up my sum.[61]

Still reviled a minute before, Ophelia has suddenly become the lovable Ophelia again, more desirable than ever. It seems that, at the very bed of her grave, Hamlet has rediscovered his desire. In any event, what follows is very clear: his change will indeed enable him to become the "bearer," the "subject of the desire of the Other" again. In other words, he will be able to take the position of revenging his father, that is, of eliminating his uncle.

What is so special about this scene, then, that it enables Hamlet to rediscover his desire? What changes Ophelia, the "object" of Hamlet's contempt in which he disapproved all lack and desire, suddenly into the "object" in which lack (phallus) and desire become again attractive to him? What makes Ophelia's unexpected appearance a pure "phallophany" that stops him from "miscognizing" all lack and desire? Simply the fact that she is dead, is Lacan's reply. Or, more accurately, simply the fact that she is mourned, and mourned, moreover, by an *Other*, Laertes. At the end of his lesson of April 15, 1959, Lacan refers to "this furious fight at the bed of the grave" as a scene

> which indicates the function of the object as what can be reconquered only at the price of mourning and of death [in order to become the again the phantasmatic support of desire].[62]

Hamlet's relation to Laertes, his bosom friend and role model (his model for identification) is thoroughly imaginary, Lacan argues. His crisis even intensifies the negative sides of his imaginary attitude. Here, too, Hamlet positions himself in his relation to his friend at a point where the mourning Laertes is almost reduced to his "lack" (i.e., to the point where he is nothing but desire for an unreachable—dead—ultimate object). For this is the best position for miscognizing this lack and putting himself forward as a remedy against that lack. However, in the bizarre churchyard scene, this imaginary strategy fails. Modeling himself on Laertes, Hamlet can no longer identify with him as though he, Hamlet, was Laertes' object of desire (which would enable him to transform Laertes' *symbolic* desire into an *imaginary* Demand). Face to face with the *dead* Ophelia, he now identifies with Laertes insofar as he explicitly *desires* Ophelia, that is, an object with which he, Hamlet (and also Laertes) *cannot* coincide. Here, the imaginary conflict between Hamlet and Laertes does not so much bridge the distance toward the object but, precisely, *installs* that distance. This conflict reinstalls the object as a (phallic, symbolic, irremovable) lack. By identifying with the mourning Laertes, Hamlet installs a definitive distance between himself and the object he now thoroughly desires again. In this way, Hamlet's phantasm around Ophelia is restored as well as the basic condition that enables him to reposition himself as a desiring subject.

For Hamlet, the entire scene is indeed a "phallophany," an appearance of the lack *as such*. Carried to her grave, Ophelia suddenly appears to him again as the pure lack—as the Other's (castrated) phallus—which Hamlet can no longer (imaginarily) ignore (miscognize). On the contrary, he explicitly affirms that lack and allows it to fully "denote" and "signify" him. By identifying with Laertes' mourning, he actually mourns the phallus, that is, the lack with which the Other is irreparably marked (in this case, Laertes). He will no longer think he can (imaginarily) supplement this lack by means of his bold existence; now he will acknowledge it—by mourning it—as an irremovable, unsublatable object of desire.[63]

Where does Lacan's Hamlet find his "real" self? Where, in other words, does he find the desire and the lack that he "is"? Not in a *real* lack, in any case. If it were *really* lived, such a "lack-in-itself" would literally imply the death of the one who lives it. He can find himself only in a *symbolic* lack, Lacan emphasizes here. Hamlet can only find the lack from which he stems in an order that is itself marked by lack: the order of signifiers. He finds himself precisely at the place where the order lacks and where, in its (phallic) lack, it makes full circle. Begun as a flight from all lack, his "odyssee" arrives at that same lack. He discovers at the end of his quest that the emptiness of desire he once so hated in his mother and his lover is his ultimate *raison d'existence*, as well as the keystone of his identity. To his father's demand, who beseeches him to undo the lack that struck him, he finally answers by offering himself as a mere lack—as a deadly wound. He finds the answer to his question about desire nowhere else than in the emptiness of his desire. In this emptiness and this lack, he finally meets his true "self": this is the core of Lacan's interpretation of *Hamlet*.

And where, according to Simone Weil, does the miser find his true "self," that is, his desire? Not so much in the tangible riches he cherishes but in the "lack itself" that the riches stand for. Weil's miser found himself in the "emptiness" that lay hidden behind the riches, and which, for anyone who detaches himself from all his riches, could be experienced as a true fullness.

Lacan's theory of *desire*, as it gained shape over the course of his sixth seminar, *was about to "close" the whole problematic of desire and its lack in on lack itself*, a "lack" operating as both the motor and the keystone of the autonomous symbolic order. Had Lacan left his theory like this, it would hardly have changed the classical ethical paradigms. At any rate, a new, psychoanalytically oriented "ethics of desire" would have recognized the Christian mystically oriented ethic as its predecessor. Thought from the primacy of desire, the good as the object of desire would have been marked by an irremovable lack, it is true, but this desire would nevertheless have found "itself" precisely *in* that lack "itself," that lack being the "good" that it seeks. In any case, the discovery of the symbolic order as the "scene" in which the human libidinal being finds its ground encouraged Lacan to conceive such desire as a circular quest for itself (which is at the same time its lack and its "supreme good"). In this way, thinking ethics from the primacy of desire and lack—that is, from the paradigm of psychoanalysis—would have changed little. The Christian ethics drawn from Weil's mystical thought would not really have differed from the ethical consequences resulting from Lacan's theory of desire of that period.

### 5.2. . . . Under Critique

Nevertheless, things went differently. The final lessons of Lacan's sixth seminar already show how he became less and less satisfied with a purely imaginary or symbolic characterization of desire's ultimate object.[64] At the moment when he finally explains Hamlet's "phallophany," as he had long and with great pathos announced to his audience he would do, he no longer seems able to read Ophelia exclusively as the phallus. The object of desire and phantasm (in this case, Hamlet's) no longer seems able to be thought exclusively as imaginary or symbolic. What he already had been calling the "*objet petit a*"[65] for the last two seminar-sessions, he is now going to characterize as real. In the final lessons of the sixth seminar, this intent becomes more and more pronounced.

With this, he corrects his own idea that desire would close in on itself,—that is, in an empty, phallic signifier. Instead, desire stands open toward the real. By interpreting the ultimate object as something real, it was easier to develop why the object relation the libidinal being rests on never stops being a *relation* to that object, despite its radical identification with the object. To give that ultimate object—which is also the object of the phantasm—a real status radicalizes the nature of desire. In the last lesson of the sixth seminar, Lacan describes the phantasm primarily as the articulation of an "opposition," a "cut," a "disconnection" between the subject and object poles of the "object relation" that desire stems from.[66] Here he defines the object constituting the kernel of the phantasm as a (real) remainder escaping the symbolic surface of desire. In his lesson of July 1, 1959 (the final lesson of his sixth seminar), he says that the "object of desire"

> in its nature is a 'residue,' a remainder. It is the 'residue' which is dumped by 'being' [and] to which the speaking subject is confronted as such, [. . .]. And this is the way the object joins the real.[67]

Although the object still continues to function as a signifier, in the final analysis, it points not purely to other signifiers, but also to the real, or, as Lacan puts it here, "to being . . . insofar as this is marked by the signifier" (Lacan, 1996a; 534). This is to say that the object relation on which desire is founded, is a radically *open* relation.[68]

Such openness indisputably responds to the main issue of Lacan's seminar on "Desire and Its Interpretation." As opposed to the all too "moralizing" object relations theory that supposes desire to be based in the object to which one is by nature ("instinctively") attached, Lacan tries to approach this issue exclusively from the primacy of desire. It is desire that determines the object, and not the other way around. According to Lacan at the end of that seminar, this is as much as to say that the libidinal being only exists as an *openness to* an always retreating—because always *desired*—"object." In the final lesson, Lacan explicitly characterizes that ultimate object—baptized meanwhile as the "object a"—as "something open":

> The object as such, the object a of the graph, if you prefer, is something open.[69]

The analytic cure, too, essentially works toward such a kind of openness. In search of himself as the desire that he *is*, the analysand is not only confronted with the fact that he is the desire of the Other, but also, according to Lacan at the end of the same lesson, that he

> opens upon a cut, upon pure being, manifesting itself here as lack.[70]

In the closing sentences of this lesson (which, in Lacan's own words, forms a sort of "prelesson" on the theme of the following seminar[71]), he also refers explicitly to this openness. The psychoanalytic cure operates exclusively within the " 'cut' of the word," claims Lacan, but to this extent processes an "opening [. . .] towards something radically new."[72] No one who glances further through the seminar he will give a couple of months later, will misunderstand this hint: he is indisputably referring to "*das Ding*," one of the main terms in his *Ethics Seminar*.

## 5.3. An Expressly Ethical Context

It is worth remembering that the link to that following seminar is not solely confined to this single, somewhat mysterious reference to *das Ding* we find here. The entire problematic of the *Ethics Seminar*—including major themes such as the problem of the "Supreme Good," "hedonism," "utilitarianism," Aristotle's "*master* ethics"—is already announced in the first lesson of Lacan's seminar on "Desire and Its Interpretation." There, all the issues developed extensively in the next, seventh seminar, are already summed up, including his critique of the explicit moralizing suppositions behind the current object relations theory of his days.

Contained in Fairbairn's distinction between "pleasure seeking" and "object seeking" is nothing other than the classical question with which all traditional ethics have wrestled, Lacan claims, namely whether the object of one's highest striving (the good) also guarantees the greatest pleasure. In that lesson we read:

> I will, more or less, stand still with what has been the position of the philosophers in this. This has always been very exemplary [if one regards things] from the point we situate our problem [i.e., from desire]. I have been so diligent to put on top of the blackboard these three [*sic*!] terms, *pleasure-seeking, object-seeking*. Seeking pleasure [on the one hand], seeking the object [on the other]: this is the way reflection and morality always have put the problem—I mean the theoretical ethics, the ethics which expresses itself through prescriptions and rules, through what philosophers and certainly so-called ethicists promote.[73]

Is what gives us the greatest pleasure also of the highest ethical value? Is the satisfaction our desire unconsciously leads us to also the ethical good that we consciously have before our eyes? While the majority of psychoanalytic theories answer in the affirmative, it was clear for Lacan that under no circumstances could Freud's basic intuition allow this. Pleasure is polymorphous-perverse and thus "perverts" everything that is offered to it as the "supreme Good" or the "good in itself." This is the basic intuition behind his inquiry into the pleasure principle: human desire has no firm ontological ground, but is based in a principle of "ontological perversion": pleasure. So, desire is not bound to any specific good and nor is it a good in itself. It is a "mere"—that is to say, polymorphous-perverse—openness and therefore cannot be defined in terms of *what* it "opens" to—defined here, in object relations terms, as the "object." Or, in more traditional terms: even if there may be something *transcendent* about desire, desire cannot be defined or thought *through* that transcendence.

# Chapter 2

# Crucial Problems

The difficulty—at times even unreadability—of the Lacanian text is well known. Apart from Lacan's speaking style (long sentences, mannerist constructions, etc.), this difficulty is also due to the fact that he rarely if ever spells out the *precise* question or problem he is wrestling with. Yet it is only from such precise information that his entire line of argumentation can be clearly grasped. Hence, before starting a close reading of Lacan's ethics seminar, it will be helpful to list at least some of the larger questions and crucial problem areas Lacan is dealing with. Being aware of them is indispensable for gaining insight into the seminar as a whole.

A first point is that Lacan's turn toward ethics is in itself rather striking. Where he previously maintained a strict distinction between ethics and psychoanalysis, in his seventh seminar he doesn't hesitate to call the kernel of the psyche something that is "ethical through and through." He even attributes to psychoanalysis as such the status of an ethics (see below, section 1).

Second, this turn makes the problematic of moral guilt particularly complex. Where Lacanian psychoanalysis previously guaranteed desire a refuge when it extricated itself from moral guilt, in his seventh seminar he will conclude that we can also be guilty in the eyes of desire itself (see 2).

And, third, although Lacan felt compelled to grant both the psyche and psychoanalysis an ethical status, this did not stop him from claiming that psychoanalysis is incapable of formulating a new practical ethics. The same goes for the emphasis psychoanalysis puts on the erotic dimension of human existence. Despite this emphasis, it still appears that psychoanalysis has been unable to elaborate a new kind of erotics, that is, an erotic ethos founded on psychoanalytical premises (see 3).

## 1. One Ethical Demand versus Another

It is not simply the philosopher's thought that seeks to justify duty.
(S7E: 8; SF: 16)

No one has been more hostile to all forms of moral approaches to psychoanalysis than Lacan. He is too convinced that the desire that man 'is'
stems from a polymorphous-perverse drive, which is per se without any
ethical quality. Anyone who attributes an inherent morality to desire or
maintains that libidinal life is automatically directed towards an ethically
firm ego misses the true "scandal" of psychoanalysis in Lacan's eyes. To
grant desire a primary function—one of the conditions sine qua non of
psychoanalysis—is, at the very least, to presume that one must rethink
ethics beginning with the moral indifference of the polymorphous-perverse
drive. To take the opposite direction and start out from ethical premises
is to fill out in advance the drive's open, polymorphously perverse nature
with one's own wishes and fantasies, and immediately to fall into a mor-
alistic distortion of the psychoanalytic paradigm. For Lacan, ethics and
desire are strictly differentiated from one another.

In his seminar given two years earlier (*Seminar V: The Formations of
the Unconscious*), for example, Lacan explicitly states that Freud's oeuvre
brought about a break with modern theories of desire precisely because
he did not make the mistake of starting from ethical premises. Moreover,
"ethics" is something that primarily works against desire or disciplines it,
as he says in his lesson of March 5, 1958:

> I have brought to your attention how, up till Freud, that ele-
> ment as such [i.e., desire] always has been minimized and in
> a sense removed. This allows me to say that, up till Freud,
> every enquiry concerning the human libidinal economy was
> more or less based on a moral, ethical preoccupation—in the
> sense that it was less a matter of studying than of minimizing
> and disciplining desire. (SV: 251; own translation)

Here, Lacan identifies ethics with the psychological function that
restrains desire through commands, prohibitions and ideals, and which
psychoanalysis names the superego. In his eyes, ethics mainly functions
as something that turns *against* the drive and desire and therefore fails
to offer adequate access to the problematic of desire.

It is particularly striking, then, that not even two years later, in
his seventh seminar, Lacan assumes a quite different tone. Ethics, he
emphatically claims now, is not only something that must be subjected to

psychoanalytic critique. It is also the very essence of its problematic and the heart of its existence, both at the theoretical and the practical level.

In the first lesson of the seminar, Lacan says that the moral dimension of psychoanalysis lies nowhere else than in its founding experience, that is, the experience of the unconscious. This unconscious is no neutral, "mute" thing. Rather, it "speaks" and imposes itself on us. It presents itself as an unremitting appeal. For Lacan, the well known Freudian formula, "Wo Es war, soll Ich werden," means nothing less than that the unconscious makes itself knowable as an *ethical* command:

> The moral experience involved in psychoanalysis is the one that is summed up in the original imperative proposed in what might be called the Freudian ascetic experience, namely, that *Wo Es war, soll Ich werden* with which Freud concludes the second part of his *Vorlesungen (Introductory Lectures)* on psychoanalysis. (S7E: 7; S7F: 15–16)[1]

What drives us, that is, the drive that at the most fundamental level keeps us perpetually on the hop, stems from an "ought" or, as Lacan calls it, an "original imperative," a command or an exhortation that is described here as a "moral experience." To enter into a confrontation with our unconscious, to search for the desires that official morality barely tolerates, to go against the ethical ideals that rule us: at the base of all of this lies an ethical imperative for Lacan.

Yet while the appeal that comes from the unconscious might be "ethical," this is not to say it is compatible with that other, equally ethical appeal of the superego. When, in the psychoanalytic cure, an obsessional battles again and again with his superego (the problem of obsessional neurosis provokes the context for Lacan's discussion of ethics; S7E: 7; S7F: 15–16), his question is not so much how he can accommodate this ethical imperative as how, precisely, he can escape it. He fumbles desperately for ways of *dis*obeying this "foreign" law that he is bound to so painfully. He will use every means at his disposal in order to maintain a distance to the Law and its demands. In like manner he will also maintain a distance to the demands that *he* makes to the Law in return, a demand to which the law never seems to adequately respond. It is as if, beside the law he is (imaginarily) bound to with demands and counter demands, there is another law that commands him to renounce the first law. The obsessional's permanent indecision is not a back and forth oscillation between the moral and the immoral. Both sides of the alternative, according to Lacan, are ethical, and the "truly" ethical dimension perhaps lies rather in the disobedience. This is at least what he suggests when, in front of his audience, he evokes the image of the obsessional's indecision:

> Will it [i.e., the ego] or will it not submit itself to the duty that it feels within like a stranger, beyond, at another level. Should it or should it not submit itself to the half-unconscious, paradoxical, and morbid command of the superego [. . .]? If I may put is thus, isn't its true duty to oppose that command? (S7E: 7; S7F: 16)

The appeal emerging from this (unconscious) desire basically never coincides with the demands of the superego, but it is no less ethical, Lacan argues. Evidently, ethics cannot be reduced to demands coming from the outside and interiorized by the superego. In the same lesson Lacan says:

> Moral experience is not simply linked to that slow recognition of the function that was defined and made autonomous by Freud under the term of superego, nor to that exploration of its paradoxes, to what I have called the obscene and ferocious figure in which the moral agency appears when we seek it at its roots. (S7E: 7; S7F: 15)

It may be true that the superego can torment us to such an extent that we finally no longer dare to desire anything and must succumb under its pressure (think of the moral torments of the obsessional neurotic or of a saint[2]), yet the foundations of ethics are not revealed in our desire's servitude to this "vengeful and obscene" law. Ethics is not to be merely reduced to that which bridles and restrains desire. Indeed, it is by virtue of desire that ethics exists in the first place. Still in the same lesson, Lacan says that

> One can, in short, say that the genesis of the moral dimension in Freud's theoretical elaboration is located nowhere else than in desire itself. It is from the energy of desire that that agency is detached which at the end of its development will take the form of the censor. (S7E: 3; S7F: 11)

Hence, the "censor" controlling unconscious desire has its foundation *in* desire as well. The term "ethical" no longer refers exclusively to everything that keeps desire within bounds, but also to what explicitly goes *beyond* or even quite simply *against* those bounds. This is the truly new thing psychoanalysis has to say about ethics. There is an "ought" that is situated *beyond* the moral "ought" of the superego, which can even go completely counter to it and yet still be regarded as ethical.³ This is to say that the ultimate orientation point of moral action lies—more radically than a classical ethics can claim—*beyond* the law.

However, is classical ethics without any form of well-considered, "moral" transgression of the moral law? Is such an ethics not able, in some cases, to run counter to the strict rule of law when this, for example, degenerates into a purely legalistic affair? In other words, do not all ethics have their Antigone who steps beyond the legalism of a Creon's law?

With this reference to Sophocles' renowned tragedy we are, as far as Lacan's *Ethics Seminar* is concerned, on far from neutral ground. His reading of this tragedy is undeniably the culmination of the seminar. Lacan highlights the figure of Antigone as the paradigm of this type of "positive" ethical relation that goes *beyond* the moral law of the super-ego. That he so expressly focuses on Antigone obliges us to question anew just precisely what could be original about Lacan's standpoint. For already in the most classical kinds of ethics, Antigone functions precisely as a positive moral exception who shows up the shortcomings of those who keep all too strictly to the letter of the law.⁴

Here, one should not miss the crucial point Lacan makes with respect to ethics. For, indeed, while he admits that ethics must be thought as a "positive" orientation toward what lies *beyond* the formal law,⁵ this is not to say that we will find something *good* there. What lies *beyond* the moral law is not what fulfils it; we will not meet there the good the law promises. And yet, this beyond is the core of all ethics, as Lacan will repeat again and again during that seminar.

Lacan is criticizing the mistake all moralizing ethics make, including moralizing psychoanalysis, which consider Antigone as an example of a moral attitude that has overcome a formal, "legalist" approach to the law. In contrast, Lacan claims that what is unique about Sophocles' protagonist is that her transgression of the law absolutely does not stand as a model for any kind of ethical ideal or truth. It is in this thoroughly tragic position that Lacan will discover the possibility of thinking a radically anti-idealistic (and, in this sense, antimoralistic) ethics.

In the same first lesson, Lacan already remarks that, during the cure, the analyst occupies the place where the analysand supposes her demand will be answered. Therefore, it is very tempting for the analyst to respond to the analysand's demand with some ideal image or model and hold it up to her as the requested moral mirror. Here, Lacan describes at length three of these ideal models popular in the Freudian landscape of his time, in order to stress how the psychoanalytic cure has *nothing* to do with this. It is not a matter of holding up an ideal of "human love" or "authenticity" or "independence" (to sum up the three ideals Lacan cites here; S7E: 8–10; S7F: 17–19). It is not that these ideals would be wrong, but just that the fact that one wants to *hold them up* inevitably implies that they function as *imaginary* examples and that, therefore, they lead to misrecognition of what an analysis is all about, namely, desire. For, so Lacan argues, an analytic cure must relinquish all imaginary fixations and restructure them *symbolically*—that is, it must let them flow over the surface of signifiers—so that the call of *desire* can be heard. That call has its source not in the imaginary ideal (the "*Gestalt*" of the "ideal ego") but in the distance vis-à-vis this ideal, that is, in the realm of the signifiers where no signifier ever acquires the completeness the ideal suggests. Only a *symbolic* universe can enable the subject to constitute itself as desire and, in this way, do justice to the fully undetermined, polymorphous-perverse drive the subject stems from. To lend an ear to the unruly, impossible desire we "are": this was the discovery of Freudian psychoanalysis and whose explicitly ethical status Lacan will confirm here in his seventh seminar.

## 2. A New Form of Guilt?

But what does this mean, "To lend an ear to the unruly, impossible desire we *are*"? It is not only a question of whether this is possible and whether desire *as such*—apart from superego, ideal ego and other repressing formations—can exist at all. Even if this was the case, it would still be doubtful whether, from a moral perspective, it would be such a good thing. Since both the unconscious and desire evidently possess an *ethical* appeal for us, it is not inconceivable that we can also be guilty of resisting *their* demands and no longer only those of the superego. Hence it seems that, from Lacan's point of view, the "morbid realm" of guilt—according to Angelo Hesnard, psychoanalysis's exemplary domain[6]—needs to be extended. Opposing the idea that psychoanalysis can liberate man from all feelings of guilt, Lacan explicitly says:

> If there is, in fact, something that psychoanalysis has drawn attention to, it is, beyond the sense of obligation properly speaking, the importance, I would even say the omnipresence, of a sense of guilt. (S7E: 3; S7F: 11)

The avalanche of guilt that rolls daily over psychoanalytic and other therapeutic couches doesn't seem to stem exclusively from a feeling of failure with respect to limits imposed on desire by moral commandments and prohibitions. One can also be guilty in relation to the demands of desire *itself*.

This is at least the conclusion of Lacan's investigation into the "ethics of psychoanalysis." The characteristic kind of guilt the psychoanalytic cure has to deal with, and which is the core of its ethical preoccupations, is a guilt with respect to desire *itself*. "Have I not 'given ground relative to [my] desire?' Have I not let my desire be restricted and tamed?" This is the *only* question of moral guilt that counts in the analytic cure, as it appears from one of the paradoxical "propositions" Lacan highlighted in the final lesson of his *Ethics Seminar*:

> I propose then that, from an individual point of view, the only thing of which one can be guilty is of having given ground relative to one's desire [c'est d'avoir cédé sur son désir]. (S7E: 319; S7F: 368)[7]

The aim of analysis lies entirely and exclusively in a confrontation with desire and the only ethical question that counts here is whether the analysand has "acted in conformity with the desire that is in [him]" (S7: 314; S7F: 362).

None of this makes the problematic of ethics any easier. The deathly universe of guilt psychoanalysis hears about during the cure makes it conclude that we are not only guilty with respect to a moral law (the law of the super-ego), but that our guilt also refers to what lies beyond such a law, that is, to the feeling of not having satisfied our desire *as such*. Can this mean anything other than that we must henceforth *always* feel guilty? The law of the superego can never be satisfied, precisely because of the primacy of the desire that we "are." This desire is fundamentally that of the Other and never stops being "other." This is why it ceaselessly forces itself on us as a law that has *yet* to be satisfied. But who guarantees that we can ever satisfy the "beyond" of that law, the "lawless" law, so to speak, of mere desire? For this, the polymorphous-perverse libidinal being we "are" relies all too much on the symbolic, unnatural signifying world where the superego lays down the law. Without this artificial universe of signifiers, the human libido simply would not be able to live. How, then, can a confrontation with our desire *as such* (which is what the psychoanalytic cure is supposed to aim at) deliver anything other than a confrontation with our guilt in relation to this desire?

Or is it nonetheless granted to us to face our desire *as such*? In other words, is a "pure" desire possible, a desire that is able to be maintained *as such*, without the support it finds in the law, in the realm of signifiers? Does Antigone represent the possibility of a confrontation with desire *beyond* law and guilt? Does she testify to a completely "pure desire"?

We will see that Lacan's thinking does indeed head in this direction, although it immediately raises the question of whether this claim is not weakened by the tragic figure illustrating it. Antigone may well incarnate a confrontation with such a "pure desire," but she illustrates at the same time the tragic impossibility of surviving such a confrontation. Even though, in Lacan's view, psychoanalysis must uncompromisingly think through the primacy of desire, and confront man with himself as the desire he "is," the question still remains what all this might mean when only a tragedy culminating in death can give us an adequate image of it.

### 3. A New Ethics, a New Eroticism?

There also seems to be something *tragic* about the inherently ethical dimension Lacan attributes so emphatically to psychoanalysis, as is laid on the table from the very first lesson. Even though psychoanalysis presents a valuable forum for ethical reflection, and while its foundational experience as well as its praxis are ethical through and through, Lacan admits that this is not yet enough to turn it into a fully fledged ethics. For this, it lacks the means for creating its own system of values and norms, or for making a substantial contribution to an existing moral system. Lacan is clear about this from the outset. At the end of his first lesson, he frankly states that psychoanalysis

> perhaps should give up the hope [peut-être devrions nous faire notre deuil] of any genuine innovation in the field of ethics. (S7: 14; S7F: 24)

The same is also true for those areas where one seems to escape somewhat from the pressures of the universal moral rules, namely, the domain of "erotics"[8] and "perversions." Likewise, in the areas that it deals with daily, psychoanalysis seems incapable of creating a specific rulebook or a new way of living, Lacan adds. In the same breath as his previously cited claim that psychoanalysis is unable to contribute to the culturally accepted ethical code, he explains that

> in spite of all our theoretical progress, we haven't even been able to create a single new perversion.[9]

Although he now puts "love" and eros at the center of the "ethical experience" more than ever before, these do not lie at the origin of a new form of erotic culture.

Analysis has brought a very important change of perspective
on love by placing it at the center of ethical experience; it has
also brought an original note, which was certainly different
from the way in which love had previously been viewed by
the *moralistes* and the philosophers in the economy of inter-
human relations. Why then has analysis not gone further in
the direction of the investigation of what should properly be
called an erotics? This is something that deserves reflection.
(S7: 8–9; S7F: 17)[10]

Even with respect to the strict field of psychoanalytic practice, Lacan
reaches the same conclusion. Although it is a form of mental therapy,
although the demand it has to deal with is an ethical demand for the
"good" (the patient wants to "feel good" again), psychoanalysis cannot give any positive advice concerning that good. It can only assist the
patient in the search for his desire *as such*, that is, his desire insofar as
it does not coincide with the good(s) moral values and norms promise.
Psychoanalysis can offer the analysand no alternative kind of ethics and
tell him how he must deal with his desire. The only "moral act" it hopes
for is that of the analysand's, namely, that he takes sides with his desire.
Once the cure has reached this point, it can assist him no further in this
"moral act." Lacan left his listeners in little doubt regarding this. At the
beginning of the second lesson, he

point[s] out that moral action poses problems for us precisely
to the extent that if analysis prepares us for it, it also in the
end leaves us standing at the door [en fin de compte elle nous
laisse à sa porte]. [. . .] I will say right off that the limits of
psychoanalysis coincide with the limits of its practice. Its practice is only a preliminary to moral action as such [. . .]. (S7E:
21–22; S7F)[11]

The analyst can bring the analysand only "at the door" of such a
"moral action." He cannot go *through* that door with her. If the analyst
readies us for a moral act, it is so that, at the moment it must be performed, he leaves us *alone*. Here, one senses the harsh consequences of the
"ethics of distance" that we will see Lacan prescribe for psychoanalysis.
At the moment of the moral act psychoanalysis is leading toward, that is,
the ultimate confrontation with one's desire, the patient is left alone. For,
so Lacan argues, this is equivalent to a confrontation with death, and once
this point has been reached, even the most vigorous ethics has to leave
behind all its know-how and expertise. Once we reach that point, we can

"expect help from no one," Lacan writes (S7: 304; S7F 351). Here, ethics seems to meet its own finitude and develop reservations with respect to itself. In this sense it can be defined as an "ethics of distance."

But does all this not imply that psychoanalysis blows hot and cold at the same time, at least in Lacan's interpretation of it. It calls its intention to take the analysand to a confrontation with his desire thoroughly ethical (see above: 1), but once he gets that far it must, precisely for ethical reasons, leave him to his fate (see 3). Psychoanalysis thinks of desire as being rooted in (infantile) sexuality and eroticism, but when it comes to the crunch, it is unable to offer any real positive perspective or concrete advice concerning desire, sexuality or erotics (see 3): Desire does not equal the moral law, psychoanalysis professes, but at the same time it nonetheless declares "lawless" desire to be a possible cause of guilt (see 2). It maintains an ethical plea for a confrontation with "pure desire," but can only illustrate this with figures who tragically come to grief (see 2).

Once all these paradoxes and impasses are added up, one must ask whether Lacan knows precisely what he means by his concept of "desire," even after just having devoted his entire sixth seminar to this subject (*Desire and Its Interpretation, 1958–59*). Or was Lacan indeed serious when he claimed at the beginning of his seventh seminar that the previous one was not yet really finished? In any case, in this seminar he takes his reflections on "desire and its interpretation" further. The idea of desire as an opening to the "real," which was brought up at the end of the sixth seminar, is developed in the seventh. Only once he has clarified the impact of the real on the whole problematic of desire does he think it possible to clarify the impasses of the ethics of psychoanalysis correctly.

In the following chapter, we will look more closely at Lacan's renewed emphasis on the real as it was developed in the first lesson of his seventh seminar. The fact that an emphasis on the real forces Lacan to reflect on ethics should not be all that surprising. For this brings Lacan's position into the vicinity of classical ethics, since almost all traditional moral systems suppose ethics to be based in reality—that is, in the "real"—itself. Aristotelian ethics set the tone from the outset, and it will be through a confrontation with that ancient philosopher's ethics that Lacan will develop his own position. More specifically, he will read classical ethics in the light of utilitarianism (for him, the most "modern" form of ethics), so as to bring his own, contrasting position more clearly into focus.

# Chapter 3

# Aristotle Revisited

> I have discussed Aristotle because I believe that the *Nicomachean Ethics* is properly speaking the first book to be organized around the problem of an ethics. (S7E: 36; S7F: 46)

Lacan discusses Aristotelian ethics extensively in his *Ethics Seminar*, if only because today's most commonly accepted form of ethics—the "ethics of happiness"—reaches back to him. It was Aristotle who gave this ethics its natural, real foundation. If Lacan zeroes in critically and at length on Aristotle, it is not so much to search for an *other* than real foundation for ethics, as to rigorously apply our "modern" definition of the real to the founding problem of ethics. His conclusion will be that the Aristotelian paradigm has become untenable for us moderns (see below, section 1). More precisely, his renewed emphasis on the real—contrary to what one might expect—will subversively undermine the real foundation of traditional ethics (ibid.). Furthermore, this confrontation with Aristotle will lead Lacan to a profound reflection on the "modern," neurological foundations of psychoanalysis. This will enable him to better describe the impact of reality (or, what he will define as the "real") on the psyche (see 2). That description will surprisingly bring him much closer to Aristotle than one would admit at first sight. In any event, it shows how, from a psychoanalytic perspective, the relation with reality is a strictly "logical" process, and that bears a striking resemblance to the *ethical "judgment"* Aristotle describes in the *Nicomachean Ethics* (see 3).

## 1. "The Interval between Aristotle and Freud"

If Lacan founds ethics in the real, this "real" must be understood in its *modern* definition. With the emergence of modernity in the seventeenth century, the concept of the real underwent a profound transformation such that our entire image of the world and of mankind has profoundly changed. According to Lacan, it is in this historical context that Freudian psychoanalysis must be explicitly understood. Additionally, Lacan's claim that the subversiveness of an ethics of psychoanalysis is due to its anchoring in the *real* will only become comprehensible once we consider how psychoanalysis itself is, in a sense, the result of this *modern* conceptualization of the real.

## 1.1. *"Interval"*

At first sight, Lacan's thesis that the "weight" of ethics lies in the real does in fact seem fairly classical and traditional. Whether Platonic, Aristotelian, Stoic, hedonistic, or Christian, traditional moral systems always begin from the idea that the good has something to do with the way things *really* are. Moral laws rein in desire only so as to guarantee its true, *real* satisfaction. Despite their capriciousness, desires are supposed to be profoundly ethical since they bring us to our most "real" reality. No matter how idealistic a moral law may appear, it invariably legitimizes itself by referring to a true, valid reality.

When, in the second lesson of his seminar, Lacan proposes to his audience his basic thesis on ethics, it sounds little different. In his typically mannered and rather bombastic style, he claims

> that the moral law, the moral command, the presence of the moral agency in our activity, insofar as it is structured by the symbolic, is that through which the real is actualized—the real as such, the weight of the real. (S7E: 20; S7F: 28)

Although the desire we "are" rests on a imaginary and symbolic construction, the ultimately ethical "weight" of our actions will nevertheless be determined by something real. In the final analysis, what drives us ethically is not an imaginary ideal or a symbolic law but a real object. In this sense, psychoanalysis will discover the traces of its most fundamental ethical aspiration by extending the "notion of the real." This was already unmistakable from the first lesson:

> More than once at the time when I was discussing the symbolic and the imaginary and their reciprocal interaction, some of you wondered what after all was the "real." Well, as odd as it may seem to that superficial opinion which assumes any inquiry into ethics must concern the field of the ideal, if not of the unreal, I, on the contrary, will proceed instead from the other direction

by going deeply into the notion of the real. Insofar as Freud's position constitutes progress here, the question of ethics is to be articulated from the point of view of the location of man in relation to the real. To appreciate this, one has to look at what occurred in the interval between Aristotle and Freud. (S7E: 11; S7F: 20–21)

The explicit emphasis on the real is thus all the more striking if one considers how up till now Lacan situated psychoanalysis in "what occurred in the interval between Aristotle and Freud." More specifically, in the course of his previous seminars, he continually stressed how one must always interpret the stakes of Freud's oeuvre in light of the *break* with the real, a break that in his eyes is decisive for the whole of modernity *tout court*. For Lacan, psychoanalysis's characteristic "decentering of the subject" was coextensive with the decentering that our entire world picture underwent at the beginning of modernity. At that time, a far-reaching "mathematization of the real" was carried out, argues Lacan who in this is indebted to Alexander Koyré.[1] Where the Aristotelianism of the middles ages still embraced the idea that science was founded on a relation with the real *being* of things, in the seventeenth century, the idea gained ground that reality is to be approached as an autonomously operating "logical"—in this case, mathematical—system.

This idea found a first great proponent in Galileo and it decisively penetrates our physics with Isaac Newton. In Newton's eyes, science is no longer about questioning the *essence* of things. Things were the creation of an unfathomable, transcendental God and, hence, inaccessible to finite human knowledge. Science must limit itself exclusively to the way things *appear* to us. In order to grasp the movement of a falling apple, for instance, I no longer need to search for its essence in order to—teleologically—explain its falling movement. Henceforth, I must explain the falling movement *as such*, that is, regardless of its cause,[2] and simply capture, so to speak, the "formal protocol" of the movement. This brought Newton to his mathematically formalized law of uniformly accelerated movement. Kant subsequently gave this new "modern" physics a decisive philosophical legitimacy.[3]

The early Lacan already recognizes in this mathematical approach to reality an initial affirmation of the primacy of the signifier.[4] It is not our insight into their *real* kernel that explains the state of things; this is done by a self-functioning symbolic system that in itself has nothing to do with reality as such. We are no longer "bearers" (subjects) of some *real* essence (as premodern science thought), but of a *symbolic* system cut off from the real. Where thought was previously supposed to be directly and "centrally" based in the real, now the "base" or "support" (literally, *subjectum*) from where we approach reality has a "decentered" position with respect to the real. Moreover, when Freudian psychoanalysis revealed the unconscious foundation of this subject, the latter took on an *even more* radically "decentered" position. The "point" from which we relate to the world—a "point" that is the subject—is now considered to be permanently eroded in its "centrist" pretensions. In contrast to Descartes, now the subject's complete certainty about itself is disallowed. Henceforth, the subject, too, must be conceived from the primacy of the signifier, and thereby lifted out of its self-conscious and self-assured position.[5]

## 1.2. Bentham's Utilitarianism

In the just cited passage from his first lesson, Lacan evidently takes the idea of a modern break with the real as already familiar to his audience. At least he refers to the first ethics that emerged from this modern break. Out of the entire period in the "interval between Aristotle and Freud," it is Jeremy Bentham's utilitarianism he will focus on exclusively.

> To appreciate this, one has to look at what occurred in the interval between Aristotle and Freud. At the beginning of the nineteenth century, there was a utilitarian conversion or reversion. (S7E: 11; S7F: 21)

For Lacan, the importance of Bentham's utilitarian ethics does not lie in the famous maxim of "the greatest happiness for the greatest number of people." More important for him is the fact that Bentham attributed an independent status to what, in contrast to the real, he called "fiction": the things that ethics has to deal with are now to be situated at that "fictitious" level. Things we talk about in language are not exclusively the direct, perceptible "real entities" or "fabulous unreal entities"; there are also things that exist solely thanks to language. Abstract things such as quality, quantity, potency, soul, duty, the good, and so forth are what Bentham called "fictitious entities." For Lacan, it is clear that with his *Theory of Fictions*—the title of the work Lacan refers to[6]—Bentham points toward what he calls the symbolic.[7] This is not to say that Bentham already claims we must approach the *whole* of reality as fiction,[8] that is, as a signifier (as Lacan will do more than a century later), but he does at least display an unmistakable sensitivity toward the autonomous operation of language in our (as Lacan says, "dialectical") relation to reality, and toward language's capacity to generate its own fictitious "reality." According to Bentham, the good as well as everything else having to do with ethics must be thought from such a "dialectical relation between language and the real." This is how Lacan puts it in his first lesson (at least according to the "pirate version"):

> It is in the dialectical relation of language and the real that Bentham tried to give a place to the real good, i.e., to the pleasure which (as we will see) he ascribes a function that differs radically from what Aristotle meant by this. And in his emphasis on the opposition between fiction and reality, I will declare, lies the break inaugurated by the Freudian experience.[9]

Is Lacan claiming here that for Bentham the good situates itself on the "side of the real," as Jacques-Alain Miller lets him say? Does a *Theory of Fictions* imply that the ethical good is found "*du côté du réel*"? This, at least, is how it sounds in the official edition, in the first sentence of the previously cited passage:

> Bentham's effort is located in the dialectic of the relationship of language to the real so as to situate the good—pleasure in this case, which, as we will see, he articulates in a manner that is very different from Aristotle—*on the side of the real.* (S7E: 12; S7F 21–22)[10]

The difference from the just-cited "pirate" version is striking and enables us to see the blunder in the official text edition. Bentham's attempt to give a place to the "real good" immediately becomes an assertive allocation of the good to the domain of the real in Miller's edited version. Neither in Bentham's own writings nor in the other passages where Lacan refers to him is there any suggestion that the ethics of utilitarianism situates the good on the "side of the real." Miller has probably, by mistake, allowed himself to be led by the enthusiasm that Lacan has expressed for Bentham at times.[11] However, in this passage, Lacan's appreciation for this author concerns solely the weight he attributes to language, as well as the fact that he reduces all ethical matters to "fictions," that is to say, to "entities" whose existence depends entirely on language.

Here, Lacan says, we see the true significance of utilitarianism for the history of ethics during the "interval between Aristotle and Freud." Where for Aristotle, ethical action still has a "real" foundation (man's aspiration for the "Supreme Good" was regarded as an indication of his *ontological* process of completion, of his most optimal self-realization), in Bentham, that same ethics lies exclusively at the level of "fiction" or, in Lacanian terms, at the level of the signifier. Just as for Bentham, for Aristotle the moral goal of human striving was happiness (feeling good or, psychoanalytically speaking, pleasure[12]), but for the ancient philosopher, happiness still held as a *natural* indication to let man know he is on the right path toward his ontological realization.

Utilitarian ethics no longer refers to a real but to a "fictive" happiness, that is, to what most people *say* what happiness is, regardless of whether they reach their ontological destination or not. Henceforth, both happiness and the good become "fictitious." They exist solely thanks to language, in this case, thanks to the language of a majority that can chose whatever it wants to feel happy. The irreconcilable "opposition of fiction and reality"—the philosophical and scientific paradigm since Newton and Kant—is affirmed in its *ethical* implications only with Bentham. What utilitarianism makes into such an irreversible milestone in our modern moral history is thus not the maxim of "the greatest happiness for the greatest number of people," but the claim that happiness and the good are "fictitious" (i.e., purely signifiers).

### 1.3. "Bestial Desires"

But is it not precisely against this that Lacan inveighs in his seventh seminar? Is not his main claim that the entire question of ethics and the good is not located exclusively at the level of the "fictitious" (symbolic) but also—in the final analysis—at the level of the real? Can such a claim come down to anything other than a harking back to the ethical premises prior to utilitarianism? Does the "interval between Aristotle and Freud" mean anything else than a long and unnecessary detour only to fall back into a *real* foundation for ethics once again?

To invoke how Lacan maintains a typically *modern* definition of the real does not make his claim any more plausible at first sight. How can one possibly found an ethics in this modern "real" if it is a real that above all escapes our knowledge, referring us irreversibly to the domain of the symbolic? Was it not for these reasons that Lacan elevated Bentham to a genuine "landmark" in the history of morality? So, again, how can he locate the ethical center of gravity in the real, and yet not fall back into the Aristotelian position? No matter how preposterous it seems, the foundation of ethics in the real is the thesis Lacan will defend and his seminar is one long attempt to prove that.

Let us therefore follow Lacan through his first lesson once again. There, he does indeed cite Aristotle's importance as a reference point for a reflection on the ethics of psychoanalysis. However, this is first of all a *negative* point: what psychoanalysis understands by desire is *in*compatible with Aristotle's definition of it. This is at least one reason why psychoanalysis does not subscribe to an Aristotelian ethics. The desires that are central to the psychoanalytic ethical engagement fall unquestionably outside the domain of ethics for Aristotle. Already at the beginning of his lesson, Lacan draws his audience's attention to this:

> Where a certain category of desires is involved, there is, in effect, no ethical problem for Aristotle. Yet, these very desires are nothing less than those notions that are situated in the forefront of our [psychoanalytical] experience. A whole large field of what constitutes for us the sphere of sexual desires is simply classed by Aristotle in the realm of the monstrous anomalies—he uses the term "bestiality" with reference to them. What occurs at this level has nothing to do with moral evaluation. [S7E: 5; S7F: 13][13]

Although Aristotle recognizes the fundamental importance of pleasure and desire, they are in his eyes essentially rooted in the heart of being.[14] What "drives" me, according to Aristotle, is a striving for happiness, and a feeling of pleasure indicates that I am on the right path to realize my full potential. All of nature (φύσις, "*phusis*") stems from a potency of being (δύναμις, "*dunamis*") that brings it to its self-development (ἐνέργεια, "energeia"). Man's experiences of happiness and pleasure are rooted in this teleological potency. The role of ethics is to keep human strivings strictly on track in regard to mans fullest potential. Desires that do not respond to this teleological orientation of being thus fall outside of ethics for Aristotle. Everything one does that has no role in the specific realization of man's being is a reversion to the "bestial." It is not that such behavior is ethically wrong in Aristotle's eyes. It is worse: it does not even come into consideration for ethical qualification because it is corrupted at the level of its very nature—"owing to natural depravity," to quote Aritstotle.[15] The man who pursues such behavior is already damaged at the level of his ontological 'potentiality' and is therefore unable to control himself as "human *being*." He is incapable of what Aristotle defines as ethics. His desires are no longer fully attuned to human self-realization and fall under the category of "bestiality" ("θηριότης," "*thèriotès*"; Aristotle, 1994: 403).

Lacan doesn't hesitate to conclude that precisely this type of "bestial" desire is central to psychoanalysis since, from the Freudian perspective, desire is at odds with natural self-realization. Freud characterized the underlying drives as polymorphous-perverse: they *pervert* (*subvert*) every natural relation with whatever object they seek, including man's own identity. At the end of his first lesson, Lacan refers explicitly to how the idea of "nature," to which so many appeals are usually made, has acquired radically different content during the "interval between Aristotle and Freud":

> Aristotle's thought on the subject of pleasure embodies the idea that pleasure has something irrefutable about it, and that it is situated at the guiding pole of human fulfillment, insofar as if there is something divine in man, it is in this bond of nature. You should consider how far that notion of nature is different from ours, since it involves the exclusion of all bestial desires from what is properly speaking human fulfillment. Since Aristotle's time [literally: "in the interval," "*dans l'intervalle*," i.e., during "the interval between Aristotle and Freud"] we have experienced a complete reversal of point of view. (S7E: 13; S7F: 22–23)

To counter what remains an influential Aristotelianism, Lacan claims, psychoanalysis must confirm this "reversal of point of view." This is why its task is to affirm these "bestial" desires: unattuned as they are to the self-realization of being, they have to be given the "right to exist" as well as affirmed in their *ethical* dimension. Almost immediately following the second to last cited passage, Lacan explicitly says

> if one believes that the whole of Aristotle's morality has lost none of its relevance for moral theory, then one can measure from that fact how subversive our experience is, since it serves to render this theory surprising, primitive, paradoxical, and, in truth, incomprehensible. (S7E: 5; S7F: 14)

Hence already at the level of praxis, according to Lacan, psychoanalytic "experience" contradicts Aristotle. While at the conscious level, man supposes himself to strive for "natural" fulfillment, often using Aristotelian terms to express this, at the unconscious level, however, he subverts (perverts) any reference to "nature" and "fulfillment." With each alleged fulfillment, desire is only confirmed in its dissatisfaction. That is why psychoanalysis attributes primacy to desire. The satisfaction it refers to is never more than a *phantasm* that keeps desire going the moment the subject supposes itself to be entirely satisfied. Desire *itself* cannot be made compatible with any presumed selfhood that man attributes to his *being*. Rather, it is precisely what never reaches the level of *being* and therefore implies the disruption and subversion of all forms of presumed selfhood. In this sense, desire is "bestial" for, as Aristotle explains, being corrupted in its very capacity of being (i.e., its potentiality of fulfillment), it must be regarded as "bestial."

This is also why psychoanalysis cannot identify with the goal Aristotle imputes to ethics: the acquisition of good habits, that is, of mastery over one's abilities (which is what "virtues" are about). This is how man is brought to the full realization of his 'potential.' Ethics, for Aristotle, is still more fundamentally linked to the "character" ("ἦθος," "èthos") man forms by means of moral training or code ("ἔθος," "ethos").[16] "Bestial" desires thus have no place in this.

Furthermore, according to Lacan, Aristotle honors a typical "master"-ethics, that is, a type of ethics for those who, having slaves, were exempted from labor and had time to work on themselves and, in positive mutual competition, to perfect their "virtues."[17] Striving for "mastery" consisted of maintaining the "precise middle" between extremes (μεσότης, mesotes, see S7E: 292–293, 314; S7F: 339, 362), which enables man to ground himself in what should be his natural foundation. Man was thus to keep himself far away from excessive "bestial" desires. By depriving ethics of its anchoring in *being*, and reducing it to something *"fictitious,"* utilitarianism literally and figuratively "took the ground from under the feet" of this type of Aristotelian morality.

But why does Lacan continue to attach such importance to Aristotle in the course of his ethics seminar? If his estimation is so negative, why does he—as he himself says—give him such an "important place in [his] discussions" (S7E: 5; S7F: 13)? Is Lacan's break with the "essentialist" morality Aristotle venerates not a sufficient reason to opt in full for utilitarianism and its fictitiously-supported ethics? If a confrontation with this ancient philosopher only teaches us that our desires, "bestial" as they are, have no real anchor, why does Lacan then enlist something like the real at all? How can he both enlist the real and break with Aristotle? Or, to put it differently, if modernity is indeed beyond Aristotelian ethics, why continue to give it so much prominence?

One of the reasons Aristotle remains an important reference point for Lacan's reflections on ethics lies in the fact that the basic principles of psychoanalysis are brought into sharper focus through a confrontation with his thought. A concept such as (psychic) energy, for example, becomes clearer when one contrasts it with the concept of energy in Aristotle (see below, 2). More specifically, it invites one to go deeper into the way psychoanalytic theory maps the relation between pleasure and reality (see 3). While Lacan may break with Aristotelian morality on the level of content, he takes his lead explicitly from Aristotle's *Nicomachean Ethics* in his formal sketch of the relation between pleasure and reality (see 3.1). Like no other, Aristotle's book shows how the foundation of ethics must be sought in the relation between desire and reality (or, in more technical terms, between the *pleasure* and *reality principles*), a relation that implies an ethical judgment, that is, a judgment about what is good or not for the desiring subject (see 3.2). Lacan's *psychoanalytic* reading of such "moral" judgment will "de-center" the classical premises of ethics. It will bring him to a radically new definition of the ethical good and of ethics as such (see 3.3).

## 2. Aristotle *and* Freud against Bentham

### 2.1 Energy . . .

The reference to Aristotle first and foremost enables Lacan to clarify why, at the level of ethics, psychoanalysis can take no satisfaction in Bentham's utilitarianism even though in principle it agrees with utilitarianism's "fictive" foundation of ethics. Although for Bentham, too, it is about happiness (and, thus, *pleasure*), from a certain perspective Freud's pleasure principle is much closer to Aristotle's idea of pleasure and happiness. In contrast to Bentham, for Freud and Aristotle pleasure is not based in the sovereign decision of a free subject. For Bentham, pleasure is a question of a conscious, rational choice and, to his mind, the "fictitious" status that ethical values will henceforth be assigned grants this choice a heretofore unknown freedom. Neither Aristotle nor Freud will deny the moral significance of free choice, but for them, pleasure and (hence) ethics go back to a pre-conscious drive. In the final analysis, it is a matter of "energy," and for neither thinker can this be conceived in terms of a sovereign subjective freedom.

For both Freud and Aristotle, our relation to reality (including ourselves) doesn't primarily depend on our consciousness. It concerns a "natural" event, although it must immediately be said that both attribute a radically different meaning to the concept of "nature." Lacan refers to this difference in the closing sentence of the passage in the previous section, where he raises Aristotle's reflections on "bestial" desires:

> You should consider how far that notion of nature is different from ours, since it involves the exclusion of all bestial desires from what is properly speaking human fulfillment. Since Aristotle's time we have experienced a complete reversal of point of view. As far as Freud is concerned, everything that moves toward reality requires a certain tempering, a lowering of tone, of what is properly speaking the energy of pleasure. (S7E: 13; S7F: 23)

For Aristotle, "nature" is a dynamic and energetic process. Realizing myself and my world equals succeeding in putting my *possibility of being* ("*dunamis*") into energy ("*energeia*"), and in this way fulfilling the teleological destination that lies hidden in me. This positive increase in "*dunamis*" activated in "*energeia*" gives man a feeling of well-being, of happiness or pleasure. Freud, too, approaches human "nature" as a process in which "energy" is involved, and conceives of the pleasure principle underlying our drive life in "energetic" terms. However, for Freud, "energy" must not so much be stimulated as carried off, discharged. The "energy" by which an organism lives is, in principle, a negatively experienced tension that must be removed, if not totally, than at least as far as possible. For Freud, pleasure must be exclusively linked to the release or removal of the stimulant tension.[18] For Aristotle, man lives from an "energy" that must be awoken; for Freud, from an "energy" that needs moderating and "tempering." Lacan is quite justified in calling the "reversal of perspective" between Aristotle and Freud "complete."

Just like the aforesaid "interval," this "reversal" must also be interpreted from its historical perspective. Moreover, Freud's position must be situated in the context of the new paradigms that were to support the biological and subsequently also psychological (or, as Fechner put it, "psychophysical") sciences of the nineteenth century. In the wake of Newtonian physics, these sciences, too, would come to be defined by premises breaking with the Aristotelianism that had governed science since the Middle Ages. As opposed to Aristotle who thought being as modeled on "life" (in this case, an in itself, teleologically unfolding "*phusis*"), they conceived things as "dead," material externality. Now, life could no longer be approached as a vitalizing, teleologically oriented force (as Aristotle approached it), and even less could it be regarded as a mechanical "automaton" ruled by Nature, as conceived by the materialism of the eighteenth century). Henceforth, life must be approached as *what reacts to stimuli*.[19] The stimulus/reaction theory attempts to think of life in purely objective terms. On the basis of this schema, it becomes possible to replace the old distinction of dead and living beings with a new one, namely, organic and inorganic. An *inorganic* "object" gets defined as something that doesn't react to stimulation, an *organic* one as something that does.

This definition of a "living" organism emerges from a completely different perspective than the Aristotelian approach. *Energy* is no longer something "positive" that is inwardly directed to realize the inherent potentialities of an organism, but something (formally) 'negative' that is primarily suppressed, expelled or removed by the organism. In the final analysis, life finds its cause and reason for existence not in life itself, but is rather an effect of stimulations that are in fact purely *accidental*. It is no longer a matter of a life caused by itself, by its autoteleological energy, as Aristotle thought. Where Aristotelian "life" still describes an active and *essential* being, it will henceforth be thought purely as *accidental* and *reactive*.

Trained in the neurological laboratories of Meynert and Brücke, and profoundly influenced by authorities such as Helmholtz and Fechner, Freud was an expert in the (psycho-)physical tradition of his time. Once he was obliged to exchange his laboratory for private practice, he approached the problems he faced there in terms of the same stimulus-reaction paradigm. From his first scientific attempt to chart the psyche's operation (the *Entwurf* of 1895[20]) until his final metapsychological reflections, Freud approached the "(psychic) apparatus" as a stimulus/response system. Whether this stimulation is external (exogenous stimuli that accost the organism from without, such as cold or warmth) or internal (endogenous stimuli that are internal to the organism itself, such as hunger and thirst) "life," for the organism, exists solely in *re*acting to these stimuli. In itself, the apparatus is a "dead" reaction mechanism.[21] The sole—but crucial—thing Freud's psychoanalysis adds is a new reaction *principle*. Instead of the generally accepted principle of self-preservation, Freud's fundamental intuition is that this reaction is at least traversed by a *pleasure principle*, if not led by it. In the final analysis, an organism reacts not out of self-preservation but because of the pleasure it experiences in self-preservation—or in whatever, even the opposite of self-preservation. Polymorphous-perverse as it is, a libidinal being "subverts" its biological functions, even at the level of self-preservation. For these reasons, Freud will always, till the end of his days, stress the fundamentally conflictual nature of the human drive and formulate it in increasingly irreconcilable conceptual pairs, for instance the distinction between the ego-drive (self-preservation) and the object-drive (libido) at the beginning of his oeuvre, or that between Eros and death in his late phase (in *Beyond the Pleasure Principle*).[22]

## 2.2. . . . and Reality

The pleasure-driven stimulus and reaction theory underlying Freudian psychoanalysis attributes a particularly precarious but crucial role to "realities." According to the premises of the stimulus-reaction theory (which are also psychoanalysis's own), reality is that which acts on an organism as a field of stimuli and thereby effects a tension—an "energy"—inside the organism that must be discharged or abreacted as quickly as possible. It causes unpleasure that requires removal, generating pleasure. As the source of stimulus-tension—and thus of life—reality is something that in principle must be warded off. What keeps the organism alive then is due to the pleasure principle's counterpart, the *reality principle*. This principle is responsible for the organism's "positive" relation with a part of reality so as thereby to satisfy what Freud called the "Not de Lebens" (needs such as hunger and thirst).[23] Yet for Freud, the relation between pleasure and reality principles—and, consequently, between the organism and reality—is conceived as thoroughly conflictual. Any balance in the two is as contingent as it is fragile. Moreover, the organism continues to ward off the majority of the stimulus attacks from reality.

In contrast to Aristotelian physics, the energetic tension by which the organism lives does *not* imply any *essential* relation to reality. While the energy that keeps it going may in large part be the effect of reality (or, more precisely, of its influence on the organism[24]), the pleasure principle ensures that the stimulus-tension is to a large extent removed. Thus, the energy level in the organism is kept as low as possible (as indicated by Freud's "constancy principle"). But there is more. Freud's extreme step in *Beyond the Pleasure Principle* suggests that, in the final analysis, the reaction principle aims to allow all the internal energy to flow out entirely and thus bring the (living) organism back to its (dead) inorganic state. Being basically an inertia principle, the pleasure principle ultimately makes the drive into a death principle. At the end, the organism aims to discharge all tension and therefore to become completely insensate of the outside world (i.e., of reality).[25]

The introduction of the death drive gives the position of "reality" in Freud's system an even stranger character. Thus far it is clear that outside "reality" is indispensable for the organism's libidinal life, while at the same time the pleasure principle to a larger part resists reality. This does not, however, prevent the libidinal economy from secretly being oriented and driven *toward* reality by a principle that goes *beyond* the pleasure principle. This secretly operating death drive is, however, "[n]ot really in opposition to the pleasure principle, but yet independent of it," thus Freud conceives of this sort of "demonic" principle[26] revealing a self-destructive "inertia in organic life."[27] If organic life has an aim, it can only be located in a return to inorganic life, since life stems primordially from "dead" inorganic matter.[28] For Aristotle, "drive" and "reality" meet one another in the *life* from which they stem. For Freud, they meet in the *dead* inorganic. For him, the "reality" that, in the final analysis, the drive aims at as well as the "reality" from which the drive ultimately stems, is nothing other than the banal lifelessness of what since modernity we have called "the material."

This is not without an important implication. Although the stimulus/reaction theory does indeed presuppose a radical break with the real (the libidinal organism has anything but a natural harmonious relation with its environment), this doesn't mean that the real doesn't play any part in the life of the organism. On the contrary, the organism must summon up "energy" again and again to keep the "real" effectively outside. In the most radical sense of the word, the organism only *lives in and through* its reaction against the real. The "energy" it lives by only exists in an abreaction that both turns *against* and orients *toward* the stimulus field of reality, in the sense that in the final analysis its aim is ultimately to return to the inorganic.

Hence the organism continues to relate to reality, albeit it in a mainly negative way. It must constantly shield itself from this overwhelming source of stimuli, and does this by means of an energy that is partly the effect of the stimuli stemming from the "real" outside world.[29] Even more, the organism will structure itself in such a way that the outside dies off, as it were, and it will harden itself to become more or less immune to stimuli. In this manner, it becomes capable of letting in a small part of "external world charged with the most powerful energies," for the sole purpose of removing this energy—a removal that unquestionably coincides with the life principle of the organism.[30]

Psychoanalysis thus cannot relax in the logical or, if you will, "logical-positivist" comfort of Bentham's *Theory of Fictions*. Its "natural scientific" premises do not allow us to simply imagine the real as being behind us and allow us to settle in our fictive (i.e., *symbolic*) universe. This symbolic world is itself a major "reaction formation" against the overwhelming field of stimuli that is reality, the field of the "real" that keeps beating against our symbolic system. The "real" will be defined as that part of "reality" that fails to become integrated in the symbolic world, that is, in the universal "reaction formation" we live in and which is made of signifiers. This is why the break from the "real" never liberates us definitively from it. It never stops pounding on our symbolic universe, which itself never ceases to react against it. To chart this complex relation between symbolic order, reality, and the real, Lacan will take a notion from Freud's *Entwurf* called "das Ding." This is the first notion in his entire oeuvre with which he tries to give a proper status to the real in its symbolic implications.

However, Lacan's conceptualization of psychoanalysis was not exactly to take that direction. His thesis of the primacy of the signifier could easily have legitimized a theory in which the "real" had ceased to be a problem. Bentham's theory of fictions could have been a valid confirmation of this. But it was precisely this common ground with Bentham that perhaps prompted Lacan to take a different direction. In Bentham's *Theory of Fictions*, he faced an affirmation of the symbolic that at first sight leaned strongly toward his own, but with this one difference: Bentham was not forced to call on a notion such as the unconscious. To the contrary even, in his eyes the fictional status of ethical reality (among other things) gave modern man more freedom than ever to *consciously* take their fate in hand. So, if Lacan wanted to maintain Freud's basic assumption of the primacy of the unconscious, he could no longer do so solely by emphasizing the fictitious (i.e., symbolic) character of reality.

"The unconscious is structured like a language," Lacan never stopped proclaiming, but the confrontation with Bentham forced him more keenly than before to admit that this claim doesn't mean that language (symbolic order) and unconscious must be identified with one another. Language and its laws *do not equal* the unconscious. They only give us access to it. The unconscious as such lies not so much in the signifiers that can lead one so astray, but in the "reality" *behind* the signifier, a "reality" that the signifiers or the entire "psychic apparatus" must keep at bay. In his "Rome Discourse," Lacan still formulated the unconscious exclusively in terms of signifier and discourse:

> The unconscious is that part of concrete discourse qua trans-individual, which is not at the subject's disposal in reestablishing the continuity of his conscious discourse. (Lacan 2002: 50, 1966: 258)

Here, in his seventh seminar, Lacan links the unconscious to a "real" reality. This is why, in his second lesson, he focuses on a letter to Fliess (October 31, 1897) in which Freud, referring to his own self-analysis, explains that the most unpleasant things about it are the "*Stimmungen*," because they "very often hide reality."[31] Lacan will claim that this "reality" has more weight for the libidinal operation than a theory of the signifier would seem to admit at first sight. For the latter tends to privilege the primacy of the signifier and to regard the real as something definitely excluded and, therefore, unproblematic. Nevertheless, Lacan argues, this excluded 'real' reality remains the cause of the *energy* with which the libidinal apparatus maintains itself. The *energy* the libidinal being lives by is, in the final analysis, won from "reality."

It is thus too easy to consider the libidinal relation to reality as solely negative. The entire psychic apparatus is not only a defense mechanism against that overwhelming field of stimuli plaguing it from the outside. That apparatus also positively lives by the stimuli it takes in from the outside world, if only because hunger stimuli, for example, can only be alleviated by an actual ingestion of food. The psychic apparatus's relation to reality is thus not only a matter of the death drive (a tendency toward the inorganic). It is at the same time a matter of self-preservation and of pleasure principle. The libidinal relation to reality thus requires a somewhat more nuanced description. More specifically, must the reality principle still be explained in terms of its "positive" relation to the pleasure principle? Here, too, Aristotle will be one of Lacan's guides. Not only did a confrontation with his thought force psychoanalysis to rethink its concept of "energy," Aristotle will also be the point of reference for conceptualizing the formal operation of the pleasure principle. Lacan will show how the psychic apparatus operates in a way that bears close resemblance to Aristotle's description of moral judgment. The idea that psychoanalysis is a form of ethics, and that its "experience" (its praxis, the cure) is inherently ethical will thus become more explicit in Lacan through an express reference to Aristotle.

## 3. Pleasure, Reality and Logos

Although "bestial" desires have no *essential* anchor in reality, psycho-analytical theory nevertheless does not consider them to be completely disconnected from reality. Even if the pleasure principle subverts any possible *natural* relation with reality, this does not reduce the impact of the latter to *zero*. On the contrary, reality—albeit not as "essence," "nature," or "phusis"—is involved in libidinal life, even constituting a "principle," for it is from reality that the libidinal economy has to secure pleasure. Hence, in the libidinal apparatus, the pleasure principle never functions without its indispensable companion, the reality principle. Thus, like in Aristotle, pleasure and reality are inextricably connected to one another but their connection can no longer be explained in terms of an Aristotelian essentialist "physics." As a phenomenon of "modern" *epistèmè*, psychoanalysis retains a radically different concept of both pleasure and reality. If only because of this, psychoanalysis will have to thoroughly reconsider the paradigms of Aristotelian ethics. Or, as Lacan saw, it will have to read the Artistotelian problem into the metapsychological theory of the libidinal apparatus.

### 3.1 A Judgment Apparatus

This is in fact what Lacan accomplishes in the first lessons of his *Ethics Seminar*, where his comments on Aristotle lead to a reading of Freud's first metapsychological text: the *Entwurf*. That text, he claims, should be reinterpreted in the light of Aristotle's *Nicomachean Ethics*. Then it will become clear that psychoanalytic "experience"—and by this he means also the unconscious, "neuro-physiological" operation of the psychic apparatus—is profoundly *ethical*. In his second lesson, for example, referring to the *Entwurf*, Lacan asks his audience "to reread this text," adding that

> you will see that beneath a manner that is cool, abstract, scholastic, complex and arid, one can sense a lived experience, and that this experience is at bottom moral in kind. (S7E: 29; S7F 38)[32]

For Lacan, the profoundly ethical character of the psychic apparatus is due to the decisive influence of "reality." Not unlike traditional ethics, which claims there is no desire without a law that restrains it, Freud's *Entwurf* also assumes that pleasure doesn't function without a restricting and correcting principle. And, again like traditional ethics for which law is rooted in reality, for Freud, too, the principle that curtails pleasure refers to "reality." Whereas the *pleasure principle* refers to a free stream of energy (and thus, a *removal* of the tension of stimulation) defined as "*primary* process," the *reality principle* regulates the "*secondary* process" that reins in and binds this free energy—a procedure that is necessary for maintaining the libidinal economy.[33] According to Lacan, it is precisely that tensed relation between the two basic principles that makes the working of the libidinal apparatus thoroughly ethical:

> Contrary to received opinion, I believe that the opposition between the pleasure principle and the reality principle or between the primary process and the secondary process concerns not so much the sphere of psychology as that of ethics properly speaking. (S7E: 35; S7F: 45)

To understand this, one must first find out *how* reality affects the libidinal system, that is, *in what way* the reality principle regulates contact with the outside world. Here, Aristotle will be an outstanding reference for Lacan to explain the *formal* ethical status of the libidinal apparatus. For "reality" will only come into play insofar as that apparatus has *judged* it. Already that unconscious "judgment" makes a decision about good and evil, and is in this sense ethical. Our conscious relation with reality, including our moral conduct, is based on that unconscious judging procedure.

Lacan's "rereading"[34] of Freud's *Entwurf* convinced him that the operation of the apparatus must indeed be conceived in terms of an ethical judgment. Like any logical judgment, this apparatus will submit a particular premise, a "minor" one, to a more universal "major" premise in order to come to the right or (ethically) good answer. This makes Lacan turn back to Aristotle's *Nicomachean Ethics*, which he praises as "the first book to be organized around the problem of an ethics" (S7E: 36; S7F: 46). Not only does this book give a primordial place to pleasure, not only does it link this pleasure with a "reality principle," it furthermore attributes the connection between the two to a strictly *logical* process. The psychoanalytic paradigm behind terms such as "pleasure," "reality," and "logos," however, will at the same time "pervert" and undermine the Aristotelian ethical logic.

So, it is not without provocative intent[35] that Lacan compares Freud's psychic apparatus with the way Aristotle develops his theory of ethical judgment in the *Nicomachean Ethics*. He refers more specifically to a passage from the beginning of the seventh chapter where Aristotle treats an "aporia." How is it possible, we read there, that someone who has reached a high degree of insight can nevertheless act in a non-self-restrained manner?[36] This was indeed not self-evident for Aristotle's audience. That audience was primarily wedded to the Platonic idea that men can only do evil out of ignorance. Moral knowledge and moral conduct, *knowing* the good and *doing* the good, were supposed to go hand in hand.[37] But for Aristotle, this is not necessarily the case. His "logical" analysis of the knowledge process always begins from the point that, beside a purely theoretical dimension, there is also an independent *act* of judgment. In order to be realized, knowledge's "potentiality" must be "actualized," and this requires an active deed. In the field of "practical reason" the impact of an *act* judgment is certainly observable. And it is in the dimension of the act that the entire ethical weight of reason lies for Aristotle. It is precisely through the discrepancy between theoretical moral knowledge and the effective act of judgment that errors can creep in. Errors—moral errors as well—can thus be blamed on our thought *processes* and can in this sense be *accidental* in kind. They do not have to directly indicate the inadequacy of our knowledge *as such*.

In the case Lacan refers to (in an extremely obscure and misleadingly edited passage[38]), Aristotle minutely elaborates such a logical judgment process—in this case "a certain *syllogisme du désirable*." That someone who *knows* behaves in an unrestrained manner testifies not so much to his ignorance as to the fact that in a specific syllogistic reasoning, he has subsumed a particular minor premise to a universal major premise in an erroneous way under the influence of desire (ἐπιθυμία" *epithumia*). Aristotle writes:

> In a practical syllogism, the major premise is an opinion, while the minor premise deals with particular things, which are the province of perception. Now when the two premises are combined, just as in theoretic reasoning the mind is compelled to *affirm* the resulting conclusion, so in the case of practical premises you are forced at once to *do* it. For example, given the premises 'All sweet things aught to be tasted' and 'Yonder thing is sweet'—a particular instance of the general class—, you are bound, if able and not prevented, immediately to taste the thing. When therefore there is present in the mind on the one hand a universal judgement forbidding you to taste and on the other hand a universal judgement saying 'All sweet things are pleasant,' and a minor premise 'Yonder thing is sweet' (and it is this minor premise that is active), and when

desire [ἐπιθυμία, *epithumia*] is present at the same time, then, though the former universal judgment says 'Avoid that thing,' the desire leads you to it (since desire can put the various parts of the body in motion). Thus it comes about that when men fail in self-restraint, they act in a sense under the influence of a principle or opinion, but an opinion not in itself but only accidentally opposed to the right principle [ὀρθὸς λόγος, *orthos logos*] (for it is the desire, and not the opinion, that is really opposed).[39]

A *wrong* ethical action can thus, for Aristotle, also be the result of a logical judgment process, and is not necessarily the effect of ignorance, as Plato maintained. From the elements of a correct knowledge an incorrect conclusion can be drawn. The lack of restraint, being a morally reprehensible action, is thus not incompatible with a potentially optimal knowledge. It is just an effect of a mistaken application of this knowledge. It is the result of an erroneous *act* of judgment.

Aristotle's "*syllogisme du desirable*" enables us to see that moral action is the result of a strictly logical process. I can find the particular good that I want to do or experience only by making it into the object of a judgment, just as I must make my particular perception (i.e., the minor premise, "this is sweet" from our example) subordinate to the universal logical laws of thought. This latter is what Aristotle called "ὀρθὸς λόγος" (orthos logos), in this case, the universal (true) claim of our example.[40]

According to Lacan, Freud conceives the psychic apparatus as such a "judgment apparatus" working in a similarly "logical, syllogistic" manner. The only—but far-reaching[41]—difference is that here thought is considered to be an *unconscious* process, operating in a field of memory traces (and, thus, of representations), and operating according to its own proper logic. The *Entwurf* describes the neurological working of the apparatus such that the stimulus attack from the outside world searches for a way through the field of representations.[42] With each new stimulus, the apparatus leads the tensional energy along the appropriate pathways ("facilitations," "*Bahnungen*") to the associated representations that "remember" the most optimal energy discharge—that is, the highest pleasure effect. In this sense, the psychic apparatus with its field of representations forms a system with which the organism "judges" the incoming stimuli as well as their stored representations. This is the way the system thinks unconsciously and regulates its relation to reality. If it could in fact live by its pleasure principle alone, it would have no need of any reality for thanks to these representations, it could have an exclusively *hallucinated* satisfaction. But since hallucination cannot guarantee the *real* discharge of libidinal energy required by satisfaction and, secondly, since the libidinal being is *also* biological, a second principle is indispensable: the reality principle. Endogenous stimuli such as hunger and thirst are not to be diverted and even less alleviated by hallucinations. So, the pleasure-being must rely on the outside world and requires the assistance of the reality principle. It is again thanks to the system of representations that the apparatus can turn *pleasurably* to this outside world and make the fulfillment its needs compatible with its pleasure gratification. The field of unconscious representations, mutually bound through a network of facilitations (*Bahnungen*), allows an unconscious, pleasure-related judgment about reality. On this basis, the organism will apply its internal tension energy to what Freud in the *Entwurf* calls a "specific action," that is, an action through which it specifically intervenes in reality.[43]

The psychic apparatus is thus to be conceived as a judgment apparatus that enables the organism to regulate pleasure and attune it to the outside world. By means of this judgment process, it chooses the "good" it needs to satisfy its pleasure requirement. This, however, changes the status of the outside world from being merely a real entity to a "logical" discourse, a linguistically organized field of representations. Consequently, the "good" one obtains from this reality will also be something "discursive," something linguistic or symbolic. In the following section, we will follow Lacan's analysis of how already for Freud, the reality that the psychic apparatus deals with had an unmistakably discursive status. This, however, is only one side of the coin for Lacan, for he will also glimpse another type of reality that is just as operative, if less explicitly, in Freud's reality principle.

### 3.2. Reality: A Discourse

According to Freud, the operation of the judgment apparatus begins with the invasion—and, thus, the (unconscious) perception—of stimuli. This unconscious perception is located in a separate structure Freud called the "*W System*."[44] Only after going their way through the unconscious (the *Ubw System*), the stimuli—in the shape of representations—present themselves consciously (i.e., in the *Bw System*). Thus *even in perception*, the unconscious precedes the conscious. Lacan likes to say that the unconscious lies between perception and consciousness "as between glove and hand" (or, more literally, "between skin and flesh").[45]

Still, in principle, the apparatus would rather *not* 'judge.' At first, it simply wants to remove all stimuli. Hence the fundamentally "precarious" status of reality and the reality principle for the operation of the apparatus. For the outside world presents itself as an overwhelming quantum of stimulus energy that in the first place the organism wishes to reject.

Reality is precarious. [. . .] The profound ambiguity of this
approach to the real demanded by man is first inscribed in
terms of defense—a defense that already exists even before
the conditions of repression as such are formulated. (S7E: 31;
S7F: 40)

It is precisely the endogenous stimuli that force the apparatus to turn
toward the outside world. For by definition, endogenous stimuli cannot
immediately be resisted or "promptly discharged along a motor path."[46]
The organism can close itself off from sunlight (by shutting the eyes, for
example), but it cannot close itself off from hunger stimuli. Such stimuli
force themselves unhindered on the apparatus and only something from
the outside world can discharge their accumulated tensional energy. Only
real food can alleviate hunger. Yet, in the first instance, the apparatus
doesn't seek real food at this level. The apparatus is exclusively after
the satisfaction of *pleasure*, not *needs*. To remove such an endogenous
stimulus tension, it chooses the most direct path and consults the memory
representations of an earlier pleasurable discharge of tension. Once this
"perceptual identity" has been found, the apparatus doesn't hesitate to
render this representation in a hallucination so as to find the most direct
way to satisfaction—the discharge of the stimulus tension. Lacan notes
that Freud thus situates "perception" primordially under the authority of
the pleasure principle and not under that of the reality principle as one
is inclined to think:

What are we led to articulate the apparatus of perception onto?
Onto reality, of course. Yet, if we follow Freud's hypothesis,
on what theoretically is the control of the pleasure principle
exercised? Precisely on perception, and it is here that one finds
the originality of his contribution. (S7E: 31; S7F: 40)

However, this "primary process" that is based merely on the pleasure
principle (which arranges for a purely hallucinatory satisfaction if need be)
is not capable of removing the endogenous stimuli (hunger, for example),
since these are based in the necessities of life ("*Not des Lebens*"). The
apparatus will thus have to adjust this procedure. The "secondary processes" will closely "scan" the representations stored in the unconscious
(or, in the *Entwurf*'s terminology, in the $\psi$ system) and bring them into
relation with earlier memory traces, that is, exogenous stimuli perceptions
that once did bring satisfaction. This is how the organism tries to "judge"
outside reality in an attempt to find an object that can satisfy its requirements (of pleasure as well as of the "*Not des Lebens*").

Note that *only here* does reality intervene in the operation of the apparatus. Reality is thus approachable not through an unconscious *perception*, but through an unconscious *thought* process. Just like in Aristotle, here too, a minor premise (the stimulus) is subjected to an "*orthos logos*," that is, to a field of representations (signifiers) that makes up the unconscious. However, this "orthos logos" no longer concerns universal truths founded in *being* as with Aristotle, but in wishes based in the pleasure principle that are therefore strictly singular.[47] The strange thing here is that, as Lacan notes, what vouches for conformity with reality functions entirely on the basis of representations regulated by the *pleasure* principle. The reality principle thus only searches within this pleasure domain for a "*thought* identity" with the perceived stimulus:

> All thought occurs according to unconscious means. It is doubtless not controlled by the pleasure principle, but it [nonetheless] occurs in a space that as an unconscious space is to be considered as subject to the pleasure principle. (S7E: 33; S7F: 41)[48]

The "space" where (unconscious) thoughts about the reality value of a stimulus are judged is thus traversed by "primary," purely pleasure-driven processes.

Does this mean that for Freud reality comes in directly along the paths of unconscious thought to enter conscious thought (System *Bw*) and so presents itself like this to the organism? Here again, Lacan warns his audience not to jump to conclusions too quickly. The thought process gives "reality" through perception (*System W*) only in the form of an articulated expression that it brings about, a "cry," for example. And this cry, in its turn, only has meaning (reality value) because it is taken up in a network of signifiers. It is solely in expressions and sounds—and thus in fact in words and language—that reality presents itself *consciously* to the psyche:

> Freud tells us that a hostile object [i.e., a stimulus linked to a non-pleasure representation] is only acknowledged at the level of consciousness when pain causes the subject to utter a cry. The existence of the *feindlicher Object* as such is the cry of the subject. [. . .] We only grasp the unconscious finally when it is explicated, in that part of it which is articulated by passing in words. It is for that reason that we have the right—all the more so as the development of Freud's discovery will demonstrate—to recognize that the unconscious itself has in the end no other structure than the structure of language. (S7E: 32; S7F: 42)[49]

Thanks to the linguistic structure of the unconscious, the stimulus that is strictly *internal* to the apparatus (processed, there, by the "judgment process") seems to come *from outside* the psyche. Hence, our reality perception in fact stems from the linguistic nature of the unconscious. What our "Bewusstsein" (the System *Bw*) perceives is a 'discourse' and not reality itself. Or, as he formulates it further on:

> after all, we know nothing else except this discourse. That which emerges in the *Bewusstsein* is *Wahrnehmung*, the perception of the discourse, and nothing else. (S7E: 62; S7F: 76)

The "reality" that rules us as libidinal beings is perpetually marked by this linguistically structured unconscious. It presents itself as something that is articulated from the outset in words, in language. With this, Lacan repeats yet again the metapsychological reason why we cannot but relate to reality as a field of signifiers.

Pleasure and reality can thus interact thanks to the linguistic field in which they both operate. In connection with this, at the end of his second lesson, Lacan speaks of a "double intersection" ("double entrecroisement") between pleasure and reality (S7E: 33; S7F: 42). With this, he expresses precisely the structural impact of the linguistic field in which our unconscious thought performs its "judgment operation." That field makes pleasure and reality inseparably intertwined with one another.

Thus the reality that channels pleasure is a linguistic reality, a discourse, a "logos." In a sense, this was also true for Aristotle when he claimed that the "logos"—or, more precisely, the "orthos logos"—is where the pleasure principle is "*ortho*pedically" directed into good (because true, *real*) paths. This also holds for Freudian theory, Lacan argues, albeit with one last proviso: that this "orthos logos" is no longer founded in actual reality but in the polymorphous-perverse space that divides the pleasure being from its "real" nature.

### 3.3. Real versus Reality

Here we face the most important difference between the psychoanalytic conceptualization of ethics and its Aristotelian counterpart. From a psychoanalytic perspective, the good is a pleasure-invested reality or—what, in the light of the "double intersection," amounts to the same thing—a reality interwoven with pleasure. However, this means that just like reality, the good only intervenes as a "representation," as something that responds not to the hard laws of actual reality (as in Aristotle), but to the laws of the autonomously functioning linguistic logic of the unconscious. If the good is then a pleasure-inflected reality, this "good" reality only holds

in the form of a representational "inscription" (*"Niederschrift"*) of it.[50]
One can no longer speak of a *real* good reality. From a psychoanalytic
perceptive, the good, that is, pleasurable reality in which the human
libido thrives can only be attributed a *symbolic* status, that is, the status
of a signifier.

At this end of his second lesson, Lacan "nicely" summarizes his
whole exposition on the "double intersection" in a schema.[51] He catego-
rizes the different functions of the psychic apparatus in the two columns
of pleasure and the reality principles respectively, and he places the good
explicitly in the pleasure principle column:

> As far as the pleasure principle is concerned, that which pres-
> ents itself to the subject as a substance [comme substance] is
> his good [son bien]. Insofar as pleasure controls subjective
> activity, it is the good, the [unconscious] idea of the good, that
> sustains it. That is why ethical thinkers have at all times not
> been able to avoid trying to identify these two terms, which
> are after all fundamentally antithetical, namely pleasure and
> the good. But over and against that [i.e., on the blackboard,
> on the other side of the column with the reality principle],
> how does one qualify the substratum [le substrat] of reality
> of subjective activity? For the moment, I propose to put here
> a question mark.[52] (S7E: 33-34; S7F: 43–44)

"The good" is an unconscious "idea"—read, *signifier*—and only in
this capacity is it the "substrate" (or "element") on which the pleasure
principle operates. Only unconscious representations (signifiers) and not
*real* things provide content and "substance" to the pleasure we live by.
Thus, thanks only to the primacy of the signifier, the various types of
ethics were able to conceive of an inherent connection between goodness
and the experience of pleasure, between the good as what one is charged
to do and the good as something that we can enjoy. Yet, new to psychoanalysis is the idea that this relation is not guaranteed by reality itself.
*The "substrate" of the reality principle is incompatible with that of the*
*pleasure principle.* It is this point Lacan tries to explain with his scheme
on the blackboard. It is not the unconscious idea (the signifier) of the
good, but that which lies *beyond* this signifier and thus *beyond* the good,
that is the "substantial" reality the principle of the same name refers to.
For this substrate Lacan reserves the term "the real" (*"le réel"*).

The reality modifying the pleasure principle—and which gives the
psychic apparatus its ethical status—is thus essentially double. On the
one hand, it stands for the totality of memory traces and representations
that are taken up in the unconscious and which in this way give the

pleasure process a "substantial substrate." On the other hand, it is also the 'real' reality resisting the representational (i.e., symbolic) power of the unconscious. No matter how incompatible both are with respect to each other, ethics must nevertheless be conceived in terms of the impact that *both* kinds of realities have on the pleasure operation of the psychic apparatus. Thus the "real" reality also contains ethical weight in the psychic apparatus, although its substrate is no longer to be defined as "the good" but as something that is situated *beyond* the signifier and thus *beyond* "the good."

It is not simply an accident that Lacan, in the blackboard scheme, leaves the place of this real "substrate" of the reality principle empty, putting a suggestive question mark there. In the rest of his seminar he will try to explain how the real "substrate" of the ethically functioning psychic apparatus lies paradoxically beyond "the good." And, as we will see, he will increasingly make use of negative terms in order to explain this beyond. Ultimately he will define it as *evil itself*. With this "radical evil" as the *real* substrate of the inherently moral psychic apparatus—and thus of ethics *tout court*—Lacan makes a decisive break with the traditional foundation of ethics and formulates the moral consequences of the polymorphous-perverse "*skandalon*" that is Freudian psychoanalysis. Aware of the implications of this claim, he will clarify them only hesitatingly and in small doses throughout his seminar so as to divulge them to his audience only at the end in all of their "scandalous" consequences.

At the conclusion of his second lesson, Lacan only takes the first step in this direction by way of a very short reference to one of Freud's most pessimistic essays, *Civilization and Its Discontents*. There he plainly states that culture—and thus ethics—demands too much, even something impossible, from us. In exchange for obedience to its law, one is guaranteed happiness which, however, will never be realized in any *real* way. For the promised happiness can never get beyond the level of representation (i.e., of the signifier). Hence the ineradicable discontent man entertains toward his culture (its ethics included). The good he expects from it and which he is promised has no "real substrate." Or, more precisely, that "real substrate" is in no way to be defined as the good. It calls for a "new figure," Lacan suggests at the end of the second lesson:

> What is the new figure that Freud gave us in the opposition reality principle/pleasure principle? It is without a doubt a problematic figure. Freud doesn't for a moment consider identifying adequacy to reality with a specific good. In *Civilization and Its Discontents*, he tells us that civilization or culture certainly asks too much of the subject. If there is indeed something that can be called his good or his happiness, there is nothing to be

expected in that regard from the microcosm (i.e., from himself[53]), nor moreover from the macrocosm. (S7E: 34; S7F: 44)[54]

The "new figure" he talks about here will take shape in his concept of *das Ding*. Without reality, pleasure cannot guarantee satisfaction—and thus life—to man. But the fact that his pleasure—or his desire—never attains this reality *as such* and is therefore plagued by an obdurate discontent is *also* an aspect of that indispensable reality principle. It is this *real* aspect that Lacan will grasp in the "figure" of *das Ding*. This *real* *"thing"* stands for reality's own "substrate." However, in contrast to symbolic reality, it is hardly to be defined in terms of goodness or pleasure. This is why one must call on terms that point to something *beyond* the pleasure principle—and thus *beyond* the good: as something which is in principle evil. This "evil" aspect of reality will be just as—if not more—determining for the ethical operation of the psyche as the reality forged through the signifier and the discourse.

The ethical dimension of the psychic apparatus depends on its relation to reality. This reality is now discovered in its double dimension: reality as a symbolic universe of signifiers, and reality as what lies beyond this, that is, as mere (unsymbolised) real. So, in the same gesture through which the psychic apparatus brings reality into representations, the psychic apparatus must also keep the *real* reality *at distance*. This is why, although "substantially" made up of a universe of representations disconnected from the real, the apparatus is still affected by that real, if only because it constantly has to keep that real at bay. Although the apparatus has distanced itself from *real* reality, as what, from an ethical perspective, must be defined as evil, this distance continues to play an active role, if only because the good, in order to be what it is, must continually keep this "real" evil "thing" actively at bay. This is the complex structure that, according to Lacan, must be discerned in Freud's "reality principle."

Now, ethics depends on how the evil 'real' is both kept at a distance and simultaneously maintained as the main point of orientation for ethics. It is easy to see that an ethical theory built upon these premises will present numerous difficulties. The psychic apparatus may attribute its ethical status to the fact that it must take the substance of its "good" from the (unconscious) representation of reality, but its ultimate moral weight lies at the same time in the reality it unremittingly pushes away. The "good" subject's fascination with this evil real will be an adequate illustration of this, and Lacan will give it an ethical valorization. The ultimate weight of ethics will be that of a "distant thing."

## Chapter 4

# An Intimately Distant "Thing"

> It is to the extent that the commandment in question preserves the distance from the Thing as founded by speech itself that it assumes its value. (S7E: 83; S7F: 100–101)

Considering how little weight a notion such as *das Ding* is given in Freud's oeuvre, it is all the more striking how much significance it acquires in Lacan's "return to Freud." In Freud's *Entwurf*, the text Lacan retrieves it from, its place is pretty relative; it is one of the elements in the neurophysiological sketch of how judgment functions. Aside from a couple of suggestive references, it appears nowhere else in the rest of his oeuvre.[1] For Lacan, on the other hand, *das Ding* acquires the status of a general concept and is loaded, moreover, with an entire philosophical problematic that draws on thinkers such as Aristotle, Kant and Heidegger (to name only these). In fact, for Lacan it becomes a concept capable of laying bare the heart of our entire religious, ethical, aesthetic, and even scientific tradition.

It might be tempting, then, to see something weighty and "essential" in this Lacanian concept, something "transcendental" even, and to represent it as something mysterious, absolute—even as a "holy" entity for some. Although Lacan considers this concept useful for saying something *about* "transcendence" or the "absolute," it is first of all a concept critical of every claim that speaks in the name of some "transcendence or absolute." It deconstructs or decenters such transcendent claims by confronting them with their polymorphous-perverse libidinal base. And it is even less Lacan's intention to trace the polymorphous perversity of desire back to the fixed contours of a metaphysical "thing." Hence, it is important always to keep the "neuropsychology" or "psychophysical" context out of which Lacan plucked this concept in mind. In that sense, it is not without significance that he extracts this concept precisely from one of Freud's most "scientific" writings and it must therefore be interpreted first and foremost in the "neurological" way in which Lacan, in his reading of this earlier Freudian text, analyzes ethical judgment.

In this chapter, I will first briefly examine Lacan's reading of the passage in the *Entwurf* where Freud introduces this notion (see below, 1). We will only be able to understand how Lacan can connect this directly with a passage from another Freud essay, *Negation*, if we take into account the "object relations" axiom that, here again, is Lacan's basic theoretical support. Next I will examine how a concept such as *"das Ding"* primarily names the *distance* that the pleasure subject assumes in relation to it (see 2). The crucial importance Lacan attaches to this concept, as well as its ethical weight, must be sought principally in the peculiar kind of *distance* the subject maintains toward it. The importance of maintaining this distance becomes more comprehensible when one takes the impact of the death principle into account. That principle will also reveal the ultimate reason why a modern ethics of distance with respect to the "thing" must be placed at the center of moral consciousness. But it is not yet clear how such a *conscious* relation toward this principally *unconscious* distance is possible (see 3).

## 1. *"Das Ding"*

### 1.1. A Notion from a Theory of Judgment . . .

The context in which Freud raises the notion of *das Ding* is fairly prosaic. The *Entwurf* is an attempt to set out a "metapsychological" blueprint of the way the psyche functions at the most basic level. The passages in which the notion appears are attempts to map the neuropsychological structure of human thought activity, in this case, that of judgment. In this sense, *das Ding* in Freud is in no way a *general* concept that functions alongside the other psychoanalytic concepts. It is, more specifically and more limitedly, solely the metapyschological term that refers to the grammatical *subject* of a judgment or proposition. We already discussed how Freud conceives the judgment process as the unconscious processing of stimuli from the outside world or, more precisely, stimuli *complexes* (*aggregates* of stimuli). In that process, two heterogenous things are in play, as Freud explains in the *Entwurf*: on the one hand, a number of *loose* elements, predicates that can be applied to things, and, on the other, a fixed core, a *fixed* kernel, a firm "thing" these predicates can be attached to.[2]

In the passage Lacan refers to (in S7E: 51–52; S7F: 64), Freud gives the concrete example of a baby who perceives something from the outside world and is forced to reach a judgment about this impression:

> Let us suppose that the object which furnishes the perception resembles the subject—a *fellow human-being [Nebenmensch]*. If so, the theoretical interest [taken in it] is also explained by the fact that an object *like this* was simultaneously the [subject's] first satisfying object and further his first hostile object, as well as his sole helping power. For this reason it is in relation to a fellow human-being that a human-being learns to cognize. Then the perceptual complexes proceeding from this fellow human-being will in part be new and non-comparable—his *features*, for instance, in the visual sphere; but other visual perceptions—e.g., those of the movements of his hands—will coincide in the subject with memories of quite similar visual impressions of his own, of his own body, [memories] which are associated with memories of movements experienced by himself. Other perceptions of the object too—if, for instance, he screams—will awaken the memory of his [the subject's] own screaming and at the same time of his own experience of pain. Thus the complex of the fellow human-being falls apart into two components, of which one makes an impression by its constant structure and stays together as a *thing* [als *Ding* beisammenbleibt], while the other can be *understood* [*verstanden*] by the activity of memory—that is, can be traced back to information from [the subject's] own body. This dissection of a perceptual complex is described as *cognizing* it; it involves a *judgment* and when this last aim has been attained it comes to an end.[3]

As a libidinal being, in order to also satisfy the requirements of the reality principle (if only to accommodate the biological needs, "*Not des Lebens*"), the child's psychic apparatus must "judge" the incoming "complex" of stimuli, in this case a fellow man (the "*Nebenmensch*," the mother who feeds and holds it, for example). The most basic procedure of this judgment lies in making a distinction between stimuli that the organism can recognize by itself, and stimuli it cannot. These latter present themselves as an exceptional group, separate from the already familiar stimuli. Nevertheless, the judgment attempts to relate these familiar stimuli to the still unknown stimuli. This procedure involves making the most fundamental distinction ("*Ur-teil*") that is the prerequisite of any judgment (any proposition or claim) namely, the distinction of subject and predicate.

The predicates concern the content of the judgment. They stem from *representations* of earlier stimuli invasions that help the "thinking apparatus" to identify the present stimuli.[4] The "subject" or "thing" is that which can not be bound to "familiar" (stimulus) representations and therefore appears as and isolated "unknown." This "thing" is effectively dressed up in the "familiar" predicates in an effort to render it recognizable.

Lacan first remarks that, for Freud, judgment and thinking apparently come into being in an "intersubjective" context. The complex of stimuli with which the apparatus is confronted is the "first satisfaction object [. . .], the first hostile object, as well as his sole helping power"—in short, an other person, a "fellow human being." However, this "other" that the child is confronted with also "cries" (as Freud writes), a fact that is anything but indifferent for Lacan. It indicates that from the outset, the other must be interpreted as a "speaking being" and thus as a representative of the linguistic (symbolic) "big Other."[5] Only through an identificatory relation with a linguistic fellow human being does thought emerge (or, as Freud writes: "it is in relation to a fellow human-being that a human-being learns to cognize").

What interests Lacan above all is the way that object, that is, the intercepted "stimuli complex"—in this case, the linguistic other—is judiciously divided into representations (of stimuli attacks) that can be "understood by the activity of memory," on the one hand, and, on the other hand, something that escapes this grasp and (therefore) "als Ding beisammenbleibt" ("what stays together as a thing"). The "thing" judged is taken strictly as something that escapes its "attributes," which is why the latter must be applied to it. As regards content, the 'thing' thus escapes judgment and in this sense remains "alien," as Lacan—mistakenly—quotes:

> The *Ding* is the element that is initially isolated by the subject
> in his experience of the *Nebenmensch* as being by its very
> nature alien, *Fremde*. (S7E: 52; S7F: 64–65)

Although Lacan indeed is mistaken when he says he cites the word "Fremde" from the *Entwurf* (in the passage in question, this term does not appear[6]), he nevertheless quite accurately reproduces what Freud intends to say: the subject of judgment, the "thing" that is judged, is never known or named *as such*. Only the predicates that are to be applied to it are known; the thing itself—or, to say it with Kant, the "Thing in itself"—remains an "unknown."[7] A few pages further in the *Entwurf*, there is a passage which is not cited by Lacan, although it would have been a perfect support for his interpretation. There, Freud writes literally:

> What we call *things* are residues which evade being judged
> [Reste, die sich der Beurteilung entziehen]. (Freud, SE1: 334)

*1.2. . . . Applied to an 'Object Relation'*

Lacan discovers the same structure *outside* the field of judgment as well. In his eyes, it corresponds to the general way object relations function—which is one of the main reasons he gives *das Ding* much greater weight than permitted by the strict letter of Freud's text. As I said, judgment consists of loose elements, predicates that all apply to one fixed subject, a "thing." At the same time, however, these predicates never touch the thing as such; they never make the thing *itself* known. For Lacan, this procedure is the grammatical translation of what occurs at the level of the "object relation." There, too, the object itself structurally escapes the grasp of desire. The formal procedure of the "object relation" implies that the object *itself* is lost from the very beginning.

Lacan links the just-cited page of Freud's *Entwurf* to a passage from *Negation* where Freud once more explains the strange structure of the "object relation." In his eyes, the "original division [*Ur-teil*] of the experience of reality" into "predicates" and "thing" is consonant with the fact that rather than being *found*, the object must be *re*found. Referring to the analysis of judgment in the *Entwurf*, he claims:

> We have here an original division of the experience of reality. We find it as well in *Verneinung*.[. . .] That's what Freud indicates when he says that "the first and most immediate goal of the test of reality is not to find in a real perception an object which corresponds to the one which the subject represents to himself at that moment, but to find it again, to confirm it is still present in reality." (S7E: 52; S7F: 65)[8]

Strictly speaking Freud is only saying here that the libidinal being, before it even goes in search of an object in the outside world, already has this object in front of him at the level of (unconscious) representations. This is why it is able to gain pleasure from that object in a hallucinatory way,[9] even though it will indeed turn to the outside world out of necessity, that is, because of the 'Not des Lebens.' "Reality testing" thus always comes *after* the object is first endorsed as unconscious representations by the pleasure principle. Several lines further in *Negation*, one reads that:

> it is evident that a precondition for the setting up of reality-testing is that objects shall have been lost which once brought real satisfaction. [Freud, SE19: 238; SA3: 376)

Is Freud saying here that the objects are *always* already lost, as Lacan suggests?[10] Does he claim here that, from the first confrontation, the object *already* escapes in advance from the grip of the psychic apparatus and that, strictly speaking, it is even never lost since it has never been present? Not at all. According to Freud's text, the object that must be refound is one that indeed once provided "real satisfaction." Freud recognizes the primacy of (unconscious) representations with respect to reality and in this sense claims that the object must therefore be refound. But his main hypothesis is that the origin of the unconscious representations lies in an original, satisfying encounter with the object. As he unambiguously puts it, "the "lost objects once gave real satisfaction."[11]

With this latter idea, Lacan can only disagree, but it is typical of him that he takes the arguments for his critique from Freud himself. In this way, his famous "return to Freud' remained unspoiled. The *Entwurf* already showed how, in the act of judgment, the object *as such—das Ding*—is lost to our understanding. The "judgment apparatus" that we *are,* structurally denies us access to the actual object. This doesn't however mean that we do not fully coincide with our *relation* to that impossible object. Here, again, we touch the core of Lacan's thought. As a judgment apparatus, we are also—and fundamentally—an "object relation" (see chapter 1). Prematurely born into a world where nothing is geared to its pleasure requirements, the judging libidinal being bonds with a fictional object and constructs for this bond an equally fictional bearer: a subject. The gap—and, accordingly, the *relation*—between the two will not only be *imaginarily* miscognized, it will also and primarily be *symbolically* repressed, that is passed on from signifier to signifier.

Lacan thus applies Freud's analysis of judgment to the object relation and thereby brings the impact of the signifier into sharper focus. Because reality presents itself first and foremost as an unconscious representation (recall the "double intersection" discussed in the previous chapter), because, in other words, the object functions from the outset as a signifier, that object is always subdivided in advance between a "thing" on the one hand, and signifying predicates, on the other. From the outset, the object in relation to which we *are,* is marked by the original division (*Ur-teil*) of the *judgment* apparatus from which our relation to ourselves and the outside world stems. The "thing" in this sense is an effect of the primacy of the signifier in the unconscious.

It is not then a matter of seeing in *das Ding* an alternative to the "primacy of the signifier" or, to put it differently, to see a break between "the Lacan of *das Ding*" (or "object a") with the "Lacan of the signifier." Of course, there is a difference between the Lacan of the fifties, when it was all about the signifier, and the Lacan of the sixties and seventies where one sees a continually renewed emphasis on the Real. But the crucial point here is that the concept of *das Ding* is not so much a break with Lacan's emphasis on the signifier, as its intensification. The notion of *das Ding* makes the thesis of the primacy of the signifier even more provocative.[12] In any event, Lacan's line of reasoning in the seventh seminar makes it easy to see that the notion of *das Ding* is comprehensible and defensible only by maintaining the primacy of the signifier. Constructing a parallel with Aristotle's *Nicomachean Ethics* and, thus, considering the unconscious as a "machine for judgment," Lacan presumes a procedure operating entirely within a universe of signifiers. Yet, whereas for Aristotle, the "thing" stands for the essence that grants judgment its (energetic) ontological foundation, here the "thing" is a remainder of the "signifying" act of judgment. It is that which a priori escapes the "logos," that is, the universe of signifiers (the symbolic Other) in which the libidinal being is realized. This is why a concept such as *"das Ding"* is forged, precisely to stress the radical otherness of the symbolic universe and, in this sense, it strengthens the primacy of the signifier. For the mere existence of that remainder implies that the Other never achieves full self-identity and, indeed, remains always "other with respect to itself." Which is to say that, already in itself, the Other is nothing but *desire* (for whatever may be, including an impossible "self").[13]

The "origin" and "final purpose" of the Other—in other words, the point where the Other would achieve self-identity—is just as inaccessible for the Other as it is for the subject: this is the ultimate consequence of its symbolic status. It is not in an ultimate signifier that the Other resides, but in an *un*signified (and fundamentally unsignifiable) "stupid," real thing; which is to say that the Other finds utterly no rest, since its resting point lies outside itself. This is what Lacan reads in the cited passage from Freud's *Entwurf*: confronted for the first time with the Other in the figure of the mother—a linguistic Other with which it must identify in order to become a subject (of desire), the child also immediately makes an irrevocable primary division—an *"Ur-teil"*—between the Other as "thing" and the Other as a fluid aggregate of representations (or, in Lacan's terminology, as a field of signifiers).

In one passage, Lacan defines *das Ding* as the "other of the Other" (S7E: 66; S7F: 81) or as the "absolute Other of the subject": not the Other insofar as he provides me with the "coordinates," the "associations" (i.e., the signifiers) necessary to find pleasure again, but the Other insofar as it escapes these "co-ordinates of pleasure." Or, as Lacan puts it,

> The world of our experience, the Freudian world, assumes that it is this object, *das Ding*, as the absolute Other of the subject, that one is supposed to find again. It is to be found at the most as something missed. One doesn't find it, but only its pleasurable associations [its co-ordinates of pleasure; *ses coordonnées du plaisir*]. (S7E: 52; S7F: 65)

As libidinal beings, we test reality in order to *re*find something. However, this reality is entirely *symbolic* while the object to be refound is *real*. This is why we will never find the sought-after "thing," according to Lacan, but only a number of "coordinates" (signifiers) that point in its direction. The "thing" in itself we search for has always slipped away from us. For this reason, we are invariably gnawed by a degree of unrest and dissatisfaction, no matter how satisfactorily we have installed ourselves in the symbolic universe of the Other.

In this sense, *das Ding* precedes the symbolic Other. Lacan refers to it as the "prehistoric other" Freud talks about in his letter to Wilhelm Fliess of December 6, 1896, the famous Letter 52 (S7E: 50; S7F: 63). There Freud stresses how, rather than simply a discharge of stimulus tension, the hysterical episode is a directed action, addressed to an "unforgettable other":

> The hysterical attack is not a discharge but an *action*; and it retains the original characteristic of every action—of being a means to the reproduction of pleasure. [. . .] Attacks of dizziness and fits of weeping—all these are aimed at *another person*—but mostly at the prehestoric, unforgettable other person who is never equaled by anyone later. (Freud, 1985: 212–213; Freud's italics)

It is clear for Lacan that we must make a direct link between this "prehistoric other" of Freud's letter and the "thing" from the *Entwurf*. Just like in hysteria where all symptoms in the final analysis refer to a clearly sighted but "irrecoverable other," so all signifiers, more broadly, are aimed at an inaccessible, unsignifiable "thing." Although the "thing" is not a signifier, it nevertheless functions as the signifier's central point of orientation, as a point around which the entire signifying mill—and thus the entire object relation that the human being *is*—revolves.

## 2. A Matter of Distance

### 2.1. A "Topological" Problem

The whole libidinal economy *circles* around a "thing" that, no matter how *central* the position it assumes, nevertheless stands completely *outside*. This is simultaneously the most crucial and the most problematic aspect of the whole concept of *das Ding*. For the simple question is where precisely we must *locate* this "thing." On one side, it is permanently banished from the libidinal signifying economy, while on the other side, it continues to occupy a central place. In other words, does it lie inside or outside the psychic apparatus?

Do not think this was not also a thorny question for Lacan. When, at the beginning of his sixth lesson (hence, after he had already introduced *das Ding*), he tries to summarize his point in a concise manner, his "simple" explanation promptly runs up against this question and immediately lays the whole problem bare. In any event, the light irony with which he peppers his opening sentences doesn't last long:

> What if we brought a simple soul into this lecture hall, set him down in the front row, and asked him what Lacan means. The simple soul will get up, go to the board and will give the following explanation: "Since the beginning of the academic year Lacan has been talking about *das Ding* in the following terms. He situates it at the heart of a subjective world which is the one whose economy he has been describing to us from a Freudian perspective for years. This subjective world is defined by the fact that the signifier in man is already installed at the level of the unconscious, and that it combines its points of reference with the means of orientation that this functioning as a natural organism of a living being also gives him." Simply by writing it on the board and putting *das Ding* at the centre, with the subjective world of the unconscious organized in a series of signifying relations around it, you can see the difficulty of topographical representation. The reason is that *das Ding* has to be posited as exterior, as the prehistoric Other that it is impossible to forget—the Other whose primacy of position Freud affirms in the form of something *entfremdet*, something strange to me, although it is the heart of me, something that on the level of the unconscious only a representation can represent. (S7E; 71; S7F: 87; Miller's italics)

Even the "simple soul" explaining Lacan's theory of *das Ding*, immediately puts his finger on the core difficulty: how to indicate on the board that this "thing" does not belong to the symbolic universe human pleasure (and, thus, life) lives by, and yet forms the very heart of it? How to situate an *exterior* "thing" at the *center* of the apparatus and at the same time claim that it remains radically *outside*? This seems to affect the very idea of center and periphery. How do you think a center that is at the same time decentered? How to think a decentering that continues to occupy the central position?

This question continues to occupy Lacan, not only throughout his seventh seminar, but in more or less all of the ensuing seminars. His notorious and often extravagant hunt for the right "topological" formula—an obsession that will see him through to the end of his days—is an exquisite example of this.[14] Although the topological schemes he will deal with so prodigiously later on are missing in the seventh seminar, the question he raises here with his concept of *das Ding* is of a preeminently "topological" nature (in the literal sense of the word: a "*logos*" that concentrates on the "*topos*," the structural position of the object).[15]

Here, Lacan realizes that the project of mapping out the "perverted" pleasure economy inevitably starts with the "thing"-like, "excentric" center he has just discovered. The entire pleasure economy (of which the subject is both an effect and a bearer) must be explained according to what Lacan elsewhere calls "extimacy" ("extimité"),[16] a kind of "excluded interior" ("intérieur exclu"). At this moment, however, Lacan does not yet have a properly developed topological schema for this "extimate" position. He still bases his argumentation exclusively on a reflection concerning the *distance* installed between the center and the periphery. The irreducibility of this distance will nevertheless enable him to give an initial "topological representation" of this paradoxical "extimate" place of the thing. For this image clearly shows how the libidinal being, as subject (bearer) of a chain of signifiers, rests not upon itself but on its strained *distance* in relation to that ex-centric "thing." It is as if, referring mutually to one another, these signifiers persistently point in the direction of that "thing," if only so as to maintain a safe *distance* from it. Or, as Lacan puts it in the lesson where *das Ding* is first introduced:

> *Das Ding* is that which I will call the beyond-of-the-signified. It is as a function of this beyond-of-the-signified and of an emotional relationship to it that the subject keeps its distance and is constituted in a kind of relationship characterized by primary affect, prior to any repression. (S7E: 54; S7F: 67–68)

This "topological" emphasis on *distance* can be heard still more clearly in the following lesson. There, Lacan suggests that all the "facilitations" ("*Bahnungen*") governed by the pleasure principle circle around the domain of the "thing." And it is precisely through this circular movement that they maintain a satisfactory distance from it:

> The pleasure principle governs the search for the object and imposes the detours which maintain the distance in relation to its end [i.e., the object]. Even in French the etymology of the word—which replaced the archaic "quérir ("to search")"—refers

to *circa*, detour. The transference of the quantity from *Vorstel-lung* to *Vorstellung* always maintains the search at a certain distance from that which it gravitates around. The object to be found confers on the search its invisible law; but it is not that, on the other hand, which controls its movements. The element that fixes these movements, that models the return—and this return itself is maintained at distance—is the pleasure principle. It is the pleasure principle which, when all is said and done, subjects the search to encounter nothing but the satisfaction of the *Not des Lebens*. (S7E: 58; S7F: 72)

All of the vagaries of the libidinal economy are one big "detour" that lands again and again *beside* the (re-)sought-after object. For where that object should be, a signifier crops up, which invariably refers to another signifier and, in so doing, keeps the gap between the subject and the object (the "thing") in place. The unconscious field of signifiers over which psychic energy is spread circles around a central inaccessible object. The image Lacan seems to have in mind here is that of the orbit of the planets. Gravitating toward the sun, they all "fall" in its direction but always by falling "beside" it and in this way making a path *around* it. A few pages later, Lacan talks about the surface structure of the stimuli-receptive skin as the place where the signifiers must be located and which he conceives as a "sphere" that, analogous to the heavenly sphere, is indeed a kind of "gravitation":

And the sphere, order, and gravitation of the *Vorstellungen*, where does he locate them? I told you last time that if one reads Freud carefully, one has to locate them between perception and consciousness, between the glove and the hand [comme on dit entre cuir et chair]. (S7E: 61; S7F: 75)

And again on the next page, he refers to the same "topological" model:

As far as *das Ding* is concerned, that is something else. *Das Ding* is a primordial function which is located at the level of the initial establishment of the gravitation of the unconscious *Vorstellungen*. (S7E: 62; S7F: 77)

Although the "unconscious *Vorstellungen*"—that is, signifiers—oper-ate according to autonomous laws, they nevertheless appear subject to a "gravitation" exerted by *das Ding*. Beside their own, visible laws of displacement and condensation, they are ruled by an invisible law that orients them toward the "thing" and which in this way provides them with a point of gravity—with a "weight," as Lacan says. To regard the world as a surface of signifiers was already a Copernican revolution in itself. A concept such as *das Ding* in its turn strengthens this effect by explicitly placing the center of gravity of these decentered signifiers *outside* themselves. Thus for the libidinal being, it is a matter of continuously missing the "thing," of incessantly "falling" beside (and hence around) it, that is to say, of revolving around it.

In a sense, Lacan conceives the movement inside the psychic apparatus in terms of the model of gravitation Newton found at work in the universe. Again, this shows how faithful Lacan remained to his thesis that psychoanalysis realizes for the realm of subjectivity the revolution Galileo and Newton accomplished for the object world.[17] The decentering of our "objective" world that was established with modernity acquires its "subjective" counterpart in psychoanalysis. Ever since the "Copernican revolution," the place from where we relate to the world (ourselves included) lacks any central objective stability. Psychoanalysis further radicalizes this claim by also stripping the (Cartesian) subject of its fixed kernel and placing it outside the subject's reach as something "extimate." The "intimate" place wherefrom one relates to oneself and the world is henceforth located in the inaccessible exteriority of *das Ding*.

Lacan's concept of *das Ding* poses first of all a topological problem. The question is not so much what it is, but *where* it is, that is, in what "topos" of the libidinal economy it is to be located and how its distance to the subject is to be conceived. It is the "topos" of this 'thing' and the "distance in relation to it" that is crucial. The human libidinal being is the subject (bearer) of a distance that gapes between the signifiers in which he realizes himself as desire and the ultimate "thing" that desire aims at. Only insofar as he is able to be the bearer of this distance (and therefore to maintain this distance) can he repress the lack-of-being he is on the level of the real. With concepts such as *das Ding* and *object a*, Lacan tries to map the coordinates of this distance. The analysand's (like everyone's) search for his self-identity will thus amount to an attempt to find and maintain the right (imaginary and symbolic) distance in relation to the (real) "thing." Furthermore, the core of ethics must be looked for precisely in the "rightness" of this distance.

## 2.2. Subject of a Distance

Lacan's thesis regarding *das Ding* brings the paradox of the "object relation" more sharply into view. While the libidinal being may find its support in an identification with an object, at the same time it only lives through (and *as*) the distance it sustains vis-à-vis that object. It is precisely the primacy of this "vis-à-vis" and of this "distance" that makes this kernel an unsignified and unsignifiable "thing." The function of the "thing" is thus as paradoxical as it is double: it shows how the libidinal being is *simultaneously* its object *and* its relation to that object. Here, too, this paradox can be clarified by applying the Lacanian triad. In its *real* aspect, the libidinal being is nothing other than the "thing" excluded from the Other;[18] *symbolically* and *imaginarily*, it is the "distance" in relation to that real thing, a distance that it can maintain only thanks to the Other, that is, thanks to the sliding chain of signifiers. Unable to have a real existence, the libidinal being must realize itself imaginarily symbolically, that is, it must become the bearer of a signifying chain. It is in this sense that it must be regarded as the *subject* of a distance in relation to the "thing."

The function and weight attributed to the "thing" are thus inextricably bound to the distance taken with respect to it. The way this distance takes shape is decisive for what Freud called the "*Neurosenwahl*," the "choice of neurosis," that is, the unconscious choice between hysteria, obsessional neurosis and paranoia as various ways of warding off the original trauma.[19] In the lesson where he introduces *das Ding*, Lacan reformulates the "choice of neurosis" as ways of keeping the "thing" at a distance. This enables him to map the constitutive impact of this repelled original trauma more clearly. The libidinal economy lives not only from the gap in relation to the "thing" (or, what comes down to the same thing, from the repression of the original trauma); it remains at the same time oriented toward that traumatic "distant thing." Behind every object that satisfies the "necessities of life" (*Not des Lebens*), an ultimate pleasure object is concealed (the "thing") that, because it is "originally" lost, always has to be *re*found over and over again. No matter how inaccessible, the "thing" functions all the same as the main point of reference for the entire libidinal economy and in this sense grants it a final, *real* consistency. This is as true for "healthy" as for "unhealthy" psychic structures. In his fourth lesson, Lacan names four of the latter, distinguishing them according to the position they assume with respect to the "thing":

> The behavior of the hysteric, for example, has as its aim to recreate a state centered on the object, insofar as this object, *das Ding*, is, as Freud wrote somewhere, the support of an aversion. It is because the primary object is an object which failed to give satisfaction that the specific *Erlebnis* of the hysteric is organized. On the other hand [. . .] in obsessional neurosis, the object with relation to which the fundamental experience, the experience of pleasure, is organized, is an object which literally gives too much pleasure. [. . .] the obsessional [. . .] regulates his

behavior so as to avoid what the subject often sees quite clearly as the goal and end of his desire. [. . .] As far as paranoia is concerned, Freud gives us a term that I invite you to reflect on as it first emerged, namely, *Versagen des Glaubens*. The paranoid doesn't believe in that first stranger [the prehistoric other as *das Ding*] in relation to whom the subject is obliged to take his bearings. (S7E: 53–54; S7F: 67)

The hysteric's feeling of continually being disappointed stems, in the final analysis, from a strange, unconscious way of avoiding the object of desire, the "thing," and thus establishing a safe distance from the "thing." That this object always falls short in the demands of pleasure is, paradoxically, what makes the whole (hysterical) pleasure economy possible. Obsessional neurosis, on the other hand, is a procedure that protects one against an *excess* of pleasure coming from the "thing." The obsessional neurotic's scrupulous actions and thoughts form an unconscious strategy for keeping the "thing" at bay. Finally, the paranoiac installs the distance with respect to the "thing" through "forsaking all belief" in it. With his unbelief, he declares the whole problematic null and void, and in this way maintains the "thing" at a safe distance. Decisive in each of the three psychic figures is thus "the weight of a distant thing" and what distinguishes each from the other is the *way* in which this distance acquires a more or less sustainable form.

The "weight of a distant thing" not only differentiates between the "choices of neurosis" for Lacan. It also forms the heart of the generally accepted "healthy" figures in which we normally realize ourselves. Following Freud, Lacan also connects the neuroses just mentioned—hysteria, obsessional neurosis and paranoia—to art, religion, and science respectively. These latter, in which people reveal themselves as "masters of signifiers" par excellence, are also based in an (unconscious) way of keeping distance from the "thing."

In the tenth lesson, Lacan sets out the terms of this parallel:

Thus I once quoted a very short formula which brought together the respective mechanisms of hysteria, obsessional neurosis and paranoia with three forms of sublimation, religion and science. [. . .] All art is characterized by a certain mode of organization around this emptiness [i.e., the emptiness of the 'thing']. [. . .] Religion in all its forms consists in avoiding this emptiness. We can illustrate that by forcing the note of Freudian analysis for the good reason that Freud emphasized the obsessional traits of religious behavior. Yet, although the whole ceremonial phase of the body of religious practices, in effect, enters into this framework, we can hardly be fully satisfied with this formula. A phrase like "respecting this emptiness" perhaps goes further. [. . .] As for our third term, the discourse of science, to the extent that it finds its origin in our tradition in the discourse of wisdom or of philosophy, the term Freud uses in connection with paranoia and its relation to phsychic reality, the term, *Unglauben*, finds its meaning there. (S7E: 129–130; S7F 154–55)

Just like in hysteria, art tries to maintain the distance to the "thing" by emphasizing its "emptiness." In the final analysis, art highlights the way every representation refers to something unrepresentable and allows only an empty shadow to shimmer in its place. Religion, in its turn, is concerned with that same "thing" but now affirms its "fullness," albeit it in order to avoid all *direct* access to it and to install a safe distance toward it by means of its ceremonies. Finally science, too, is just as involved with that same "thing," the in principle unknowable thing, which it keeps at a distance through its disbelief in it.

The question of whether the three parallels are sustainable in every detail we will leave aside for the moment. But it is in any event clear now how, for Lacan, both 'unhealthy' and "healthy" psychic figures stem from an (unconscious) process of installing a distance from the "thing." In the final analysis, it is this distance that keeps desire—and thus the human being as such—going. To bring human beings back to "themselves"—that is, to the desire that they *are*—is to confront them with that strained distance that yawns between "them" and the "thing." Psychoanalysis aims to get human beings, whether "healthy" or "unhealthy," to confront their desire and thus to confront the "weight of that thing at a distance." In this lies both the specific ethical demand as well as the very reason for psychoanalysis's existence for Lacan.

Hence ethics, in Lacan's eyes, is not a domain *alongside* art, religion or science (or, by the same token, *alongside* hysteria, obsessional neurosis and paranoia). Ethics is an attempt to confront man, regardless of whether he realizes himself in "sick" or "healthy" psychic forms, with the desire that he *is*. The "standard" according to which desire must be measured is to be sought in the distance the subject takes from the "thing." According to Lacan, Freudian psychoanalysis offers both the theoretical instruments and the practical framework for confronting humans with this "standard" and, in so doing, offers them the chance to respond to it in an ethical way.

## 3. How Much Does a Thing Weigh?

### 3.1. An Unconscious and Lethal Weight . . .

The question is still whether such an ethical task can have any meaning at all. Why *must* we track down the measure of our desire? Does not the "distance" this measure refers to emphasize precisely the radically unconscious nature of the "thing" around which the psychic apparatus revolves? Not only are the "representations" in which the psyche moves completely unconscious, but these representations themselves gravitate around a point that ceaselessly escapes them. What, then, would be the benefit in searching for it? If one is weighed down by hysterical, obsessional, or paranoid symptoms, one can understand why it might be worth embarking on the exhausting search for one's desire. In that case, a confrontation with that unmanageable 'distant thing' could be useful and, in that sense, ethically good. But why should one go after such a confrontation when it concerns livable and relatively "healthy" psychic figures such as art, religion and science? Even if there are parallels with the specified "choices of neurosis," these figures are not necessarily painful and unlivable. Why, then, should it be one's ethical duty to go in search of "desire's measure" operative in art, religion and science? Why confront these livable kinds of pleasure economies with this strange distance with respect to that "thing," which *in any case* escapes their grasp?

Because there is something wrong with this "in any case," Lacan would reply. Although we cannot consciously manipulate this distance, this doesn't imply that it is immune from all interventions on our side. Despite everything, this distance, as the ultimate guarantee of our pleasure economy, is far too unstable and brittle. What counts for hysterics, as for artists, for obsessionals and paranoiacs as for mystics and scientists, counts for every libidinal being: while the distance that cuts it off from the "thing" may be constitutive, it shares in the contingent, temporary character that is specific to every libidinal solution, and, strictly speaking, lacks any truly solid basis. That is to say, the gap separating the subject from the "thing" is not *forever* irremovable. A *real* abolishing of this distance might indeed imply the death of pleasure's subject, yet this doesn't make it impossible.

What is more, the libidinal being is itself cursed with both a stubborn and unconscious inclination to abolish its distance from the "thing." This is what the Freudian notion of the death principle comes down to, according to Lacan: the *lethal* tendency to overcome the distance toward the "thing."[20] Yet, it is only a tendency. For normally, the libidinal economy does not smash into pieces on the "thing" but keeps circling around it. Thanks to the autonomous, "lateral" operation[21] of signifiers—that is, thanks to the fact that they continuously refer to one another—they interminably keep missing their sighted target (the "thing"), and in this sense continuously fall "around" it. This fruitful failure is the work of the pleasure principle. In relation to the pleasure principle, the death principle assumes a place just as "extimate" as the "thing" is with respect to the pleasure economy. Or, as Lacan explicitly puts it:

> Note the following: Freudian thought directs us to raise the problem of what it is exactly that one finds at the heart of the functioning of the pleasure principle, namely, a beyond of the pleasure principle [. . .]. (S7E: 125; S7F: 150)

Right at its most intimate kernel, the entire pleasure economy is haunted by what can destroy it. It is kept going thanks to the distance it maintains from the "thing" while nonetheless always being pushed in the very direction of the "thing."

With the concept of the death principle, psychoanalysis clearly emphasizes the conflictual, shaky and (therefore) finite character of our libidinal relation to the world as well as to ourselves. It indicates how we are the subject/bearer of a drive cluster that is not entirely compatible with our wish for self-preservation. Libidinal satisfaction at the level of the organism does not principally coincide with libidinal satisfaction at the level of the subject. Hence libidinal satisfaction can also occur at the *cost* of the subject. The satisfaction of the drive can reach a level that is no longer compatible with the level established by a (by definition fictitious) subject in order to manage an equilibrium in its libidinal economy. This is where the pleasure principle turns out to go "beyond" the limits of the subject's economy and to become a death principle.[22]

In the *Ethics Seminar*, Lacan gives the Freudian concept of the death drive a proper "topological" formulation. The "thing" names the "topos" around which the entire pleasure economy gravitates but it also stands for the "topos" where the economy shatters once it can no longer maintain the necessary distance from it. Freud defined the death principle as the organism's regressive tendency to return to an inorganic state. Lacan defines it, more broadly and more topologically, as an inclination to merge with the real (the "thing").

So to forget that the "thing" one is after is radically inaccessible is to unchain lethal libidinal forces, Lacan claims. Recalling Heidegger's critique of *technics*, he states that the danger threatening modern man lies in his spontaneous tendency to overlook this radical inaccessibility of the real. Trusting in his limitless power, technologically developed man forgets that it is precisely his infinite power that confronts him with his finitude. The threat of nuclear war, for example, shows precisely how the limitlessness of technical power enables us to destroy ourselves.[23] In Lacanese, man becomes a threat to himself if he gives free rein to his tendency to endlessly grasp after the real. He then denies precisely that to which he owes his existence: the distance from the real.[24]

In his lesson of January 20, 1960, Lacan offers up a slightly ironic science-fiction version of this kind of eschatological threat:

> Nevertheless, the weapon suspended over our heads which is one hundred thousand times more destructive than those which came before—just imagine that rushing toward us on a rocket from outer space. It's not something I invented, since we are bombarded everyday with the news of a weapon that threatens the planet itself as a habitat for mankind. Put yourself in that spot, which has perhaps been made more present for us by the progress of knowledge than it was before in men's imagination—although that faculty never ceased to toy with the idea; confront that moment when a man or a group of men act in such a way that the question of existence is posed for the whole of the human species, and you will then see inside yourself that *das Ding* is next to the subject. (S7E: 104–105; S7F: 125)

The weapon suspended over our modern heads is nothing other than the omnipotence of our advanced technological ability, evoked here in the grisly but real possibility of deciding about the continuation of mankind's existence. But this anxiety, too, must first of all be approached from the Lacanian methodological distinction between the symbolic, imaginary and real. For our modern omnipotence doesn't imply that we henceforth shall have a grasp of the *real* totality of our existence. On the contrary, just like everything else, this totality, too, must be understood as a *symbolic* entity, that is, as a universe of signifiers. It is precisely *because* we, moderns, regard everything as signifiers that we are able to make our hold on the world more radical and total. Reality has lost its essence and, therefore, allows us to do whatever we want with it. It has become the tractable object of our unlimited creativity. But for this precise reason, we can reduce it to nothing and literally annihilate it. The idea of being able to decide the future existence of the human race illustrates this terrifying possibility. According to Lacan, this is also why, from an historical perspective, a concept such as the death principle is possible only with modernity—that is, only with the transformation of the world into signifiers.

In the lesson just before the beginning of his commentary on *Antigone*, Lacan again stresses the explicitly *historical* necessity of a notion such as the death drive. Now that our world has become a universe of signifiers, our desire is open to an infinity unknown prior to then (since it is no longer held together by the infinite God). One of the consequences, however, is that we can now also desire to reduce everything that is, including ourselves, to zero. This is what the Freudian notion of the death drive translates into psychoanalytical terminology. After Lacan makes a connection between the mathematization of our world picture (responsible for the becoming-signifier of our universe), the omnipotence of our *technics* and the place of human desire in this, he asks:

> if the discourse of physics, as engendered by the omnipotence of the signifier, will reach the point of the integration of nature or its disintegration. This fact strangely complicates the problem of our desire [. . .]. Let us just say that, as far as the man who is talking to you is concerned, it is there that one finds the revelation of the decisive and original character of the place where human desire is situated in the relationship of man to the signifier. Should this relationship be destroyed? [. . .] I take it that you might have heard [. . .] that it is in that direction that the question of the meaning of the death drive lies. It is insofar as this question is tied to history that the problem is raised. It is a question of the here and now, and not *ad aeternam*. It is because the movement of desire is in the process of crossing the line of a kind of unveiling that the advent of the Freudian notion of the death drive is meaningful for us. The question is raised at the level of the relationship of the human being to the signifier as such, to the extent that at the level of the signifier every cycle of being may be called into question, including life in its movement of loss and return. (S7E: 236; S7F: 277)[25]

One can desire anything. Desire has no *real* relation to anything, nor has it a *natural* aim or end. This is why, confronted with the possibility of attaining everything (the "totality of being"), it can also choose *nothing*. Desire goes that far. This is why in the end desire is desire for death and for nothing. The Lacanian "thing" names this stubborn kind of "nothing" one can continue to desire when an infinity of signifiers lies open before us. It is the "nothing" that would survive us even if we satisfied our (death) desire with the entire world. It is, thus, the kind of nothing we should keep at distance in order to save the desire we *are*.

The ethical task of psychoanalysis is to guard this distance and bring it to the center of our attention. This distance is the most basic condition of the desire we are. Psychoanalysis's ethical interest in confronting man with the weight of his desire holds not only for hysteria, obsessional neurosis, and psychosis, but also for the "healthy" psychic figures of art, religion, and science. Both at the strictly individual and the more general cultural level man must, if he doesn't want to succumb to the deathliness of his drive, track down the "measure" of his desire as that which can maintain the "right" distance from the ultimate "thing" that, as a libidinal being, he seeks.

### 3.2. . . . *Consciously Weighed*

While the idea that we must go in search of the measure of our desire—namely, in search of the distance that separates us from the "thing"—may be a moral imperative for Lacan, this doesn't yet answer the question of whether we are capable of doing this. How can one imagine a *conscious* confrontation with a radically *unconscious* "thing"? How on earth can one *consciously* measure this *unconscious* distance vis-à-vis the "thing" of one's desire?

Although the psychoanalytic ethics Lacan wishes to draw attention to will stand or fall by this question, he doesn't immediately have a cut-and-dry answer. Such an answer will require a long and difficult path and even at the end will not be entirely free from ambiguity.

Take, for example, the already cited parallel he observes between hysteria, obsessional neurosis, and psychosis, on the one hand, and art, religion, and science on the other. One is inclined to define their difference according to whether or not they represent a conscious or unconscious relation toward the "thing." On closer examination, however, *both* appear to rely on *unconscious* structures. In the previously cited passage, science for instance stands for a completely unconsciously miscognized relation toward the "thing." Yet this is not to say that one can therefore treat both groups in the same way. Where the "unhealthy" group can be described as forms of "repression" or "miscognitions," Lacan characterizes the "healthy" group of art, religion, and science as so many forms of "sublimation."[26]

It is here that Lacan's argument will make a strange twist. For the *unconscious* procedure of sublimation will be described as having active, *conscious* capacities at the same time. This will not always benefit the clarity of his argument, although he is proud of having given this Freudian concept a more solid foundation. For Freud had never succeeded in giving the concept the clarification it required.[27] With Lacan, on the other hand,—and preeminently in his *Ethics Seminar*—the concept of sublimation acquires not only a univocal and consistent meaning, but also a central place in the whole of his reflections on ethics (and, thus, on psychoanalysis, since the latter is profoundly ethical, as Lacan repeats over and over). More precisely, "sublimation" will be defined by reference to the "thing" and its distance with respect to the subject. It will, however, remain unclear whether sublimation is a conscious or an unconscious process.

Art, religion and science are described as different types of sublimated relations with respect to the "thing" and to this extent are unconscious. This nevertheless doesn't prevent them—but not all, and this is precisely the rub—from having a *conscious* idea of this *unconscious* distance.

It is already apparent from the previously cited passages how science stems from a blind (because) unconscious miscognition of the distance that separates us from the 'thing.' Although such blindness—or, as Freud would say, such an "illusion"—is not absent from religion either, Lacan seldom seems to reduce it to this. And least of all is this the case with art. As the superior form of sublimation, art in Lacan's analyses (just like in Freud, by the way) is presented as a *conscious* procedure that gives insight into the distance between man and his 'thing.' In any event, the examples of sublimation illustrating his ethical vision all come from the aesthetic realm and point unambiguously in the direction of a *conscious* confrontation with the hidden structure of desire. To his mind, the tragedy of *Antigone*, with which his seventh seminar culminates, will stage the conflict between human desire and the 'thing' in a lucid and conscious fashion, and he will explicitly name this staging a sublimation. However, the other sublimation, science, is supposed to function as an outstanding example of a stubborn blindness with respect to the "thing." Lacan thus uses the concept of sublimation both in the sense of blinding and of illuminating. It seems as if sublimation is a way of warding off the core paradox of psychoanalysis itself, namely, the thesis that the unconscious is both irrevocable and undeniable.

Moreover, the concept of "sublimation" anticipates the problematic ambiguity that will affect the kind of ethics Lacan distills from psychoanalysis. On the one hand, the human libido is ethical through and through, since the psyche operates according to the model of a moral judgment apparatus. Ethics, in this sense, is already an unconscious business evading our conscious grasp. On the other hand, however, this necessitates a conscious, active, ethical position. For precisely moral reasons, one must actively and consciously keep the 'thing' at distance.

Once more it is clear how close this paradox of the "ethics of psychoanalysis" is to the traditional ethics that it claims to "subvert." Just like in classical ethics, Lacan links ethics to a real dimension, albeit (in contrast to classical morality) because humans no longer correspond in any way to that real. Where classical ethics can posit such a correspondence, for psychoanalysis it is closed off. According to psychoanalysis, with the arrival of modernity, the distance or gap that separates man from the real has become unbridgeable: this gap has become constitutive of the modern subject. But because this *unconscious* constitution is fundamentally unstable, it is never really superfluous to keep it under *conscious* vigil. From a theoretical perspective, it remains nonetheless difficult to imagine a *conscious* vigilance over the *unconscious*. The whole rhetoric of Lacan's *Ethics Seminar*, culminating in his concept of sublimation, is perhaps no more than a (fruitless?) attempt to avoid this paradox—one of the most stubborn paradoxes in psychoanalysis.

Here we come up against one of the most problematic questions raised by Lacan's *Ethics Seminar*: How can one *consciously* weigh the unconscious deadly weight that gives ethics its measure? How can one take what is *unknowable* par excellence as the guiding principle for our ethical *knowledge*? How can one *consciously* maintain a principally *unconscious* distance from the "thing"? Only a closer look at Lacan's concept of sublimation will provide clarification here (see chapter 8).

Yet it will first be necessary to reexamine the unconscious kernel around which the whole psychic economy revolves—and thus also examine the question of ethics—namely, the unconscious deadly weight of that "thing" where, according to Lacan, the "measure" of our desire is to be found. This is why, in the rest of his seminar, Lacan focuses on a work from the modern ethical tradition he had already mentioned in his sixth lesson as a crucial reference point for all modern reflections on morality, namely, Immanuel Kant's *Critique of Practical Reason*. He wishes, more specifically, to revise the project of a "critique of moral reason" in an even more radical way than Kant. The conclusion of Lacan's "critique" is his famous and provocative thesis that the unconscious truth of the ethical law—of both the Christian love of one's neighbor and of the Kantian categorical imperative—is to be found in the Marquis de Sade: in other words, that the truth of what for centuries we have called the supreme good must henceforth be identified as radical evil.

Chapter 5

# Critique of *Pure* Practical Reason

Well now, the step taken by Freud at the level of the pleasure principle is to show us that there is no Sovereign Good—that the Sovereign Good, which is *das Ding*, which is the mother, is also the object of incest, is a forbidden good, and that there is no other good. Such is the foundation of the moral law as turned on its head by Freud. (S7E: 70; S7F: 85)

Ethics itself knows how difficult it is on the whole to comply with the pledges with which it binds us. Although it claims that even its harshest rules lead to happiness and the good life, it is nonetheless aware how often one's sacrifices go bitterly unrewarded. Yet no ethics would throw away all laws and rules just for this reason (with the exception of Sade's libertinism, which we will discuss shortly). Even from those who, believing the law to be far too inhibiting of desire, try to free themselves from its yoke, you will not often hear an argument against the existence of rules and norms *as such*.

Nor will you from psychoanalysis either. The fact that it conceives the entire ethical problematic in terms of desire is precisely why it places all the more emphasis on the importance of law and rules. Precisely because we *are* desire, man's bondage to the law is taken extremely seriously. In Lacanese, we are the "subject" (the "bearer") of the desire of the *Other*, that is to say, of an ever receding, *symbolic* Other that with each new signifier slips further and further away and which, for this reason, we experience as a perpetually dissatisfied, alien law. The fact that "I is an Other," as Lacan formulates it with Rimbaud, means above all that I will permanently *have to be* an "other"—and that this imperative will never be realized. In this sense, as the "subject" of the (desire of) the

Other, I am forever "subject" to its law. My attachment and resistance to the moral law both derive from this structure. The distressing feeling we have at times of being eternally subject to the alien law feeds on my sneaking suspicion that none of the goods promised me by the moral law will become reality and that the law in all of its cruelty will continue to "weigh" on me.

Earlier ethical systems could still ward off this suspicion because they were convinced that happiness and the Good were part of reality's essence. Aristotelian morality supposed humans and law to have the same foundation in *being* and, hence, that the observation of ethical laws goes hand in hand with one's own self-realization. The efforts of keeping to the right path and the pain inflicted by this hard law vanish into thin air once people gain insight into the essence and the final purpose of their existence. So, too, could the ethics of medieval Christianity guarantee its "subjects" that there can be no comparison between the earthly pangs accompanying their striving for goodness and the bliss of infinite, holy grace.

With the arrival of modernity, such Aristotelian and Christian morality fell into crisis. The waning of the Christian-Thomist anthropology brought the theological and ontological reference point of the ethical law into discredit, while the Enlightenment's merciless critique of religion did the same with all idea of heavenly salvation. The new, anti-essentialist physics of Newton did not allow one to look for "salvation" in nature, all of Rousseau's odes to Nature with a capital "N" notwithstanding. Freed from all essence (founded in God or not), henceforth the Enlightened subject himself was to stand in for the ethical law. Nevertheless, this moral emancipation could not prevent him from being tormented by the fear of losing access to a real, actual good, for the good could no longer be defined as the *foundation*, but only the *effect* of the moral law: such is the "Copernican" revolution of modern ethics. The "good" became anything the free subject names. All the same, freedom could not be defined as mere arbitrariness, otherwise ethics would lose all guarantee and become impossible. So the question was how to make freedom the basis of a law limiting that same freedom. What, in other words, would still be capable of providing a *free* ethics with its solid "weight"?

For Lacan, this sums up the crucial moral problem we are still dealing with today. That is to say, we have not yet fully put the ethical crisis of the Enlightenment behind us.[1] Hence, any reflection on ethics must inevitably return to this period, specifically to the final years of the eighteenth century (the "high point of the ethical crisis," as he puts it; S7E: 76; S7F: 92–93) where the problem is posed in remarkably diverse and precise ways. Lacan points first of all to Kant's *Critique of Practical Reason* of 1788, in his eyes an unmistakable reference for anyone wishing to understand what psychoanalysis has to say about ethics. At the same time, however, he lays a similar emphasis on Sade's *Philosophy in the Bedroom* that appeared in 1795. This infamous book might seem utterly incompatible with the exalted ethics of Kant's *Second Critique*, but for Lacan it comprises just as unmistakable a reference for understanding both the ethical crisis of modernity and the wider moral implications of Freudian psychoanalysis. For it is only the light of these *two* highly incompatible oeuvres that one can uncover the unconscious foundation of the moral idea so prevalent in the public opinion of that time: the ideal of universal love. The entire French revolution can in fact be seen as a laicized, political actualization of the ancient Christian love of one's neighbor. The psychoanalytic light Sade shines on Kant enables Lacan to penetrate into the darkest, unconscious foundation of our entire—Christian and post-Christian—moral history.

In this and the following chapter, I will sketch out the relation Lacan discovers between Kant (see this chapter), Sade (see later, VI, 2), and the love of one's neighbor (section VI.3). Here, the notion of "enjoyment" ("*jouissance*")—which acquires the status of a full concept in the *Ethics Seminar*—will be central.

## 1. Kant's Critique of Morals

The key problem for modern ethics is to ascertain where a *free* moral law might acquire its "weight" so as to prevent it from lapsing into mere arbitrariness and subjective voluntarism. In his *Critique of Practical Reason*, Kant is the first to extricate this "weight" from what is traditionally called the "essence" of reality. For, since that essence is unknowable (as Kant showed in his first *Critique*), human morality would then be subjected to something "alien," keeping man unfree. But, again, if ethics is free, free even from any essence, what can provide it with its "weight"?

The question of freedom was not at stake in Kant's First *Critique*, the *Critique of Pure Reason* (1781). The limitation of human knowledge with respect to phenomena was precisely why one should not conceive of theoretical (scientific) reason in terms of freedom. Instead, reason must be subjected to a rigorous transcendental-critical investigation in order to establish the laws it must satisfy to be necessarily and universally valid.

In his "critique of moral reason," Kant sets to work from the opposite side and proceeds directly from supposed freedom. The desire to act ethically in a specific situation immediately confronts reason with its desire to apply the highest (*noumenal*) principles directly to the most concrete (*phenomenal*) questions. Confronted with a moral question, the "fact" ("Faktum") of its freedom becomes evident immediately. If someone wants to know how to act ethically in a specific situation, they need only to apply the premise of reason's universal applicability to this specific context. The point of departure for practical reason in a concrete situation must be the same as what holds for a universal ethics: this is one of the definitions of what Kant called the "categorical imperative."[2] In contrast to theoretical reason, practical reason thus directly enforces its own law and, by that "fact," offers proof of its freedom.[3] What supplies a free ethical judgment its definitive "weight" is nothing other than free, self-determining reason.

This is, at least, assuming that we are dealing with—and only with—*practical* reason. According to Kant, reason is incapable of having *theoretical* knowledge of its freedom, because that would transgress the limits established by the *Critique of Pure Reason*. This *Critique* limited the range of scientific reason exclusively to *phenomenal* reality. *Noumenal* ideas such as the Ideas of Reason (the subject, the world, God) or the "thing-in-itself" fall irrevocably outside its scope. At first sight, this limit seems to disappear when reason asks itself practical-moral questions. It seems as if, in that case, reason is able to rise above its sensible, phenomenal tendencies and legislate directly according to its highest (noumenal) principles. It thus itself imposes the law it must obey, immediately proving that it is free. Yet, by this it only proves *that* it is free and not *what* this freedom is. Its knowledge is restricted to the *fact* of its freedom. Its content—its "essence," its thing-in-itself,[4] if you will—remains unknown. As a consequence of its *noumenal* nature, one does indeed suspect that practical reason has something to do with the noumenal "being" of reality, and that the freedom it appears to have "*in fact*" is no mere illusion. However, *in principle* it is unable to conclude this theoretically and (thus) scientifically.

While the weight of ethics may lie in reason itself, it also seems that the weight of reason lies exclusively in ethics. Isn't reason too closely entwined with ethics, then, to be able to function as its ultimate guarantee? Because reason can only be sure of its noumenal freedom at a *practical-ethical* level, it is unable to form a link with the similarly noumenal thing-in-itself—this is, with the rational essence of the outside reality. Despite its moral certainty, reason therefore always remains a bit unsure whether it is not simply a fantasy that has been torn loose from reality. Only an anchoring in reality itself, only the thing-in-itself, can ultimately guarantee its moral certainty, but the limits of theoretical reason deprive it of any of this certainty. Everything seems to indicate that ethics has something "essentially" to do with the rational (noumenal) core of reality. However, moral reason can have no theoretical knowledge of this "essence." The freedom proven by its "*Faktum*" in moral reason remains theoretically an unknowable and unknown thing-in-itself. And yet, everything indicates that this "thing" constantly plays a part in the background of Kant's ethics and, in the final analysis, constitutes the unknowable, unconscious "weight" of ethics.

Certainly Kant would never give in to the temptations of this final conclusion. His entire *Critique of Practical Reason* is written precisely to discourage us from this. Still, this is where the interest of Kantian ethics lies for Lacan. In his eyes, it is the first ethics to have taken the "weight of the thing" as its point of departure. To be able to find this in Kant, Lacan is obliged to seek refuge in a seriously "forced" reading. In the following section, we will look more closely at that reading[5] and see how he interprets the *Critique of Practical Reason* above all in terms of the premises of the *Critique of Pure Reason*. In this way, he will be able to lay the "weight of the thing" at the heart of practical (moral) reason.[6]

## 2. Lacan and the *Critique of Practical Reason*

Lacan situates his founding thesis concerning ethics—namely, that the "thing" is what constitutes its 'weight'—explicitly in the wake of Kant's *Critique of Practical Reason*. In his sixth lesson, for example, where he deals extensively with Kant for the first time, he turns to his audience and, mentioning the title of Kant's book, declares:

> It is impossible for us to make any progress in this seminar relative to the questions posed by the ethics of psychoanalysis if you do not have this book as a reference point. (S7E: 72; S7F: 88)[7]

A little further on, he names Kant's *Critique* in the same breath as his central thesis:

> My thesis is that the moral law is articulated with relation to the real as such, to the real insofar as it can be the guarantee of the Thing. That is why I invite you to take an interest in what I have called the high point of the crisis in ethics, and that I have designated from the beginning as linked to the moment when *The Critique of Practical Reason* appeared. (S7E: 76; S7F: 92–93)

Here Lacan seems to suggest that in Kant's *Critique of Practical Reason*, one can find a supporting argument for his central thesis that the ethical law obtains its orientation and final "guarantee" in the real "Thing" (the *thing-in-itself*). Yet, in Lacan's subsequent line of reasoning, while he may cite a points of comparison between Kant's thought and his own analyses, he will not be able to claim that the guarantee of ethics lies in the "thing." In this context, the sentence following the previously cited passage speaks for itself:

> Kantian ethics appears at the moment when the disorienting effect of Newtonian physics is felt, a physics that has reached a point of independence relative to *das Ding*, to the human *Ding*. It was Newtonian physics that forced Kant to revise radically the function of reason in its pure form. And it is also in connection with the questions raised by science that a form of morality has come to engage us; it is a morality whose precise structure could not have been perceived until then—one that detaches itself purposefully from all reference to any object of affection, from all reference to what Kant called the *pathologisches Objekt*, a pathological object, which simply means the object of any passion whatsoever. No *Wohl*, whether it be our own or that of our neighbor, must enter into the finality of moral action. (S7E: 76; S7F: 93)

Here, Lacan expresses his appreciation for the Copernican turn ethics took with Kant when he placed the center of the moral act in the subject. Man's ethical behavior must be governed by nothing that comes from the outside, by no "pathological object," by no "good in itself."[8] Thanks to the autonomous power of his *Reason*, man is able to extricate himself from the passions that bind him to the phenomenal realm, thus providing a glimpse of a noumenally grounded freedom. At the moral level, he need not be led by everything that happens to feel good ("*Wohl*"), but by a freer and more persistent type of goodness ("*das Gute*") that is a direct effect of his autonomous moral reason.[9] Just as Newtonian physics distanced itself from the pretence to know the essence of things (the thing-in-itself) so, too, did ethics win its independence from the "good *in itself*" with Kant. Such a substantially conceived "good" would throw man back into his old lack of freedom. And, as is well known, according to the "enlightened" Kant, our moral duty is to not allow this to happen.

The question, however, is whether this Kantian thesis supports Lacan's claim that morality is to be defined in terms of its "orientation to the real as such"? Rather the opposite seems to be the case. Here Kant illustrates how ethics has left precisely all orientation to the real—to the *Ding an Sich*—behind. It no longer searches for its ultimate "guarantee" in something outside itself, but only *in* itself, in the autonomy of its own reason, which is precisely independent from all foreign authorities, including the one of "*das Ding an Sich*." So, it is striking how little it seems to hinder Lacan that his reference to Kant illustrates precisely the opposite of what he wants to show. Further along in the same passage, he praises Kant precisely for the "radicalism" with which he persisted in his break with "*das Ding an sich*"—in the *Critique of Practical Reason* as well. About the categorical imperative and the *Critique* more generally, he says the following:

> That formula, which is, as you know, the central formula of Kant's ethics, is pursued by him to the limits of its consequences. His radicalism even leads to the paradox that in the last analysis, the *gute Wille*, good will, is posited as distinct from any beneficial action. [. . .] one must have submitted oneself to the test of reading this text in order to measure [its] extreme, almost insane character [. . .]. (S7E: 77; S7F: 93–94)

As is well known, Kant's ethics of duty breaks with the idea that an ethical act can be good because it "does good," that is, because of its inherently beneficent, salutary effects. Morality based on pure reason refuses to be determined by anything "pathological" and thereby proves its complete autonomy. For the first time, Kant also formulates an ethics that no longer defines itself in terms of the *attainable*, or the *possible*. Ethical duty is not founded in the ability to realize the Good, but solely in the duty to do it, even if the (noumenal) good that your duty calls you to is not (phenomenally) realizable. Right up until his final lesson, Lacan focuses on what is irrevocable in the Kantian turn:

> A decisive step is taken there. Traditional morality concerns itself with what one was supposed to do "insofar as it is possible," as we say, and as we are forced to say. What needs to be unmasked here, [. . .] is nothing less than the impossibility in which we recognize the topology of our desire. The breakthrough is achieved by Kant when he posits that the moral imperative is not concerned with what may or may not be done. To the extent that it imposes the necessity of a practical reason, obligation affirms an unconditional "Thou shalt." (S7E: 315; S7F 364)

After Kant, the moral maxim is no longer "you can (realize the Good) therefore you must" but just the other way around: "you must, therefore you can."

Lacan will take this central line of thought from Kant's ethics beyond what the letter of Kant's text permits. Freed from every patronizing "thing," he claims, reason is also delivered from human essence, from the "human *Ding*" as Lacan called it in a passage we already cited

(S7E: 77; S7F; 93). In other words, it has delivered itself also from what Kant called the postulate of the "immortal soul." Unlike Kant, Lacan will carry this Kantian skepticism toward these kinds of ideas of "pure reason" from the first *Critique* over to the second *Critique*. The first *Critique* had removed all guarantee that "noumenal" ideas such as an "immortal soul" really exist. But what if there is no such thing as an "immortal soul"—understood as "man himself," as the "human thing"— *and, yet, Kant's formal ethics of duty remains valid*? Man, then, would still coincide with his obedience to a "free law," but this law would only liberate *itself*, even *at the cost of mankind if need be*. In that case, in the final analysis, man would be defined as a *substanceless*, "apathetic" servant to the moral law.

Of course, it is Lacan, not Kant, who takes this "extreme, almost insane" leap of thought. Anyway, you will not find any trace of it in Kant. Perhaps only the famous pathos in which his odes to freedom and duty are steeped can be read as an attempt to avoid this "almost insane" implication Lacan claims to uncover here. To perceive this implication, Lacan suggests, we need only view the categorical imperative in the light of contemporary science, which has progressed considerably since Kant's time and, accordingly, left *"das Ding an sich"* even more drastically behind:

> Henceforth, given the point we have reached in the light of our science, a renewal or updating of the Kantian imperative might be expressed in the following way, with the help of the language of electronics and automation: "Never act except in such a way that your action may be programmed." All of which takes us a step further in the direction of an even greater, if not the greatest, detachment from what is known as a Sovereign Good. (S7E: 77; S7F 94)

Here, although Lacan goes beyond the letter of Kant's text, his "charged" reading unmistakably pursues a line of thought that comes directly from Kant. In fact, all he has done is make Kant's famous idea of the autonomy of reason "harsher" by uncoupling it from the "human thing," from any kind of human "essence." Kant still believed that man and reason were "essentially" attuned to one another and that reason's perfection also presupposes man's. The fact that he maintains the immortality of the soul as a postulate of pure practical reason already indicates this. In contrast, from the perspective of Lacan's psychoanalytic theory of the subject, "reason"—"logos" thought here in its materiality as the field of signifiers—is regarded as autonomous with respect to man. With his thesis that man is *only* the subject (the bearer) of symbolic "reason," Lacan precisely wishes to emphasize how "reason" operates separately from human consciousness; that is, it responds to its own, autonomous laws that can also, in principle, run counter to the interests of the subject. At its extreme, this in fact implies that man, insofar as he wishes to perform his duty as subject of the (symbolic) law, is purely programmed and *as such*—as a "human thing"—is of no more account. In any case, it is not in this "accidental" bearer that the finality of the symbolic law lies, and the law can turn just as easily against him.[10] Here, the fundamental principle of autonomous reason is thus also, in the final analysis, the death principle.

In this way, Lacan removes every *"an sich"* element from reason. This is true, too, for the "thing" that, for Lacan, as well as for Kant, reason stems from. Like Kant, Lacan explicitly wants to maintain *das Ding* as "unknowable." He even fully endorses the idea that this unknowable "thing" nonetheless remains reason's ultimate point of orientation. But for Lacan, it is no longer the anticipated point where man and reality are finally *"an sich,"* enjoying a noumenal fullness that they lack in the phenomenal world. According to the premises of his subject theory, something like an *"an sich"* or a fullness of being is not only unthinkable, it is downright impossible. For Kant, man is still the subject (the *"Ich denke,"* the "I think") of a reason that allows him to hope—and only to hope, that is, never to know with certainty—that, in the final analysis, everything (mankind, the world, God) fits together and possesses an ultimate ontological foundation, a "Thing in itself." In Lacan, the "reason" of which man is the bearer (the subject), no longer has any point where it is hoped that it will all come together. This is precisely why man is defined as the subject of the Other, as the "bearer" of a "logical" order that defers all selfhood to the infinite, and fundamentally lacks any *"an sich"* dimension. Nothing in the symbolic universe can stop our incessant sliding from one signifier to another.

## 3. The Lacanian "Critique of *Pure* Practical Reason"

In his book, *Le don de la loi* (*The Gift of the Law*), Jacob Rogozinski observes that the *Critique of Practical Reason* is not entirely a "critique" in the strict Kantian sense of the word (Rogozinski, 1999; 47–48). According to Rogozinski, it lacks an analysis of the "transcendental illusory appearance" (*"transcendentale Schein"*) that pure (practical) reason can provide. In the *Critique of Pure Reason*, Kant explains that, when reason appeals *solely* to its highest faculty, that is, to pure reason,[11] it spontaneously reaches for the ideas that may *appear* to be objective, but which cannot endure "critique."[12] Moreover, the idea that reason itself exists as an objective reality in-itself is an example of such a "transcendental illusory appearance." *Hypothetically*, it is possible, but because reason is unable to be an object of perception (*Anschauung*), it cannot be the object of true, objective knowledge.

Yet such an investigation into the "logic of appearances"[13] is completely superfluous for moral reason, Kant writes at the very beginning of his *Critique of Practical Reason*. There, the existence of reason immediately presents itself as "*Faktum*," as a fact. Whether it exists in itself or not cannot remain an open hypothesis for moral reason the way it is for scientific reason.[14] Without any foothold in the phenomenal realm, moral reason from the outset is forced to suppose (to postulate) itself, in its pure noumenality, as a fact. This is why there is no risk of moral reason going beyond the limits of phenomenality and losing itself in "illusory appearances."[15] On the contrary, the moral question has to start from beyond phenomenality; it has to proceed from the universality of noumenal reason. So, ethics can—and must—be founded in reason itself. The highest formal demand of reason, as operative in the categorical imperative, offers ethics instant access to the practical certainty of a well-founded Good. This is not a Good that reason has to submit itself slavishly to. Neither is it a Good dependent on how good one feels about it (*das Wohl*), but a Good (das Gute) that is indubitably the effect of our rational freedom.

Such an autonomous, rational ethics nevertheless remains susceptible to a "critical" analysis into the "logic of appearance." At least, this is what Lacan, against Kant, foregrounds in his *Ethics Seminar*. In this sense, as Rogozinski argues, the overall approach of this seminar can be understood as an attempt to work out Kant's unwritten *Critique of Pure Practical Reason* (Rogozinski 1999: 47). The tone is already set at the beginning of the lesson on December 23, 1959, where, for the first time, Lacan examines Kant closely. This passage, which will be our focus now, is already known to us (see above IV.2.1). Lacan uses a fictional "simple soul" to set out his theory of the "thing" and as a result brings that "thing" into relation with the "prehistoric other" Freud talks about in a letter to Fliess (S7E: 71; S7F: 87). This "presymbolic other," this "thing" can never be *present*, but only *re*presented through what Lacan, using a Freudian term, calls a "*Vorstellungsrepräsentanz*"—a notion that he (mistakenly[16]) interprets as a "representation that represents how everything is only a representation (signifier)."

> It is a matter of that which in the unconscious represents [. . .] representation as a function of apprehending—of the way in which every representation is represented insofar as it evokes the good that *das Ding* brings with it. But to speak of "the good," is already a metaphor, an attribute. (S7E: 71–72; S7F: 88)

Despite the problematic use Lacan makes of the Freudian notion of "Vorstellungsrepräsentanz," the context here is clear: the entire signifying chain that is driven by the pleasure principle (the whole of the unconscious representations) revolves around that "extimate thing," "the prehistoric Other," thereby evoking the "Good" that one can expect coming from this direction. Note that it only "evokes" this Good, as Lacan immediately corrects himself. To think that the "thing" corresponds with the Good would be to jump to a conclusion too quickly. In this case, "to speak of 'the Good' " is only a manner of speaking—"a metaphor, an attribute"—and it doesn't yet enable us to claim that the "thing" would also *really* be good. Neither does it allow us to consider the Good as something *real*. On the contrary, for Lacan, the Good is indeed a manner of *speaking*, that is to say, a *symbolic* Good. At the unconscious level, the Good must be regarded as the effect of autonomously operating signifiers (separate from the real), as Lacan concludes two sentences later:

> It is only that way [i.e., by means of unconscious representations, signifiers] that the subject relates to that which represents itself on the horizon of the good [son bien]. His good is already pointed out to him as the significant result of a signifying composition that is called up at the unconscious level or, in other words, at a level where he has no mastery over the system of directions and investments that regulate his behavior in depth. (S7E: 72; S7F: 88)

In Kantian terms, the "Good" is determined here not by the noumenal but by the phenomenal. It is something that we are pathologically bound to, and to which we unconsciously owe duty even before we can consciously and rationally choose it. It is something that does us good, something that responds to our pleasure principle. It is thus a matter of what Kant calls "*das Wohl*," and not "*das Gute*," Lacan concludes a little further on:

> It is then, to be explicit, the Kantian term *Wohl* that I propose in order to designate the good in question. (S7E: 72; S7F: 88)

In this way, Lacan has everything in place for his "critique" of the "transcendental appearance" of the ethical Good. It is now clear that the Good must be conceived primarily in terms of the pathological "*Wohl*"; but the question is whether the aspiration for the Good—"*das Gute*"—*beyond* the "*Wohl*" can be legitimized. That it does exist as aspiration, as *idea* (or, in psychoanalytic terms, as *phantasm*) is clear for Lacan, too, but the question is whether there is any referent for this idea. This cannot be the Good in itself, Lacan must conclude in accordance with what he had previously said, but it certainly is the "thing." A few lines later, Lacan refers to the "thing,"

> which at its heart already gives rise to what we may call *das Gute des Objects*, the good object—following the Kantian example, as the practitioners of psychoanalysis have not failed to do. (S7E: 73; S7F: 89)

Note that the "thing" *seems* to be the "Good" desired in every object. And that "Good" is also effectively interpreted by most psychoanalysts as the moral certainty of a Kantian "*Gute.*" But, for Lacan, it is not immune to a critique of its transcendental illusory appearance. The "thing" *beyond* all "well-being" ("*Wohl*") can just as easily be something bad, "the bad object" of Kleinian psychoanalysis, for example, as Lacan says a few lines farther on:

> This is why, on the level of the unconscious, this *Gute* is also at bottom the bad object that Kleinian theory is concerned with. (S7E 73; modified translation; S7F: 89)[17]

The "thing" does indeed bear close resemblance to what Melanie Klein calls the "bad object," the thing that must be warded off from the outset. Although the entire pleasure system is directed toward this "thing," the subject must first and foremost avoid it. It is the "source of all well-being," Lacan states, but immediately adds that it is a matter of keeping a safe distance from that "source"—something the symbolic universe makes possible. Thanks to the signifying chain of which the subject is the bearer, Lacan explains earlier on the same page,

> the subject regulates his initial distance to *das Ding*, the source of all *Wohl* at the level of the pleasure principle [. . .]. (S7E: 72; S7F: 89)

So, it is the autonomous sphere of the signifier that "makes the law" (lays down the law) for the desiring subject. This is Lacan's way of claiming that the law originates *only in the law itself*, not in what lies *beyond* the law. It doesn't originate in a "Good" that will arrive as soon as one fulfills the law's prescriptions. It doesn't come from the happiness one expects to get from that law. Instead of the anticipated "good *in-itself*," what lies beyond the law is the evil "thing." There, instead of the law's fulfillment, lies its complete opposite: radical evil. If the law laid down to us proceeds from the supposed "good" beyond the law, it proceeds from the "thing." In fact, in this case, the law proceeds from radical evil. Then, instead of giving us the "good" we hoped for, it will make us its victim. On this same page, Lacan says that, in such a case, the

> verbal phrase "makes the law" [is given] the emphasis it receives in one of the most brutal games of elementary society [. . .] that is evoked in a recent book by Roger Vailland. It is a capricious and arbitrary law, the law of the oracle, the law of signs in which the subject receives no guarantee form anywhere, the law in relation to which he has no *Sicherung*, to use the Kantian term." (S7E: 73; S7F: 89)

The reference to the "recent book by Roger Vailland," *The Law* (1957)[18] cannot be misunderstood. If the law is made from the supposed Good, that is, from its beyond, it instigates precisely the kind of reign of evil and injustice this novel describes. Lacan analyzes this "making law" ("faire la loi") as something that operates directly from the "thing." The novel sketches life in a southern Italian city where the social order and the mafia are inextricably intertwined. Everyone is constantly trying to assert power over everyone else—or, as it says in the novel, "to make law"—such that the distinction between law and crime, order and corruption, is completely blurred. More concretely, the novel's title refers to a popular party game of the same name. "The law" is a game of chance where the winner may speak to the others or be silent, to insult them or praise them, torment them, reduce them, rebuke them, curse them. In short, he may freely "make law." The losing players, those on whom the law "is made," must submit without protest.[19] Accordingly, such a "capricious, arbitrary, oracular" law presents nothing in the way of a moral footing.

Vailland's novel sketches a situation in which the law is made from a point *beyond* the law (the "thing") and enables us to perceive how this point does not appear to be the place where the ethical promise of that law is fulfilled (and, hence, where goodness and happiness reign). On the contrary, it seems that *beyond* the law lies the reign of an evil lawlessness. Once men are no longer confined by the rule of law, instead of fulfilling its promise of happiness and the Good, one finds a rabid lack of restraint. After Lacan's "critical analysis" (in the Kantian sense), the idea of an absolute Good supposed to lie *beyond* the law turns out to be an illusion. Even if ethics still spontaneously clings to it, this idea is nothing but a "transcendental illusory appearance." Regardless of what Kant claims, ethics can and must not be founded on the basis of this idea. A law that establishes itself directly on the alleged noumenal "thing" leads to the sort of community Vailland describes, and makes any form of the good impossible. Only a law that can keep that evil "thing" at bay, and which does not pretend to come from that noumenal 'thing' beyond the phenomenal law (of the signifiers), can guarantee us a measure of goodness.

This is why the law may only posit itself *symbolically*. It cannot be performed from the supposed Good it promises; it can only proceed from the pure "letter," its naked signifier. Due to its nature as a signifier, the law can never realize its promise. A bearable law and a livable good are possible thanks solely to the infinite deferral of the signifier. The *idea* of an absolute good can only function here insofar as it persists in its status as a *transcendental appearance*. And, just like the symbolic law itself, this appearance is part of a strategy that "lies" about the evil beyond the law. The idea that the law promises us the good is a transcendental lie that casts a veil over the evil "thing" at which the law aims. The entire signifying chain, including its subject, is a defense system against that dangerous "extimate thing." On the same page, Lacan wonders how one can conceive of such a defense. Not in the self-mutilating way a crab amputates an intimate "bad object"—a foot, for example—he says ironically, but with the help of the signifying order, defined here as a way of "lying about evil":

> But the defense or mutilation that is proper to man does not occur only at the level of substitution, displacement or meta-phor—everything that structures its gravitation with relation to the good object. Human defense takes place by means of something that has a name, and which is, to be precise, lying about evil. On the level of the unconscious, the subject lies. And this lying is his way of telling the truth of the matter. (S7E: 73; S7F 89–90)[20]

At the most fundamental level—that of drive and pleasure—man "lies." He supposes the ultimate object of desire to be the fulfillment of that desire, while in fact it is something that, once it has been pulled out from under that transcendental veil, can only be defined as evil. Note that it is not a matter of evil "in-itself," but something that is evil, if only because the subject cannot stand the proximity of that "thing" nor even simply experience it. It is the incompatibility between the subject and the "thing" that makes the latter a radical evil. Even if the "thing" should be described as something good (because it is situated in the place where the moral promise is ordinarily located), one ought to define it as so over-whelmingly good that it turns out to be intolerable for the subject—and, hence, evil. It is in this sense we must understand Lacan when—a few lines before the previously cited passage—he states even more plainly that the "thing" is not an experiential object since it is not a signifier:

> Although it must be said that at this level *das Ding* is not distinguished as bad. The subject makes no approach at all to the bad object, since he is already maintaining his distance in relation to the good object. He cannot stand the extreme good that *das Ding* may bring him (. . .). (S7E: 73; S7F: 89)

Desire, in other words, is incompatible with its object by definition, even with its ultimate object that grants the subject (as an object relation) its consistency. The subject desires the good, but what one traditionally calls the "supreme good" is nothing other than a "transcendental appearance" that whisks the final and fatal object out of sight. Henceforth the "supreme good" that previously served as the basis for ethics loses all positive determination and can only be defined negatively, as something irrevocably prohibited. Only as something forbidden can this object generate desire and grant its consistency. The "Good" is now exclusively the forbidden "thing" and, in this sense, is evil by definition. This, for Lacan, is the ethical consequence of the incest prohibition that Freud postulated as the foundation of desire as expressed by the Oedipus complex. At the end of the previous lesson, Lacan had already put this in no ambiguous terms:

> Well now, the step taken by Freud at the level of the pleasure principle is to show us that there is no Sovereign Good—that the Sovereign Good, which is *das Ding*, which is the mother, is also the object of incest, is a forbidden good, and that there is no other good. Such is the foundation of the moral law as turned on its head by Freud. (S7E: 70; S7F: 85][21]

After Lacan's critique, the *beyond* of the moral law, where Kant postulated what he called a noumenal Good (*das Gute*), houses a prohibited evil. Where Kant claimed that ethics is only possible through a positive referral to the idea of a noumenal Good, Lacan claims that ethics demands precisely a negative referral: that "thing" must be kept at bay if one is to avoid the evil that lurks in its promise. In other words, evil can just as easily lie on the side of the so-called absolute good. To the extent this idea functions only as a "transcendental appearance," it causes no problems for our ethical well-being, but as soon as ethics tries to put this idea into reality, or to define itself directly from it, the dark powers whose presence we had little suspected behind the transcendental appearance are unleashed.

The question, however, is whether Lacan's "Critique of Pure Practical Reason" is complete now. Is it sufficient to posit the "thing" as a negative, evil entity and to claim that the supreme good for which ethics strives is this very evil "thing"? Is it not also ethics' task to achieve a *positive* relation toward the "thing"? Surely an "ethics of psychoanalysis" ought to shed light on this affirmative dimension. After all, in its own words—and counter to an entire tradition—it aims to place the naked, finite dimension of desire at the very heart of ethics. One might expect, then, that the ultimate object of that desire (the "thing") could somehow be assessed positively.

Lacan will in fact grant the libidinal being a positive relation to its ultimate object of desire. It will be able to fully enjoy that object, even if this enjoyment remains consistent with Lacan's Kantian reserve with respect to the "thing." In order to deal with this paradox, Lacan will elevate enjoyment—*jouissance*—into a fully fledged concept, one of the most important in his whole conceptualization of psychoanalysis. In his seventeenth seminar, for example (*L'envers de la psychanalyse*, 1969–1970), he casually lets slip how, if he should be remembered for one thing, it will be for the domain of "*jouissance*," although he has few illusions about this. After having mentioned the term, "field of enjoyment" ("*champ de la jouissance*"), he adds

> [. . .] it will unfortunately never be called the Lacanian field, because I certainly will not have the time even to sketch the fundamentals, but I would indeed have liked to. (S17F: 93; my translation)[22]

# Chapter 6

# The Weight of Enjoyment

This place is called Jouissance, and it is Jouissance whose absence would render the universe vain.[1]

## 1. Pleasure

### 1.1. When Pleasure . . .

The term "jouissance" appears only sporadically throughout Lacan's seminars in the fifties and doesn't yet possess the proper conceptual weight it will acquire in the sixties and seventies. Initially, it is no more than the French translation of "*Genuss*," the word Freud uses to refer to an intense satisfaction at the level of the ego, in contrast to the term "*Befriedigung*" which he employs as a concept reserved for individual drives and wishes. Needs, drives or wishes can be satisfied, he says. The ego, on the other hand, *enjoys*. From a Freudian perspective, however, the experience of "enjoyment" is not without paradoxes. For, despite the fact that the entire pleasure economy rests upon an unsublatable lack, enjoyment names the experience that enables the libidinal being to imagine that its lack is entirely overcome.

Already in the first seminars, Lacan neutralizes this paradox of *jouissance* by means of the "imaginary-symbolic-real" triad. At the imaginary and symbolic level, the subject can cancel out all lack while simultaneously continuing to remain marked by it at the level of the real. In this sense, the lack is not really gone, just (imaginarily) miscognized or (symbolically) repressed. This is why enjoying the desired object is possible.

Indeed, enjoyment is about the ultimate object in relation to which the libidinal animal is constituted; and this object can present itself as an image or a signifier, but never as something real. The "experience of complete satisfaction" at the level of the subject can thus be more clearly defined by referring to the object relation whose "bearer" the subject is. The fact that a subject "enjoys" means that it has the object completely at its disposal. Originally, the French word "*jouissance*" means "possession," "usufruct," "profit."[2] Here, however, it is the "possession" of something phantasmatic, not real. A *real* capture of the desired object would mean the end of the object relation and, hence, the end of the *subject* (bearer) of that relation. The fact is that the subject is still able to enjoy because it does so phantasmatically, and thus exclusively at the imaginary-symbolic level.

In the first six seminars, this notion of enjoyment is still fully dependent on Lacan's concept of "phantasm" and, for this reason, was not a proper concept.[3] When the subject (as "bearer" of an object relation) loses itself in its object, as occurs in enjoyment, it continues to be entirely carried by the phantasm, a signifying scenario that provides an ultimate consistency to the pleasure economy. This phantasm provides that economy with a final support should the subject itself "fade away" in the object relation that it "bears." This is precisely what happens in enjoyment. *Phantasmatically*, its fundamental lack is canceled out and the subject takes such complete and intense possession of the object that it seems about to disappear into that event. At the level of the *real*, however, both the subject and the object remain intact, separate from one another, and the all-devouring "usufruct" does not take place. The subject *only seems* to have overcome the order of lack (and hence, of the signifier). In reality, however, it has never left this order and the lack has never been overcome (and will never be overcome). For the subject in orgasm, for example, (and Lacan refers explicitly to sexual "coming"—in French, "*le jouir*"—as an exemplary form of *jouissance*), it seems that all lack has been overcome and that it has taken complete possession of the desired object, so profoundly even that as a subject it seems to "disappear" in this "possession." But it only *looks like* this is the case. From the perspective of the real, the subject does not disappear into the object at all, but remains irreconcilably separated from it. The state of lack characteristic of desire is only *phantasmatically* overcome in the moment of enjoyment.

If one were to bring the unconscious structure of enjoyment *consciously* into the picture, the object of desire would appear as "a thing of nothing." The "signified" to which the entire signifying chain refers would seem to be an empty, meaningless signifier. That is to say, the object that the subject (of the object relation) pursues would appear as a mere lack.

This is what happens in comedy, according to Lacan. It is not a coincidence when, in his lesson of March 5, 1958, he focuses explicitly on *jouissance* for the first time in his entire seminar project,[4] his chief point of reference is comedy (S5F: 252). At the same moment when the protagonist in the comedy Lacan refers to (*The Balcony* by Jean Genet) finally gets what he wanted, his entire drama ("douleur d'exister," S5F: 256) is also reduced to an absurd, naked, empty signifier, which is in this case a phallus. The fact that the latter plays the same role in the ancient comedies (in Aristophanes, for example) confirms his theory of the phallus, Lacan argues. With this concept, he aims to convey how the (symbolic) identity of a desiring subject stems purely from a signifier.[5] Seeking "himself," the dramatic subject of comedy confronts this "self" when he stands face to face with a mere, empty signifier. In ancient comedies, this is often the moment of a full-blown "phallophanie."[6] The subject's quest for himself is thus concluded only with a fictitious artifact. His identity is reduced to an artificial thing of nothing and, in that quality, laughed away. What is both revealed and repressed at the phallophanic moment is the way the entire drama, in the end, is about a tautological signifier that signifies merely itself and, hence, nothing. One's laughter at this obscene epiphany enables the empty signifier to come to light at the very moment it is again repressed. In so doing, it keeps desire alive. At the moment one laughs, the disconcerting idea that it is all about an empty signifier—and thus, about nothing—is immediately repressed.[7]

Comedy clearly shows how, in the final analysis, the desiring subject only enjoys an empty object, a thing of nothing. Yet, for this very same reason, enjoyment does not imply the end of desire. Thanks to the primacy of the signifier, the lack lying at the base of desire remains intact, even if in enjoyment, the subject experiences its overcoming. In this sense, *jouissance* is not the other pole ("l'autre pole") of desire, as one might mistakenly understand from how Lacan expresses it in this lesson of March 5, 1958, but an element supporting it. Each time he speaks about enjoyment, it is primarily to explain the primacy of desire. Still at the end of the sixth seminar, he claims that *jouissance* affirms desire in all its "frailty," in its capacity of making the subject enjoy the symptoms under which she suffers. Enjoyment does not extinguish desire, but heightens and stimulates it. It reconfirms it as a "desire to (continue to) desire." Speaking of the neurotic, Lacan says that

> his structure, which is the most current one, in the end makes
> one desire desire and that he, then desires what? Something

which in the end enables him to support his desire itself in
all its frailty. And without being aware this is the function
of every phantasmagoria, i.e., that the symptoms are the very
locus where one finds his enjoyment, how little satisfying they
may be in themselves. (June 10, 1959; S6F: 484)

No matter how empty or comical, *jouissance* is in service of desire
and protects it against its inherently conflictual nature. It helps to make
the phantasm possible and in this way sustains the imaginary "support" on
which the precarious pleasure economy lies. Enjoyment in this sense is one
of the strategies for maintaining the libidinal balance and thus follows the
pleasure principle. This is why, from the perspective of morality, *jouissance*
is to be considered good, irrespective of how empty and futile it may be.
All the same, an ethics founded on such enjoyment undermines all classical
ideas about the good. It confiscates all dreams of a divine Good (Christianity), a "kingdom of ends" (Kant) or an ethical community realizable
in the here and now (Hegel). Nonetheless, on this kind of empty, purely
"transcendental idea" of the good, an ethics can still be constructed. Even
if the enjoyment we strive for may be a vain thing of nothing, it nevertheless supports our desire, and in this way is fundamentally good.

This is true, at least, if the object of *jouissance* is in fact only an
empty signifier. But what if the object lies *beyond* the order of signifiers? What if the ultimate point of the object relation (that man *is*) is
no symbolic or imaginary signifier, but something *real*? Is not the entire
pleasure economy then handed over to the dangerous and destructive
abyss of the "thing"? And how would it be possible to build an ethics
on such an abyss?

### 1.2. . . . *Becomes Pain*

We already know by now that with his seventh seminar, Lacan is indeed
heading unmistakably in this direction. He no longer approaches the void
around which human desire revolves as an (empty) signifier, but as a real
"thing." Similarly, the site of desire's satisfaction, previously regarded as
an empty, ground zero of the Good, is now characterized as a categorical
evil. This latter then also deprives ethics of its most elementary reference:
satisfaction and enjoyment are no longer at the service of desire and thus
no longer automatically favor the subject. Or, as Lacan puts it in his
fourteenth lesson:

> [. . .] it is enough for *jouissance* to be a form of evil, for the
> whole thing to change its character completely, and for the mean-
> ing of the moral law itself to be completely changed. Anyone

can see that if the moral law is, in effect, capable of playing some role here, it is precisely as a support for the *jouissance* involved; it is so that the sin becomes what Saint Paul calls inordinately sinful. That's what Kant on this occasion simply ignores. (S7E: 189; S7F: 222–223)[8]

The Good we consciously long for is, at the level of the unconscious, a radical evil. This is what escaped Kant, according to Lacan. Instead of happiness, the ultimate satisfaction of our ethical desire brings us evil and (self-)destruction. Here, enjoyment can no longer be situated inside the limits of desire and the pleasure principle, but is to be regarded as an exponent of the *death drive*. It shows how man is impelled by a drive that, in the final analysis, corresponds not with his self-preservation, but with his death.

Yet, the form of "death" that comes with enjoyment is, at least in principle, phantasmatic, and thus, not *really* bad for the subject. In other words, when I enjoy, I am not *really* but only *symbolically* "destroyed." The moment I "fade away" in the desired object, I do so in my existence qua symbolic subject, not as a real person. It is solely as a subject of desire that I am absent in the very moment of enjoyment. That is to say, enjoyment itself is only granted insofar as it is completely unconscious and assumes no *real* proportions.

Here we can locate the radical change in "the meaning of the moral law," as Lacan puts it. This is not so much the effect of *jouissance* as such, but *a change in the relation between enjoyment and desire*; or, more specifically, of the predominance of enjoyment over desire. Prior to the seventh seminar, desire was ascendant over enjoyment. The enjoyed object was defined as an empty signifier that only stimulates desire, as Lacan's theory of comedy, referred to above, clearly shows. The empty and vain (i.e., phantasmatical) nature of enjoyment ultimately favored desire. The seventh seminar, however, reverses this relation. Desire now comes to stand in the service of enjoyment. The center of gravity lies no longer in desire itself, but in its *transgression*, or, what amounts to the same thing, in the real *beyond* desire, that is, in enjoyment. Now desire is in fact nothing more than a necessary step toward enjoyment. To reach its "aim," desire must not only follow the path of the laws it responds to; in the end it must transgress them. The ultimate "sense" of desire—and of the ethical law, too—comes to lie in a *transgressive* gesture. The symbolic law the subject (also morally) clings to ultimately serves as something to be transgressed. Enjoyment no longer serves desire and (hence) the Good; from now on, the Good and desire are, in the end, instruments of an evil (because) transgressive enjoyment. In his lesson of March 16, 1960, Lacan expresses this finding in a formula:

Without a transgression there is no access to *jouissance*, and [. . .] that is precisely the function of the Law. Transgression in the direction of *jouissance* only takes place if it is supported by the oppositional principle, by the forms of the Law. (S7E: 177; S7F: 208)[9]

Although at the level of experience this transgression remains purely phantasmatic, it nevertheless has repercussions for the way we deal with the symbolic law. Unconsciously, it seems to serve solely as something that one must transgress as intensely as one can. In Judaic-Christian terms, it appears as though our entire desire for moral perfection only serves to intensify our proclivity for evil and sin. At one moment in his seminar, Lacan does in fact literally express himself in these terms, ascribing enjoyment to the place sin used to inhabit in the Christian doctrine. More specifically, he refers to the famous seventh chapter in the *Letter to the Romans*, where Saint Paul analyses the nefarious dialectic between sin and law. There he describes how the law—meaning the Judaic law as written down in the Old Testament—ultimately plays into the hands of evil. Thanks precisely to the law, sin takes on its true (i.e., transgressive) proportions and becomes "exceeding sinful." For Lacan, the relation between *jouissance* and the symbolic law can easily be put into the same terms. In the just-cited passage from his seventeenth lesson, Lacan brings up an earlier reference to the *Letter to the Romans* where he illustrates the relation between the "thing" and the law. This is how he began, unannounced, to cite that *Letter* at the end of his sixth lesson, just after he had again alluded to his basic claim that the "weight" of ethics lies in the "thing":

Is the law the Thing? Certainly not. Yet I can only know the Thing by means of the Law. In effect, I would not have had the idea to covet if the Law hadn't said: "Thou shall not covet it." But the Thing finds a way by producing in me all kind of covetousness thanks to the commandment, for without the Law the Thing is dead. But even without the Law, I was once alive. But when the commandment appeared, the Thing flared up, returned once again, I met my death. And for me, the commandment that was supposed to lead to life turned out to lead to death, for the Thing found a way and thanks to the commandment seduced me; through it I came to desire death [m'a fait désir de mort]. I believe that for a little while now some of you at least have begun to suspect that it is no longer I who have been speaking. In fact, with one small change, namely, "Thing" for "sin," this is the speech of Saint

Paul on the subject of the relations between the law and sin
in the Epistle to the Romans, Chapter 7, Paragraph 7. (S7E:
83; S7F: 101)[10]

Paul can go that far in his analysis of the relation between law and
sin, because he already knows that God's heavenly plan will ultimately
make everything turn out all right. The law may well have led to sin and
death but Christ's sacrificial death signifies the fulfillment of the law, after
which all we (the faithful) need to do is to wait for freedom and eternal
life. Although, according to Lacan, this messianism is a "transcendental
illusory appearance" behind which lurks the deadly "thing," this doesn't
affect the inner value of Paul's analysis. It reveals the deadly intertwining
of law and sin/enjoyment, in which the "death principle" plays a major
role.[11] For what binds desire to the law (or what binds us to the "law
of desire") is, in the final analysis, the death drive: the inclination to
transgress the law that is the only thing that can guarantee us libidinal
comfort. Here, in this unholy enjoyment, lies the "weight" of our desire
and also, simultaneously, the "weight" of the (symbolic) law that desire
clings to. It is precisely our inclination to go beyond the law that keeps
us both so irrevocably and destructively bound to it.

Such a malign kind of enjoyment is already in Freud's "myth" of
the primal horde in *Totem and Taboo*. Inspired by Darwin, here Freud
outlines how in prehistoric times a leader comes to dominate the human
herd, seizing all libidinal satisfaction (all women, i.e., all objects of *jouissance*) and murdering or castrating every male rival (in this case his own
sons).[12] In order to gain access to *jouissance*, the sons murder their brutal
father, the myth continues. However, each time the mutual struggle to
take his vacant place brings a similar titan to power so that in the end
only a posthumous rehabilitation of the dead leader is able to restore
peace. In this way, the once so-hated prohibition (to enjoy the father's
wives, that is, all wives of the clan) was definitively put back in place.
With this requirement for exogamy, culture could begin, Freud concludes.
Henceforth, *jouissance* exists exclusively insofar as it is forbidden. The
prohibition against incest takes the "original" object of satisfaction away
from man and makes it the object of a fundamentally forbidden enjoyment. This clears the way for desire controlled by law; in other words,
it enables civilization.

Lacan leaves the phylogenetic suppositions of Freud's theory without
comment and considers it exclusively as a "myth" in the structuralist sense
of the word: a fable of paradigmatic value, revealing the structure that
organizes society and its culture.[13] The Freudian myth shows how it is
solely prohibition that gives both enjoyment and the law their definitive
place. Accordingly, enjoyment is only possible as something that *must* not

exist, and it is precisely this impermissible enjoyment that binds us all the more tightly to the law (a law that is the indispensable support of our desire). The primal murder Freud's myth discusses is an attempt to put precisely this paradox into a paradigmatic image, says Lacan in his lesson of March 16, 1960:

> All the mystery is in that act. It is designed to hide something, namely, that not only does the murder of the father not open the path to *jouissance* that the presence of the father was sup- posed to prohibit, but it, in fact strengthens the prohibition. The whole problem is there; that's where, in fact as well as in theory, the fault lies. Although the obstacle is removed as a result of the murder, *jouissance* is still prohibited; not only that, but the prohibition is reinforced. This fault that denies is thus sustained, articulated, made visible by the myth, but at the same time it is also camouflaged by it. That is why the important feature of *Totem und Taboo* is that it is a myth, and, as has been said, perhaps the only myth that the modern age is capable of. And Freud created it. (S7E: 176; S7F: 207–208)

For Lacan, it is a matter not of a death that occurred in a far distant past, but of a violence inherent to the structure of our desire as such. Our desire is structurally oriented toward a forbidden enjoyment. In this way, we are forced to continuously *keep on* desiring. Only in this way can we maintain ourselves as bearers/subjects of desire. However, this enjoyment is not solely the void that heightens desire, as Lacan claimed in his lesson on *jouissance* in his fifth seminar. Now it is at the same time a factor that, at the very moment it boosts up desire, disorders that very desire. The law that is "supposed to lead to life" will indeed stimulate desire and, thus, life; but it will at the same time "turn to lead to death" as well by means of the same *jouissance*.

It is this "hitch" in the logic of the law—this "*faille*," this "fault" as it is called in the cited passage, this "displacement," this "crack"—that interests Lacan here. Enjoyment binds us to the law of desire precisely by means of its transgression. Putting us in debt to the law, enjoyment is thus responsible for the guilt that binds us so closely to that law. We are not only guilty because we transgress the law in our enjoyment; enjoy- ment creeps into our most faithful obedience to the law itself: hence the "hitch," the "crack," the "displacement" in the logic of the prohibition of enjoyment. In this lies precisely the immense "interest" of this "fault" ("*faille*"), says Lacan. In the at first sight particularly enigmatic sentences preceeding the previously cited passage, we read:

It is important to grasp what is embodied in this fault [cette
faille]. Everything that passes across it is turned into a debt of
the Great Book of debts. Every act of *jouissance* gives rise to
something that is inscribed in the Book of debts of the Law.
Furthermore, something in this regulatory mechanism must
either be a paradox of the site of some irregularity [lieu de
quelque dérèglement], for to pass across the fault in the other
direction is not equivalent. (S7E: 176, S7F: 208)

The irregularity (*dérèglement*) Lacan mentions here refers to what
Freud called the "paradox of good consciousness." It is the paradox of
the one who, so scrupulously obeying the moral law (that as Saint Paul
said is "supposed to lead to life") ends up being so tortured by guilt he
finds himself on the brink of suicide. In this case, *jouissance* has penetrated
into the very fidelity to the law. Such a person is, so to speak, boundlessly
bound to the law, that is, bound in the excessive way that is characteristic of enjoyment. Enjoyment, then, also seems to be the hidden motive
behind the "obscene and ferocious" superego (S7E: 7; S7F: 15). Hence
it is not surprising that the ego is persecuted by the *excessive* demands
emanating from it. This is also the reason for civilization's permanent
"discontent." The harder that culture tries to restrain human desire and
prohibit enjoyment, the more the excessive nature of enjoyment slips *into*
the prohibition itself, and disturbs the libidinal equilibrium of the subject.
It is this idea that Lacan articulates in the lines following the previously
cited passage:

Freud writes in *Civilization and Its Discontents* that everything
that is transferred from *jouissance* to prohibition gives rise to
the increasing strengthening of prohibition. Whoever attempts
to submit to the moral law sees the demands of his superego
grow increasingly meticulous and increasingly cruel. Why isn't
it the same in the other direction? (S7E: 176, S7F: 208)

Indeed, why does it not in fact work the other way around? Anyone who complies with the demands of enjoyment rather than the law
winds up not with an excessive enjoyment, as one would expect, but is
confronted equally with the limits imposed by the law.[14] Despite its best
efforts, psychoanalysis has never found a single analysand capable of
being definitely released from the pressure of the law. We all are subjects
of a desire that is not our own (because it is the Other's) and which
therefore forces itself on us as a law. Desire's excessiveness can only be
experienced in the form of the excess of a law that scolds us and makes

us unhappy. We are unable to experience such excess in our enjoyment, although it undoubtedly forms the very essence of enjoyment. For we are only granted such enjoyment *phantasmatically*. The moment we experience it, we disappear as subjects; this is, as we already saw, the very structure of enjoyment.

> Why isn't it the same in the other direction? It is a fact that it isn't the case at all. Whoever enters the path of uninhibited *jouissance*, in the name of the rejection of the moral law in some form or other, encounters obstacles whose power is revealed to us every day in our experience in innumerable forms, forms that nevertheless perhaps may be traced back to a single root. (S7E: 176–177; S7F: 208)

To pursue, like a true libertine, solely enjoyment and to *consciously* go in search of it is to be duped. Enjoyment presents itself only as what is forbidden by law and only granted to us in *fantasy*. Anyone who wants to *truly* experience it will inevitably run up over and over again against the obstacle of the law.

On the other hand, anyone who follows the law and nothing but the law will sooner or later be confronted with the excess of enjoyment, since that enjoyment is the secret driving force behind his scrupulous fidelity to the law. Only, it will not appear to be *his* enjoyment, but that of the Other. It is the enjoyment of the excessively commanding law that reverberates throughout the symbolic order. We only experience this excess in the form of the pain caused by the "obscene and ferocious" imperatives of the superego.[15] This proves how the law addresses itself to us from the place of a criminal enjoyment that lies, in the final analysis, at its very base (as formulated in *Totem and Taboo*).[16]

What gives the law of desire—and thus of ethics—its ultimate "weight" is *jouissance*. This is Lacan's conclusion in his seventh seminar. However, this enjoyment is no longer to be approached solely as a phantasm, as a void that fans the flames of the subject's desire and thereby provides it with extra support. It is something that simultaneously erodes the very self-preservation of that desire—and thus of the desiring subject. This is why from now on Lacan will treat *jouissance* as a proper concept.[17] The void at stake in enjoyment will no longer be considered purely as an empty signifier, but will involve something *beyond* the symbolic, that is to say, something *real*.

Lacan henceforth considers the point that gives desire its ultimate meaning and orientation as a "thing" that desire can fatally smash itself on. More strongly, this deathly "thing" also proliferates in the heart of the law that desire is forced to lean on. While the subject must constantly keep this "thing" at a distance, it must do so by means of a law that secretly proceeds from that very "thing." This "thing" is the law's ultimate sense, a sense that we can only "obey" by transgressing that very law. Since it is thus the law itself that secretly prompts us to transgress the law, we are *excessively* guilty with respect to it, just as we are *excessively* bound to it.

Is it really impossible, then, to escape this kind of *guilty* excessiveness? Is there no way we can enjoy that excessiveness in a nonguilty way? Is it really only the Other—the law—that is capable of excessive enjoyment by asking too much from us, while the subject itself remains barred from its enjoyment through the inaccessibility of its phantasm?

To illustrate this persistent impotence of the desiring subject, Lacan turns back to a figure who, like no other, collided with the limits of his phantasm in his search for a "guilt free" and limitless enjoyment. It is the work of the Marquis de Sade, far and away the most scandalous in the libertine tradition, that enables Lacan to show how persistently the law remains standing even at the very point where it is most flagrantly transgressed. Through Sade, Lacan will demonstrate how enjoyment remains dependent on both law and phantasm. Moreover, Sade will enable Lacan to clarify the evil that hides behind the "transcendental idea" of the Kantian Good.

## 2. Sade

### 2.1. Sade: The Truth of Kant

Lacan puts the emphasis on the radically *un*sentimental, *a*pathetic or, as he calls it, "*a*pathological" nature of Kant's ethics. Moral action is ascribed exclusively to pure Reason and is detached from all phenomenally bound "inclinations" by definition. In Lacanese, this means that the ethical law is dictated by the autonomous symbolic order, regardless of whether or not it works toward the self-preservation of the subject. In this respect, I already cited the lesson of December 23, 1959, where Lacan ventures an updated formulation of Kant's categorical imperative: "Never act except in such a way that your action may be programmed" (S7E: 77, see above 5.2). Only, Lacan now remarks that Kant does not let this imperative apply to the actual community, but to what he calls "nature." The contemporary version of the categorical imperative, as Lacan puts it:

> takes us a step further in the direction of an even greater, if not the greatest, detachment from what is known as a Sovereign Good. Let us be clear about this: when we reflect on the

maxim that guides our action, Kant is inviting us to consider
it for an instant as the law of a nature in which we are called
upon to live. [. . .] note that he affirms the law of *nature*, not
of *society*. (S7E: 77; S7F: 94; Miller's italics)

It is true that for Kant the ethical law does not refer to the subject's
actual community. The latter belongs to the "phenomenal" realm where
the laws of pure (noumenal) Reason are inevitably trampled on. The
world that the ethical law refers to is the inviolable, ideal "nature" of
pure reason.[18] Significantly, directly after this reference to the Kantian
concept of nature Lacan abruptly introduces Sade:

So as to produce a kind of shock or eye-opening effect that
seems to me necessary if we are to make progress, I simply
want to draw your attention to this: if *The Critique of Practical
Reason* appeared in 1788, seven years after the first edition of
the *The Critique of Pure Reason*, there is another work which
came out six years after *The Critique of Practical Reason*, a
little after Thermidor in 1795, and which was called *Philosophy
in the Boudoir*. (S7E: 78; S7F: 94–95)

Here Lacan's suggestion must be taken in all of its radicalness. Only
Sade's call for an unbridled "natural" freedom can uncover what hides
behind Kant's "nature." Only a scandalous work like *Philosophy in the
Boudoir*—describing how a girl is "educated" into the worst perversions
in five days—reveals the truth of what Kant so beautifully termed the
supersensible world of the noumenal. A bold thesis, to say the least.

The first reason Lacan gives as to how it might even be possible to
discuss two such heterogeneous oeuvres on the same page is a remarkable
*formal* similarity. Although there is nothing remotely reconcilable about their
individual content, it is striking how both "enlightened" thinkers exclude
all forms of feeling from moral judgment. The wholly un-Kantian "moral"
message of Sade nevertheless formally honors the same hard rationality,
and is just as averse to all "pathological" sentiment. By saying both Kant
and Sade promote an apathetic morality, Lacan is in the tradition of the
most prominent Sade critics of his time. Georges Bataille, Pierre Klossowski, Maurice Blanchot, Max Horkheimer, and Theodor Adorno all in
their own way emphasize the specifically apathetic nature of the lawless
libertine in Sade's oeuvre.[19] As illustration of Sadean "morality," Lacan
evokes the famous political pamphlet from *Philosophy in the Boudoir*, "Yet
Another Effort, Frenchmen, If You would Become Republicans," where Sade
employs every possible logical argument to persuade the reader that only
incest, adultery, theft, murder, sodomy, rape, slander—in short, everything

that the most elementary moral law rejects—are in fact the true "values" of the emergent new revolutionary society of that time (S7E: 79-80; S7F: 95–97).[20] Sade stresses how nothing is more hampering than feelings if one is to arrive at the level of these "virtues." "Never listen to your heart, my child," the libertine philosopher admonishes his young pupil after having read the pamphlet out loud, "it is the most untrustworthy guide we have received from Nature."[21] A man can be a great libertine, for Sade, only if he is able to completely dispose of his feelings. This is also what Maurice Blanchot points out in his essay "Sade's Reason," one of Lacan's main sources.[22] For Sade, it is thus a matter of complying exclusively with one's reason and of founding one's actions on strongly held maxims. Only, these are completely at odds with the rules of traditional morality such as, for instance, the Ten Commandments:

> If you adopt the opposite of all the laws of the Decalogue, you will end up with the coherent exposition of something which in the last instance may be articulated as follows: "Let us take as the universal maxim of our conduct the right to enjoy any other person whatsoever as the instrument of our pleasure." (S7E: 79, S7F: 96)

This is how Lacan formulates the cardinal rule of Sadian morality. Sade's "rational ethics" also refers to a nature in the strict Kantian sense of the word, that is, not to our concrete society, but to an abstract "nature" as presupposed by our laws of reason.[23] However, the sort of nature that responds to Sade's pure, rational imperative is no supersensible goodness, but a universe of absolute cruelty. A purely formal ethics, Kant's being the first, is thus also capable of generating a sadistic universe, as Lacan concludes from the parallel he discerns between Kant and Sade.

> If one eliminates from morality every element of sentiment, if one removes or invalidates all guidance to be found in sentiments, then in the final analysis the Sadian world is conceivable—even if it is its inversion, its caricature—as one of the possible forms of the world governed by a radical ethics, by the Kantian ethics as elaborated in 1788. (S7E: 79; S7F: 96)

In this sense, it is significant for Lacan that the only *substantial* element the two conflicting oeuvres have in common is *pain*. The apathy that both "moral" systems require from us turns pain into a sort of a priori principle. In Sade, it is the result of the terror spread by the hero. In Kant, it appears in the discomfort inherent to every ethical conscience. The latter explicitly mentions pain as the only a priori feeling that can come into consideration for a rational ethics. Lacan refers his audience to the relevant passage in the *Critique of Pure Reason*:

> In effect, Kant acknowledges after all the existence of *one* sentiment correlative of the moral law in its purity, and [. . .] it is nothing other than pain itself. I will read you the passage concerned [. . .]: "Consequently, we can see *a priori* that the moral law as the determining principle of will, by reason of the fact that it sets itself against our inclinations, must produce a feeling that one could call pain [Schmerz]. And this is the first and perhaps only case, where we are allowed to determine, by means of *a priori* concepts, the relationship between a knowledge, which comes from practical pure reason, and a feeling of pleasure or pain [zum Gefühl der Lust oder Unlust]." (S7E: 80; S7F: 97; Miller's italics)[24]

Both works refer the "ethical" subject to a "nature" that does not correspond to its actual environment and whose access presumes an intractable pain. It is precisely here that both works intersect on a more than purely formal basis: what each strives for (for Kant, the noumenal good, for Sade evil enjoyment) is only experienced in the pain that arises in the one who is, paradoxically, unable to "really" feel the target of his striving. The ultimate *real* object of desire is only experienced *negatively* in pain because of the impossibility of experiencing it. Kant failed to realize that this pain is therefore, in the final analysis, a *positive* feeling. The bearable pain caused by an unfulfilled ethical desire protects us from the completely unbearable pain that a truly satisfied desire implies.

Although this latter idea is not explicit in Sade, his oeuvre is unique in showing how, in reality, the state of satisfied desire comes down to an apotheosis of pain. Only, this pain is flagrantly denied at the very moment it is caused, and is regarded as a pure enjoyment. This is precisely what is perverse about Sade's fantasy. The hero simultaneously disavows all of the pain he carves into his victim's skin and turns it ("perverts" it) into the pinnacle of enjoyment. The same thing happens when the sadist himself is the victim: he continues to disavow the pain and affirms it as *jouissance*.[25]

In other words, the Sadian fantasy disavows the impasse that is the inevitable end of an unrestrained satisfaction of desire, although it grants us a glimpse of the truth behind this disavowal. In this sense, Lacan can claim that Sade is the "truth" of Kant.[26] In fact, hidden behind the Kantian Good is the terror of evil, and the moral law is not so much a step—a inevitably painful step—toward the Supreme Good as a dam that protects us precisely against the unutterably greater suffering that lies in wait should we go beyond this step, that is, the suffering that lies in wait behind this transcendental appearance of the anticipated good. Sade is Kant's truth in the sense that he lets us see—albeit it in a gesture of pure disavowal—what Kant's noumenal concept of *nature* hides from view: the evil that our most ethical desire ultimately aims for.[27]

### 2.2. Kant: Sade's Truth

Although Lacan never literally formulates it like this, he regards Kant, in turn, as the "truth of Sade." Kant's rejection of the idea that we should be able to realize the good in the phenomenal world is proved correct by the manifest failure of the Sadean project. As a child of the Enlightenment, Sade believes in the radical freedom of man, a freedom he situates not in some kind of noumenal *beyond*, but in the here and now. For him, the path to freedom is not, in the first place, realized through *pure* reason, but through an unrestrained liberation of the passions. In this, Sade is the proponent of enlightened, eighteenth-century libertinism par excellence. Such libertinism holds not only to the idea that human nature is pure freedom, but also that, practically speaking, this freedom is attainable. To do so, man has only to break with all existing laws and rules and to give himself over to his passions without inhibition. Works by Mirabeau, Diderot, and Sade—to name only the three writers mentioned in the first lesson where Lacan raises the issue of libertinism (S7E: 3–4; S7F: 12)—are inspired by the ideal of the "man of pleasure" ("*l'homme du plaisir*"), the sole figure who in their eyes is in complete obedience to his true "nature." Lacan characterizes libertinism as a movement that devotes itself to a "*natural* liberation of desire" (S7E: 3; S7F: 12). To the libertine, to do justice to free nature comes down to liberation from all restraints and is synonymous with giving free reign to our wildest passions. Lacan's verdict on this project, given already in the opening lesson of this seminar, is as clear as it is devastating:

> The naturalist liberation of desire has failed historically. We do not find ourselves in the presence of a man less weighed down with laws and duties than before the great critical experience of so-called libertine thought. If we find ourselves led to consider even in retrospect the experience of that man of pleasure—through reflection on what psychoanalysis had contributed to the knowledge and the circumstances of perverse experience—we will soon see that in truth everything in this moral theory was to destine it to failure. (S7E: 4; S7F: 12)[28]

The overwhelming guilt psychoanalysis daily confronts on its couch lays bare the failure of the whole libertine project. In spite of the ongoing success of its most fanatical writers such as Sade, we are unable to free ourselves from laws and norms. This is simply a fact.

Furthermore, anyone who takes a closer look at Sade's work is immediately convinced of the inherent contradiction hidden in this "natural liberation of desire." Certainly, the Sadian heroes break with the most elementary social and ethical laws (including the incest prohibition) and in this way profess to give free rein to the orgy of excess and crime that represents in their eyes the free reign of nature.[29] However, simply the fact that they must endlessly repeat that the law no longer rules already in itself provides a sort of negative proof of how the law remains immune from all transgression. The fact that Sade's heroes must declare *time after time* that the law is null and void indicates that it has never really been cornered, proving its inviolability by default. Perpetually repeating how all laws are empty nothings and God a hideous delusion only makes it clearer how persistently the law and the lawgiver always remain standing. The "sublime" corporality of the victims the next morning who, even after the bloodiest orgy, still hold onto that youthful bloom that so inflames the sadist, further emphasizes the futility of his transgressive violence (S7E: 202; S7F: 238).

One is struck by a similar contradiction in the theoretical arguments accompanying the endless series of gruesome scenes in Sade. At a certain moment in his seminar, Lacan reads out one of these pages of theory. It concerns a passage from *Juliette* that, following Pierre Klossowski (who is clearly his source here), he calls "the system of Pius VI."[30] Before this libertine pope delivers himself and Juliette over to yet another orgy, he first takes the time to explain his radical *natural* philosophy. What initially still sounds evangelical—a critique of the arrogant self-conceit of men—quickly turns into an ode to the most pitiless form of cruelty. The church leader charges that man must stop regarding himself as the ultimate sense of Creation. Just like everything else in the universe, he is nothing but a gratuitous product that escaped from its unbridled creativity by pure accident. He is, Sade has him say, just like "vapor" and "steam [which] derives its existence from a foreign element and has in itself no intrinsic value." It therefore makes no sense to feel grateful to creative Nature, as religion preaches. "Man thus has no relationship to Nature; nor Nature to man," Pius VI adds (Sade 1968: 766–767; 1987 IX: 167). Moreover, the natural laws themselves are just "foam" splashing up from an effervescent Nature that could just as well have established radically different laws—or even no laws at all. Hence, for radical libertine natural philosophy, every self-preservation reflex of man—right up to the level of reproduction—is an unnatural act. Love and procreation sabotage the excessive orgy that is Nature. Only crime, destruction, and murder testify to a true faith in Nature.

It is clear that the Sadean idea of man also supposes a formal obedience to a law. This excessive Nature functions for Sade, too, as an imperative and reduces the most unusual orgies to an act of conformity. As for Kant, here freedom also comes down to a faith in the "*law* of freedom*." Even a libertine will allow himself to be ruled by a law and he, too, will never be able to fully satisfy its demands. For him too, law and lack go hand in hand. Therefore, just like everyone else, he will attribute a transcendental bearer or subject (a "God") to his law, to the "Other" that rules him, that is, to someone who, at the very least, will one day be able to take away his lack. Yet, the Sadean God is a "Being Supreme in Wickedness" defended by another Sadian hero, a certain Saint-Fond, during a theoretical intermezzo in *Juliette*.[31] To believe in a Supreme Being and in hell is not to forsake one's libertinism, he explains in detail to his skeptical companion, Juliette. Rather, such dogmas are true, albeit it with this proviso: that God is enthroned in hell and reigns as an incurable, thoroughly *evil* Supreme Being in whose name man must murder and steal rather than love and do good.

Furthermore, Pius VI reveals this formal alignment with a law in a more specific way. At the end of the same page, the perverse pope lets out a "sigh": although we do everything to give in to Nature's murderous excesses, it seems that our murdering remains grievously insufficient. It is as if our crimes never manage to reach that level of sublime criminality Nature demands of us. After he has demonstrated how nondestructive even our greatest excesses in fact are, at least from "nature's" perspective, Pius VI explains:

> What am I saying? The service of nature requires far more total destructions . . . destructions much more complete than those we are able to accomplish. Nature wants atrocities and magnitude in crimes; the more our destructions are of this type, the more they will be agreeable to it. To be of even greater service to nature, one should seek to prevent the regeneration of the body that we bury. Murder only takes the first life of the individual whom we strike down; we should also seek to take his second life, if we are to be even more useful to nature. For nature wants annihilation; it is beyond our capacity to achieve the scale of destruction it desires. (S7E: 211; S7F: 249–250)[32]

For the libertine pope, it is evidently not enough just to kill our fellow man. His death, as far as nature is concerned, is simply a metabolic process by which one form of existence is exchanged for another. His disintegrated matter immediately continues to live on in thousands of other life forms. Yet, in the eyes of the libertine, nature commands us to break this law as well. We must also stop the bodies we kill from regenerating in another natural form. The murder must strike at the circle of life and death itself. It must murder "productive death" as well. We must therefore kill our victims *twice*, once as a living being and once as a dead one. Several lessons later, Lacan explicitly takes up this idea of a "second death" which goes on to become a standard term in the course of his later seminars. In his lesson of May 25, 1960, he speaks of

> the second death imagined by Sade's heroes—death insofar as it is regarded as the point at which the very cycles of the trans- formations of nature are annihilated. (S7E: 248; S7F: 291)[33]

Lacan focuses in particular on this idea of a "second death" because it clearly illustrates the way the whole Sadean fantasy plays itself out at the level of the signifier and how the entire drama of that fantasy is unable to go *beyond* that signifier. Furthermore, it is only the signifier that can introduce difference into the *indifferent* natural order, where life and death exist interchangeably side by side. Only in this way can both life and death be related to one another and interpreted as, for example, a productive cycle. Trying to strike at this cycle and destroy it, the sadist is in fact aiming at the signifier. He is not content with the "simple" (natu- ral) death of his victim; he wants to strike him even in his death, even as dead, that is, he wants to strike and destroy him as a (dead) signifier. His aim is to make it as though his victim had never existed—not even as dead.[34] He wants to bring it back to the unyielding "nothing"—the "thing"—that lies *beyond* the signifier.

Although Sade continually makes the opposite claim, every page of his "fantasy" testifies to how the sadist irrevocably fails in this. No Sadean hero ever operates beyond the signifier, no libertine succeeds in destroy- ing his victim as signifier. Crushed by the sadist's orgiastic violence, the victim continues to emerge beautiful and unscathed from under the horror, remaining the radiant "signifier" that entices the sadist to perform new acts of enjoyment. It is precisely this that makes the sadist so unspeakably cruel, since he is constantly provoked to reduce his victim to that abso- lute nothing beyond the signifier. Each time, he seeks to strike his victim with a "second death"—a death that aims for the signifier itself—and each time he is forced to disavow his inability to do so. A fantasy like Saint Fond's where the victim is tortured for eternity in hell supposes an unconscious fear that the victim will never be completely destroyed. The desire to torture someone in eternity and the wish to make someone disappear so definitively that it seems as though he never existed are, in this sense, simply two variations of the same aim, namely, the disavowal of one's inability to leave the signifier behind.[35]

One finds the same disavowal in Sade's own writings. His philosophy aims to "say it all," something he can achieve only by denying on every page the impossibility of ever doing so.[36] Driving Sade's writings is the idea that one day he will have successfully said everything and that, once beyond the signifier, he will be able to embrace nature in the real. His is a classical philosophical goal whose absurdity is involuntarily revealed in his work. In this sense, too, Sade's thought can be understood as a kind of critique in the Kantian sense.

The "drama" of the Sadean hero (a drama that evidently causes him little difficulty since he *disavows* it) lies in his failure to go beyond the signifier. The evil law that commands him to kill his victims "twice" (S7E: 232; S7F: 272) and, thus, to destroy them in their quality as signifiers, nevertheless continues to operate at that same signifying level. In this sense, even the sadist remains the subject (bearer) of a persistent fidelity to the law, illustrating in this manner the primacy of the law and the symbolic order. The Sadean fantasy thus inversely confirms Kant when, with all the pathos that he can muster, he glorifies the exalted status of law (read: the symbolic order).[37] The primacy of the law persists even in the wildest transgression of its rules.

Yet, on the other side, the Sadian fantasy is able to give us a clear view of the ultimate target of the Kantian law—at any rate, a clearer one than Kant himself gives. Although inaccessible, this target lies beyond the law, in the "real," which even Kant still regards in the traditional, metaphysical way. Even for Kant, the law promises the essence of the real, that is, a freedom and a happiness that are both based in being itself. Of course, we cannot have scientific certainty of this, but in our moral acts, we cannot but postulate our freedom as grounded in being's own essential freedom or free essence. This is what we may reasonably hope when we obey our duty, that is, our freedom. Sade involuntarily reveals the futility of that hope, for he shows us the cruel and destructive "nothingness" that is the real *beyond* the signifier. However, Sade does not conclude from this that we must keep that real—the "thing"—at a distance. On the contrary, in his eyes, it is our "duty" to do everything we can to get to that "thing" beyond the signifier and to embrace the cruel universe his fantasies dish up so abundantly.

That cruel universe is not only the truth of Kantian, but also of Christian ethics. The latter's ethical command also explicitly exhorts us to orient our desire beyond the law. In his *Letter to the Romans* we already cited, Saint Paul highlights *love* as the "beyond" of—and alternative to—the law. Christ has brought us a love that overcomes the limits of the (Jewish, Old Testament) law and, in that sense, fulfills the law. With this claim, Paul indubitably formulates the kernel of Christianity. Nevertheless, rather than expressing the actual state of things, this love expresses how things will be if we obey the *commandments* of that love. That is to say that here, love is no less a law than the law it claims to have overcome. It is in that sense that, again, Sade can reveal the real truth behind that love, that is, behind the command to love one's neighbor as oneself. And since, in a laicized version, this command comprises the kernel of the ideals lying at the foundation of the French Revolution and thus of our contemporary society, Sade has still something to say about our contemporary ethical culture.

### 3. The Commandment to Love Your Neighbor

#### 3.1. Happiness as a Political Factor

There is, indeed, a direct link between the French Revolution's rallying cry of "fraternity" and the "brotherly love" at the heart of Christianity. Together with "freedom" and "equality," it offers an alternative to the feudal serfdom that supported the political power of the ancien régime. Of course, "love" is no longer the name we give to that modern fraternity, but, just like love, the latter explicitly refers to something that is situated *beyond* the law. The new politics no longer limits itself to maintaining the existing order, but tries to realize the *happiness* of everyone, *beyond* the formal law. For the first time in history, the aim of politics was defined as the "well-being of all." It is not by chance that Robespierre governed from a "Committee of Public Safety" ("*Comité de Salut Public*"). One of its members, Saint Just, put it strikingly when he claimed that from now on "happiness has become a political matter."[38] Henceforth the aim of politics is no longer to safeguard a power elite, but to meet every citizen's aspiration for happiness. "Citizen" is henceforth a title that applies to everyone without exception and is no longer, as previously, a numerically limited segment of the population.

According to Lacan, Saint-Just's comment that happiness has become a political factor provides the telling sociopolitical background in which psychoanalysis is to be situated. In his eyes, the demand coming from the analysand on the couch does not really differ from the political demand of the modern citizen. It is the simple question of happiness. The expectation of both psychoanalysis and politics is that they will make mankind happier. It is not that they think they can offer him happiness on a plate, but they try at least to offer him the framework and means to move in that direction and to achieve some kind of free self-realization.

Today, too, happiness and self-realization commonly function as synonyms and this is precisely where the problem lies, Lacan explains. This association still betrays a persistent *Aristotelianism* at odds with our modern, post-Newtonian world-picture. We still spontaneously believe we aim at our self-perfection, while science has long given up thinking of man as the naturally generating, self-unfolding "energetic" essence taught by Aristotle centuries ago. From a psychoanalytic perspective, we think of man as an unrealizable, unsatisfiable desire. Thus, if modern man *demands* happiness and self-realization, he is in fact searching for the satisfaction of his *desire*. And we know by now how it is precisely this satisfaction that by definition escapes him.

Moreover, Lacan's analysis shows how demand is *in itself* already an imaginary strategy for suppressing what is unsatisfiable in desire. As an *imaginary* procedure, any *demand* presupposes the answer in advance. This is precisely what we, as desire, will never get. Now, if politics is incessantly plagued with such (imaginary) demands, and the entire political order must live by a desire that is wholesale *miscognized*, one can understand how "things have [indeed] not become easier," as Lacan remarks in one of his final lessons:

> It is not the fault of analysis if the question of happiness cannot be articulated in any other way at the present time. I would say that it is because, as Saint-Just says, happiness has become a political matter. It is because happiness has entered the political realm that the question of happiness is not susceptible to an Aristotelian solution, [. . .] "There is no satisfaction for the individual outside of the satisfaction of all." (S7E: 292; S7F: 338)[39]

As Lacan already in his first lesson indicated (S7E: 11–12; 23; S7F: 21, 32), the "Aristotelian solution"—an ethics of *happiness*—does not have the entire community but only a privileged class of "masters" in mind. Such an ethics is conceived for those who, freed from work, had the time to discipline their *demand* (and thus also their *desire*) so that it could be geared toward the supreme good.[40] Although in principle this kind of ethics was open to everyone, it did not have the pretensions to universality of modern (Kantian or utilitarian) ethics. Slaves and townspeople respected the ethical endeavors of their "masters" without wanting to be their equals. The latter, in working for their own limited "good," felt connected to the Supreme Good and, in this way, to the ontological ground it represents. This enabled a sort of ethical hierarchy between people without depriving the less "perfect" of their connection to ethics' ontological base. By the same token, the scholastics of the Middle Ages used Aristotelianism to legitimate the "social"—that is, feudal—hierarchy of the time. Once this ontological reference disappeared with the loss of Aristotelianism, the social hierarchy that was based on it also fell into discredit. The French Revolution completed this turn. In a society where everyone is treated as equal, an ethics of the master as presented in Aristotle becomes an anomaly. Henceforth, no one can seize their happiness at the expense of others, at least theoretically. Happiness must be for everyone, if not, it is unjust. "There is no satisfaction for the individual outside of the satisfaction of all." It is not surprising, then, that the first postrevolutionary ethics is utilitarian. There, for the first time, morality is based on a happiness that is exclusively "democratically" founded. If happiness has lost its ontological ground and yet must still remain the aim of ethics (and politics), it can only be defined as what guarantees the greatest number of people—and virtually all people—the greatest feeling of happiness.

But what makes happiness so difficult, now it has become a political factor? Why "hasn't everything become easier," as Lacan put it in the context of the above citation. Here, one is inclined to point the finger at our selfishness. Isn't it this that threatens every project for collective happiness? Is it not our individual interests that continually undermine social equality? Lacan explicitly addresses this objection at length, albeit only to reject it immediately:

> I began my lectures this year with the onerous topic of the utilitarians, but the utilitarians are quite right. They are countered with something that, in effect, only makes the task of countering them much more difficult, with a sentence such as "But, Mr. Bentham, my good is not the same as another's good, and your principle of the greatest good for the greatest number comes up against the demands of my egoism." But it's not true. My egoism is quite content with a certain altruism, altruism of the kind that is situated on the level of the useful. And it even becomes the pretext by means of which I can avoid taking up the problem of the evil I desire, and that my neighbor desires also. (S7E: 187; S7F: 220)

For Lacan, it is not my selfishness that sets me against others and threatens the happiness I henceforth must rely on. At the structural level, even the most selfish ego stems from an identification with others. Originally, the human pleasure animal relates to its own ego in the same way as it relates to another, as Lacan showed already in his theory of the mirror stage, providing his own formulation of Freud's concept of narcissism. Accordingly, a major part of human solidarity is attributable precisely to narcissism and selfishness. Because we inevitably identify with others, it is not unthinkable that, within the limits of our self-preservation, we stand up for them as for ourselves. Precisely our narcissistic structure enables us to regard others as equals, and to think that the good that *we* want mirrors the good that *they* want.[41] Although this *imaginary* identification undeniably calls up its own kind of aggression (see above I.3.1.), it is not here that the greatest difficulty for happiness once it has become a political matter lies. This is rather to be sought in the *desire* that hides behind the imaginary relation. For it is not enough for the subject to recognize itself in the other in order to satisfy this. On the contrary, it aims for something that lies *beyond* the other of imaginary recognition, and *beyond* even the symbolic, desiring Other. It is directed toward a real "thing" that, in the event of a real satisfaction, would certainly mean the death of the subject—which is why that "thing" must be described as pure evil. It is not so much my selfishness that is the evil factor threatening the social happiness—happiness as a political matter—but the *desire* operative in it, and more specifically, the *enjoyment* desire aims at.

The sociopolitical context does indeed bring the "evil" that our enjoyment is oriented toward out into the open. As a rule, the self-destructive nature of enjoyment is not revealed in any one individual's singular experience of enjoyment since the subject as such "disappears" into it (and its role as support of the pleasure economy is taken over by the phantasm). While here, too, the pleasure animal goes (self-destructively) *beyond* the pleasure principle, there can be no direct perception of it because of the phantasmatic nature of the experience. In a social context, on the other hand, it is much easier to see this evil dimension beyond the pleasure principle. There, the enjoyment one seeks in another all too often and obviously goes beyond all possible limits. Situations where one person derives all his enjoyment from persecuting another and making their life hell are common. When Lacan says in the above quotation that what both I and my fellowman ultimately desire is "evil," he is referring to a well-known passage in Freud's *Civilization and Its Discontents*. Running counter to any humanistic idealism, Freud describes how man would act toward his fellow man if he no longer felt any pressure from law and culture:

> The element of truth behind all this, which people are so ready to disavow, is that men are not gentle creatures who want to be loved, and who at the most can defend themselves if they are attacked; they are, on the contrary, creatures among whose instinctual endowments is to be reckoned a powerful share of aggressiveness. As a result, their neighbor is for them not only a potential helper or sexual object, but also someone who tempts them to satisfy their aggressiveness on him, to exploit his

capacity for work without compensation, to use him sexually
without his consent, to seize his possessions, to humiliate him,
to cause him pain, to torture and to kill him. *Homo homini
lupus*. Who, in the face of all his experience of life and of
history, will have the courage to dispute this assertion? (Freud,
SE21: 111; SA9: 240)

Lacan's analysis of selfishness as a flawed argument against utilitarianism comes in the context of a reflection on this passage in *Civilization
and Its Discontents*. Lacan explicitly connects Freud's raw, realistic vision
with his concept of *jouissance*:

As a result, if we continue to follow Freud in a text such as
*Civilization and Its Discontents*, we cannot avoid the formula
that *jouissance* is evil. Freud leads us by the hand to this point:
it is suffering because it involves suffering for my neighbor.
[. . .] He wrote *Civilization and Its Discontents* to tell us this.
(S7E: 184; S7F: 217)

Weighed up against this evil *jouissance*, selfishness is thus still, all
in all, a welcome strategy for binding people together. It is precisely one's
egotism that maintains the conditions under which we can see another as
our equal. It is only when one, in the thrall of enjoyment, goes beyond
one's ego (and thus beyond one's self-preservation principle), that the
social relation falls victim to that abyss of the deadly beyond at which
all desire aims.

Naturally, I am in search of happiness and—as an egotist—can recognize the identical aspirations in my fellow man. But the demand for
happiness that makes us the same is traversed by a desire that stretches
beyond happiness and equality, and is ultimately aimed at evil. My fellow
man and I also share this same desire and it thus forms the foundation
on which we must base our political happiness. However, the evil that
is the ultimate aim of desire prevents us from forming a tranquil society
of "equals." It is precisely for this reason that happiness cannot really
give society a solid foundation. In the final analysis, man believes that a
political order that promises *happiness* (and since the French Revolution,
this is the promise of all politics) will satisfy his *desire*. Yet this satisfaction of desire lies not in happiness, but *beyond* it, in a point that from
the perspective of any ethics of happiness can only be seen as evil. In a
culture of "well-being for all" like our own, politics will thus by definition not be able to satisfy people's desire. The discontent it professes to
combat is at the same time already a defense against the much greater
calamity that would be the "perfect" satisfaction of desire.

## 3.2. The Commandment to Love Your Neighbor

In this light, Lacan has no problems understanding Freud's pointed reserve with respect to the commandment to love one's neighbor. In the fifth chapter of *Civilization and Its Discontents*, Freud expresses his amazement that the "world-famous demand" to love our neighbor as ourselves—a demand we inherited from Christianity but which is "undoubtedly older"[42]—can continue unabated to this day. Filtered through the ideals of the French Revolution, among other things, this command remains the foundational form of our sociopolitical culture.

It was not so much the idea of neighborly love itself that stuck in Freud's throat as the fact that it is a *command*, in other words, that it *requires* us to love everyone without distinction as ourselves. While it feeds our political ideal of a general well-being, it is precisely this that makes it nonsensical, dangerous even, in Freud's eyes. How can culture demand that I love everyone—anybody, no matter who—as myself and my loved ones? Although nothing is perhaps more beneficial for man than a love relation (who is more convinced of this than Freud?), it is precisely for this reason that these are limited and that we are very choosy about them. To love everyone the same as my beloved or my best friends is simply impossible. Moreover, it is in fact dangerous because I am unsure whether my love will be returned with an equally generous love. By throwing it away, I degrade both my love and love in general and make social happiness even more impossible than before. Let us be honest, says Freud: if we hand ourselves over to our fellow man with such naïveté, we stand a much greater chance of being abused than being loved. It is in this context that he puts forward the pessimistic sketch of mankind I cited earlier. Precisely the precariousness of love ensures that a world in which everyone loves everyone else can only be a sadistic universe. Lacan feels completely supported by Freud when he claims that the universe beyond the law is not one of heavenly good but diabolical evil. The true world of Kantian ethics, in other words, is rightly envisioned only by the fantasies of the Marquis de Sade.

Lacan, however, goes a step further than Freud here. While it is true that he shares Freud's idea of the cruelty concealed in neighborly love, he doesn't yet refer to it as an unbearable anomaly. On the contrary, in his eyes, this command also contains a hard, unmistakable grain of truth. Precisely in its vicious consequences, it lets us see the foundation and ultimate stakes of any moral law. The dangerous "nonsense" that Freud encountered in that command is undoubtedly the very "sense" of ethics itself. It lets us feel how a moral law wants what it forbids, namely, a *jouissance* which, should it really happen, would destroy the desiring subject. It is to this constitutive function of enjoyment that Freud remains blind. But this doesn't prevent him from granting us, nevertheless—if only through his expression of his amazement at it—a glimpse of this ultimate "sense" of our moral preoccupations. Referring to that famous fifth chapter from *Civilization and Its Discontents*, Lacan says:

> Freud makes comments about this that are quite right, moving comments on the subject of what is worth loving. [. . .] The whole Aristotelian conception of the good is alive in this man who is a true man; he tells us the most sensitive and reasonable things about what it is worth sharing the good that is our love with. But what escapes him is perhaps the fact that precisely because we take that path we miss the opening on to *jouissance*. (S7E: 186; S7F: 219)

By failing to examine the cruelty we fear in our neighbors, Freud misses how this very cruelty inhabits every one of us at the structural level. The enjoyment our ungrateful neighbor takes in abusing our love gives us an unsolicited image of the enjoyment we also desire. It reveals how the desire that drives us, takes *us* beyond ourselves. The enjoyment we, too, seek makes us break the law. To reach the real, "extimate" object our desire aims at (which is the definition of *jouissance*), the symbolic law must be transgressed—while the law forms precisely the indispensable support of our desire. In the final analysis, our enjoyment responds to a death drive that makes us fade away as subjects at the moment of enjoyment, which is why we can only "bear" it at that moment by means of our phantasm. Like any phantasm, our love is an imaginary ruse that both orients us towards that "extimate" object of enjoyment and keeps us at a distance from it. In this way, we *continue* to desire and maintain ourselves as subjects (of desire).

The *jouissance* I fear in my neighbor refers to that "extimate thing" around which my desire circles as well. That which I fear and recoil from in my neighbor ultimately stands for my own most real "self," that is, for that real "thing" that is in me more than myself (read: *imaginary* and even *symbolic* self). Two sentences further in the same lesson, Lacan explains the step that takes him *beyond* Freud:

> [. . .] every time that Freud stops short in horror at the consequences of the commandment of love one's neighbor, we see evoked the presence of that fundamental evil which dwells within this neighbor. But if that is the case, then it also dwells within me. And what is more of a neighbor to me than this heart within which is that of my *jouissance* and which I don't dare go near? For as soon as I go near it, as *Civilization and*

*Its Discontents* makes clear,[43] there rises up the unfathomable aggressivity from which I flee, that I turn against me, and which in the very place of the vanished Law adds its weight to that which prevents me from crossing a certain frontier at the limit of the Thing. (S7E: 186; S7F: 219)

The fear of my neighbor hides the more fundamental fear of my own intimate self: the fear of my real kernel that constitutes my *jouissance* for as long as I maintain myself in the signifying universe but which, were I to coincide with it, would mean my death. It is thus only the feared enjoyment of my fellow man that confronts me with my own. Of all the ethical commandments, "Love your neighbor" forces us the most to such a confrontation. In this sense, it is the moral law that enables us to see most clearly what constitutes the ultimate weight of ethics. Every ethical demand for the good is, in the final analysis, a desire for enjoyment. However, just like fear, the good is at the same time a means for maintaining the requisite distance from this enjoyment and its "extimate" kernel.

It is in this context that Lacan arrives at a strict (pleasure) economic definition of "the good." He reserves this term for that dimension of (symbolic) order in which supply and demand are geared to one another in an exchange that meets the needs of the subject. Here the "good" ("*le bien*") stands for "the domain of goods," meaning both spiritual (e.g., moral) values and purely material values (commodities).[44] As a signifier, one good can always be exchanged for another, enabling the desiring person to achieve a certain degree of satisfaction. However, the desire for the good, as well as the exchange system of goods in which this desire takes place, is a defense mechanism against the demand for the ultimate object that lies beyond the good(s), namely, (noneconomical) enjoyment. Although the command to love one's neighbor is always interpreted within the logic of the good(s), it is precisely the cruel connotations Freud mentioned that push it into the field of a *jouissance* unresponsive to any economic laws.

Lacan finds an outstanding example of this in the legend of Saint Martin, a parable that illustrates one of the works of mercy, namely, "clothing the naked."[45] In this story, the naked one's demand to the young Roman officer is usually understood as a demand for clothes, thus situating the entire gesture within the sphere of the economic goods. He is asking for a piece of cloth with which to clothe himself. But the question remains whether Saint Martin has thereby met all of the beggar's wants. What if the latter is asking not so much for goods (economic goods, cloths to clothe himself with) but for love and enjoyment in the *erotic* sense of the word? What if his nakedness is precisely a come-on to the young, good-looking Martinus—an erotic advance? Referring to the pessimistic image of man that Freud sketches in *Civilization and It Discontents*,[46] Lacan goes even further: What if the naked beggar demands that Saint Martin should kill him? The passage where Lacan formulates his "scandalous" interpretation of this story (immediately after the previous citation) is hard to misunderstand:

> As long as it's the question of the good, there's no problem; our own and our neighbor's are of the same material. Saint Martin shares his cloak, and a great deal is made of it. Yet it is after all a simple question of training; material is by its very nature made to be disposed of—it belongs to the other as much as it belongs to me. We are no doubt touching a primitive requirement in the need to be satisfied there, for the beggar is naked. But perhaps over and above that need to be clothed, he was begging for something else, namely, that Saint Martin either kill him or fuck him. In any encounter there's a big difference in meaning between the response of philanthropy and that of love. (S7E: 186; S7F: 219)[47]

No matter how scandalous Lacan's treatment of one of the most classic parables of neighborly love, it does at least offer a clear illustration of his interpretation. In the final analysis, neighborly love is *love*, "eros." Like all love, this can be interpreted from a psychoanalytic perspective as a desire for enjoyment whose only satisfaction is found in a transgression of the law. However, unlike Freud in *Civilization and Its Discontents*, Lacan here ascribes this desire for enjoyment not to the aggressor but to the one who is needy. In Lacan's interpretation of the parable of Saint Martin, a destitute man demands not so much that one respond to his needs as to the erotic call of his naked body. In this case, the beggar's request becomes a (*non*economic) demand for eroticism and enjoyment that transgresses the realm (and law) of the "good" and "goods." Here the demand that one alleviate someone's needs is traversed by an erotic demand and it is this dimension, according to Lacan, that makes up the ultimate weight of ethics. *Beyond* the demand for clothing, the naked beggar always demands something else, an enjoyment that, even with the help of the most expensive clothes, will never completely be satisfied, even should Saint Martin literally give himself as a lover. Behind the ethical reproach "I was naked and you didn't clothe me" thus lies an underside that is as polymorphous-perverse as it is impossible: "I was naked and you didn't fuck me," or, even worse, "I was naked and you didn't kill me."

It is this reproach that inspires the "hunger artist" in the well-known story by Franz Kafka. A highly successful artist, who made universally admired works of art through his practice of fasting, suddenly sees his success plummet and reproaches his vanishing audience: "I was hungry and you didn't admire me."[48] In this absurd reproach, that other work of mercy, "feeding the hungry," reveals its polymorphous-perverse underside. In short, what Lacan's provocative interpretation is designed to clarify is the way that in every ethical demand one can also hear an impossible and repressed demand for enjoyment. Although there is no place for this enjoyment in the normal (symbolic) universe, it haunts it unmistakably all the same. Kafka's tales are unique in revealing precisely how the most law-abiding normalcy is traversed by this "perverse" craving for enjoyment.[49]

Lacan's provocative interpretation of the legend of Saint Martin is less a flouting of Christian thought that one might imagine. In any case, there is a recognizable strain within the Christian tradition in which neighborly love is explicitly experienced in the transgressive erotic sense. This is true primarily for the array of mystical tendencies that have always been customary to Christianity. Further on in the same lesson, Lacan illustrates this with a reference to two female mystics:

> It wouldn't be difficult at this point to take a leap in the direction of the excesses of the mystics. Unfortunately, many of their most notable qualities always strike somewhat puerile. No doubt the question of the pleasure principle, in the place of the unnameable Thing and of what goes on there, is raised in certain acts that provoke our judgment, acts of the kind attributed to a certain Angela de Folignio, who joyfully lapped up the water in which she had just washed the feet of lepers—I will spare you the details, such as the fact that a piece of skin stuck in her throat, etc.—or to the blessed Marie Allacoque [sic], who, with no less a reward of spiritual uplift, ate the excrements of a sick man. The power of conviction of these no doubt edifying facts would vary quite a lot if the excrements in question were that of a beautiful young girl or if it were a question of eating the come of a forward from your rugby team. In other words, the erotic side of things remains veiled in the above examples. (S7E: 187–188; S7F: 220–221)[50]

Precisely these exaggerated forms of neighborly love show us the largely excessive "erotic side" that lies concealed within it. For Angela da Foligno, helping a fellow man means a total, boundless surrender to him. The transgressive nature of her ethical desire reveals the self-destructive enthusiasm with which she absorbs herself into her gesture. It becomes clear here how what one loves in one's neighbor is, in the final analysis, not the person himself, but a "partial object," an abject "thing," that escapes the economy of the good(s) and appeals to the (noneconomic) waste called enjoyment.

To conceive of ethics from the primacy of desire (Lacan's unshakable axiom), is also to situate its center of gravity—its "weight"—in the satisfaction of that desire. This is not to be found in happiness or in the good, nor in the greatest happiness for the greatest number of people, as utilitarianism (not without some reminiscence of neighborly love) holds. It is to be found in *jouissance* that escapes by definition the good and happiness of all. Previously invisible, it is this that comes to light in the Christian love of one's neighbor, coming even more clearly into view each time this love takes on unusual forms. Although Freud was not averse to a certain Christo-centrism,[51] it is this that escapes him, particularly at the moment when he deals directly with neighborly love.

However, does this mean that, in contrast to Freud, Lacan does *not* recoil from the command to love one's neighbor, elevating the excessive *jouissance* into the ultimate content of ethics? Is our universal duty henceforth to love in the same erotomaniac, life-endangering manner as Angela da Foligno loved her lepers? Absolutely not. This excessive example Lacan pulls from the mystical tradition merely gives us an *image* of the *Beyond* that the most ethical desire is oriented toward. It is therefore not an *example* to be followed. No less would Saint Martin's ethical responsibility toward the naked beggar be to comply with his erotic or suicidal tendencies. For Lacan, too, to do a leper or a beggar good comes down to doing something that benefits them and he, more than anyone, has stressed precisely how, by definition, enjoyment is unable to do this.

But why then, promote *jouissance* as the ultimate weight of ethics? Why is it so important for us to know that neighborly love can take us to the point of a self-destructive surrender to another person? Why am I not allowed to lose sight of the fact that the needy always demand something that stretches *beyond* their need and appeals to an enjoyment that is no longer concerned about goodness and goods? Because precisely *beyond* the good, the dimension of desire becomes visible in all its clarity: this, in a nutshell, is Lacan's thesis in the seventh seminar. This is the main task of psychoanalysis: to bring the dimension of desire to light. The analysand may demand happiness and goodness, yet, this demand hides a search for his desire, and it is the ethical duty of psychoanalysis to give the repressed dimension of desire back to the analysand. Wrestling with her demand, the analysand will come to terms with the fact that goodness and happiness can only be *desired*. Goodness and happiness are promised her everywhere, but in the end she will find out that her desire falls outside the scope of these promises and that only there will she encounter the true identity she was looking for. There, in that outside position beyond her demand for happiness and goodness, she will meet the desire that she ultimately *is*. To map out this strange outside position, Lacan forged his concept of the "thing" and made *jouissance* into a proper concept.

The only concrete thing that psychoanalysis does, then, is "grant" the analysand this kind of outside position. It "lets" her desire, even when this desire doesn't entirely fit into the symbolic universe in which it is realized. It offers her the chance to tarry with the lack that stems from the Other's desire (whose subject/bearer she is). For psychoanalysis, the ultimate ethical act comes down to assuming this lack. The analysand is to take upon herself how, in the final analysis, she corresponds to what escapes the Other (in which she realizes herself as desire). In this, the analysand is radically *alone*. As Lacan already emphasized in his second lesson, the cure can only lead the analysand to the "*threshold*" of this ethical act.[52] In the act itself she is absolutely singular, and she assumes desire to the extent that it stems from what the Other lacks. Hence the emphasis on the "thing" that above all escapes this Other, and on enjoyment through which the subject disappears into that "thing." In this "thing"—as in enjoyment—man escapes the universal law of the symbolic order. The "nothingness" of enjoyment notwithstanding, it is precisely in that "unground" that man comes upon the traces of his desire and, in this way, is able to reconcile himself with the unsolved question (i.e., the desire) that he *is*.

To act in accordance with the "ethics of psychoanalysis," Saint Martin should not necessarily comply with the naked beggar's erotic or suicidal appeal. On the contrary even: should he satisfy this demand, he has precisely miscognized his desire. Nevertheless, he should indeed remain open to the appeal that stretches beyond his demand. Only in this way can the beggar in question obtain the space he needs to follow the traces of his desire and confront it freely. Hence Saint Martin should neither comply with the beggar's suicidal or erotic solicitations nor should he simply reject them. Rather, he should create a space in which the desire that is hidden in the beggar's solicitation can come to light. To accomplish this, a self-critical auto-analysis of Saint Martin's *own* desire (i.e., of the analyst) is essential. This is the only way he can guarantee the necessary space for the other's desire. This "space" is not to be reduced only to the symbolic (exchange) order the analysand and analyst share with one another and in which "goods" can be exchanged. It is, rather, a space in which each are absolutely singular, and it is this singularity that psychoanalysis focuses on both theoretically and practically. Enjoyment is the figure par excellence of this singularity. Thanks to this *jouissance*, man does not simply coincide with what the universal law of the symbolic tells him he ought to do. Thanks to *jouissance*, he does not coincide with his moral duty. Nevertheless there, in that transgressive enjoyment, lies the ultimate "weight" of morality. This is the new insight psychoanalysis brings to ethics.

Up until now we have described *jouissance* and its impact on ethics primarily in negative terms. Sade's fantasies have shown us a world in which this enjoyment assumes a destructive shape, precisely because this negativity is disavowed. At the end of the lesson of March 23, 1960, cited at length earlier, Lacan was at the point of showing us the full stakes of what Sade means for ethics. But for lack of time, he postpones this to the following lesson and examines instead the two fables with which Kant illustrates his ethics of "free duty." It is in this context that he comes to a "positive" formulation of what it means for *jouissance* to constitute the "weight" of ethics. More specifically, here he focuses on the singularity whose necessary space ethics wishes to preserve. In the following section we will take a closer look at this passage.

## 4. An Ethics of Singularity

### 4.1. *Kant before the Gallows*

At the end of the lesson of March 23, 1960, Lacan postpones until the next time the "Sadean threshold" he has yet to take up. His intention had been to set out the entire Sadean instrumentarium in an attempt to make the "weight" of ethics quantifiable, but he determined that there was too little time remaining. In the meantime, he returned, by way of a short detour, to the Kantian tool kit. He can do so, since in a previous lesson he had already taken a thorough look at the Kantian reference involved (S7E: 108–109; S7F: 129–131). It concerns two concrete situations discussed by Kant in his *Critique of Practical Reason*.[53] These illustrate the real possibility of moral freedom. For Kant, it is moral reason itself that constitutes "the weight of the law" (S7E: 188; S7F; 221: "*le poids de la loi*"). As a rational being, man is able to control his passions and other 'pathological' motives so as to respond solely to the categorical imperative, that is, to the law that corresponds with his own freedom. To illustrate the "weight" of this rational freedom, Kant offers two fables that Lacan summarizes as follows:

> The first concerns the individual who is placed in the situation of being executed on his way out, if he wants to spend time with the lady whom he desires unlawfully [. . .] The other case is that of someone who lives at the court of a despot and who is put in the position of either bearing false witness against someone who, as a result, will lose his life or of being put to death himself if he doesn't do it. (S7E: 188–189; S7F: 222)

For Kant, things are clear: face to face with death, the first individual no longer dares to claim that he is not in control of his passions. He will shrink from the gallows that await him, thereby showing that man can indeed be free from the demands of his passions. With the second individual, freedom will appear capable of transcending even the fear of death. Here freedom emerges as the faculty able to choose its own "noumenal" law (the categorical imperative) over the law of the phenomenal.[54]

When Lacan discusses Kant's line of reasoning, he comes to very different conclusions. First, he notes that in the first fable, Kant implicitly places both the *pleasure* the man can have with his lady and the *pain* of the gallows under the same denominator:

> The striking significance of the first example resides in the fact that the night spent with the lady is paradoxically presented to us as a pleasure that is weighed against a punishment to be undergone; it is an opposition which homogenizes them. (S7E: 189; S7F: 222)

Here, enjoyment and pain are weighed up against each other as though they were positive and negative aspects of the same element, an element that, with Freud, one can call the pleasure principle. However, according to Lacan, the question remains as to whether they can indeed both be thought of on the basis of the same pleasure principle. For, to recognize the death principle in enjoyment is enough to give the story a completely different meaning:

> But it is important to note that one only has to make a conceptual shift and move the night spent with the lady from the category of pleasure to that of *jouissance*, given that *jouissance* implies precisely the acceptance of death [. . .] for the example to be ruined. (S7E: 189; S7F: 222)

Where does the individual discover the ultimate "weight" of his ethical choice? Not necessarily in the pleasure or life principle, as Kant imagined. The individual can also make a choice that goes *beyond* the pleasure principle, thus heading explicitly for *enjoyment*. In this lies the entire sense of the moral law for Lacan. Its significance lies not in the law itself, as Kant claimed, but in the fact that the law, precisely through its prohibition, makes *jouissance* possible. The law's promise is not to be found in the "good" it proclaims but in the enjoyment the law makes possible through its transgression. Just as the law, according to Paul, serves to makes sin *excessively* sinful, so, too, for Lacan, the sense of the moral law lies in the radical excess of enjoyment. Hence, according to Lacan, it is possible that an individual will use the law and its prohibitions simply in order to make his enjoyment of its transgression even more intense.

In the second fable, Lacan notes a logical slip with respect to the first, which subtly strengthens the a fortiori effect that Kant has in mind with this "double apologue":

> In the first case, pleasure *and* pain are presented as a single packet to take or leave, in consideration of which one avoids the risk and gives up *jouissance*. In the second case, there is pleasure *or* pain. It's not insignificant that I underline it, for this choice is destined to produce in you a certain effect of *a fortiori*, as a result of which you may be deceived about the real significance of the question. (S7E: 189–190; S7F: 223; Miller's italics)

In the first case, the man's choice remains within the limits of the pleasure principle. Should he choose to spend the night with his lady, he will gain both pleasure (making love to her) *and* unpleasure (the gallows). In the other choice, too, there is both pleasure (he remains alive) *and* unpleasure (he renounces the enjoyment of a night of love). The choice thus amounts to a calculation: one pleasure (or unpleasure) can be weighed up against the other. According to Kant, the individual in question then also immediately perceives that a single night of love cannot be weighed against the bald fact of staying alive. So, for Kant, this demonstrates that human action is free and, in the final analysis, undetermined by the passions to which it nonetheless seems to be so subjected.

In the second case, the calculation is less evident. There, the man must choose between pleasure *or* unpleasure. If he gives a false declaration, he will have pleasure since by doing so he can save his own skin. If he doesn't, *all* that remains to him is unpleasure, and in its most extreme form: death. For Kant, the fact that despite this he can still consider choosing death so as not to be unfaithful to the categorical imperative is an illustration of the fact (the "*Faktum*") of his free, pure reason. Reason, it seems, can allow itself not to be limited to the laws of the phenomenal world, even when death is involved. Even in the face of death, reason can choose the law that in complete freedom it imposes itself. However, Kant doesn't mention the fact that in the second case, the man has made absolutely *no* calculation. In this case, he hasn't weighed pleasure and unpleasure up against each other. On the contrary, he has precisely shown himself to be independent of all calculation. He does not begin from an established "weight" before choosing between two ethical possibilities. He has immediately (nonphenomenally) felt the "weight" of the very possibility of choosing, and has in fact chosen this possibility. He has chosen nothing other than his own reason to the extent that it doesn't allow itself to be determined by anything quantifiable (anything phenomenal).

Lacan claims that Kant has posited a *false* analogy between both stories as if the calculation of the first case would also hold for the second. In this way, it seems more acceptable that a man would freely choose something that would nonetheless cost him his life. And all this, while already the first case is in opposition to Kant's own concept of ethics that forbids one to make "calculations of weight" in moral questions. Thanks to this seeming analogy between the two stories, the evident calculation in the first case has kept hidden the lack of evidence in the second.

Furthermore, Lacan continues, there is another snake in the grass in that "double apologue" and it is precisely this that truly ensures that we are "deceived about the real significance of the question" (S7E: 190; S7F: 223). More specifically, this (false) analogy ensures that the reader's attention will pass over a major question, a question that is raised by the problem laid out in the second fable. If we take as a universal rule that one must not obey a despot if he commands us to bear false witness, who do we think this rule is good for? Is it for the *subject* of the universal moral law, that is, he who (freely) obeys it? Or is it for the law's *object*, that is, he to whom some good must be done? According to Kant, this would of course be an unnecessary and misleading distinction, because for him the subject and object of an ethical law essentially concerns the same rational free man. The one for whom the ethical law is intended to benefit is precisely the "bearer" of it, the universal as well as the particular subject. Free and enlightened (*aufgeklärt*) as modern man is, he is conscious that the law to which he is subjected is in the end his own autonomous reason.

For Lacan, in contrast, this distinction between the subject and the object of an ethical law is anything but unnecessary or false, since for him these can *never* be equated with one another. For ethics (like desire) aims at an object that lies *beyond* the subject, an object that is, so to speak, closer to the subject than the subject itself. In other words, ethics aims at the "thing" that represents the domain of *jouissance*. Yet the subject will never reach that object of desire, even when he explicitly takes *himself* for that "object." It irreparably remains an always already lost object that, precisely in this capacity, stimulates desire and makes up its ultimate ethical "weight."

In this respect, it is not at all redundant to ask who precisely Kant has in mind when he discusses the possibility whether I must obey a despot who forces me "of either bearing false witness against someone who, as a result, will lose his life or of being put to death himself if he

doesn't do it" (S7E: 188–189; S7F: 222). Is it *me* he has in mind, the I
who stands before the dilemma, whether or not I obey what the universal law demands? Or is it the *other* on whose rights I might or might
not trample? Is it about me, the *subject* of the ethical act, or about the
other, its *object*? Lacan sharpens this dilemma by slightly changing the
story and, strangely enough, adding a touch of truth. What if the despot
asks me to give a *true* deposition against someone who might receive the
death sentence because of it?

> What's at issue here? That I attack the rights of another who
> is my fellow man in that statement of the universal rule, or
> is it a question of the false witness as such? And what if I
> changed the example? Let's talk about true witness, about a
> case of conscience which is raised if I am summoned to in-
> form on my neighbor or my brother for activities which are
> prejudicial to the security of the state? That question is of
> a kind that shifts the emphasis placed on the universal rule.
> (S7E: 190; S7F: 223)

At first sight, Lacan has just reinserted the possibility of "calculation"
and seems to want to weigh the things against each other. Now I must
make a different choice, not between the truth and a lie but between two
truths: either I remain faithful to the universal truth that forbids me to lie,
or I choose the truth that the other is my equal and that he, just like me,
loves life more than truth. For Kant, the two alternatives coincide because
my comparison with my fellow man is mediated by the universal law of
my reason. However, such is not the case for Lacan. The comparison with
my fellow man may operate according to the symbolic law (we are both
the subject of a signifying chain), but what connects us to each other is
something that reaches fundamentally *beyond* the symbolic. What binds
me to my fellow man (and even to myself) *beyond* the symbolic law is the
"thing," the ultimate, completely *singular* object of desire. This is precisely
why my fellow man is not only my equal, but simultaneously—and in a
more fundamental sense—my "neighbor." What binds him to himself, what
binds me to myself, what binds us together at that level is a symbolically
*non*interchangeable, singular "thing." Precisely because (like myself) my
neighbor is ultimately based in such a "thing," the truth to which this
"neighbor" refers no longer corresponds to the truth of the universal (symbolic) law. It is this latter, purely singular truth that already in the second
lesson Lacan declared as the object of his entire investigation.

> This truth that we are seeking for in a concrete experience [i.e.,
> an analytical cure] is not that of a superior law. If the truth

that we are seeking is a truth that frees, it is a truth that we will look for in a hiding place in our subject. It is a particular truth. [. . .] it appears [. . .] with the character of an imperious *Wunsch*. Nothing can be compared to it that allows it to be judged from the outside. [. . .] The *Wunsch* does not have the character of a universal law but, on the contrary, of the most particular of laws—even if it is universal that this particularity is to be found in every human being. (S7E: 24; S7F: 32–33)

However, both "truths," that of the symbolic law and that of my neighbor (or the "thing") can no longer be weighed against each other, since one is universal while the other is not. More precisely, one is true *because* it is universalizable, while the other concerns a truth that escapes the universal and in this sense must be called "singular" rather than "particular" (as Lacan does). One of the truths is Kantian, the other is what Lacan is trying to formulate. The latter kind of truth is no longer founded in the universality of the signifying universe in which the pleasure animal realizes itself as a subject, but in the rigid singularity of that subject's ultimate and irretrievable object. Consequently, it is not a truth that I can share equally with *all* others. I can only share it with one or a few others at the most, and even then I will not be able to speak out that truth, not even to myself. It is too intimate, too "near" to me to relate to or even be aware of. This is why I need the evil "neighbor" (as Freud described it) in order to divine its presence.

It is only by keeping this in mind that the stakes of Lacan's variation of Kant's second fable can be understood. Imagine, for example, that given the premises of that apologue I choose to give true testimony. In such a case, I choose the first, Kantian form of truth and regard my fellow human as my "equal" in the proceedings. By obeying the categorical imperative, the Kantian I am reasons, I subject myself to the emancipatory reason in which all men participate and which enables everyone to treat each other as an equal. Or, in the utilitarian version of this kind of ethics: should the majority of people opt in such a case to give true testimony, then it cannot be anything other than the best choice. The fact that this means the death of the singular man or woman I am giving true testimony about must then be regarded as a both tragic and inevitable sacrifice with which a (noumenal) universal (phenomenal) truth is occasionally befouled.

If, on the other hand, I choose the alternative position in this moral dilemma and refuse to give (true) testimony, I choose in favor of my "neighbor." I choose the other insofar as he escapes the universal law by which everyone is "equal" to everyone else. I do not choose my "equal" in the other; I choose the "neighbor" in him, that is, that which goes *beyond* anything we can share (i.e., imaginary identity and the symbolic law). That is to say I choose his *jouissance*. Out of ethical consideration, I grant my neighbor his singular enjoyment by which he falls outside the universal of the ethical law. In the name of ethics, and remaining within the limits of the moral law, I permit the other—my neighbor—a transgression of that law. I thus consciously reserve a space for what must fundamentally be labeled "evil." More strongly, I even affirm this enjoyment as the ultimate point of reference of my ethical desire. I give sanction to the fact that the core of ethics lies, in the final analysis, *beyond* the good: not in a (noumenal) plenitude of sense but in what, from its side, negates all sense—the nonsense of evil. I affirm that which the law is made for: enjoyment. While ethics cannot but forbid *jouissance*, still I find that ethics must realize that it is never able to eradicate it. On the contrary, by way of its own limits, by affirming its own finitude, ethics must "permit" man his desire, including the evil of his enjoyment. This is the paradox of an "ethics of psychoanalysis."

### 4.2. *Lacan before the Gallows*

But is this possible? Can ethics work in favor of *jouissance*? Can it demand the *right* to enjoyment? The very singularity of enjoyment simply seems to preclude this. How could we ever speak for such a singular truth, if this truth escapes any discourse as the symbolic order? Is such a truth not already denied the very moment it is expressed?

Lacan's reflection on Kant's double apologue does not avoid confronting this question. On the contrary, a passage at the end of his lesson of March 23, 1960 (which we have been closely following here) shows how this very question suddenly begins to weigh on Lacan. Given the abyssal nature of this question, it is striking after all that he does not flinch from presenting it to his audience. Here is the final paragraph of the lesson, a passage that relates directly to an earlier citation, which I provide again for the sake of utter clarity:

> And what if I changed the example a little? Let's talk about true witness, about a case of conscience which is raised if I am summoned to inform on my neighbor or my brother for activities which are prejudicial to the security of the state. That question is of a kind that shifts the emphasis placed on the universal rule. And I who stand here right now and bear witness to the idea that there is no law of the good except in evil and through evil, should I bear such witness? The Law that makes my neighbor's *jouissance* the point on which, in bearing witness in this case, the meaning of my duty is balanced. Must I go toward my duty of truth insofar as it preserves the

authentic place of my *jouissance*, even if it is empty? Or must
I resign myself to this lie, which, by making me substitute
forcefully the good for the principle of my *jouissance*, commands me to blow alternatively hot and cold? Either I refrain
from betraying my neighbor so as to spare my fellow man or
I shelter behind my fellow man so as to give up my *jouissance*.
(S7: 190; S7F: 223)[55]

From this particularly dense and obscure passage, there is in any
case one thing we can conclude: Lacan applies his modified Kantian apo-
logues to his own situation. He problematizes himself as the "subject" of
the discourse he is describing. And notice how he immediately feels the
"weight" of what he is claiming here. If one wants to save Kant's endan-
gered man from the despot's clutches, one must above all remain silent
and bear *no* witness. Any word—and particularly any *true* word—would
betray the neighbor as one who escapes the universal law, thereby con-
demning him. But what is Lacan himself doing, he who tells us that the
ethics of psychoanalysis (and ethics in general) goes *beyond* the universal
and "permits" the other his singular desire, that is to say, the evil of his
enjoyment? He does what he absolutely must not do: he speaks, witnesses,
explains. This mere fact incorporates the fragile singularity of enjoyment
into the universal order and, thus, denies it. Publicly speaking for the singularity of enjoyment immediately makes it unacceptable, since it escapes
the public, universal order by definition. This order cannot but forbid the
transgression which all enjoyment ultimately comes down to.

Lacan's question unmistakably betrays the way he suddenly becomes
aware of himself as standing in the position of the despot he was intend-
ing to rail against. Purely by opening his mouth about the neighbor, he
has signed that person's death warrant and no further plea will be of
any avail. By the same token, this question reveals how Lacan realizes
that the neighbor, too, listening to the pleas in his defense, feels what it
means only to be a neighbor and, within earshot of a virtual universal
audience, to be reduced to what lies *beyond* this universality. Lacan himself
suddenly feels what it must mean for his neighbor to be an undefended,
perpetually lost "thing." His attempt to keep him out of the clutches of
the universal law deprives the neighbor precisely of his last hope. Like no
other, Lacan realizes that he cannot bring up the singular truth he wishes
to defend without immediately contradicting himself.

Anyone who understands the abyss in Lacan's question "if [he]
should bear such witness" (*"dois-je porter ce temoinage?"*) can imagine
how he must have reeled at that moment. It is not coincidental that,
immediately after this abyssal question with which he undermines himself
as the 'subject' of his discourse, he seeks recourse in the strict limits of the

Kantian double apologue. He stops applying the story directly to his own discourse and enters again into the position of the courtier who is forced to betray the other by giving a *true* declaration. From this perspective, so Lacan continues, I observe that the entire sense of "my duty" revolves or, more precisely, oscillates around the "other's *jouissance*." My "ought" is not longer founded in the *subject* that I am, as in the Kantian "*Pflicht*," but revolves, wavers, oscillates, "balances" around my ethical "object," that is, around an untouchable and indefensible "thing" that I would like to leave untouched in my "neighbor."

For what am I supposed to do with such an "ought," such a "duty of truth" (*devoir de verité*)? The truth is that my fellow human is not my equal but my neighbor, a truth that obliges me to grant his essentially evil *jouissance* a place. This immediately obliges me also to "reserve the authentic place of my *jouissance,* even if it is empty." While keeping my own *jouissance* empty (i.e., refusing to enjoy myself), for ethics' sake, ethics nevertheless obliges me to recognize an "immoral" *jouissance* in myself, in the core of my ethical desire. It is only on this basis that I am able to recognize and "grant" the truth of the other's enjoyment.

But can I speak up for this truth without immediately betraying it? Can I bear witness to it in front of everyone? But also: can I remain *silent* about it? Can I be silent about this truth if being silent means saying what the universal already says and consequently lying about the truth of *jouissance*? "Must I resign myself to this lie?" as Lacan asks in the cited passage. Must *jouissance* be replaced by "the good"? Must I act as if ethics is not marked by a radical finitude, as if it gives us "the good" it promises? And if I was indeed to establish that "good," would I really have found a way out of my shaky moral position, my unbearable oscillation or "balancing"? Doesn't this "lie" (i.e., speaking about the "good" when it is in fact a matter of *jouissance*) make me "blow hot and cold"?

On the one hand, by putting the good in the place of my *jouissance*, I can, in the name of that good, shrink from "betraying my neighbor so as to spare my fellow man." In that case, I refuse to betray him because I recognize him as my equal and find him, like myself, too good not to save. On the other hand, in the name of that same good, I can also do exactly the opposite and betray him by telling the truth. In this case, too, I recognize him as my equal but "I shelter behind my fellow man so as to give up my *jouissance*." I use the other to disavow my own *jouissance*, my own finitude. Unmasking the *jouissance* in the other, I deny in myself this dimension *beyond* the law that is its ultimate point of reference and (forbidden) aim, that is, that "evil" *in* which and *through* which a "law of the good" is possible.

If I do in fact wish to grant my neighbor his singular enjoyment and, thus, affirm the radical finitude of my ethical impact on him, it is impossible for me to define ethics exclusively in terms of the good. Such a point of departure still makes me blow "hot and cold." The ultimate aim of the moral endeavor is a completely singular enjoyment and, since this escapes the moral law by definition, it cannot but be defined as "evil." Nevertheless, this doesn't prevent the ethical dimension of psychoanalysis from granting a place precisely to this enjoyment. It can do so only insofar as it recognizes its own limits, its own finitude. That is why psychoanalysis, first, must start from the position that it cannot fulfill the analysand's demands. Instead of the good the analysand demands, it can only confront her with her desire for an enjoyment *beyond* every good. Second, psychoanalysis must realize that it is able to lead the analysand only to the "threshold" of her singular *jouissance* (S7E: 22; S7F: 30). Once there, the analyst must for ethical reasons let the patient go: it is up to her to assume the lack of her desire, which is for psychoanalysis the "ethical act" par excellence. It is only in this way that one can grant the other her desire and her singular enjoyment in the name of an "ethics of psychoanalysis."

But, according to this same "ethics of psychoanalysis," under no conditions may the one who stands in the place of power—and this is true, too, for anyone invested with moral authority, thus also for the analyst—allow himself such enjoyment. No one who speaks in the name of a universal law (or, in Lacanese, of the "big Other"), may permit himself any enjoyment. If they do, they fall into the situation evoked by Kant in his apologue of the despot, or into the state described by Robert Vailland's novel *La Loi*. The law then literally enters the service of someone's transgressive enjoyment and, even worse than before, makes everyone's enjoyment impossible, except for that of the despot. Just like the leader of the primal horde in Freud's *Totem and Taboo*, such an enjoying despot imposes the law in a criminal way on the entire community.

The ethical task of psychoanalysis is to safeguard a place for enjoyment. For that reason, however, it must refuse every supposed grip on that enjoyment, and in no way may it operate *from* that very enjoyment. It is even impossible to express this insight or to "bear witness" to it, as we have seen in the passage we discussed. How can such an ethics say that its "weight" lies in the "evil" and singular truth it forbids? Does it not immediately sublate the latter in the pretentions of a universal truth? Does it not disavow the singular truth it wants to defend, and this simply by speaking about it?

Already the mere fact that it bears witness to this disables this kind of ethics from bearing the "weight" of the truth it speaks about. Already under the weight of any "witnessing," it threatens to wither away. It is also possible, however, that by refusing to witness, the ethical authority secretly occupies the place of *jouissance* all the more, there taking on a perverse role analogous to that of the despot in Kant's fable.

How does one relate to this *jouissance* that is as implausible as it is unavoidable? How does one obey the law of enjoyment without participating in the evil this enjoyment represents? How can one act in the name of this enjoyment yet without becoming a perverse tyrant? How to affirm the singular truth concealed behind the universal love of one's neighbor, and yet not get trapped in the pit of a "evangelical perversion," that is to say, in the dangerous lie that proclaims "good tidings for the whole world"?

Lacan's position in regard to the "ethics of psychoanalysis" emerges from these kinds of questions that betray first and foremost the impasse they threaten to fall into. In the *Ethics Seminar*, he not only tries to clearly formulate these questions, he also hazards a positive answer for them. That answer focuses on a central concept, sublimation. In the following chapter, I will examine this concept in more detail, although it will become clear as well that the impasses posed by these questions are warded off rather than answered.

# Chapter 7

# Sublimation

## 1. From Doom to Dame

Paradoxically, as we learned in the previous chapter, the ultimate purpose of the moral law is to be transgressed. The satisfaction of our desire (which is why we obey ethical rules) lies not so much in the good as in an excessive enjoyment that cares nothing about the good. This is why even the most ethically inspired action only makes the moral lack—the impossibility of realizing the good—more profound. In the final analysis, even such action aims for evil *jouissance*. This is Lacan's way of saying that the most fundamental drive behind our moral conscience is the death drive. "The commandment that was supposed to lead to life turned out to lead to death"—thus Lacan in his lecture of December 23, 1959, quoting literally from Saint Paul's *Letter to the Romans* (Rom. 7:10):

> The dialectical relationship between desire and the Law causes our desire to flare up only in relation to the Law, through which it becomes desire for death. It is only because of the Law that sin, ἁμαρτία [*hamartía*]—which in Greek means lack and non-participation in the Thing—takes on an excessive, hyperbolic character. (S7E: 83–84; S7F: 101)

But are we therefore doomed to be the perpetual victims of this fatal dialectic? Must we simply remain blind to the diabolical ruses that traverse all of our moral aspirations in such a subversive way? Immediately after the previously cited passage, Lacan asks this question directly. In light of the emphasis he has placed on this subversive structure of moral conscience, his answer sounds surprisingly optimistic:

Freud's discovery—the ethics of psychoanalysis—does it leave us clinging to that dialectic? We will have to explore that which, over the centuries, human beings have succeeded in elaborating that transgresses the Law [on the level of the νοῦς ("nous," Greek for "raison")],[1] [i.e., that which] puts them in a relationship to desire that transgresses interdiction, and introduces an erotics that is above morality. I don't think you should be surprised by such a question. It is after all precisely something that all religions engage in, all mysticisms, all that Kant disdainfully calls the *Religionsschwärmereien,* religious enthusiasms—it is not an easy word to translate. What is all this except a way to rediscovering the relation to *das Ding* somewhere beyond the law? There are no doubt other ways. (S7E: 84, modified translation; S7F: 101)[2]

The impasse we reach through the dialectical tension between the law and desire does not have to weigh on us as an unshakable blind fate, Lacan argues. Although this impasse structures our desire, a certain stance *toward* it is nevertheless possible. At the unconscious level, there is the *jouissance* that enables our phantasm to escape it (albeit in a purely symbolic, and thus "fake" manner). At the conscious level, too—that is, at the level of understanding, of νοῦς (nous), as Lacan indicates with the Greek term—one can take a certain stance in relation to the impasse without having to be crushed by it. Eroticism, religion and certain other forms, Lacan assures us here, offer a way for desiring that deals with the transgression it aims at. These are forms that our νοῦς (nous), our rational faculty, has developed to enable us to consciously manage the transgressive link that binds us to the moral law.

By comparing it with the original stenograph of the seminars, one can see how Miller's editing simply dispenses with the Greek word νοῦς, and thus dispenses with Lacan's explicit reference to reason in this context. It must have escaped Miller that Lacan most probably read this word from out of the Greek text of the New Testament that was lying open at that moment on his lectern and from which he had just plucked the quote from Saint Paul he had surprised his audience with. That he is indeed referring to the Greek text can be inferred from the fact that he cites the New Testament word for sin, ἁμαρτία [hamartía].[2]

In the passage from the *Letter to the Romans* Lacan invokes here, Paul makes a strict distinction between "reason" [νοῦς, *nous*] and "flesh" (σαρξ, *sarx*): the former is in the service of the "law of God" while the latter responds to the "law of sin."[3] Obviously, Lacan's reference to the term νοῦς [*nous*] must be read as a critical comment on Saint Paul's text. Against the latter, he states that it is not just sin that is able to stand in for a transgressive relation with the law. Reason, too, has worked out ways of giving form and place to this transgressive relation.[4]

In this context, it is a pity that Miller drops the Greek word 'νοῦς' (*nous*). Precisely with this word, Lacan indicates that it is possible to approach the evil, transgressive dimension of desire *consciously* and *rationally*. This diabolical dialectic between the law and its *beyond* is no longer confined to the unconscious, phantasmatic phenomenon of *jouissance* that escapes the universal order by definition. That order itself, in its turn, can allow for a conscious confrontation with this dialectic. For this, Lacan reserves the term sublimation.

In fact, his comments on religion and eroticism in his lesson of December 23, 1959 are not casual side remarks intended to fill in the remaining time. Given the results, it seems clear that at that moment he was already introducing the theme of sublimation, which subsequently took no fewer than six lessons to elaborate. With this concept, he will explain how an "ethics of desire" is not just limited to the space of the psychoanalytic cure, but can also offer a contribution to the wider domain of a universal, cultural *Bildung*.

Although here, in this lesson, religion is briefly mentioned, it is already clear that Lacan considers eroticism the privileged phenomenon capable of revealing the structure of sublimation. In any event, his unannounced introduction to this concept is entirely devoted to the erotic. Implicitly, he is already referring to Courtly Love which he will later call a "paradigm of sublimation" (S7E: 128; S7F: 153). Immediately following the long, previously cited quotation, he claims:

> What is all this except a way to rediscovering the relation to *das Ding* somewhere beyond the law? There are no doubt other ways. No doubt, in talking about erotics, we will have to talk about the kind of rules of love [*des règles de l'amour*] that have been elaborated over the centuries. (S7F: 84, S7F: 101–102)

The phrase, the "rules of love" is already a striking expression of the paradox Lacan is trying to grasp with his concept of sublimation. Erotic love is the domain of *jouissance* par excellence where laws and rules only hold insofar as they are simultaneously transgressed. The erotic play installs "rules of transgression" and turns them into the stakes and the object of "culture." Driven to enjoyment by desire, all culture in fact stems from such a dubious but nevertheless well-regulated game with the law, a game in which the law is repeatedly transgressed only to be each time reconfirmed.

In the singular experience of enjoyment, that game occurs unconsciously. With sublimation, the stakes are a *conscious*, more general cultural phenomenon. Sublimation enables us to relate consciously and "rationally" to the impossible structure of our desire. A little further along, he refers to the ethical space that Freud opened up for the erotic relation, shedding light on the basic structure of eroticism along the way. From what follows in his seminar, it will become apparent how here he already describes the sublimation process in a nutshell:

> It is true: Freud placed in the forefront of ethical enquiry the simple relationship between man and woman. Strangely enough, things haven't been able to move beyond that point. The question of *das Ding* is still attached to whatever is open, lacking, or gaping at the center of our desire. I would say—you will forgive me the play on words—that we need to know what we can do to transform this dam-age into our "Dame" in the archaic French sense, our lady [qu'il s'agit pour nous de savoir ce que nous pouvons faire de ce dam pour le transformer en dame, en notre dame]. (S7E: 84; S7F: 102)[5]

The moral law places the ultimate object of desire under prohibition, thereby sealing the "damage" or, also, "doom," "damnation" ("*dam*") characteristic of desire. It seals the "wound" (other meaning of "*dam*") that irreparably cuts the subject off from its ultimate object (the "thing"). By keeping this wound open, by affirming the lack on which the entire drive economy rests, desire is kept alive. In order to keep that ultimate "thing" at a distance while still remaining oriented toward it—in other words, to continue aiming at the "doom" the "thing" stands for—this "doom" can be granted the attraction of a "dame," an inaccessible "Lady" who attracts as the erotic object of desire.

What Lacan describes here is nothing other than courtly love as a form of sublimation, as elaborated in his next lesson. Like every sublimation, this highly developed and coded form of eroticism performs the paradox of desire "in culture." The object aimed for is posited on the place of the "thing," that is, of desire's ultimate object. The "dame" becomes the "doom" that keeps desire unsatisfied; and, in the same movement, the "doom" becomes a "dame" that inflames our desire. It is sublimation—in this case, courtly love—that gives this paradoxical relation shape.

It is already clear that Lacan will define sublimation by reference to the "thing." By installing the ultimate object of desire, (the object constitutive for the object relation that we *are*) in the place of the "thing," sublimation simultaneously both inflames and brakes desire. This is to say that Lacan defines sublimation exclusively in reference to the object, that is, in terms of his own object relations theory.

## 2. An "Object Relational" Concept of Sublimation

### 2.1. The Premises of Object Relations Theory...

It is well known that Lacan's view of sublimation diverges sharply from Freud's. Although it would be interesting, of course, to explain Freud's conceptualizations of sublimation and to examine the ways Lacan differs from them, it would not be expedient here. Not only are Freud's numerous attempts in this area seriously heterogeneous in themselves (such that an inventory alone would take up too much time and space[6]), but Lacan's emphasis on the object in his definition of sublimation finds no direct precedent in Freud.

With the notion of "sublimation," Freud always had a more or less "positive" concept in mind. It names the process by which an originally sexual drive energy is diverted from its sexual aim to become the driving force behind art, science, and other typical cultural activities.[7] In this sense, Freud characterizes sublimation as a vicissitude of the drive that must be distinguished from repression.[8] Generally, he describes it as a change of sexual aim and not of object (as Lacan will claim).[9] As a rule, he takes the energy that is in play to be sexual although this does not stop him from several times explicitly calling sublimation a process of desexualization.[10] Aside from all its contradictions and the irregularities in Freud's text, sublimation can be summed up as a "positive" vicissitude through which the drive chooses a different, nonsexual aim in order to gain pleasure.

What is striking is the way Lacan only appropriates the first, general characteristic of Freud's concept. Lacan's concept of sublimation focuses on a modification of the drive *object* and not of the *aim*, as Freud (nearly) always held. Moreover, in contrast to Freud, for Lacan it is quite conceivable for sublimation to be about an explicitly *sexual* object. Anyway, it is in this sense that he will interpret courtly love—for him, the prototypical example of sublimation.

With this concept, Lacan—who is at this moment still advocating a "return to Freud"—seems to be seriously diverging from his master. Nevertheless, on closer examination, his divergence is not really so striking, certainly not for anyone who reads Lacan's theory of sublimation according to the basic paradigm on which his entire conceptualization of psychoanalysis is built, namely, object relations theory. From this angle, it is not only the sexual, erotic nature of the sublimated object that will become, if not defensible, then at least comprehensible. The difference between "change of aim" and "change of object" will also be put into perspective. It is Lacan himself who declares that we must consider the whole problematic of sublimation from the standpoint of object relations theory. He steers his audience toward it with an explicit appeal to the foundation of what psychoanalysis is for him: "object relations" (S7E: 90; S7F: 109). A closer examination of this passage is illuminating.

After having prepared the topic of sublimation in his lesson of December 23, 1959 (without, however, mentioning the term as we already saw), he comes straight to the point in the following lesson (January 13, 1960). He stresses the importance of a concept like "sublimation" for the entire topic of his seminar, if only because it brings the question of value based ethics on board.

> Sublimation is, in effect, the other side of the research that Freud pioneered into the roots of ethical feeling, insofar as it imposes itself in the form of prohibitions, of the moral conscience. It is the side that is referred to in the world in a manner that is so improper and so comical to a sensitive ear—I mean in the world outside the field of psychoanalysis—as the philosophy of values. (S7E: 87; S7F: 105)

It may still be possible, the concept of sublimation seems to suggest, for our appreciation of moral values to be grounded in our drive life in a positive way. Perhaps, on the mere basis of a polymorphous-perverse anarchy, the drive is *spontaneously and of its own accord* able to form a drive attachment to ethical values. In this case, ethics would not stem from prohibition or laws that curb the free drive but from a *spontaneous* potential *inherent* to the drive itself to transform itself into natural goodness, that is, to "sublimate" itself. In other words, a concept like sublimation would, in one and the same movement, give ethics both a drive-based and a natural foundation (S7E: 88; S7F: 106).

Of course, Lacan does not agree with this characterization of sublimation. Here, too, he criticizes any attempt to grant the drive a natural or less perverse nature. This also accounts for the negative tone he immediately gives the term "philosophy of values." Nevertheless, this doesn't prevent Lacan from agreeing that a notion like sublimation can indeed found ethics and ethical values in the drive. However, for Lacan, this drive can in no way be approached as something natural. According to Lacan, the "drive" refers to a polymorphous-perverse "*driving away*" from nature, *away* from the biological function onto which it is grafted. This accords with Lacan's methodological starting point: the primacy of the signifier. To construct a science of the human, what is called nature must be approached as a universe of signifiers. So, when he goes into the relation between sublimation and the drive in the lesson of January 13, 1960, his starting point is precisely the signifier's primacy.[11] After claiming again that the "drive" should in no way be confused with "instinct" (the "*Trieb*" and not the "*Instinkt*"), he states:

> The *Triebe* were discovered and explored by Freud within an experience founded on the confidence he had in the play of signifiers, in the play of substitutions. The result is that we can in no way confuse the domain of the *Triebe* with a re-classification of human beings' associations with their natural milieu, however new that reclassification may seem. The Trieb must be translated insofar as possible with some ambiguity, and I like sometimes to say *dérive* in French, "drift." It is in any case "drive" that is used in English to translate the German word. That drift, where the whole action of the pleasure principle is motivated, directs us toward the mythic point that has been articulated in terms of an object relation. We have to be precise about the meaning of this and to criticize the confusions introduced by ambiguities of significations that are much more serious than the signifying kind. We are now getting close to the most profound things Freud has to say about the nature of the *Triebe*, and especially insofar as they may give satisfaction to the subject in more than one way, notably, in leaving open a door, a way or a career, of sublimation. (S7E: 90: S7F: 108–109)

The drive "drives away." It continually "drives away" its energy (thereby generating pleasure) because this is siphoned over from signifier to signifier. However, Lacan argues, this manner of representation takes us to "a mythical point," a point that must be interpreted explicitly in terms of object relations theory. What Lacan has in mind here has become familiar to us in the meantime: the entire "drive system" in which the drive flourishes at the level of the signifier drives, in its turn, away from the ultimate object called the "thing." The libidinal being is an object relation that never reaches that "thing" and can therefore never definitively "drive away" the energy that is to be removed. The term "drive" thus refers to an energy fluctuation that never stops "driving away." What keeps a drive going and what, in the final analysis, grants it its consistency is thus also this cut-off, "extimate" object. The drive thus stands for this fundamental, permanently irreconcilable and forever drifting detour that the pleasure animal must take on its way toward its ultimate object, a detour by which—like a planet, as it were—the drive is taken in an orbit around its object.

This image literally lies at the basis of Lacan's conceptualization of sublimation. If the drive is cut off even at a real level from its object (and this is what Lacan concludes from Freud's *Entwurf*), one cannot conceive of the drive's satisfaction in terms of arriving at its object. Of course, at the *imaginary* and *symbolic* levels, the desiring subject can have this impression, namely in the experience of *jouissance*. At the level of the *real* however, the drive does not reach its "thing." On that level, the drive must be conceived as a perpetual, "pulsating" circling around the "thing," and its satisfaction as an unrestrained missing-out of that "thing." The vicissitude of drive called sublimation must literally be conceived of with reference to this structure, according to Lacan.

## 2.2. . . . *Applied to Sublimation*

Lacan defines sublimation as a change not so much at the level of the drive's aim, as Freud generally did, as of its object. And this change gives satisfaction not so much at the individual level (which involves *jouissance*) as at the broader, more general cultural and social level. Here, too, as a positive (non-neurotic) operation at the level of the drive, sublimation presupposes a successful, more or less satisfying *object* relation. But for Lacan, objects function as perpetually interchangeable signifiers. So, where can one find an object that corresponds to this kind of positive, satisfying[12] operation that is sublimation? What, in other words, turns something into an object of sublimation?

It is as a result of this question that Lacan discusses Freud's theory of sublimation for the first time. In his lesson of January 13, 1960, he invokes one of Freud's answers to this question:

> [. . .] [S]ublimation is characterized by a change of objects, or in the libido, a change that doesn't occur through the intermediary of a return to the repressed nor symptomatically, indirectly, but directly, in a way that satisfies directly. The sexual libido finds satisfaction in objects; how does it distinguish them? [Freud answers this question] [q]uite simply and massively, and in truth not without opening a field of infinite complexity: as objects that are socially valorized, objects of which the group approves, insofar as they are objects of public utility. That is how the possibility of sublimation is defined. (S7E: 94, modified translation; S7F: 113)

Because of the repression that hinders the drive from conquering the sexual object, the repressed always comes back in the form of some pathogenic symptom. Sublimation can avoid such symptom formation because the sexual object can be exchanged for an alternative object that is just as satisfying. Up to this point, Lacan agrees with Freud. But he does not agree with Freud's argument concerning why a nonsexual object can be equally satisfying. According to Freud, in the absence of explicitly sexual objects, an object can also give satisfaction for the sole reason that it is generally appreciated and held as an established value. Unable to have sexual relations, the poet hopes to achieve satisfaction later in the form of the public's acclaim for the sublime poetry where he sings of his impossible love. The nonsexual enjoyment that accompanies social or cultural recognition gets interpreted as a compensation for the individual's sexual deprivation.[13]

For Lacan, this kind of "compensation theory" is much too rash[14]—as if the social could unproblematically compensate for the individual's lack. As if the larger group's acclaim is sufficient to forge the individual's discontent into a sense of well-being.[15] In any event, Lacan's reflections on the relation between individual and community—read: between the subject of the drives and the symbolic order, the Other—presents things in a more nuanced manner. In the first place, the individual is *always already* situated in a community—or, in Lacanese, in the Other—and it is always via that Other that he obtains his drive satisfaction. Second, what he can get from the Other as remedy for his lack is, in the final analysis, equally lacking. The Other, too, is based on an irreconcilable lack. Hence what the community can give the artist or the celebrity is, in the last resort, nothing but lack. It is not by chance that fame is extremely fleeting or that the most harrowing libidinal dramas are reserved for the most successful *megastars*. The social recognition of their "sublimation" doesn't necessarily deliver greater pleasure.

Moreover, such a compensation theory seems to be based on the idea that something in the outside world can directly connect to the lack at the level of the drive. The public's acclaim is supposed to intervene decisively at the level of the artist's drive life. With this, Freud contradicts his own basic intuition, which denies any direct "natural" relation between the libido and the outside world, and therefore leads him to call the principle that "drives" the drive (namely, pleasure) polymorphous-perverse. It is no surprise then that Lacan, in this context, dwells once more on the complete absence of a "natural" relation between the "microcosm" of the drive economy and the "macrocosm" of the outside world (full of objects the helpless pleasure animal relies on; S7E: 92; S7F: 110–111). If Freud defines sublimation as a direct relation between drive and culture, Lacan asks a little further on, why does he in the very same text call it a "reaction formation,"[16] a term indicating that culture repudiates (sexual) drive and, thus, refers to repression rather than sublimation? In short, for Lacan, the criterion for what enables an object to become the center of sublimation must in no case be sought in its social valuation.

But must we then search for this criterion solely in the individual realm? Must the mechanism of sublimation be thought as laying wholly within the internal workings of the drive economy? This is, in any event, where Lacan's line of reasoning is heading when, immediately in connection with the previous idea, he claims it is only Freud's theory of narcissism and its associated "second topography" that can map out the problem of sublimation.[17]

> In truth, the problem Freud raises relative to sublimation only comes fully to light at the time of his second topography. We will have to approach that from *Zur Einführung des Narzissmus* ("On Narcissism: An Introduction"), a work that not only is an introduction to narcissism, but also the introduction to the second topopgraphy. In this text [. . .] you will find the following comment: "What we have to seek is that which now presents itself to us concerning the relations to this formulation of the ideal to sublimation. Sublimation is a process that concerns object libido." (S7E: 95, modified translation; S7F: 114)[18]

Freud thus regards sublimation here as a figure for the "object libido." According to Lacan, this new outlook offers a way of getting around the anomalies of Freud's first theory of sublimation (i.e., the compensation theory). His new theory enables him to locate the object of sublimation exclusively inside the narcissistic "microcosm." It lies in the ideal that the libidinal being must put forward in order to maintain its identity, an ideal that must be conceived as the object of narcissistic libido. Indeed, the not-directly sexual object that is capable of giving satisfaction must be a narcissistic, imaginary object. There the libido finds "itself," that is, the object that supports its entire drive economy with a positive "pleasure balance." The consistency of the desiring subject is not only the effect of an imaginary object—an *ideal ego*—but also of a symbolic object—an *ego ideal*—that the subject incessantly pushes ahead, from one signifier to another.[19] Henceforth, Lacan argues, what Freud called sublimation must be understood in terms of this new narcissistic and "object related" conception of the human libido.

Does sublimation lie, then, in the reinstallation or reparation of such a narcissistic object? This is in any event the direction that Melanie Klein's theory of sublimation heads. She interprets sublimation as a *reparation* of the object, in this case, the maternal body, in relation to which the pleasure being *"is."*[20] But according to Lacan, besides the fact that Klein fails to take the status of that object into account (whether it is imaginary, symbolic or real), he also finds it a strange idea that sublimation is supposed to "repair" something—as if sublimation is meant to connect the drive to a repressed origin after all. In this way, one again neutralizes the "scandalon" of Freud's intuition, namely, the polymorphous-perverse nature of the drive that cuts it off from any origin. And if there is one thing Lacanian psychoanalysis opposes, it is precisely this.

Is the object around which sublimation revolves to be identified with the symbolic object, then? In other words, must this Freudian concept also be conceived in terms of the primacy of the signifier? Lacan's answer to this question is affirmative. Like all Freudian concepts, for Lacan, sublimation must also be understood on the basis of that primacy. Yet this does not mean that we must regard its object as something that is *purely* symbolic. Precisely because the object refers incessantly from one signifier to another, the *ultimate* object must escape the realm of signifiers and be approached as something real. For Lacan, sublimation finds its support in the tension that is aroused between the object as a symbolic, always receding entity and the object as a real, always already lost "thing."

The object that supports sublimation belongs to the microcosm of the drive economy. In other words, it must be understood in terms of the narcissistic structure assumed by the libidinal being. But that object is neither the imaginary ideal ego, nor the symbolic ego-ideal, but the object that escapes their dialectic, and which therefore provides them with their ultimate consistency. Or, as Lacan puts it in the lesson of January 13, 1960:

> It is through this mirage [i.e., imaginary, narcissistic] relation that the notion of an object is introduced. But this object is not the same as that which is aimed at on the horizon of the instinct. Between the object as it is structured by the narcissistic relation and *das Ding*, there is a difference, and it is precisely on the slope [la pente] of that difference that the problem of sublimation is situated for us. (S7E: 98; S7F: 117)

If the mechanism of sublimation comes down to a displacement at the level of the object—the claim Lacan is defending here—this must be situated in the "slope" (the "course," the "space": "la pente") that lies between the object as an imaginary or symbolic ideal self and the object as a real "thing." The term "slope" is not without import here. It is one more indication that the drive always continues to operate *in the course of* its aim/object, without ever having access to it. The sublimated drive maintains itself in the space between the level of the imaginary and symbolic objects on the one hand, and that of the "thing" on the other. Only by operating in the space of this difference can sublimation give the drive's true nature a chance. Just prior to the passage in the next lesson (January 20, 1960) where Lacan gives his most formal definition of sublimation, he refers to this one more time:

> The sublimation that provides the *Trieb* with a satisfaction different from its aim—an aim that is still defined as its natural aim—is precisely that which reveals the true nature of the *Trieb* insofar as it is not simply instinct, but has a relation to *das Ding* as such, to the Thing insofar as it is distinct from the object. (S7E: 111; S7F: 133)

In sublimation, the true "nature" of the drive comes to light, namely, that it is not directly anchored in nature but operates according to a polymorphous-perverse distance from it. In other words, it makes clear that the drive's "nature" is unnatural. The sublimated (and therefore satisfying) figure of the drive thus reveals itself in the distance from the "thing" with which it "is" a relation. All of the objects through and by which the drive lives (as an "object relation") are marked by this distance.

This is the context in which Lacan situates his "most general definition" of sublimation. A few lines later we read:

> Thus, the most general formula that I can give you of sublimation is the following: it raises the object—and I don't mind the suggestion of a play on words in the term I use—to the dignity of the Thing. (S7E: 112; S7F: 133)

Sublimation "raises the object [. . .] to the dignity of the *thing*": a definition that is as brief as it is enigmatic. While a close reading of the context gives us a sense of how one might begin to interpret it, so far little has actually been said about it. In any case, it doesn't illuminate the contradiction that is already expressed by the terms of this "formula." How can Lacan attribute a "dignity" to the "thing"—and a *high* dignity, since the object must be "elevated"—while keeping it outside of all value by definition? For the realm of the "thing" is *jouissance* and, as such, exceeds the order of all values and goods. Perhaps this is why Lacan draws his audience's attention to the word play that enables one to hear the German-sounding "*Dingität* (or *Dingheit*) in the French word "dignité," as if he was trying thereby to soften gravity of his "formula" and give it an ironic twist. Anyway, it seems to be in keeping with one of the examples Lacan uses elsewhere to illustrate his concept of sublimation. The object Jacques Prévert "elevates to the dignity of the thing" is nothing other than a series of banal, empty match boxes placed end on end to decorate his room, as Lacan comments in his lesson of January 20, 1960 (S7E: 114: S7F: 136; Wajcman, 1999: 53–54).

The contradictions in Lacan's definition of sublimation are not limited solely to the formula alone. Particularly because the term "sublimation" sometimes applies to the most divergent things, the concept seems to empty itself out. Not only are religion, art, and science sublimations (S7E: 130; S7F: 155), ethics too (S7E: 87; S7F: 105), or concepts such as the drive and death principle[21] and even Freudian psychoanalysis as such (S7E: 214; S7F: 253) are given this label. There are so many that it seems the term can guarantee little conceptual power. And yet, this is not a reason to set it aside as meaningless, for it contains the contradictions and paradoxes that reveal the most crucial problematic of the whole of Lacanian psychoanalysis.

This is why it is worth reflecting more on this concept if we are to follow Lacan's not-always evident train of thought. To penetrate what Lacan has in mind with his concept of sublimation, we must look explicitly at the example he uses so strikingly often to illustrate it, namely, courtly love.[22]

## 3. Courtly Love

### 3.1. "Fin'Amor" . . .

Nearly every time Lacan brings up the topic of sublimation, he refers explicitly to courtly love. He already did so when he introduced the topic without mentioning it by name (S7E: 84; S7F: 101–102; see above 7.1), and he does so in the lessons where he develops the concept. He even readily admits afterward that it was not without cause he highlighted precisely courtly love as the first example of sublimation.[23] Similarly, his critical "formula" of sublimation (just-cited) is immediately followed by the first more developed reflection on courtly love:

> [. . .] it [i.e., sublimation] raises the object [. . .] to the dignity of the Thing. That is significant, for example, in relation to something that I alluded to at the limit of our discussion, something I will get to next time, the sublimation of the feminine object. The whole theory of the *Minne* or of courtly love has, in effect, been decisive. Although it has completely disappeared nowadays from the sociological sphere, courtly love has nevertheless left traces in an unconscious that is sustained by a whole literature, a whole imagery, that we continue to in

habit as far as our relations with women are concerned. (S7E: 112; S7F: 133–134)

The "object" raised to "the dignity of the *thing*" is directly illustrated by the object courtly love puts in the center of its particular eroticism.

We do not have to take it pejoratively that the word "object" in this context refers to woman. Here Lacan is only alluding to the fact that in almost all traditional cultures (concerning love relations or marriage agreements), the woman is assigned the place of a (passive) object rather than of an (active) subject. Generally, the latter falls to the man. In marriage cultures without free partner choice, the man is said to marry while the woman *is given in marriage*. Even in a culture with free partner choice, the woman remains the one who *is* courted, seduced, and *taken*, while the man is more commonly given an active role. In order to increase the power of his object-directed theory of sublimation, Lacan thus reaches back to a phenomenon which, for the first time in our (Western) history—and with positive consequences—touches fundamentally on the traditional object position of woman. From a male-dominated "object," woman becomes an "object" that now dominates men.[24] Inside a fully feudal culture that saw woman reduced to a matrimonial object of exchange,[25] a new, courtly culture suddenly created a position for her that completely broke away from that marriage economy and, in time, even forced the existing marriage culture into a specific historical direction.

The influence of courtly love undeniably stretches into our time and therefore—and solely therefore—plays a part in everyone's unconscious.[26] Still, Lacan refers in the first place to a *historical* phenomenon, namely, the highly erotically tinged courtly culture of "fin'amor":[27] a refined form of erotic culture that sprung up with the Provencal and Aquitanian troubadours of the twelfth century, and that disappeared again several decades later following the destruction of this area (during the crusade against the Cathars, 1208–1215).[28] The direct influence of "courtly love" on the rest of Western Europe, the *trouvères* culture in Northern France, as well as that of the *Minnesänger* in the German Empire only lasted until the first quarter of the thirteenth century (S7E: 145; S7F: 174).

In the midst of a harsh feudal culture where the woman was primarily a matrimonial object, necessary for reproduction and (thus) for the continuation of the family estate, a culture unexpectedly burgeoned forth where that same woman became the center of a lifestyle that was as playful as it was refined, and whose influence covered all aspects of existence. Even though the woman in the new culture still remained a legal wife as well as, in this respect, her husband's "possession" (and thus the guarantee that his property will remain within the family), nevertheless an explicitly erotic culture blossomed up around her where young troubadours and jongleurs courted her and sang their love for her in frank terms. However, this doesn't mean that they intended to marry her at all costs. On the contrary, most of them held her husband and master in more than the usual esteem. It was, after all, often at his invitation that they were guests at his feudal seat and paid as jongleurs. Still, this did not prevent the love-sick troubadour from competing with undisguised erotic seriousness for his Lady's favor. Neither did it prevent him from loving other mistresses, nor from having his own family with a legal wife.[29]

In other words, here we are dealing not so much with an amorous sensibility as such, as with a highly nuanced, long-drawn-out culture, rich in reflections, rules, and methods for stylizing and refining that sensibility. While every courtly lover dreamed of spending a night with his Lady,[30] his entire culture of courtly love was designed to make that night, if not impossible, then at least postponed for as long as possible.[31] This is why he must first "deserve" his lady's love which, given the highly codified nature of that love, was no easy thing to do. The sovereign place assigned to the woman in this code obliged the lover to approach her with both the most ardent desire and the greatest caution. It was above all his "duty" to immediately acquiesce to her most capricious whims and commands. These, too, were prescribed by the code of courtly love—recall the "love trials" and the so-called *asag*—and may not be shirked, no matter how impossible to execute they were.[32] It is courtly love's very nature to make the *asag*—and the entire code—particularly difficult, since this confirmed the inaccessible place of the Lady. The code was nothing other than a "scholastics of unhappy love" where the love object is cultivated as if she were already lost and mourned by the courtly lover (S7E: 146; S7F: 175).

But again, courtly love was a culture that had not so much to do with the feeling as such as with the stylization and refined forms to which it gave rise. The hallmark of the courtly lover lay not so much in the authenticity of his sentiment as in the degree of artistry with which he was able to express his desire for his inaccessible Lady. Courtly love was an "art," not a feeling. It was a clearly artificial mode of life, love, and desire, three things that were interchangeable for the ideal "construct" of courtly culture. For this reason, too, the unshrinking fidelity that bound the courtly lover to his Lady was simultaneously both stronger and weaker than the marriage bond. It was stronger because, aside from any marriage and hence property-economies, it testified to a radical disinterestedness and selflessness. But it was at the same time weaker insofar as the lover was never really bound to her. For that, courtly love was too artificial, and too easily exchangeable for a still greater fidelity to an even more sublime Lady. Guilhem IX of Aquitaine (Count of Poitiers, 1071–1126), for instance, the first-known troubadour in history, was in fact a Don Juan–like womanizer, while his poetry literally makes a great song and dance about fidelity to the one and only inaccessible Lady. Even a glimpse of real infidelity makes an appearance in his poetry, albeit never without being "sublimated" and refined, thus emphasizing the internal tension in the courtly love grammar as such.[33]

Seen from this perspective, it does not matter whether the famous *cours d'amour*—the "female court" that passed judgment on matters of courtly love—is a matter of historical accuracy, as Andreas Capellanus suggests in his *De amore* (written around 1185), one of our preeminent sources for the study of *fin'amor*.[34] If this was indeed so, these "courts" function as a game, intended in the first place to entertain. In any case, at no moment do they bring the accepted marriage laws into question. Courtly love must thus be primarily regarded as an artistic—and hence artificial—"construction," a set of "artifices," as Lacan puts it (S7E: 151; S7F: 180).[35] Nevertheless, it will be precisely on this aspect that he will lay the ethical significance of this courtly love culture. And since, for him, courtly love functions as a prototype of sublimation, he will attribute the ethical dimension of everything that is called sublimation primarily to that artificial nature. However, let us first look at what Lacan has in mind when he calls courtly love a sublimation.

### 3.2. . . . and Sublimation

As always, Lacan's point of departure here is the primacy of the signifier, which is why he places so much emphasis on the artificial character of courtly love. In his eleventh lesson, for example, where he examines this topic at some length, he asserts:

> On this subject all the historians agree: courtly love was, in brief, a poetic exercise, a way of playing with a number of conventional, idealizing themes, which couldn't have any real concrete equivalent. Nevertheless, these ideals, first among which is that of the Lady, are to be found in subsequent periods, down to our own. The influence of these ideals is a highly concrete one in the organization of contemporary man's sentimental attachments, and it continues its forward march. Moreover, march is the right word because it finds its point of origin in a certain systematic and deliberate use of the signifier as such. [. . .] Of interest to us from a structural point of view is the fact that an activity of poetic creation was able to exercise a determining influence on manners at the time[36] [twelfth century]—and subsequently in its historical consequences—when the origin and the key concepts of the whole business [i.e., of courtly love] had been forgotten. (S7E: 148–149; S7F: 177–178)

Lacan does not explain how courtly love has influenced both our marriage ethics and our morality in general, let alone how it has elevated mutual love into a conditio sine qua non for marriage relations. He does not even introduce sufficient elements for a first attempt at such a sketch.[37] But he does venture a hypothesis regarding the origin of this ethically significant change. This, he claims here, has everything to do with "an activity of poetic creation," with a specific "systematic and deliberate use of the signifier as such."

Once again, the whole point of Lacan's thesis lies in the final addition, "the signifier *as such*." At the turn of the twelfth century, the status of the "female object" changed, not by giving her another *real* position (she stayed more than ever man's "possession" and "object"), but by playing consciously with the signifier that makes this position possible. The entire fixed field of signifiers that made woman "what she was" in this culture was shaken up, and became the stakes of a creative poetic game. Just as much as the rediscovered intimacy of erotic desire (the yearning for love), the crude social reality (the woman as guarantor of inheritance and property) was brought back to what Lacan calls its true ground: the autonomously operating field of signifiers. The poetic revolution of courtly love reworked, rearranged, remodeled, and refurbished the set of signifiers that regulated sexual difference at that time. The troubadour, as a jongleur, juggled with words, and, "out of nothing"—*ex nihilo*—created a new culture. Courtly love thus does not stem from a supposed medieval "soul" ("the famous great soul of the blessed Middle Ages"; S7E: 112; S7F: 134), nor from a mystical experience akin to those of Hindu or Tibetan cultures, as Denis de Rougemont, one of Lacan's sources, claims.[38] It is an *artificial* creation, a *poetic* insurrection incited by a small "literary circle," a revolution at the level of the signifier and, in this capacity only, does it influence marriage morality or ethics and culture in general by way of a "veritable social epidemic" (S7E: 126; S7F: 151).

All cultural renewals—and in this sense, all of culture itself too—are thus, in Lacan's eyes, the results of sublimation in the sense of what he repeatedly calls a "façonnement du signifiant," a "fashioning" (retooling, styling, modeling) of the signifier.[39] In this sense, all cultural realizations—including ethics—come down to a "creation ex nihilo," that is, to signifiers that, thanks to their "negative" power, can break with what exists—and with the real as such—so as to call something new into life purely on the basis of their autonomous operation.[40]

When Lacan defines sublimation as the "elevation of an object to the dignity of *das Ding*," this implies first that the object in question has the status of a signifier. The fact that it involves the "elevation" of the woman in courtly love is not because she represents an absolute value in herself but precisely because she *does not*. In other words, it is because she is an arbitrary, displaceable, signifier that is interchangeable by definition. But precisely for this reason, she can, at a certain moment, be "elevated" above all other signifiers and become the central value of a renewed symbolic system. Because such a system has no real ground, "woman" can become the signifier in which that system reconstructs its own consistency. Furthermore, this single signifier also bears the clearest traces of this break with the real. It is as if in this signifier one can still feel this break, Lacan suggests. In other words, it is as though at this place the real still noticeably "suffers" under the gesture by which the signifier broke with it. In this sense, the "supreme value" that an entire symbolic universe depends on—in courtly culture, for example, the Lady—is marked by the real, by the "thing," by "that which in the real suffers from the signifier" as Lacan formulates it repeatedly here.[41]

This is why this kind of supreme value—the sublimated object—locates itself strictly *outside* the symbolic system. The Lady is literally "absolute" (from the Latin verb "absolvere": to set free, to disconnect) and "transcendent": she is beyond the acceptable, she transgresses the normal. Lacan alludes to this when he says that an object is elevated "to the dignity of the 'thing,' " a "thing" that by definition falls outside the field of signifiers but around which, as the "extimate" center, everything rallies. Whence the unassailable position assigned to the Lady of courtly love.[42] But whence, too, the *empty, stereotypical* impression she makes. In the lover's perception, she functions not as a concrete person but as an empty ideal. She has become a pure signifier that all the other signifiers derive their meaning from, but which itself signifies only "itself"—and therefore nothing. She provides sense to every gesture, every feeling, every word of the courtly poet, while emptying herself of all content. This is the case for all sublimations: the elevated "object" in whose light everything else acquires sense is itself empty and senseless. This is how sublimation functions at the unconscious level. At the conscious level, the sublimated significance is felt precisely as the utmost meaning and ultimate value.

From a structural perspective, sublimation is thus purely the result or, better, the creation of the autonomous operating signifier. It is as if sublimation corroborates the monotheistic myth that everything was created by the word—and hence "out of nothing". As a "creation ex nihilo," sublimation in fact repeats the primary cut of the signifier in the real. Again, a signifier brings a difference, a lack, an emptiness into the indifferent real onto which a new autonomously operating system can graft itself.[43] However, this system is incapable of filling in the lack it has introduced into the real, and is therefore, in its turn, plagued by that real as if with an irreconcilable lack. The term for that real lack is the "thing" and the sublimated object is "raised to the dignity of the thing."

In this sense, a sublimation creates the "*ex*timate" center of a symbolic system. Just as a jar is only a jar insofar as it gives form to the emptiness inside it (an image Lacan borrows from Heidegger) so, too, can a symbolic system only maintain itself thanks to an "internal outside" around which it incessantly revolves. However, one must realize that, as the "essence" of a jar lies in its emptiness, this emptiness can no longer be conceived as a substance in itself to which "attributes" can then be ascribed. On the contrary, in this case, the attributes *predate*, as it were, the entire ontological process, so as to *retroactively* create the "jar." In an essay that bears precisely the title of "Das Ding," and to which Lacan explicitly refers here (S7E: 120; S7F: 145), Heidegger describes this inversion of the ordinary (metaphysical) way of thinking of the jar (this "Destruktion" of what is classically called its "essence"). One does not "first" have the thing, in the sense of something original that, then, is given form by the symbolic reality. "First" is the (by definition) unoriginal signifier. The signifying cut only *retroactively* turns the real into the emptiness that gives the floating corps of signifiers its stabilizing center; this, at least, is how Lacan interprets the Heideggerian idea.[44]

In other words, it is not that one first sees an intrinsic value in the Lady, around which a courtly universe is subsequently constructed. Rather, according to Lacan, one first discovers that the woman and all other values in a culture are (only) signifiers, sliding entities in a universe that in itself offers no foothold. It is only by allowing all existing values and norms to "float" that a center becomes vacant in the midst of this cultural storm that can serve as an anchoring point for this unstable universe. The sublimation of the female object lies in artificially associating the signifier "Lady" with this type of "extimate" (beyond the signifier) center, this "thing" in the middle of the rotating whirl of signifiers.

The usual psychoanalytic interpretation of sublimation is that it involves a more or less successful satisfaction of pleasure. While he is not insensible to the neurotic appetites testified to by the courtly love poets, still, for Lacan, courtly love *as such* is not a neurotic affliction that threatens to drag the individual under the vicissitudes of his pleasure economy. Rather, like other forms of sublimation, courtly love is a solution to this type of problem. In this, Lacan undeniably follows Freud's line on the concept. By "raising an object to the dignity of *das Ding*," a sublimation such as courtly love can proffer the pleasure animal a more or less adequate answer to the desire that it *is*. However, such an "elevation" of the object amounts in the first place to an emptying of it. Precisely because "in this poetic field, the female object is stripped of all real substance," as Lacan puts it in his lesson of February 10, 1960, sublimation can provide an answer to the demand that in the most fundamental sense of the word we *are* (S7E: 149; S7F: 179). And we must take the word "demand" here in the "technical" sense the term has acquired in Lacanian psychoanalysis. Only then does his conclusion become somewhat clear:

> Here we see functioning in the pure state the authority of that place the instinct [la visée tendentielle] aims for in sublimation. This is to say that, that what man demands, what he cannot help but demand, is to be deprived of something real. And one of you, in explaining to me what I am trying to show in *das Ding*, referred to it neatly as the vacuole. [. . .] Were, in effect, is the vacuole created for us? It is at the centre of the signifiers—insofar as that final demand to be deprived of something real is essentially linked to the primary symbolization which is wholly contained in the signification of the gift of love. (S7E: 150; S7F: 179)

What does sublimation give the demanding libidinal animal? An empty place, a void. It does not give us the desired "object" itself, the "thing" we seek; it refers us solely to the place where the object lies and, further, keeps this place explicitly empty. Sublimation must thus be strictly distinguished from *jouissance*. There, the libidinal being takes possession of the thing, albeit not without disappearing as a subject in this process. Sublimation, on the other hand, manages to keep the subject intact and gives it, if not the "thing," then at least a signifier that covers over the empty place of that absent "thing." What the subject *demands* of sublimation is the (imaginary) fullness of love (that is, the filling in of its lack). What the subject *gets* from it is the paradoxical fact that it will be perpetually deprived of something: the real "thing." Only in this way does it give us what we in fact demand: our (symbolic) desire, that is, the polymorphous-perverse openness that we are the bearers of, an openness that does indeed have an aim but will never reach its destination. That aim is the singular "thing" desire seeks; it is that which is desired in every object because no object can give it. This hard, "objectal" negative, this thinglike openness acquires a satisfying form in sublimation, affirming desire in a positive, bearable fashion. In this way, the human pleasure animal gets the one thing it can live off: a gift that continually gives *nothing*, and therefore stimulates its desire.

But along with this "thinglike" nothing, sublimation simultaneously gives an "artifice," an artificial element. The sublime *nothing* it hands to us implies first and foremost an entire torrent of signifiers that enables us to keep the place where this "nothing" is given to us empty. In this sense, Lacan can suggest, it is as though, in courtly love, the signifier "Lady" "colonizes" the "field of the Thing" as it were (S7E: 99; S7F:

119). That signifier occupies the place of the "thing" and draws the courtly lover's desire toward it. But instead of granting him access to that domain, the "Lady" simultaneously functions as a hindrance, a terrifying "doom" that deters him from it. In this way, the domain of the "thing" remains empty.[45] Constantly groping for still more signifiers, the courtly lover perpetually circles *around* his Lady. No matter how unsatisfying it seems –and how removed it is from what takes place in *enjoyment*—this process keeps desire alive (albeit never more than temporarily) without putting the individual at risk. It is in this sense that sublimation offers a satisfying solution to the unstable drive economy.

## 4. Culture as Sublimation

### 4.1. Culture . . .

Sublimation comprises the basis for the wider, more general field of "culture." Following Freud, Lacan distinguishes three subcategories of culture: art, religion, and science, which stem respectively from ethical, religious, and scientific sublimations. In the already-cited passage from his tenth lesson where he calls on the earlier Freudian text, he links this "healthy" drive vicissitude to its pathological counterparts, namely, hysteria, obsessional neurosis, and paranoia.[46]

The process described in courtly love is characteristic of an *aesthetic* sublimation.[47] The beauty with which desire allows itself to be seduced functions as a veil that suggests something sublime behind it without ever actually showing it. It is as if the beautiful simultaneously blinds one to what it implies will be unveiled. The ravishing Lady sets the lover's heart on fire but the entire courtly code is designed to make her beauty operate as a veil that will never be removed. In this sense, aesthetic sublimation has something of hysteria about it, Lacan says in a previously described passage (S7E: 130; S7F: 155). However, this is the "healthy" side of hysteria, not the side that succumbs to repression. Refusing all concrete content of desire, leaving every ultimate object as empty and unfilled as possible, consciously organizing the entire desiring trajectory around a void so as to keep it infinitely alive: these are features of both hysteria and aesthetic sublimation. It is as if courtly love reforges—sublimates—the hysterical procedure as a conscious form of culture. The void that makes the hysteric suffering becomes the stakes in a controlled and refined *fin'amor* in the case of the courtly love poet.[48] In aesthetic sublimation, the hysteric's pain in feeling the weight of desire's lack becomes a richly creative process or a gripping aesthetic experience. Yet, in a way, beauty has an identical function to the hysteric's symptomatic pain. In one and the same movement, it keeps the desiring subject both aimed at and away from the "thing." And in the same gesture, the courtly lover cultivates his cherished "Lady" into a "doom" that forever denies him the "thing" he seeks. Beauty is both the allure that attracts desire and the dazzling blindness it recoils from.

Aesthetic sublimation is not the only form of sublimation. Religion, too, is a type of sublimation for Lacan, albeit as the "healthy" reverse of obsessional neurosis, according to that same passage from his tenth lesson (S7E: 130; S7F: 155). As he cites from a draft Freud sent to Fliess, the primal scene of obsessional neurosis stems from an experience of an "excess of pleasure" that must be warded off at all costs. The obsessional then organizes his desire around a supposed fullness toward which he feels guilty and worthless. No matter how much he wishes to redeem this guilt, the obsessional thoughts that plague him only increase it, forcing him to institute still more defense mechanisms. Where the hysteric could still place the lack in the desired object, in the obsessional neurotic it lies entirely in himself. The obsessional idea that it is he, rather than the Other, who falls short is a way of avoiding the fact that it is in the first place the Other who is marked by lack. Yet, while the obsessional feels this as a terrible weight, religious sublimation delivers humans from such suffering, even if it acts in a similar way. The scrupulously regulated (and hence easily transgressed) rituals, the fantasies of an inaccessible, heavenly realm absent of all lack, the guilt that increases the more we think we can escape it: these are features common to both obsessional neurosis and religion. In religion, however, they are accompanied with no painful effects. There, they prevent people from succumbing to the anomalies of their by definition unstable drive economy. By burdening the domain of the "thing" with all kinds of divine prerogatives, religion keeps it at bay, and thus reserves the necessary space desire needs to flourish. But this very veil of holiness and divinity, on the other hand, keeps that same desire aimed at the impossible "thing" and in this way gives it the requisite consistency.

On the same page (S7E: 130; S7F: 155), Lacan distinguishes yet a third form of sublimation: science. From the days of ancient wisdom, crossing the long philosophical tradition and arriving at the different kinds of scientism of our day: from a libidinal perspective, these are all ways of keeping the domain of the "thing" out of consideration by way of a stubborn "disbelief." They each have something of the paranoiac's way of imagining himself to be the master of reality, Lacan says, plucking again from Freud's same text to Fliess. The paranoiac does not believe in the trauma with which he wrestles, something that, in the final analysis, is also true for the "thing" that traumatically attracts and deters him. The paranoid ideas that typically give him his inalienable certainty are all part of a strategy for foreclosing the "thing's" existence. "Foreclosing" here has a specific meaning, distinguished from "repression." In the two previous neurotic forms, the finitude of our grasp of reality (the impossibility of ever reaching the "thing") is *repressed*, and to this extent in a way also confirmed. Both in their own ways, the hysteric and the obsessional reserve a *space* for the "lack" and (hence) for desire (albeit an empty, "*extimate*" space). The paranoiac, on the other hand, forecloses this empty realm of the "thing" and imagines that his grasp of reality is complete. The same "disbelief" in the structural limitations of desire is also characteristic of science, according to Lacan. While science, too, relates to the domain of the "thing," it does so in a strictly negative way. Here is how Lacan puts it in his lesson of February 3, 1960:

> The discourse of science repudiates [the perspective and[49]] the presence of the Thing insofar as from its point of view [i.e., from this repudiation] the ideal of absolute knowledge is glimpsed, that is, something that posits the Thing while it pays no attention to it. [. . .] The discourse of science is determined by this *Verwerfung* [. . .]. (S7E: 131; S7F: 157)

Believing in the omnipotence of the signifier (an omnipotence that has indeed taken on massive proportions with the mathematization of the modern world, see above: 3.1.1), for science there is only one unknown: that which it doesn't *yet* know, and thus imagines it *will* one day *be able* to know. Its perspective is thus nothing less than "absolute knowledge," as Lacan calls it here with Hegel. With this kind of "madness," science remains blind to the structurally unknowable and unconscious support on which its entire knowledge is based and which Lacan conceives here in terms of the domain of the "thing."

But being no less a sublimation than art or religion, science enables us to deal with our desire in a "healthy," satisfying way. Its "disbelief" is way of giving form to our relation to that distant "thing" in a manner that saves us from individual neuroses. "Foreclosing" the "thing" also keeps the place of the ultimate reference point of our desire empty and, in this way, keeps desire perpetually alive. However, through its obstinate belief, this kind of sublimation ensures that such a "thing" doesn't exist and that, in other words, "nothing" escapes its grasp.[50] Rather, it has unconsciously expelled that unruly "thinglike nothing" in advance, and thus kept the place of that voidlike "thing" open. Science speaks of reality as if it is (at least virtually) master of it but it can do so only because it has kept this point of mastery—the ultimate "object" it desires—open in advance. Ultimately, it is only for this reason that science can maintain "itself," that is, the desire that it *is*. Science is thus also a way of enabling us to see the "object relation" we *are* in all of its paradoxes. As a result of this type of sublimation, man imagines himself lord and master of reality, yet he continues to yearn for a still greater mastery. It is as if he is simultaneously the object he seeks *and* his relation to that object. In short, the scientific sublimation permits him to be the "bearer" of the distance toward the "thing." In other words, it makes it possible for a libidinal being to realize itself as the "subject of desire."

This is true of every sublimation. Aesthetic, religious or scientific, all sublimations enable us to give what is in principle the impossible object relation with which we correspond a form that is nevertheless livable. They centralize the object and thereby confirm how fundamentally dependent the (in-itself totally helpless) pleasure animal is upon an object outside itself. At the same time, they clearly keep that same object *at a distance* and in this way guarantee the irreconcilable relation that we "are" toward that object. The way an aesthetic sublimation achieves this is by seducing us with a beauty that constantly slips away from us. A religious sublimation achieves this by demanding such immense respect for a deity that we cannot help but disappoint, with the result that we owe him even more respect. Science achieves this by remaining blind to the fact that what, from its perspective, it characterizes as an absolute knowledge only exists precisely because that absolute knowledge—in the shape of the "thing"—has been excluded from its purview in advance. In short, the entire cultural field in the broadest sense of the word (including more contemporary phenomena such as sport, relaxation, amusement, work, social work, and suchlike) is a field of sublimations that enable us to avoid the individual neuroses and to more or less successfully give form to the impossible pleasure animals that we are.

## 4.2. . . . and Its "Polymorphous-Perverse" Foundation

By the same token, this also means that, at the most fundamental level, man is only connected to his culture precisely *because* it stems from sublimations. We cling to our culture, not only because it is of vital assistance to us, but primarily because its sublimations allow us to deal with our *desire*. And this occurs not because sublimations give full satisfaction to our desire but precisely because they don't; because they only *keep us dangling*, and delude us into thinking our desire *will someday be* satisfied. It is as if culture, precisely in its quality of sublimation, is able to lie when it comes to desire, enabling us to go on desiring in a more or less satisfying manner. It is as though, precisely in its capacity as sublimation, culture is able to tell us lies with enough imagination and promise such that we make peace with the discontent that haunts us. At the end of his lesson of January 13, 1960, the first full reference to the problem of sublimation, Lacan says:

> At the level of sublimation the object is inseparable from imaginary and especially cultural elaborations. It is not just that the collectivity recognizes in them useful objects [i.e., objects of common interests]; it finds rather a space of relaxation [*champs de détente*] where it may in a way delude itself on the subject of *das Ding* [*se leurrer sur* das Ding], colonize the field of *das Ding* with imaginary schemes. That is how collective, socially accepted sublimations operate. Society takes some comfort from the mirages that moralists, artists, artisans, designers of dresses and hats, and the creators of imaginary forms in general supply it with. But it is not simply in the approval that society gladly accords it that we must seek the power of sublimation. It is rather in an imaginary function, and, in particular, that for which we will use the symbolization of the phantasm ($ \$ \lozenge a $), which is the form on which depends the subjects desire. (S7E: 99: S7F: 118–119)

Collective and other forms of sublimations "work" because they accommodate not so much what we need in order to live but our unconscious fantasies. They conjure up the object of our fantasies, the ultimate object from which all our desire stems, and keep us fixated at that imaginary level. In sublimation, we dangle a lure in front of ourselves ("*se leurrer*") and delude ourselves with visions of a fata morgana we can yearn for, thereby sustaining our desire. Culture may thus have no real foundation—as the creation of a polymorphous-perverse libido it may well be built "on nothing"—nevertheless, it is precisely for this reason that it is more or less able to satisfy the libidinal being. It is precisely this that makes it compatible with the drive that, at the most fundamental (i.e., *real*) level, never reaches its object but only circles around it.

In the same way, the satisfaction offered by ethics comes back, in the final analysis, to the fact that it has something of an artificial illusion about it. According to Lacan, it derives from a "morally fabricated hallucination," and only in this capacity is it satisfying. It is only to the extent that, as a "creation ex nihilo," it is not a fixed entity that it appeals to the "free space" that divides man from the object his drive (as an object relation) aims at. In the final analysis, desire discovers its most fundamental support only in this "space" (this "distance," this "gap"). Sublimation grasps this gap in an imaginary way through an image (a "mirage," an illusion, a hallucination). If it installs an object (a signifier) in the center of this "free space," it is not in order to subdue desire but rather to make it circle around it more intensely. Sublimation can give desire the satisfying feeling that it has got (an imaginary) hold of its ultimate object while at the same time maintaining a distance from it. The mere glimpse of his Lady already brings the courtly lover into ecstatic enjoyment[51] while, nonetheless, his desire continues unabated. Solely this "illusion," solely this "earliest" truth-founding lie provides the ultimate guarantee that his desire will have the space it needs.[52] To the extent that this "free space" acquires form in our moral values, these values escape the neurotic activity that desire so often generates and we are able to experience desire in a more or less satisfying way. It is only this kind of open space that permits our drives to function in a more or less "healthy" fashion inside culture without succumbing to the frequently neurotic demands emerging from it.

Culture proffers itself as a law. As a helpless, libidinal creature, man is irrevocably dependent on this law (or, what comes down to the same thing, on the symbolic order). It is the sole element that can guarantee our existence as desiring beings. But in the final analysis, what the law offers is an "open space" *beyond* itself, a space that permits us to transgress the law, if only phantasmatically. What binds us to culture, what binds us mutually in culture to others, is the transgressive space of our fantasies. Desire's ultimate guarantee is not the universe of signifiers that lends it its indispensable law, but an object that lies *beyond* it. Culture can stand in for this guarantee because it stems from sublimations, from signifiers or objects that it has rendered in the place of that transgressive "thing." Such an object elevated to the level of the "thing" not only provides an ultimate reference point for the whole drive economy; sublimation also keeps the space around that "thing" open and free so that desire, too, can move around freely in a realm that escapes the symbolic law. Sublimation's incapability to absolutize an object to a "thing" is thus meant to give desire free space, that is, a space where it performs a certain freedom vis-à-vis the symbolic law (however indispensable that law is).

Note that while culture may stem from sublimations, sublimation as such is an *active* process whose satisfying effect is owed to this aspect. Once established, it loses much of its sublimating power and its chances of operating neurotically increase. Sublimations only provide satisfaction to the extent that they are perceived in their transgressive dimensions. It is as if by perceiving a (religious, artistic, scientific) value, we simultaneously perceive its "foundation," its "creation ex nihilo" and thus sense the way it springs from a realm where our desire proceeds *beyond* the law and circles around an ungraspable and (in this sense) absolute "thing." Only in this way does it become compatible with the most fundamental structure of the drive: a pulsating movement where everything revolves *around* a central, empty "thing." In this way, a cultural value is brought back to the polymorphous-perverse starting point from which the human libidinal creature perceives it. Courtly love's sublimation springs not so much from the lover's authentic love as from the play of fidelity and transgression set down by the courtly code. It is only thanks to this "perverse" *play* with the law that he encounters the frequencies of his most fundamental drive structure and is able to bind himself to his "culture" with a fully libidinal stake.

As I mentioned, in the final lesson of his sixth seminar where he announces the theme of the following seminar (the "ethics of psychoanalysis"),[53] Lacan already explicitly talks about "sublimation" in the transgressive, even "perverse" sense that we have traced here. "Culture," he says in this context, is not purely the means by which an individual fits himself into a society but is also something that authorizes a mobile *counter* "dialectic." Of course, man is dependent on society. He is so already as a "sujet logique," as Lacan formulates it here, as a logical subject, as the "bearer" *of* the *logos*, that is, of the linguistic, symbolic Other (Lacan, 1999a: 538). But this doesn't prevent this society, precisely through the agency of the individual, from having an inclination towards "entropy" and dissolution, since the individual always sets himself in opposition to its norms at the same time (ibidem). Although society offers models with which he must inevitably identify, he remains at the same time recalcitrant toward them. It is precisely in this "protest" that desire reveals itself most clearly, that is, in the polymorphous-perverse nonconformity the human drive stems from:

> What, in the society, presents itself as culture [. . .] is something that establishes a movement, a dialectic, which opens the same gap inside of which we try to situate desire. It is in that sense we can qualify what is produced as perversion, i.e., as the reflection, the objection on the level of the logical subject, of what the subject undergoes on the level of identification, insofar as identification is the relation which commands, which establishes the standards of social stabilisation [. . .]."[54]

It is in this context that the term "sublimation" appears a couple of lines farther on:

> In the sense that we could say that something is established as an interaction [circuit tournant] between what we could call conformism [. . .] [and] perversion, insofar this [i.e. perversion] represents [. . .] all that, in conformisation, performs as protest in the proper dimension of desire as the relation of the subject towards its being—this is the famous sublimation

about which we maybe will talk next year. For this is truly
the most extreme notion, the most justified of all what I am
presenting to you [. . .].[55]

Note how Lacan's subsequent formulation of sublimation can already
clearly be seen here. Sublimation concerns the relation of the desiring
subject toward his "being," that is, to the real (the "thing") that lies
*beyond* the (symbolic) world of signifiers in which it moves. This relation
is explicitly linked here with the subject's "perversion" and its "protest,"
that is, with the way in which the subject falls short in his identification
with the Other that he needs for survival (i.e., with the models and
norms that society supplies him with). Sublimation must be framed in
a "circuit," an "interaction" between conforming to the norm, on the
one hand, and a "perverse" (inverting all norms) "protest" on the other.
This interaction reveals how desire forms the basis for culture and its
norms; how it, too, in the final analysis is founded in the polymorphous-
perverse pleasure animal that is man. This is what connects culture and
sublimation: both show that the subject's immersion in the symbolic order
nevertheless leaves open a "free space" that allows this "protest," making
it precisely for this reason possible for the subject to circulate in that order
as a *radical desire*. For this reason, sublimation allows the subject to be
interpellated into society in a more or less satisfying way. It is able to
keep the interaction between "conformity" and "perversion" sufficiently
livable that the subject can conform to the law without relinquishing the
radical desire that he "is."

## 5. Sublimation and Ethics

### 5.2. Sublimation versus "Perversion"

Lacan remains completely faithful to what he said at the end of his sixth
seminar. His investigation into "desire and its interpretation" (*"Le désir
et son interprétation,"* the title of that seminar) concludes that also at the
macrolevel of culture, desire (as well as the polymorphous-perverse drive
structure it stems from) remains the most basic factor. It is no surprise,
then, that in his following seminar that same sublimation plays a crucial
role. It will deliver a concept that enables him to avoid having to define
the "ethics of desire" entirely at the microlevel of the psychoanalytic
cure, but also let it apply to the wider level of culture. One must understand a culture's values as "objects elevated to the status of a *thing*," as
signifiers that thus come to occupy the "*ex*timate" empty place around
which the entire drive economy revolves and in this way keep desire alive.

The reason why ethical laws and obligations do not necessarily have to be neurotic, neither at the microlevel nor at the macrolevel, is because they stem from a sublimation, that is, from an imaginary structure that is linked to the polymorphous-perverse nature of our most fundamental drive-life: an interminable revolving around a "thing" with which we "are" an (object) relation.

Still, it is worth looking more closely at a passage in Lacan's seventh seminar where he talks explicitly about this strange interweaving of sublimation, perversion and ethics. This will show that the confrontation of sublimation with the ethical problematic will force further refinements of Lacan's reflections on "perversion." Here he lays the basis for what will later become a specific theory of perversion, where the term can no longer be confused with "polymorphous-perverse" but, instead, indicates one of the three major psychic structures (alongside neurosis and psychosis).

The passage in question is from his lesson of January 20, 1960. At a certain moment, he emphasizes the contingent, "historical" nature of sublimation, which he therefore characterizes as something "cultural" rather than "collective" or "individual," that is, as something through which the individual's recalcitrant singularity carves itself "dialectically" into the collective. It would be difficult for anyone who had attended the final lesson of his sixth seminar to hear Lacan's use of the term "culture" here in a neutral way:

> You don't paint in Picasso's time as you painted in Velazquez's; you don't write a novel in 1930 as you did in Stendhal's time. This is an absolute essential fact that does not for the time being need to be located under the rubric of the collectivity or the individual. Let's say we will place it [i.e., sublimation] under the rubric of culture, for what we question here is precisely its relation to society—i.e., what satisfaction society can find in it.[56] The problem of sublimation is there, of sublimation insofar as it creates a certain number of forms, among which art is not alone, [. . .]. (S7E: 107, modified translation; S7F: 128–129)

As a sublimation, art comes into being in a context where individuals extricate themselves from the accepted demands of society while nevertheless producing things in which that society can subsequently recognize itself. However, as Lacan suggests here, art is only one of the sublimations for which this applies. It is just as applicable for ethics Lacan argues later. Ethics, too, stems from a contingent, historical moment during which an individual goes outside the existing ethical order so as to create, as if from nothing, a new moral value. If society subsequently recognizes itself in this, this recognition is linked from a libidinal perspective to the "creative" origin of that value. *What binds people to these values is the phantasmatic transgressive space out of which they spring*, a space that responds to the most basic, polymorph perverse drive structure of their desire.

It is here that for the first time Lacan cites the passage from the *Critique of Practical Reason*, already discussed at the end of the previous chapter, where Kant presents two fables to illustrate the "weight of reason" in ethical questions.[57] It is no coincidence that in both of the cases it involves a singular individual who explicitly sets himself *against* the law and has the chance to "protest" against it and even to transgress it. In the first fable, Kant invokes a man who has the opportunity to spend a night with his mistress with the proviso that, if he takes up this offer, he will later be hanged. In the other fable, a person finds himself in a position where he must disobey the moral obligation to always tell the truth: he can send his fellowman to death with a false declaration, with the proviso that, if he fails to do so, he will himself be killed.

In his analysis of this passage, in which he limits himself for the most part to the first case, Lacan stresses how there is one thing that Kant fails to see. For Kant, it is clear that, having to choose between a night of enjoyment or saving his life, a man will opt for the latter without question. According to Lacan, what escapes Kant is that the man in question *may well be a courtly lover*. For such a person, it is in no way senseless or immoral to value his mistress over his own life. What is of "weight" in his ethical dilemma is not "reason," as Kant claims (S7E: 108[58]; S7F: 130), but his Lady. From the standpoint of courtly love, she is, from an ethical perspective as well, his "mistress," his "Domina," the one who is so good as to "dominate" him. Kant was unable to imagine that the man in question might just as easily choose the fatal night of love, not so much because he cannot control his passions but because, on account of his courtly ethos, he owes her his obedience and fealty. And this ethos originates not in the unshakable transcendental structure of human reason (as held by Kantian ethics), but in a poetic revolution—"historically specific" (S7E: 109; S7F: 130)—in which troubadours conjured up out of nothing a new, female-friendly eroticism.

Kant's fundamental error, according to Lacan, is to remain blind to the fact that in the final analysis an ethical relation stems not from the "weight of reason," nor from the autonomy of the law, but from a "dialectic" (ibid.) between the subject and the law. This "dialectic"—as he teaches us at the end of the sixth seminar—puts the subject *against* the law and thus in a certain sense *outside* it. The subject stands in the transgressive place where the law is *made* as if out of nothing ("creation ex nihilo") (as one "makes" literature and poetry, as still found in the strong meaning of the Ancient Greek word for "to make" ['ποιεῖν,' *poiein*]). In other words, Kant failed to see that ethics stems from a sublimation. Or, as Lacan puts it in a difficult and uncivilly long sentence (only the basic skeleton of which is translated here):

> Our philosopher from Königsberg [. . .] doesn't seem to have considered that under certain conditions of what Freud would call *Überschätzung* or overevaluation of the object—and that I will henceforth call object sublimation—under conditions in which the object of a loving passion takes on a certain significance (and, as you will see, it is in this direction that I intended to introduce the dialectics through which I propose to teach you how to identify what sublimation really is), under certain conditions of sublimation of the feminine object [. . .] [as in] courtly love [. . .], that under certain conditions of sublimation, then, it is conceivable for such a [transgressive] step to be taken [as described in Kant's apologue]. (S7E 108–109; S7F: 130)

For Lacan, it is thus not impossible that the character in Kant's fable would, for ethical reasons, choose a night of love with his lady above his own life. In this case, in the name of the courtly ethic, he transgresses the usual ethical law, even if he must put his self-preservation at risk for this. It is only in this transgressive "step" ("*franchissement*"), according to Lacan, that it becomes clear how ethics stems from a sublimation, that is, from a "dialectical" relation *with* the law.

But, Lacan adds in this unseemly long sentence, this same free space beyond the law makes it "not impossible" that the man transgresses the law out of a *fidelity to evil*, and falls into an intolerable, pure criminality:

> All of which leads to the conclusion that it is not impossible for a man to sleep with a woman knowing full well that he is to be bumped off on his way out, by the gallows or anything else, [. . .]; it is not impossible that this man coolly accepts such an eventuality on his leaving—for the pleasure of cutting up the lady concerned in small pieces, for example. (S7E: 109; S7F:131)

The site *beyond* the law is thus evidently not exclusively reserved for sublimation. Crime, too, operates from here, Lacan claims. The place *beyond* the law that is the place of the "thing" and that constitutes the center of every sublimation is, at the same time, the domain out of which a criminal interaction with the law operates. Recall Roger Vailland's description of the village of mafiosi in his novel *La Loi* where the law is established directly from out the "thing," as Lacan's analysis demonstrated (see 5.4). Here, too, man operates explicitly on the basis of a transgressive realm, albeit in an exploitative manner where terror reigns in the name of the law.

It shouldn't surprise us, then, that Lacan can no longer allow his notion of "perversion" to be associated with the universal "polymorphous-perverse" human condition. So as to distinguish sublimation and crime from one another, both of which operate from out of the same transgressive space of the "thing," the term "perversion" will be reserved solely for crime and is no longer employed to characterize sublimation, as it was at the end of his sixth seminar. Several lines further, we hear how

> I have outlined then two cases that Kant doesn't envisage, two forms of transgression beyond the limits normally assigned to the pleasure principle in opposition to the reality principle given as a criterion, namely [on the one hand], excessive object sublimation and [on the other] what is commonly[59] known as transgression. (S7E: 109; S7F: 131)

Operating from out the "thing" *beyond* the law, there are thus two possibilities for human action, one negative and one positive: either perverse lawlessness, or sublimation.[60]

However, this does not mean that, at the level of content, Lacan strips sublimation of the "perverse" nature he had attributed to it at the end of his sixth seminar. It remains "perverse" here, too, in the sense of being a figure of that polymorphous-perverse distance the pleasure being assumes with respect to the law. It remains, in other words, a transgressive game with the law. However, in sublimation this occurs in a *positive* fashion; the transgressive space beyond the law is explicitly kept open.

Here we bump up against what is undoubtedly the most crucial point of Lacan's concept of sublimation. Why does sublimation enable us to relate to this "lawless" space beyond the law without thereby falling into pure crime? It is because there, in that transgressive domain, *only our object is posited*. In no way are we present as *subjects*. That which sublimation elevates to the status of a "thing" is *exclusively* the object: something that the subject desires but with which it can never coincide. In crime, on the other hand,– in "perversion" as defined here—what is posited in the place of the transgressive "thing" is the *subject*. In this case, the subject itself takes the place of the "thing" and in this way sublates the distance that divides it from the object (or at least acts *as if* that distance has been sublated). Whenever this kind of person directs herself toward others, it is not surprising that the absolute evil the "thing" stands for will come to the surface as well. The way the maffiosi in Vailland's novel imagine themselves *above* the law speaks volumes in this context. Anyone who "makes law" out of the transgressive "thing" that lies at its foundation inevitably sows terror.

## 5.2 Sublimation and Transgression

Generally speaking, one could claim that, through the notion of sublimation, Lacan has attempted to conceptualize the lawless, "mystical" ground of the law (to use Montaigne's and Pascal's term[61]). His aim is to chart the way the foundation of ethics perpetually escapes ethics' own ethical grasp and how the law—as remedy against crime and evil—itself, in the final analysis, derives from crime and evil. Freud sketched out this "mystical," unconscious foundation of the law in *Totem and Taboo*. In this essay, the law emanates from the unrestrained libido of the primal father who, dominating everything and everyone, is consequently murdered by the oppressed sons. However, this doesn't stop the criminal "law" that curtails the libidinal life of his sons from being permanently forged into the ethical law after his death, binding them more powerfully to the "criminal" law of the father through their sense of guilt. Lacan's "ethics of psychoanalysis" is an attempt to allow this "mystical," transgressive space that lies at the basis of the ethical law to come into its own right because it is there, par excellence, that desire and the polymorph-perverse drive it derives from are revealed.

However, Lacan's concept of sublimation makes it clear that one must not assume this space *as a subject*, if only because, as Freud's myth suggests, one would lapse into the unholy violence of the primal father. In that case, the distance that separates the libidinal being from its ultimate object would be destroyed. The object relation libidinal economy is based on would collapse, bringing about the death of the subject. When this is about to happen, the sole means of survival lies in the way the subject diverts the violence away from itself and abreacts it onto others. Then, the subject acts *as if* there is no longer any gap between itself and the "thing" whereas, in fact, the evil hidden inside it becomes abreacted onto others and the subject imagines itself as sovereign as the maffiosi in Vailland's novel or as the heroes in Sade's fantasies. For this latter outlet, where the subject operates directly from the position of the transgressive "thing," Lacan reserves the term "perversion," although it will take another two years before he arrives at a fully developed theory of perversion.[62]

An "ethics of psychoanalysis" such as Lacan presents here uncompromisingly aims to do justice to desire and must therefore affirm the transgressive origin of the law. For this reason he focuses on the "thing," on this transgressive space that prevents the subject from merging with the symbolic law, enabling it to take a certain position vis-à-vis the law. It is the only possible way a subject can more or less satisfactorily hold out in a world filled with "neurotic" laws and norms. Precisely as a sublimation—as a "creation ex nihilo"—"culture" maintains contact with the free space of the "thing" and connects to the most fundamental polymorphous-perverse structure of the human drive. But for sublimation to maintain contact with this transgressive "thing" simultaneously means keeping the subject at the necessary distance from that "thing." Here, the fully ethical dimensions that Lacan attributes to sublimation become clear. *That sublimation must elevate precisely the* object *to the status of a thing comes primarily as a result of the fact that the* subject *must not assume this place.*

Here, we face one of the most fundamental reasons why Lacan, unlike Freud, conceives his theory of sublimation entirely from the perspective of the object pole. The "object relational" grammar enables us to see more clearly the paradoxical gesture that sublimation stands for. The *object* of the object relation that we *"are"* lies *beyond* the limit of the law, while the *subject* of this relation remains on *this* side of the law. In this way, it becomes more or less comprehensible why, as libidinal beings, we remain both devoted to the law *and* fixated on what lies *beyond* it. Lacan's object-relational version of sublimation articulates how it is possible to maintain contact with the domain of *Jenseits*, beyond the law—a necessary requirement in order to allow desire to come into its own and, hence, in accord with an "ethics of psychoanalysis"—without the subject "itself" transgressing the limit of the law. Sublimation keeps the drive open towards an object that lies beyond the law while simultaneously allowing us to maintain ourselves as subjects (bearers) of that symbolic law. It is only sublimation, considered from the object relational perspective, that enables us to think the relation between law and desire as a "dialectic," albeit a dialectic that—in contrast to what Hegel maintained—never overcomes ("sublates") its antagonistic operation.

*Only the object*—and *never the subject*—is elevated to the status of the "thing" in sublimation. In the very gesture of transgressing the limit of the law (the symbolic order) and establishing an object above the law, the subject is prevented from participating in this transgression. Only a sublimated *object* can keep the space beyond the law open (and so sustain the most radical dimension of desire) without dragging the subject along with it into that dangerous openness. It was in this way that the courtly lover could trample on the ordinary laws and open up a space beyond, while at the same time be prevented by the Lady (i.e., the sublimated object) from handing himself completely over to that space. In what is "commonly" called perversion (as Lacan puts it in the passage cited above), this space is not respected and the *subject itself* takes the place of the "thing" from where he then literally lays down the law for others. The maffiosi in Vailland's novel relate not to an object *beyond* the law but put themselves (as subjects) literally outside or above the law from where they lay down the law to their fellow men with a sovereign capriciousness.

Now it becomes clear how sublimation brings the founding paradox characteristic of the object relation sharply into the foreground. On the one hand, man "is" the object he desires: only in that object "is" he what he desires to be. However, on the other hand, his 'being' is posited as nothing other than an *object*, as a point of reference that perpetually withdraws behind the limit and which makes us infinitely desire the object that we "are," thereby confirming ourselves as an (object) *relation*.

This also clarifies the ethical stakes of sublimation: sublimation stands as a guarantor for desire precisely by making the irreconcilable gap between subject and object the engine of "culture." An object elevated to a "thing" affirms the transgressive dimension of our desire while simultaneously preventing us from being dragged along by that transgression, since the subject is explicitly evacuated from the law-transgressing gesture. In this way, sublimation gives acculturated man the chance to connect with the polymorphous-perverse nature of his drive life while preventing him at the same time from falling into the monstrous position of perverse criminality (where we believe ourselves to be the "thing"). Sublimation thus combines a more or less satisfying positive gesture with an active fight against the lawless evil perversion leads to. This, for Lacan, is indisputably the essence of its ethical dimension.

## 5.3. The "Function of the Beautiful": An Ethical Function

The sublimatory character of our culture appeals to the fundamental drive structure of our desire. From a psychoanalytic perspective, it is only in this sense that culture fulfills its ethical function. Each in their own way, art, religion, and science—the three major sublimations Lacan, following Freud, distinguishes—keep this space *beyond* the symbolic law open. In this way, they arouse desire at its most radical level, that of the drive. In this way, too, Lacanian psychoanalysis is able to give a positive moral valorization to all three.

Nevertheless in his Ethics Seminar, Lacan expresses a clear preference for one of these three sublimations, namely, the aesthetic. Here the structure of desire is most clearly revealed. For this reason, according to Lacan, one must attribute a particular ethical task to the aesthetic sublimation. In fact, not all of the three sublimations Lacan itemizes (following Freud) yield up their secrets in the same clear fashion. Science does so least of all for, paradoxically, it only "reveals" the "extimate" space around which its desire is centered by foreclosing its existence in advance. There, this space can only be deduced from the irrepressible zeal with which it pursues "absolute knowledge." That zeal makes science blind to the fact that such knowledge must remain infinitely postponed. Religion is much clearer about this because it explicitly reserves a place for this radical space of desire. There, the transgressive nature of our relation to this space is unmistakable. The limit religion installs between the sacred and the profane functions as the perpetual object of a highly regulated, spiritualized form of transgression. Only, religion organizes these transgressions as rituals (which is the sacred side of religion) or—other possibility—condemns them as sin and evil (which is religion's moral side).

According to Lacan, it is in fact the aesthetic realm that offers the most far-reaching view of sublimation's transgressive game. Art comes up with the most "enlightened" way of bringing the structure of our desire and our drive to light. Of course, the aesthetic acts as a veil, but for this very reason it most clearly betrays how that veil continues to hide something, and is therefore *only* a veil. For Lacan, courtly love is paradigmatic of sublimation (S7E: 128; S7F: 153) because the veil cast over the Lady (as representative of the "thing") is what points most clearly to her (and hence to the "thing").

Lacan speaks about aesthetic sublimation as a "function of the beautiful," which he distinguishes from the "function of the good" (S7E: 218, 231; SVII: 257, 271). It is not in the latter function (the good) but in that of the beautiful that one must seek the kind of ethics psychoanalysis has in view.

In the meantime it has become clear that with a notion such as the "function of the good"—to clarify this first—Lacan is not referring to the "good in itself" or the "supreme good." Rather, he has the entire *symbolic* world in mind as both the material and spiritual "values" and the "goods" to which we are libidinally bound. For him, the "domain of the good" is also directly "the economy of goods."[63] And these goods not only meet our needs (as people still believed up until and including Bentham's utilitarianism, see among others S7E: 228; S7F: 269), but primarily our pleasures and desires. More specifically, they answer to the desire we "are" and which—according to the foundational axiom of Lacanian theory—"is that of the Other." In order to become a subject at all, the libidinal being must assume the desire of the Other, including all of the "goods" he or she may desire. In so doing, we always desire what the Other desires. Consequently, anything we have is always something that we have in fact held back from an other. This is the reason why "the domain of the good(s)" is so rife with power and violence. At the end of the lesson that Miller titled "The function of the good," Lacan maintains:

The domain of the good is the birth of power. The notion of control of the good is essential [. . .]. To exercise control over one's goods, as everyone knows, entails a certain disorder, that reveals its true nature, i.e., to exercise control over one's goods is to have the right to deprive others of them. [. . .] For the function of the good engenders, of course, a dialectic. I mean that the power to deprive others is a very solid link form which will emerge the [specific dimension of the] other as such. (S7E: 229; S7F: 269–270)

My good is thus in principle just as much the other's good. Whence, too, my natural tendency to distrust that other and fear he will take "his" good away from me. At the same time, I am also jealous of that other and imagine he has precisely what I so pointedly lack (S7E: 237; S7F: 278). No matter what good I have, I naturally believe that the other is the only one who has the *real* good, and it bugs me that he seems to have at his fingertips the very good I am pining for in vain.[64] Although the realm of the goods possesses a logic of envy, it is nevertheless constitutive for our desire. It binds us to the order of the Other and keeps us at a distance from the "thing." Moreover, in the final analysis, our desire is not for a "good" but for a "thing," although it can only maintain itself thanks to the distance it takes from that "thing." Even our most severe attachment to a possession is still just a means of keeping us away from our ultimate object of desire.

Just recall the miser and his riches in Simone Weil's *Gravity and Grace*. He, too, can only maintain himself as a desiring subject, as Lacan's analysis in his sixth seminar has it, to the extent that he denies himself all enjoyment of his riches. For himself even more than for others, his riches remain a forbidden and (only for that reason) desired fruit (see 1.3.5). In this sense, the dimension of the good or the goods forms a "wall," a "barrier" (S7E: 216; S7F: 256) that holds desire back in its push toward enjoyment.[65] Or, as Lacan puts it elsewhere, playing on the double meaning of the French word "*défendre*":

There is a fact observed in experience that one always has to remember in analysis, namely, what is meant by defending one's goods [défendre ses biens] is one and the same thing as forbidding oneself from enjoying them [se défendre à soi-même d'en jouir]. The sphere of the goods erects a strong wall across the path of our desire. (S7E:230; S7F 270)

Possessions, including the envious struggle that inevitably accompanies them, form a "strong wall" against *jouissance*: this is "the function of the good." Nevertheless, this doesn't mean that this function solves all problems. On the contrary, the blind envy that characterizes this realm keeps man perpetually in bondage to others. Unable to find the hoped-for "good" in myself (for the simple reason that, because it is enjoyment, it can in no way ever be appropriated), I will covetously imagine the other has it. I will envy him and literally take it from him if need be. His inability to give it to me only strengthens my suspicion that he is in fact withholding it from me, and this makes me hate him all the more. In his lesson of May 18, Lacan says this about the spiral of jealousy:

> Isn't it strange, very odd, that a being admits to being jealous of something in the other to the point of hatred and the need to destroy, jealous of something that he is incapable of appre-hending in any way, by any intuitive path? The identification of this other virtually in the form of a concept may in itself suffice to provoke the movement of malaise concerned; and I don't think one has to be an analyst to see such disturbing undulations passing through subjects' behaviors. Now we have reached the frontier. What will enable us to cross it? One finds at this frontier another crossing point, which enables us to locate precisely an element of the field of the beyond-the-good principle. That element, as I have said, is the beautiful. (S7E: 237; S7F: 278)

If the good protects us from the dangerous realm of the "thing," it does so in blind fashion that lands us in a spiral of envy and aggression. The "function of the beautiful," according to Lacan, is to arm us against this. The beautiful operates *beyond* the limit of the good although, like the good, it also serves to prevent us from gaining access to that "thing" beyond. The beautiful is thus also a "barrier." But it is a barrier that, by blinding us with something beautiful, prevents a blind fight for the "good." It keeps us under the spell of a beauty that paralyzes, for a moment, our envious struggle for the good. At the end of his lesson on "the function of the good," where he makes the transition to the "func-tion of the beautiful," we read:

> Beyond the place of restraint constituted by the concentration and circuit of goods, a field nevertheless remains open to us that allows us to draw closer to the central field. The good is not the only, the true, or the single barrier that separates us from it. What is that second barrier? [. . .] The true barrier that holds the subject back in front of the unspeakable field of radical desire that is the field of absolute destruction, of destruction beyond putrefaction, is properly speaking the aes-

thetic phenomenon where it is identified with the experience of beauty—beauty in all its shining radiance, beauty that has been called the splendor of truth. It is obviously because truth is not pretty to look at that beauty is, if not its splendor, than at least its envelope. (S7E: 216–217; S7F: 256)

If we go beyond the "barrier" of the circuit of goods, we do not immediately enter the realm of the "thing," the "field of absolute destruction" where the subject disappears. Beyond the first barrier is a second barrier: the beautiful. There we are brought to a halt, not by the "thing" itself, but by a "splendor," a brilliant radiance that, drawing our attention toward the "thing," simultaneously pulls it out of our direct sight.

In Lacan's line of reasoning, the barrier of the beautiful takes on a double and, in a sense, ambiguous function. On the one hand, it is the subject's final obstructive limit in its search for its "radical desire," that is, for its extimate and deathly "*radix*," that is, the "thing." On the other hand, it opens up a "field" that enables us to "draw closer" to the "thing." It is thus a barrier that is at the same time an access. Precisely in this lies its difference from the barrier of the good. For as long as we dance before the limit of the good, we keep on blindly imagining that the other has our "thing" in his possession, and thereby fall prey to an irremediable jealousy. In this sense, the good threatens and deceives us. But if we transgress the limit of the good and stop before the limit of the beautiful, we get a glimpse of that impossible, unreachable and destructive "thing." We are no longer confronted with an absolute good possessed only by the other but now see it more clearly as something that, if it cannot be had, can also not be tolerated.

The beautiful in its strange function with relation to desire doesn't take us in [ne nous leurre pas], as opposed to the function of the good. It keeps us awake and perhaps helps us adjust to desire insofar as it is itself linked to the structure of lure [leurre]. (S7E: 239; S7F: 280)

The beautiful thus does not deceive us in our desire, precisely because it is already in itself deceptive. Beauty also shows how it is only an appearance, a representation, without ever letting us see the "thing" as such. Seducing us, it doesn't deceive us for it explicitly presents itself as an unattainable good. In this sense, the beautiful provides a more fitting image for desire insofar as, despite everything it grasps for, it remains perpetually unsatisfied.

This is precisely the moral function that, tracing out an ethics of desire, Lacan will ascribe to the beautiful. More so than the good, the experience of beauty prepares us for a confrontation with our desire *as such*, with this futile movement that constantly misses the "thing" it desires and thereby circles perpetually around it. In the beautiful, the deception of desire at least becomes *visible* and therefore helps us avoid becoming entangled in the good's deceptions. From this perspective, the beautiful is "better" than the good, because it lets us see that the "better" we continually strive for is not the fulfillment but the destruction of the good. Lacan cites the French saying, "the better is the enemy of the good."[66] The beautiful preserves us from that "better than the good" by allowing us to see it in its petrified cruelty.

Sublimation appeals to the most fundamental structure of the drive and therefore gives an extra (transgressive) space to the desire that has been aroused by the symbolic law. It is here that the ethical dimension of sublimation lies. An explicitly *aesthetic* sublimation only makes the *ethical* dimension more distinct. It gives us the clearest picture of what is at play in sublimation, in desire and in the drive. Precisely because it deceives us less than other forms of sublimation, its ethical dimension is more pronounced, says Lacan. More than the others, it grants us a glimpse of the "thing" we seek, a glimpse that, while always making us recoil, at the same time—precisely through its beauty effect—"consciously" keeps it in place. In the first allusion Lacan makes to sublimation in his *Ethics Seminar*, he had already this *conscious, lucid* aesthetic sublimation in mind. As we saw at the beginning of this chapter, he was concerned with

> that which, over the centuries, human beings have succeeded in elaborating that transgresses the Law [on the level of the νοῦς ("*nous*," Greek for "raison")], [i.e., what] puts them in a relationship to desire that transgresses interdiction [. . .]. (S7E: 84; S7F: 101; see above 7.1)

Lacan, already talking about sublimation without mentioning the term, approaches it as a "conscious" means for affirming the transgressive relation between the desiring subject and the symbolic law. Sublimation is announced as a positive, nonrepressed affirmation of desire's transgressive structure, an affirmation at the level of the νοῦς [*nous*, understanding, reason, thought, consciousness].

Yet this does not prevent precisely the "conscious" nature of aesthetic sublimation from being highly problematic. For how can we imagine such an aesthetic confrontation between desire and its own "extimate" object? While it might be situated on the level of the νοῦς [nous], the "function of the beautiful" certainly cannot be defined as the becoming-conscious of the unconscious. In that case, Lacan's theory would lapse into a traditional philosophy of consciousness and would misrecognize the most essential point of psychoanalysis, namely, that the unconscious is consciousness's very base and, thus, structurally "unsublatable." The mere fact of the "thing's" unknowable nature confirms this fundamental idea.[67]

But still this does not answer the question of how such a conscious, aesthetic contemplation of the unconscious, unsublatable "thing" can have an ethical function. What am I supposed to do with that "beauty" that gives me a glimpse of that unbearable yet at the same time irresistible "thing" my desire unconsciously seeks? In the following chapter we will see how the entire problem with which we ended the previous chapter—that is, the unpronounceable singularity of an "ethics of desire"—rears its ugly head again. For, even when the ethical function of an aesthetic image is to make desire visible, the question remains whether we can therefore make that image function as an aesthetic demand or a moral law. Can one even remotely take an ethical stance on the basis of an aesthetic image? Or does the singularity of desire as affirmed in that image make this impossible?

To deal with these questions, Lacan will comment on an exemplary aesthetic sublimation that makes desire visible. The example in question is the well-known (also from an ethical perspective) ancient tragedy, Sophocles' *Antigone.*

# Chapter 8

# Radiant Antigone

Beauty, too, has its rights.

—Balthasar Gracian

## 1. An Anamorphic Glance at Tragedy

### 1.1. Beauty: . . .

"The splendor of Antigone"—such is the title Jacques-Alain Miller invents
for the first lesson of Lacan's commentary on the tragedy bearing this name
(S7E: 243; S7F: 285). The title suggests the image of a beautiful young
woman, "radiant" in the center of a fatal catastrophe, and it sends us
directly to the heart of Lacan's interpretation. What, to his mind, makes
the central figure the main theme of Sophocles' tragedy is indeed her
beauty, her irresistible radiance. When he asks at the beginning of his
reading, "What does one find in *Antigone*?" his answer is instantaneous:
"First of all, one finds Antigone" (S7E: 250; S7F: 293). Her "unbearable
splendor," her harsh "beauty," this is what the tragedy is about (S7E:
246; S7F: 290).

> The articulation of the tragic action is illuminating of the
> subject. It has to do with Antigone's beauty. And this is not
> something I invented; I will show you the passage in the song
> of the Chorus where that beauty is evoked, and I will prove
> that it is the pivotal passage. (S7E: 248; S7F: 290)

It is typical of Lacan's often sloppy teaching method that he never explicitly fulfills this promise. From the context, however, he almost certainly had the third Chorus song in mind (verses 781–805). He comes back to it frequently and with great emphasis.[1] It does indeed concern beauty, albeit not specifically of Antigone herself, but of young girls in general. The radiant bloom on "a girl's soft cheek" (v. 784) is a sign, the Chorus sings, of the irresistible power of "Eros," "never conquered in battle" (v. 782).[2] Yet, in the given context, this ode to Eros is rather striking. A furious Creon just sentenced Antigone to be buried alive, and already the choir starts up with a song of praise to erotic love. In Roberts Fagles's translation, the brusque transition in the text is clearly evident:

CREON:	I will take her down some wild, desolate path
		never trod by men, and wall her up alive
		in a rocky vault, and set out short rations,
		just the measure piety demands
		to keep the entire city free of defilement.
		There let her pray to the one god she worships:
		Death—who knows?—may just reprieve her from death.
		Or she may learn at last, better than ever,
		what a waste of breath it is to worship Death.
		(*Exit to the palace*)
CHORUS:	Love, never conquered in battle
		Love the plunderer laying waste the rich!
		Love standing the night-watch
			guarding a girl's soft cheek [. . .][3]

For Lacan, this brusque transition from a death sentence to a hymn to Eros is highly significant. What shimmers along with the figure of Antigone at that fatal tragic moment is also Eros or—in Lacanian terms—desire. A little later in the Chorus' song, we find the term on which the core of Lacan's interpretation hangs: ἵμερος ἐναργὴς [himeros enargès], "the visible desire that comes from the eyes of a beautiful girl (v. 795–796).[4] Antigone, her crime and the carrying out of her death sentence: for Lacan, each of these are aesthetic figures, figures of beauty through which desire becomes "visible" and whose power glows and "radiates." Referring to the moment just after Creon seals Antigone's death, Lacan claims:

> It is precisely at this moment that the Chorus says in so many words: "This story is driving us mad; we are losing our grip; we are going out of our minds; as far as this child is concerned we are moved to. . . ." what the text, using a term whose appositeness I ask to remember ἵμερος ἐναργὴς [*himeros*

*enargès*] [. . .]. Ἵμερος ἐναργὴς is literally desire made visible.
(S7E: 268; S7F: 311)[5]

Despite—or, more strictly, *because* of—the hideous context in which
she is situated, the power of desire "radiates" from Antigone's appearance. The entire play is a ghastly tableau that, as Aristotle puts it, elicits
only "pity and fear,"[6] yet in Lacan's eyes it serves primarily to give us a
sharper image of the harsh beauty of desire.

It goes without saying that Lacan's reading of Antigone raises some
critical questions. Since Aristotle, has it not become clear that tragedy's
essence lies primarily in the tragic *drama*,[7] rather than in the personality
of the protagonist? Anyway, the emphasis on Antigone's beauty is absent
from Sophocles' text itself, as is any reference to her specifically erotic
radiance. Rather, the tragic poet depicts Antigone as a cold, unfeeling
character.[8] Following the letter of the text, it is only her fiancé, Haemon,
who shows any sign of erotic distress. When he falls on his sword at
the end of the play, it is out of genuine love for his beloved. Antigone
herself doesn't let any of love's considerations stop her, unless it is her
love for her brother, but this is not given the slightest erotic interpretation by Sophocles.

However legitimate, this type of criticism does not really bring us
closer to understanding Lacan's train of thought, which is our primary
concern. For this purpose, even his misreadings can be illuminating.
Remember his reading of *Hamlet* in the sixth seminar (see above I, 5,
1–2), where it became clear that his comments on this major canonical
text are primarily meant to force his own theory into sharper relief. From
this perspective, a confrontation with Antigone will allow him to reflect
on what the "ethics of desire" is about. His reading is thus colored in
advance and my intention is to judge that "color," not by its accuracy to
the original text, but by what it contributes to the theory currently being
formed here. Hence it makes sense to follow Lacan's highly charged—at
times even erroneous—reading of *Antigone* very closely within the lines
of thought he is developing in his Ethics Seminar.

## 1.2. . . . *Ethical, But Not Good*

In the course of this seminar, Lacan has explained in various ways how
the supreme good is in fact a radical evil and that the "goods" we deal
with on a daily basis are perpetually sliding *signifiers* that deceptively
keep us away from that evil "supreme good," the ultimate "thing" our
desire aims at. In that deception, he had identified the "function of the
good" and had added "the function of the beautiful" as the next step in
his reasoning. In the beautiful—an artwork, a creative play with signifiers

(a "façonnement du signifiant" as he sometimes calls it)—the capricious, deceptive structure of the good whose work normally goes unnoticed comes to the surface. Or, as Lacan expresses it in the passage cited at the end of the previous chapter:

> The beautiful in its strange function with relation to desire doesn't take us in, as opposed to the function of the good. It keeps us awake and perhaps helps us adjust to desire insofar as it is itself linked to the structure of lure. (S7E: 239; S7F: 280)

Beauty unmasks the deception through which we realize ourselves as (subjects of) desire. On a conscious level, it grants us a view of the "thing" and in this way supports our unconscious fascination with it. At the same time, beauty supports the necessary distance in relation to that dangerous "thing" that even our best intentions unconsciously aim for. In this lies the expressly *ethical* function of the beautiful for Lacan.

This is why Lacan now tries to show how the "function of the beautiful" does indeed operate ethically in a work of art. In his eyes, Sophocles' *Antigone* seems particularly well-suited for this, if only because of the explicitly ethical character of its scenario. Rarely is the question of the meaning of the moral law and man's relation to it so clearly delineated than in the conflict between Antigone and Creon. Moreover, the long history of ethical reflection accompanying the reception of this tragedy enables Lacan to position himself against the entire ethical tradition.

Yet precisely because of the explicitly *moral* nature of this tragedy, Lacan's commentary can easily be misinterpreted. His point is that its ethical power is found not so much in its moral content as in its formal beauty and the way that this beauty "works." Lacan latches on to *Antigone* primarily because it is a *work of art* and appeals to our sense of beauty. *Solely* in this capacity is it able to tell us something essentially new about ethics. Consequently, it is senseless to hunt for exactly what it is that Lacan finds ethical or unethical in Antigone's decision to bury her brother in defiance of Creon's prohibition. It makes just as little sense to ask why he doesn't emphasize Creon's own moral dimension more. Regardless of how interesting such further discussions might be (and the entire reception of *Antigone* up till now is proof of this[9]), Lacan nevertheless puts the emphasis on something completely different. For Lacan, the ethics of this tragedy lie not in Antigone's motive, nor in the potentially unethical nature of Creon's death sentence. The ethical must be exclusively sought in the "beauty" of the play, that is, in the purely aesthetic effect that it has on the audience.

Do not imagine that this makes Lacan's thesis any easier to grasp. His claim will not only require us to go patiently through the often confusing explanations of his seminar, it will also remain problematic within the lines of his seminar's own logic. For what could a specifically *ethical* function of the beautiful mean? That it is morally *good* to look at beauty and be captivated by art? That the beautiful gives us a more adequate ethical model than the good and that from a moral perspective the beautiful is "better" than the good?

Although Lacan's argument seems to point in this direction at first sight, the very logic of his reasoning can only forbid such a conclusion. For if the *good* is bound up with the *beautiful*, this immediately risks reducing the beautiful to a *good*, that is, to something that deceives us in our desire. How can we still claim, then, that it is precisely the beautiful that *reveals* the deceptive strategies hidden in the domain of the good? It is easy for Lacan to attribute a fully ethical function to the beautiful, but what else could this mean than that the beautiful is a *better* good than the good, that it thus inevitably belongs to the good and has the same function? To grasp Lacan's point here, we should understand how the beautiful can be more ethical than the good, without therefore being "better"—which takes us to one of the thorniest question in the *Ethics Seminar*.

## 1.3. An Anamorphosis

In his first two lessons devoted to *Antigone* (May 25 and June 1, 1960), Lacan limits himself to a scene by scene overview of the text, occasionally pausing on a fragment discussed by such major figures as Goethe and Hegel (to name only these two). These latter provide him the opportunity to present, bit by bit, his own interpretation. Regarding his general approach and the method that directs his reading, for the moment, the reader is left guessing. It is only on June 8, in his third and final lesson on *Antigone*, that we hear something about this.[10] However brief and casual this may be, it is of decisive importance for understanding Lacan's entire commentary.

In this lesson, he observes that the structure of a tragedy is comparable to an anamorphosis, a painting whose image can only be recognized once one has found the right perspective.[11] Such a reference would not have been entirely surprising to his audience given that he had already spoken about anamorphoses earlier in his seminar, again in relation to the aesthetic. More specifically, on the third and tenth of February he had displayed an anamorphosis borrowed from his friend Jacques Prévert and given a fairly detailed explanation of it. This was a cylindrical or tubular anamorphosis, a remarkable example of artistry made from a flat support where all one sees at first is a chaotic mess of color until one places a cylindrical mirror in the middle of it and looks into that mirror from a particular angle. At that moment, a full image emerges out of the chaos. In the case of the anamorphosis in question, this was a miniature copy of a crucifixion by Peter Paul Rubens.

This is the anamorphosis Lacan is referring to in his third lesson on *Antigone*. After a long digression on the other Sophoclean tragedies that have overcome the ravages of time (S7E: 271–272; S7F: 316–317), he unexpectedly displays this little artefact so as to promptly promote it into a methodological paradigm for his reading of tragedy. This is what he says:

> Let us return to Antigone [. . .]. On one occasion I showed you an anamorphosis; it was the finest I could find for our purpose, and it is indeed exemplary, far beyond anything one could have hoped for. Do you remember the cylinder from which this strange phenomenon rises up? It cannot properly speaking be said that from an optical point of view there is an image as such. Without going into the optical definition of the phenomenon, one can say it is because an infinitesimal fragment of image is produced on each surface of the cylinder that we see a series of screens superimposed; and it is as a result of these that a marvelous illusion in the form or a beautiful image of the passion [Christ's passion] appears beyond the mirror, whereas something decomposed and disgusting spreads out around it. That is the kind of thing that is involved here. What is the surface that allows the image of Antigone to rise up as an image of passion? [. . .] Tragedy is that which spreads itself out in front so that that image may be produced. When analyzing it, we follow an inverse procedure; we study how an image had to be constructed in order to produce the desired effect. (S7E: 272–273; S7F: 318)

How does Lacan regard tragedy? Not in the way Aristotle does for whom it primarily concerns a highly complex "plot" that at a specific moment tragically "explodes." For Lacan, a tragedy is first of all an arbitrary set of disparate facts and events that, precisely in and through these confusing impressions, generate an image that is lit up with an "éclat," a radiance. It is in this sense that tragedy resembles the painted surface of an anamorphosis. There, in an "ugly and diffused" way, everything collides with one another while nonetheless succeeding in finding a unity, albeit not so much in the narrative plot line as in the persistent flickering image that emerges out of that chaos (if one can still call it an "image," Lacan adds). Out of an anarchy of death and misery, Antigone emerges as an ultimate epiphany of beauty that persists through to her living grave, through to what Lacan, with Sophocles, calls her *Atè* (see 3.1). In the eyes of the audience, her "radiant" image holds out despite it all. For Lacan, the epiphany of this radiance is the rationale of every scene and of the play in general.

*Analyzing* a tragedy for Lacan, then, is not so much a matter of looking for the logic behind the plot as studying how, despite—or, better, thanks to—its confusing spectacle, each scene generates that flickering image. Only, this kind of analysis must pursue that procedure in the "inverse" direction. Unlike the audience who allow themselves to be dragged along by that fascinating image, the analysis Lacan proposes suspends the operation of that image so as to reveal the chaotic surface of the tragedy and to show how each of its pieces "does its job" in conjuring the central epiphany into being. Now that we understand Lacan's anamorphotic view on tragedy, it is clear what he had in mind during his confusing, two-lesson-long "articulations of the play"[12]: not a discursive analysis of the plot but a study that focuses individually on each scene to see how they successfully conjure up that central image.

Or, to put it in Lacan's own terms: he examined each scene in its capacity as *signifier*, generating its arbitrary *signified* only through its mutual play with other *signifiers*. Usually a signified is generated *immediately* and hence *unnoticeably*. A tragedy, in contrast—and by the same token any artwork and the entire domain of "the beautiful"—is constructed in such a way that the viewer makes the link between the signifier and signified less rapidly. This is why, in the tragic scene, a series of mysterious tableaux (signifiers) appear whose secret is not immediately divulged, making the gap between signifier and signified tangible and demonstrable. In this way, a tragedy enables us to see how signifier and signified are encountered not by nature but by chance and, in the case of tragedy, even by fate.

According to Lacan, the anamorphic structure that one can recognize in tragedy not only allows the gap between signifier and signified to be seen. It also neatly shows where the *subject* is placed within these coordinates. For Lacan, the "bearer" (the "subject") of an anamorphosis, that is, this entity where all of its elements coincide, the point where it "is what it is," lies not in its dappled ground surface, nor in its mirror, but *behind* the mirror. In the real anamorphosis Lacan is referring to, the crucified Christ looms up out of this dark tain. In the same way, in Lacan's eyes Sophocles' tragedy creates the central but inaccessible space out of which Antigone looms up and "radiates." It is in this space that Lacan will locate the precise place of the subject, the load bearing but fictive point on which the entire libidinal construction rests.

And, last but not least, does Lacan's reference to anamorphosis tell something about the way we should look to tragedy, that is, as if we were looking at ourselves in a mirror? In contrast to an image generated by a flat mirror, however, an anamorphic image does not give one the illusion that it is reflecting reality itself. On the contrary, an anamorphosis immediately shows that the image is *only* an image, a haphazard effect of intrinsically meaningless spots. Precisely for this reason, such an image will not be allowed to function as an example that we ought to follow in our real lives. For such an image undermines any link to reality in advance: it does not reflect *reality* (as does a flat mirror), nor even ideals or prefigurings of an anticipated future reality. It reflects only meaningless "spots," "stains," or, in Lacanese: signifiers.

It is now clear that when Lacan attributes an ethical function to tragedy and interprets it as an anamorphosis, such tragedy by definition must not be interpreted as an *example*, no matter how spontaneously one is inclined to do so given the ethical context we are in. While *Antigone* may well have something important to say about ethics, it neither functions in Lacan's ethics seminar as a moral example, nor does the tragedy permit one to draw a moral lesson from it.[13] In this respect, as we will see later on, it makes no sense for us to debate, for example, whether we ought to be *like* Antigone ethically, and whether it is she or Creon we should take as our example when confronting a moral choice. If fictional figures such as Antigone or Creon possess a moral function, it is purely and simply as an "image" that, precisely, *cannot* serve as an example. Because of its anamorphotic operation, such an image "decenters" or deconstructs our tendency to take them as moral examples. The ethics of psychoanalysis, so Lacan will argue, lies in this very decentering or deconstruction of "normal" ethics.

In what follows, we will first look more closely at the way Sophocles' tragedy offers an anamorphotic image of our situation as *subjects of signifiers*. Only then can we understand what motivates the ethical conclusions Lacan draws from it. More specifically, it will become clear how Lacan's anamorphotic analysis of *Antigone* forms an illustration for a more general decentering of ethics.

## 2. The Subject in the Picture

### 2.1. "My life has long been dead"

From the very beginning of the play, Antigone is literally in a fatal position. She realizes that burying Polyneices equals her own death sentence, but at the same time she knows she will bury him anyway. It is clear to her that giving her brother final honors implies she is already dead. Both his funeral and her death are the two sides of the same choice for her. This is evident, for instance, in what she snaps at Ismene in the opening dialogue of the play: "but I shall bury him: It is honorable for me to do this and die [. . .] I shall lie with him." And she is even clearer about this when, standing before Creon, she accuses her sister: "Yes, you chose life, and I chose death."[14] When she cries to Ismene a little later on, "You are alive, but my life has long been dead" (v. 559),[15] she aptly expresses how she regards herself at the beginning of the play. It is as though she can only do what she does precisely *because* she already considers herself dead. In any event, this is what Lacan takes from the text. He is struck by how Sophocles depicts in Antigone a figure who proclaims in full consciousness to be in fact already dead.

Describing Antigone's song of complaint in his lesson of 8 June (S7E: 280–281; S7F: 326–327), he cites the numerous commentators who find it difficult to understand how, after hearing her official sentence, Antigone, the cold, "inhuman" heroine bursts into tears, complaining bitterly about her fate. Reacting to the repeated suggestion that this passage is perhaps a later addition, Lacan fulminates:

> It is an absurd misinterpretation, for from Antigone's point of view life can only be approached, can only be lived or thought about, from the place of that limit where her life is already lost, where she is already on the other side. But from this place she can see it and live it in the form of something already lost. (S7E: 280; S7F: 326)

The explanation for Antigone's unexpected complaint is to be sought neither in the plot nor in the main character's psychology, says Lacan. According to the logic of Lacan's anamorphotic reading, this complaint turns out to be just another expression of Antigone's position. The fact that she was always already dead is now shown less ambiguously. As the audience, we can no longer get around the fact that she is indeed what she says she always already was: dead. It is a means of emphasizing the "dead" position from which she operates. And this is just as true for the long, tense scene as a whole where she penetrates the "caverns of the dead" (v. 920). There, according to Lacan, is revealed a

> fate of life that is about to turn into certain death, a death lived by anticipation, a death that crosses over into the sphere of life, a life that moves into the realm of death. (S7E: 248; S7F: 291)

Lacan's emphasis on the "dead" position from which Antigone operates ought not to surprise us. In any event, it should not have surprised his listeners, since with this he broaches the main theme of his previous seminar (*Desire and Its Interpretation*)—and even of his entire oeuvre. For the idea that a human being, as a real being, is always already "dead" lies at the heart of the Lacanian theory of the subject. Being the subject/bearer of signifiers, human beings have left behind their real being and only live by grace of the signifiers that represent them. In his commentary on the passage where the choir calls Antigone "autonomous" (v. 821) in the lesson of 8 June, Lacan calls up—as if in a flash—this theory of the subject:

> Antigone appears as αὐτόνομος [*autonomos*, autonomous], as a pure and simple relationship of the human being to that of which he miraculously happens to be the bearer, namely, the signifying cut that confers on him the indomitable power of being what he is in the face of everything that may oppose him. (S7E: 282; S7F: 328)

As the image of "the pure and simple relationship of the human being to [. . .] the signifying cut," Antigone gives us an image of the subject as such, that is, of the fact that, as a libidinal being, man is the bearer of a break with his "being." As explained earlier, for Lacan the very ruse of the pleasure economy lies in how the unbearable lack that we "are" on the level of the real is replaced by one at the level of signifiers that work precisely on the basis of a lack. An *impossible* real lack is replaced with an operational, linguistic lack (which is what primary repression comes down to for Lacan). This is to say that the human "self" only exists as something that can be *re*presented by these signifiers, without however really being "present." Hence Lacan's thesis that "I is an Other"; as a *real* being it is "always dead" because it has always already disappeared beneath the chain of (*symbolic*) signifiers. To put it into the metaphorics of *Antigone*, the subject is, strictly speaking, always "buried alive."

Lacan's anamorphic cylinder is an excellent illustration of this. At the base, all spots (signifiers) conjure up the dying Christ, but this image certainly does not find its "bearer" either in a real Christ or in the chaos of spots in front of the mirror. It finds its bearer in an ungraspable point *beyond* this mirror out of which Christ suddenly, in a brilliant "éclat," appears. He exists only insofar as he is the "subject" of a chaos made up of reflected fragments and colors (signifiers). He is there only insofar as is he represented. At the place where the representation suggests a *presence*—in our case, in the empty central space behind the mirror—there is nothing at all: this is the precise locus of the subject. Lacan reads *Antigone* according to the model of this anamorphosis. The bearer/subject of the whole play is at the same time what disappears behind its central, looming image. Just before the previously cited passage, Lacan explicitly says that he situates Antigone precisely at this point: "a victim at the center of the anamorphic cylinder of the tragedy."[16] By situating her in the hollow kernel behind that tubular mirror surface, Lacan clearly indicates how she disappears beneath the play of signifiers that represent her, while on the other hand it is only in this capacity that she is the subject (bearer) of that signifying play.

Nevertheless, the passage cited above where Lacan invokes his theory of the subject tells us more. Lacan not only suggests that Sophocles' protagonist shows us what it is to be the "bearer" of a symbolic order. He also, in so many words, speaks about an "autonomous" Antigone, an Antigone who has "the indomitable power of being what [s]he is in the face or everything that may oppose [her]" (S7E: 282; S7F: 328). This somewhat mysterious formulation seems to indicate that a space is conferred on her in *opposition* to the signifiers of which she is the bearer. She may "always already be dead"; she may always already have disappeared under the signifiers that represent her, yet she still seems to be characterized in opposition to them and therefore to be able to "do what she wants." More strongly, she even seems capable of autonomously choosing her always already dead condition. At least this is the direction Sophocles' text seems to point since she is said to have "autonomously" chosen death.[17]

Before we look more closely at Lacan's interpretation of this paradoxical, tragic freedom (see 2.4), we must first examine Antigone's autonomy in its more usual sense. Is she not completely autonomous because she resists what in her eyes is an illegitimate law? Does her freedom not lie first of all in the fact that she buried Polyneices in defiance of Creon's explicit prohibition? Is she not free primarily because she dared to champion her brother who was branded an enemy of the state? Lacan's answer to this question is indisputably positive. However, he will show how her choice of Polyneices and of her own death comprise two sides of one and the same decision. To clarify this, we must first examine the introduction and the stakes of Antigone's autonomous act and investigate why precisely she makes such an unconditional commitment to Polyneices.

## 2.2. "My brother is my brother"

It is clear that Antigone takes up a autonomous position vis-à-vis the Creonean law. But the question is how this autonomy is to be understood. Does it indicate that Antigone acts in the name of a law other than Creon's? Does she defend the law of the family in opposition to one of the "polis," as Hegel believed?[18] Her appeal to an "unwritten law of the gods" in her dispute with Creon could point in this direction (v. 454–455). Or is her autonomy that of her own, personal free will that does not want to be absorbed by the tyranny of a universal law? In that case, burying Polyneices primarily expresses her own individual freedom. Support for this might be found in the implacable and uncompromising way she tirades Creon. Or, third possibility, does the play show us primarily that Creon's law is simply wrong and her autonomous act is a cry for a better, more humane law? For this, too, there is something to be said, particularly if one recalls how, at the end of the play, Creon himself is plainly forced to recognize his mistakes.

However, the key question around which these and other interpretations usually turn is the question of why Antigone takes Polyneices side so unconditionally. What binds her to such an extent to her dead, "number one enemy of the state" brother that she shrinks from no prohibition and radically and autonomously opposes the established law? If Sophocles had mentioned somewhere in his play that Polyneices had explicitly begged his two sisters not to leave him unburied should he die (as was the case in *Oedipus at Colonos*[19]), the entire thing would be less enigmatic. But in Sophocles's play we get not the slightest allusion to this element from the myth, thus only strengthening the impression that she does everything "autonomously" and from her own sovereign inclination.

A *discursive* analysis would peel everything back to this underlying conviction in an attempt to understand Antigone from the inside, as it were. Hegel, for example, finds in her a fidelity to the family law which, in that specific period—classical Greece of the fifth century B.C.—was still at odds with the general law of the "polis." Lacan's *structural* analysis resists such an interpretation because it erroneously professes to be able to look *behind* the text. As often, here too, he repeats: "Garder vous de comprendre": "Don't think that you can look beyond the text to grasp its supposed underlying essence."[20] According to Lacan, an analysis can only explore the text's surface and an interpretation can only be supported by the way the elements relate amongst themselves on that surface. How, then, does Lacan interpret Antigone's unconditional choice of her dead, enemy brother? What is her direct motive in his eyes? In the lesson of June 8, he examines this closely (S7E: 277–280; S7F: 323–326) and indicates first and foremost that she doesn't feel obliged to give Creon much explanation. This already demonstrates her "autonomy":

> When she explains to Creon what she has done, Antigone affirms the advent of the absolute individual with the phrase: "That's how it is because that's how it is." (S7E: 278; S7F: 323)

Yet Lacan will give a particular interpretation of what he calls Antigone's "absolute individuality." For he links Antigone's autonomous act to the act of her brother, and to the autonomous position that *he* assumes in relation to good and evil or to the law in general. Polyneices may have acted in an unjustifiable way, but for Antigone this is still no reason not to give him the "final honors" once dead. A little later, Lacan explains Antigone's argument with Creon as follows:

> My brother may be whatever you say he is, a criminal. He wanted to destroy the walls of his city, lied his compatriots away in slavery. He led our enemies on to the territory of our city, but he is nevertheless what he is, and he must be granted his funeral rites. He doubtless doesn't have the same rights as the other. You can in fact, tell me whatever you want, tell me that one is a hero and a friend, that the other is an enemy. But I answer that it is of no significance that the latter doesn't have the same value below. As far as I concerned, the order that you dare refer me to doesn't mean anything, for from my point of view, my brother is my brother. (S7E; 278; S7F: 324)

"My brother is my brother"—this, according to Lacan, is why Antigone buries Polyneices. This, too, is what is at stake in her sovereign, autonomous act. What, however, might this mean? A little later, in her song of complaint, she herself gives a explanation, although it does not make us that much wiser. Had it been a husband, she argues, I could have taken another; had it been a child, I could have had another, but because it is my brother and my last remaining brother since my mother and father are dead, he is irreplaceable.[21] It is a strange argument that many commentators have found incomprehensible. Goethe even doubted the authenticity of this passage.[22] Lacan, on the other hand, professes to find it less problematic. The passage continues immediately as follows:

> That is the paradox encountered by Goethe's thought and he vacillates. My brother is what he is, and it's because he is what he is and only he can be what he is, that I move forward toward the final limit. If it were anyone else with whom I might enter into a human relationship, my husband or my children for example, they are replaceable [. . .]. But [. . .] this brother is something unique. Ant it is this alone which motivates me to oppose your [i.e., Creon's] edicts. (S7E: 278–279; S7F: 324)

The motivation of Antigone's autonomous act lies in her brother's uniqueness. Her father and mother are dead, thus she will never again have a brother to whom she can render the final honors. While Lacan may let fly at all those who cannot cope with this argument, he, too, will have to "translate" it before being able to say something about it. For

Lacan, Polyneices' uniqueness cannot strictly be derived from the place he holds in the genealogical line of the family but stems from the mere place he occupies in the symbolic order, regardless of anything he has or has not done. What makes Polyneices unique, in other words, is the pure fact that he is a signifier, as is evident in the long and difficult sentence that follows the above passage:

> Antigone invokes no other right than that one, a right that emerges in the language of the ineffaceable character of what is—ineffaceable, that is, from the moment when the emergent signifier freezes it like a fixed object in spite of the flood of possible transformations. What is, is, and it is to this, to this surface, the unshakeable, unyielding position of Antigone is fixed. (S7E; 279; S7F: 324–325)

Antigone calls on what it is that makes Polyneices unique, something he is simply and purely because *he* is. She alludes to the "ineffaceable character of what [he] is," to his own unique *being*. But, Lacan immediately adds, this unique value does not lie in what he *really* is, but in the signifier that "freezes" him to something firm over and above his own real, amorphous facticity ("above this stream of every possible change"). The unique value of Polyneices, affirmed in Antigone's funereal rites, lies not in the actual (real) kernel of being but in the (symbolic) signifier he "is" and which he "remains" after his death. A little later on, Lacan puts this more clearly:

> [. . .] Antigone's position represents the radical limit that affirms the unique value of his being without reference to any content, to whatever good or evil Polyneices may have done, or to whatever he may be subjected to. This unique value involved is essentially that of language. Outside of language it is inconceivable, and the being of him who has lived cannot be detached from all he bears with him in the nature of good and evil, of destiny, of consequences for others, or of feelings for himself. (S7E: 279; S7F: 325)

By burying Polyneices, Antigone honors him not for the good or evil that he may have done but for his existence per se. The value her brother has in himself is separate from any of his good or evil acts, but it is also separate from his brute, real, natural facticity. Polyneices's value for Antigone is not of the order of the natural, nor of the real in the Lacanian sense (and thus does *not* derive from what Lacan called *das Ding*), but of the order of the signifier. Polyneices "is what he is" even when he is

no longer real, that is, after his death as well, and this is only because
he is named, because he "is" a name and a narrative—because he "is" a
signifier. Of course, a person and language are not exchangeable entities
but, as a libidinal being, man is "what is he" because he has a name
and, precisely as a name, a signifier, he never coincides with his facticity
on the level of the real. Hence a dead Polyneices may well be dead but
he is not gone, and one may not act after his death as though he never
existed. He has existed as a signifier and in this capacity exceeds the
facticity of his death. It is the signifier that has torn him loose from the
natural order of life and death (from "the stream of possible changes")
and thereby ensures that his value does not disappear along with him
when he dies.

This signifier, moreover, is also separate from the meaning ("signifieds," "*signifiés*") he generates. No good or evil that Polyneices ever
accomplished coincides with the ultimate ground of his existence, which
is the pure, senseless signifier that he is. This is the dimension that Antigone sees in the reviled body of Polyeices, Lacan argues. She adopts the
position of the pure signifier that he is: "pure" not in the moral sense
of the word but because it has been detached (purified) of all meaning,
all signifieds, even the meaning of "state enemy number one." Antigone
takes her stand as it were in the "cut" between language and "meaning," in the fault line that ensures that no single signifier can pretend to
ground "being." In the final analysis, meaning comes from nothing,—"ex
nihilo"—from the "cut" that language makes in the real. This is what we
hear immediately after the previously cited passage:

> That purity, that separation of being from the characteristics
> of the historical drama he has lived through, is precisely the
> limit or the *ex nihilo* near to which Antigone takes her stand.
> It is nothing more than the break that the very presence of
> language inaugurates in the life of man. (S7E: 279, translation
> modified; S7F: 325)

Antigone, who is going to bury Polyneices at any cost, thus wants
to honor her brother in the capacity of an unbound signifier arising out
of nothing. It is not Antigone herself (or her "attachment" to him) who
makes Polyneices into something unique. He is unique because the law
tried to expel and destroy him. If Antigone takes up the cause of this
unique "expelled" one, it is to show that it is precisely his status as a
signifier that makes him immune to the law's destruction. The law cannot
make it as though Polyneices had never existed. If it tries, it will only
make him persist all the more visibly as a signifier. It is this status as a
signifier that Antigone wants to affirm with her autonomous act.

Put another way, it is precisely this status that Creon does not want to recognize in Polyneices. For Creon's attitude shows even more clearly that what is at issue in the entire confrontation about Polyneices' funeral is in fact the signifier. Creon wants more than his death; he wants his body to rot away or to be left as carrion for the dogs and birds, leaving no traces of him behind. Eteocles, Creon's predecessor in the war, was elevated as a hero in a state burial, but Polyneices' signification is to be reduced to nothing. He is to disappear from history as if he never existed. It is for this reason he will not grant Polyneices a grave with his name. But it is precisely here that Creon runs up against the harsh materiality that lends Polyneices his ultimate value, namely, the "ex nihilo" on which he rests, the signifier that he is and which cannot be undone by any bestowal of meaning, no matter how negative or destructive. Even after Polyneices' death, (hence, as a corpse), Creon wants him to face what Lacan, following Sade, calls the "second death," that is, a death that destroys him as a signifier (S7E: 254; S7F: 297). But the entire tragedy shows that this "second death," the murder of the signifier, is a lethal impossibility. It is precisely the signifier as such that Creon, whose own power he owes to the signifier, cannot touch.

Creon does indeed stand for "the law without limits, the sovereign law, the law that goes beyond or crosses the limit," as Lacan emphatically puts it elsewhere (S7E: 259; S7F: 301). But precisely because the law, too, works with signifiers, it is finite, bound as it is to the limits of the signifier. In the last resort, Creon can exercise power and establish a difference between good and bad, right and wrong, friend and enemy thanks to the signifier. But he is unable to go beyond the signifier; he cannot decide the "being" of Polyneices beyond the signifier that represents him. He cannot send Polyneices back to the real. Here the law must acknowledge its finitude and admit that it can only intervene at the level of the signifier, without being able to touch the signifier *as such*. It is this structural powerlessness that Creon fails to see.

It is precisely this powerlessness Antigone illustrates by her autonomous gesture. She asserts herself not *against* Creon's law as such but consciously stands at that law's *limit*, at the precise place where the law encounters its material support: the pure signifier, in this case, presented in the dead body of Polyneices the enemy. She resolutely goes to where the law can no longer realize its pretensions so as to show how that law threatens to run up against its own limits. It is thus no surprise that Lacan invariably associates Antigone's position with a boundary, a "radical limit" as he calls it in the passage cited above (S7E: 279; S7F: 325) or a condition of "the-race-is-run" as we already cited.[23] He describes her not so much as someone who resists Creon's law as if from the outside but rather as someone who advances to the limit of the law from within—"toward the fatal limit" as Lacan calls it (S7E: 279; S7F: 324)—so as to take a position at this "radical limit," the limit that is at the same time the material "core" ("radix" in Latin) of the law: the signifier.

## 2.3. Antigone: Decentering the Subject

At that radical limit, we also encounter that which binds us as libidinal beings to law and the signifier: desire. Antigone also shows us the desire that we *are*. In contrast to our daily experience, at the unconscious level, law and desire are not that opposed to each other, as Lacan explains in detail throughout this seminar. For the desire that we *are* is primarily that of the symbolic Other, which is imposed on us from outside, telling us what *have to* be *or have to* do. Although we project the fulfillment of our desire onto the Other (which is why we always remain more or less attached to its law) we at that same time repress the Other's impossibility of doing so (this is "primal repression"). In fact, it is precisely because the Other will invariably fail in this, that it is so constitutive for our libidinal economy. Only in this capacity does it *keep* us desiring. We reflect ourselves in the symbolic Other precisely because it is at one and the same time both desire and lack, and it exists only insofar as we are the subjects/bearers of that desire and lack. To repeat the basic claim of Lacanian psychoanalysis: we have replaced the unbearable real lack with a livable symbolic one (the Other as "order of the lack"). It is thus essentially the lack in the Other that makes us desire.

Still, this is only one side of the coin. The Other not only makes us desire; in another sense, we *also make the Other desire*. As bearer/subject of its lack, we situate ourselves precisely in that symbolic field of otherness where it is marked by a lack. By taking this place, by "subjectifying" the lack of the Other, we keep the Other open and arouse its desire. And because the Other proffers itself as a law, we thereby affirm the law's constitutive inadequacy, finitude and lack (including that of the ethical law). As subjects of the desire of the Other—and hence as subjects of the law—we are at the same time an affirmation of the lack of the Other and its law.

Here we arrive at the heart of Lacan's interpretation of *Antigone*: it is precisely this aspect of his theory of the subject that his reading of this ancient tragedy is meant to illustrate. In his previous seminars, Lacan had already explained that man is the subject of the desire of the Other. Recall his sixth seminar (*Desire and Its Interpretation*) where he interprets *Hamlet* as a tragic attempt to become the subject of the Other's desire and law (see above 1.5.1). If he then focuses on *Antigone* in his next seminar, it is to develop an aspect of his subject theory that has not yet been fully clarified. Here the protagonist's catastrophe makes it clear how the Other, too, is primarily radical desire and therefore marked by lack and finitude, even if this Other proffers itself as an absolute law. Antigone is the subject of the Other's desire, a desire that clearly appears here as the law: as the daughter of the previous king, her existence is completely determined by the political (symbolic) order. But this is not what the play brings into focus. It rather presents Antigone in such a way that she makes clear how the entire order, with its power and law, is at one and the same time desire *and* lack. Under circumstances where the law appears omnipresent and all-powerful, she assumes precisely the place where the law comes up against its own limits, thereby revealing how it cannot give or realize what it promises.

Creon functions in the play as the representative of the law (or, in Lacanian terms, the Other) trying to restore order in a "polis" recently ravaged by war. Where the two brothers had brought the city to the brink of the abyss by their capricious desire, Creon's wish is for the law to prevail over desire, a law that—as Lacan formulates it elsewhere—has the "good of all" in mind ("le bien de tous," S7E: 258, 259; S7F: 300, 301). By the end of the play, to his own dismay and shame, he will be forced to realize that the law—that is supposed to restrain desire—itself stems from desire. Then Creon finally understands what Antigone had shown him by opposing his law so vehemently: the lack of his *own* desire, more precisely the lack and the desire lying at the base of the law. Before his tragic fall, he considered himself the true "subject," the true "bearer" of the law. Following the death of both pretenders to the throne, he has become responsible for the good of the *polis*. It was up to him, then, to separate good from evil again, to identify friends (in this case, Eteocles) and enemies (Polyneices), and treat each accordingly. At the end of the play, it becomes evident how wrong he was, however noble his intentions were. For, it was not *he* who was the subject and bearer of the law but the one whom he had expelled on the basis of the law, Antigone with her lawless desire.

The play in fact stages what Lacan would call the "decentering" of the ethical subject. It is not Creon's certainty about the good that shows us the point where the ethical law finds its fundamental support, but Antigone's stubborn and unfulfilled desire. Creon reveals the law as supported by desire, by a desire to destroy all evil and to create real goodness. The confrontation with Antigone's inflexible desire will make him—and the audience—conclude that indeed, his law can only desire such a thing; that his law, too, in other words, stems from just as obstinate a desire as that of Antigone's. The good the law promises can only be desire, and it is in this desire that the law finds its ultimate ground.

## 2.4. *"Autonomous"*

It should now be clear that the key to understanding Lacan's commentary on *Antigone* lies in his theory of the subject even though he rarely refers directly to it. As we saw, at the end of his lesson of June 8, he alludes to it in connection with the "autonomy" he attributes to the figure of Antigone. Although this passage was cited and commented on already, we can now understand it more clearly. "Antigone," he claims here,

> appears as αὐτόνομος [*autonomos*, autonomous], as a pure and simple relationship of the human being to that of which he miraculously happens to be the bearer, namely, the signifying cut that confers on him the indomitable power of being what he is in the face of everything that may oppose him. (S7E: 282; S7F: 328; see above 2.1)

As we now know, what makes Antigone autonomous for Lacan is the signifier. She has taken her stand at the very locus of the "signifying cut," that is, in the gap between the signifier and the real. Neither the real as such nor any of the established meanings lay down the law to her, which gives her "the indomitable power of being what [s]he is in the face of everything that may oppose [her]." Does this mean that now she can choose to be what she is out of her own free will? Not at all.[24] Her autonomy is not that of a free subject in the voluntarist sense of the word, but that of a subject insofar as it is the "bearer" of a desire, a desire, note, that is that of the (symbolic) Other. Neither the real, nor the fixed signified, but the *signifier* and (which amounts to the same thing) the "desire of the Other" lay down the law to her. But if this is the case, how can she then be free? How is precisely a law able to make her into a rebel?[25] How can she be both obedient to the law of the signifier and the rebel who tramples autonomously on every law? It is because this autonomy is not only hers, but also and primarily that of the law itself. The autonomy Antigone testifies to in her tragedy is—technically speaking—not that of the ego she imagines herself to be but that of the subject she is, and this is something completely different for Lacan. Of course, Antigone is for him, too, an autonomous liberated rebel; however, in his eyes she can only be this thanks to an autonomy and freedom that is also characteristic of the law she opposes. *She is the subject/bearer of an autonomy of the Other and (thus) of the law.* In this sense, the conflict in Sophocles' *Antigone* is not between autonomy, on the one hand, and the law on the other, but a confrontation of the law (or, which amounts to the same thing, the symbolic order) with its own autonomy and the anomalies that mark it. In Antigone's rebellion, the law itself is confronted with the problem of its own autonomous foundation.

In fact, from Lacan's perspective, the law (and the symbolic order in general) must be regarded as a radically autonomous entity that stems neither from some kind of essence nor from something real. It is only supported by signifiers that have been cut off from the real and determine what we call "reality." In other words, it is the signifier that makes the law an autonomous power. Still, it is also the same signifier that is responsible for the radical finitude of this autonomous power and ensures that the law will never realize its pretensions and promises. Any signifier that promises to realize the law projects this anticipated autonomy in a signifier that is forever to come so that the realization of autonomy remains infinitely deferred. Since the autonomy of the law is only symbolic—because it derives from signifiers—the law remains desire longing for itself, although its function is precisely to channel all desire and put it onto the right path. It is solely because the law can only desire rather than realize the fulfillment of its promises, the human libidinal being is able to be its bearer (subject). Because, in other words, the law remains "other to itself" as well, the (from a real perspective) impossible and unlivable libidinal being can nevertheless find shelter and realize itself as "other" (as Lacan calls it referring to Rimbaud's "I is another").

Against this background, it is now clear why Lacan immediately associates Sophocles' word "autonomous" with the fact that Antigone is the "bearer of the signifying cut." The freedom with which Antigone resists Creon's law and even chooses death is nothing other than the freedom and autonomy of the symbolic order and of the law as such—which are free, also in the sense of "freed from the real." However, this symbolic order or law can only sustain itself by repressing this radical groundless freedom at every turn. Antigone's tragic gesture breaks through this repression and confronts the law and the entire symbolic order with its groundless ground: with an unattainable otherness or, what amounts to the same thing, with a radical and unfulfillable desire.

Thus "desire" is also the term Lacan uses here to think the finitude of the ethical law. That law must inevitably profess the realization of its promised good, but can in fact never do anything more than make us long for it. This is the desire, says Lacan, that shines in the figure of Antigone. It is not coincidental that, following this allusion to his subject theory, he talks about Antigone's tragic gesture[26] and interprets it as a radical act of desire:

> [Antigone] pushes to the limit the realization [accomplissement] of something that might be called the pure and simple desire

of death as such. She incarnates that desire. (S7E: 282; S7F: 328–329)

Antigone's act is one of pure desire. "Pure," because all elements that usually keep desire repressed are set aside.[27] The discursive order of significations that provide this unrestrained desire with a protective meaning falls away. The metonymic displacement of signifiers also strands itself on the one literal dead signifier "Polyneices." Even the subject of this desire (Antigone) is so carried away by that desire that it forgets its function of bearer and is at risk of disappearing. The "accomplishment" ("realization") Lacan talks about here does not mean the fulfillment of desire in the sense of *jouissance*. Rather, it is a matter of keeping that desire going "to the limit," a limit behind which both the Other and the subject who bears that Other disappear. In this way, desire becomes a "pure and simple desire of death," a desire that goes *beyond* the self-preservation of the subject. Here, "accomplishment" thus does not mean that desire, now purified of all foreign elements, has come to the end of its odyssey and finally attained itself.[28] On the contrary, the death principle means that desire never comes home, and its support (i.e., the locus where it lies and from where it operates) by definition lies not in itself but in the symbolic Other—an Other that, in its turn, has its "subject" (the place where it "finds itself") only in the fictional place from which the drive regulates its libidinal economy.

In the ethics seminar, Lacan forges a concept for mapping this paradox of desire in a more nuanced way. With "Das Ding," he names desire's inability to really come full circle and gives it a specific locus in the libidinal economy. As a radical exteriority, the "thing" nevertheless forms the central point around which the whole economy revolves and at which desire aims, a "topological" paradox for which he forges the term "extimité" (S7E: 139; S7F: 167). While the "thing" indicates the point at which desire aims, as if at "itself," it is also what would destroy it as soon as it was reached. This is why the "thing" is an indispensable element in the cartography of desire. *Antigone*, for Lacan, offers a particularly apposite illustration of this.

## 3. Desire in the Picture

### 3.1 "Atè"

Although fundamental for the argument, the term "*das Ding*" is nowhere to be found in Lacan's comment on *Antigone*. In the course of the previous lessons, Lacan had come step by step closer to the "extimate" domain of the "thing." In the session on "enjoyment" (April 27), we read that only transgression gives access to that domain and in the following lesson (4 May, on "the death drive") the reference to Sade showed how evil and diabolical that realm is. The next lessons, "the function of the good" (May 11) and "the function of the beautiful" (May 18), developed two ways of maintaining us at a distance from the "thing" despite our orientation towards it. If, Lacan, argued, "the good" does so in a "deceptive" way, the "beautiful" at least permits something of that ultimate domain at which our desire aims to shimmer through. The latter will be of great interest to an ethics based on the primacy of desire.

A work of art such as *Antigone* grants us a vision of the domain of the "thing": this will be the next step in Lacan's line of reasoning. This tragedy reveals how the limit of desire is transgressed and gives us a certain view of the "thing" that lies beyond this limit. There, a domain emerges where our desire can indulge itself uninhibitedly but where, precisely for this reason, nothing or no one can survive, neither can any ethical desire to do good. We already saw this in a previously cited passage where Lacan characterizes Creon's tragic fault as the misrecognition of the limit that separates us from the "thing." In Creon, Sophocles gives us a man who wants to let the good rule without any constraint or limit; too late, he realizes how he has unleashed the apotheosis of his own fate:

> His error of judgment [. . .] is to want to promote [. . .] the good[29] as the law without limits, the sovereign law, the law that goes beyond or crosses a certain limit, [his mistake in judgment is] that he doesn't notice that he crosses this famous limit [. . .]. (S7E: 259, modified translation; S7F: 301)

A little later on, Lacan derives the following from this:

> The good cannot want to[30] reign over all without an excess emerging whose fatal consequences are revealed to us in tragedy. What then is this famous sphere that we must not cross into? We are told that it is the place where the unwritten laws, the will or, better yet, the Δίκη [*Dikè*, legal order] of the gods rules. (S7E: 259; S7F: 301)

Here, in Sophocles' text, we have the equivalent of what Lacan calls "the domain of the thing." The "famous sphere" we reach once we transgress the limit of our desire is nothing other than what the ancient Greeks meant with the will, the law, the justice (the "*Dikè*") of the gods. The terms "law" and "justice" are rather deceptive since the ancient "gods" refer not to something symbolic but indicate a field that lies beyond it and which must unquestionably be called the "real" (the "thing"). This is at least what Lacan claims here, and he will affirm it in one of the first lessons of his next seminar (*The Transference*, 1960–1961). There, he will repeat that what the Greeks called "gods" must be understood as "the real" and differs radically from the monotheistic God which is of the order of the Word and, hence the symbolic. During his third lesson of the seminar (November 30, 1960), he questions his audience:

> What after all do you think about gods? Where are they situated with respect to the symbolic, to the imaginary and to the real? [. . .] the gods it is quite certain belong obviously to the real. The gods are a mode of revelation of the real. (S8F: 58)[31]

In brief, Lacan's interpretation of Creon comes down to this: by trying to realize a limitless good, the mortal Creon goes beyond his limits, imperceptibly landing in the domain of the gods—the real—and is there confronted all the more bitterly with his own limits and his own mortality. What interests Lacan here, however, is how the audience meanwhile obtains a glimpse of the transgressive space the Greeks described as the domain of "the gods," which he indicates with his terms, the real and the "thing." For this is what tragedy consists of, for Lacan: a staging of signifiers in such a way as to allow the real, gaping beyond the symbolic field, to shine through.

How, then, can this transgressive space appear through a figure such as Antigone? Isn't she precisely the one who respects the space of the gods, and resisting Creon's law, defends the inviolability of their particular kind of law, their "*Dikè*? Does she not try precisely to safeguard the domain of the gods from any transgression, that of the audience included? How, then, is she able to reveal something of this transgressive space that the "thing" stands for?

It is at this point Lacan breaks away from the majority of interpretations of *Antigone* to opt for a reading that, if we are to believe George Steiner, is the furthest from the "Sophoclean tenor" (Steiner, 1986; 93). Everything comes down to the interpretation of one verse in Sophoclean play, the verse where Antigone refuses to go along with Creon's edict:

> Yes it was not Zeus who made this proclamation [to me], nor was it Justice who lives with the gods below. (v. 450; Sophocles, 2002: 45)

According to the usual interpretation, Antigone is challenging the legitimacy of Creon's law: he has no mandate from the gods for his edict. Like in many other translations, Hugh Lloyd-Jones also neglects to take the word "μόι" [*mói*, me] into consideration.[32] Once one does so, however, the text can also be translated as "neither Zeus nor any other god asked this of me," where the pronoun "this" refers not to Creon's decree but to Antigone's own "crime."[33] Lacan defends this latter reading vigorously and says, with reference to Antigone:

> She denies that it is Zeus who ordered her to do it. Nor is it Δίκη [*Dikè*], which is the companion or collaborator of the gods below. She pointedly distinguishes herself from Δίκη. (S7E: 278; S7F: 324)

In this interpretation, Antigone thus claims that *no god* ordered her to bury her brother, that is, she did it purely by herself, "autonomous" as she is. The autonomous nature of her act shows how she observes no limit between mortals and gods and, like Creon, is also guilty of an unlawful transgression.

For Lacan, Antigone's transgressive nature is revealed by yet another element in the text: the often repeated theme of "*atè,*" blind fate. When Lacan describes Antigone in his lesson of 1 June, he links her immediately with this "*atè*":

> By way of introduction, I would just like to make a few remarks. And I will come right to the point in stating the term that is at the center of Antigone's whole drama, a term that is repeated twenty times, and that given the shortness of the text, sounds like forty—which, of course, does not prevent it from being read—ἄτη [*atè*]. (S7E: 262; S7F: 305)

As is typical in such cases, Lacan exaggerates a little. The term appears not twenty but ten times[32]—stamping the whole play all the same—and is not the main topic of the passages at hand. But Lacan has gone so deeply into one passage that it colors his reading of all the others. It concerns a number of verses[33] from the second stanza, the choir's song where they complain about the fate that, after having mowed down all the other members of the "house of Labdakos" now strikes Antigone. In the final strophe we hear:

> He was a wise old man who coined
> the famous saying: "Sooner or later
> foul is fair, fair is foul
> to the man the gods will ruin"—
>     He goes his way for a moment only
>         free of blinding ruin. (v. 620–625; Sophocles, 1984: 89)

"Blinding ruin" translates (correctly, by the way) the Greek "atè." However, in Lacan, this word acquires a more specific meaning because he reads it in relation to the preposition that accompanies this word here (as it does in a number of other verses). In one verse, man is led "towards *atè*"—"πρὸς ἄταν [pros atan]"—in another one finds oneself ("for a moment only") "beyond atè"—"ἐκτὸς ἄτας [ektos atas]."[34] For Lacan it is clear: the *atè* stands here for a limit, a border. Human existence moves toward a limit that, once transgressed, brings us into a domain where we cannot maintain ourselves. At the beginning of his third lesson on *Antigone*, Lacan focuses on the verses from the second stanza:

> Ἐκτὸς ἄτας [*Ektos atas*] has the meaning of going beyond a limit in the text. And it is around this notion that the Chorus's song is developed at that moment in the same way that it says that man goes toward πρὸς ἄτας [*pros atan*], that is, toward *Atè*. In this business the whole prepositional system of the Greek is so vital and so suggestive. It is because man mistakes evil for the good, because something beyond the limits of *Atè* has become Antigone's good, namely, a good that is different from everyone else's, that she goes toward, πρὸς ἄταν [*pros atan*]. (S7E: 270; S7F: 315)

Antigone's act involves a clear transgression. She has gone beyond the limit of "atè," beyond the limit inside which life and goodness are possible. By "mistak[ing] evil for the good," by choosing what falls outside the law, she is beyond *atè* and, like Creon, sets her destiny in motion. Note that this "choice" does not refer to a decision of will, nor an error of judgment on Antigone's part, but to a structural element in desire. Coming back in the following lesson to this passage in the second stanza, Lacan states:

> It is because she goes toward *Atè* here, because it is even a question of going ἐκτὸς ἄτας [*ektos atas*], of going beyond the limit of *Atè*, that Antigone interests the Chorus. It says that she's the one who violates the limits of *Atè* through her desire. [. . .] *Atè* is not ἁμαρτία [*hamartia*], that is to say a mistake or an error [la faute ou l'erreur]; it's nothing to do with doing something stupid [une bêtise]. (S7E: 277; S7F: 322–323)

One can still blame Creon's transgression of "atè" on a mistake (as the choir explicitly states at the end of the play[35]). It is literally, as they say, his own "ἁμαρτία [hamartia]." But we never hear that word—which is nevertheless essential to tragedy for Aristotle[36]—about Antigone. Her transgressive step beyond the "atè" is evidently not the result of an error but, according to Lacan, to be blamed purely on "her desire." The way she is presented in the play does not make us look for her fate's cause (as is the case with Creon) but confronts us directly with her desire and, more precisely, with the autonomy of that desire in the sense that we have outlined. Her tragedy lies, then, *not in the way* she deal with her desire but *in that desire itself*. In Antigone, it becomes clear how desire only exists thanks to the limit that separates it from the real that it nevertheless aims for. This limit is nothing other than the signifier itself, the sign of both the autonomy and of the finitude of desire. In the play, Antigone seeks this "pure" signifier and, therefore, takes her stand at the limit of the symbolic order and its law. Appearing in this limit, she reveals how, despite being completely dependent on this order and law, desire still tries to go *beyond* it and aims at the real, the "thing," that is, that domain where the subject of desire (its bearer) disappears. Her commitment to Polyneices reveals the tragic locus of the signifier, that is, the limit that desire both props up and is incited to transgress in order to lose itself in the real. *Antigone*, the play, shows desire as aiming at a *Beyond* where the subject is unable to sustain itself. There, desire appears as what is always at odds with what limits and constrains it; in the final analysis, it coincides with the very irreconcilability of that tension.

Both Creon and Antigone transgress the constitutive limit of the law and thus confront the audience with the transgressive structure of desire. Does Lacan, then, make no distinction between Creon and Antigone? Do both represent two equivalent ways of bringing desire into the picture? And in this sense do they both have the same moral validity for the "ethics of desire" Lacan is outlining here?

### 3.2. "Apotheosis of Sadism"

Although they both go beyond the limits of "atè," Antigone's and Creon's transgressions are not the same. Antigone is fully conscious of the limit and, transgressing it, she does so in complete awareness that she is sealing her fate. Creon, on the other hand, remains blind to this limit, regarding the law he defends as unlimited. Only when it is too late, only when his wife and son have been mowed down by fate, will he take notice of that limit. Until then, his arrogance denied that his law was limited by the material it consists of (i.e., signifiers). In so doing, he remained blind to the same "wild" desire that underlies his own law, but which he initially saw solely in Antigone.

According to Lacan, this type of conscious blindness is not as foreign to us as we might think. It is in fact our very own, if only because monotheism and, more specifically, Christianity have such a strong influence on us, regardless of whether we are religious or not. In a previously cited passage where Lacan compares the domain of the "thing" with "*atè*," he links our ignorance of the ancient gods immediately to our Christian origins:

> What then is this famous sphere that we must not cross into? We are told that it is the place where the unwritten laws, the will or, better yet, the Δίκμ [*Dikè*] of the gods rules. But we no longer have any idea what gods are. Let us not forget that we have lived for a long time under Christian law [sous la loi chrétienne], and in order to recall what the gods are, we have to engage in a little ethnography. (S7E: 259; S7F: 301)

Monotheism elevates the denial of the domain of the gods (that as an individual Creon testifies to) into the principle of a new religion and, in the shape of Christianity, lays the foundation for Western culture, modernity included. For the gods are idols and hence non-existent, so monotheism claims. Only God is God—a God who is to be considered as Word. With this, the word itself acquires a divine and (hence) infinite status. The divine no longer lies beyond the word, as with the Greeks, but has now become the word itself. It is through the divine omnipotence of the word that all of creation came into being.[37] And after creation fell into sin and death through the pride of man, that same word—now become "flesh" in Christ—is going to save us.[38] In the foundational texts of Christianity, the savior is explicitly called the "logos," reforging in this capacity all lack, death and finitude into the infinity of an "eternal life." Through him—in the terrestrial world too—the "logos" becomes unlimited and no operation hampers its power, not even death. The entire philosophical and scientific tradition is supported by this unlimited belief in "logos" whose influence continues undiminished, even after Christianity lost its dominant role in our culture.

Thus our scientific culture (certainly following the mathematization of our world picture; see above: 3.1.1) and our religious tradition both suppose an unlimited belief in the "logos."[39] "Unlimited," precisely because it denies its radical finitude and, in so doing, consciously remains blind, like Creon, both to the limit on which this "logos" is built (the Greek "atè," the Lacanian signifier) and to the domain that yawns beyond this "logos" (for the ancients, the gods, for Lacan the domain of the "thing"). Both monotheistic and scientific traditions have extracted all content from "the gods," declaring them unreal chimeras. Several lines later, Lacan says this about the "domain of the gods":

> In other words, this whole sphere is only accessible to us from the outside, from the point of view of science and its objectivation. For us Christians, who have been educated by Christianity,

it doesn't belong to the text in which the question is raised.
We Christians have erased the whole sphere of the gods. And
we are, in fact, interested here in that which we have replaced
it with as illuminated by psychoanalysis. In this sphere, where
is the limit? A limit that has no doubt been there from the
beginning, but which doubtless remains isolated and leaves its
skeleton in this sphere that we Christians have abandoned. That
is the question I am asking here. (S7E: 260: S7F: 302)

Here, Lacan argues, psychoanalysis at least allows a consideration of
the limit of that suppressed domain of the gods (and hence also the limit
of the "logos"). Note that psychoanalysis itself is a full consequence of the
primacy of the "logos" that has determined our culture since the rise, first,
of Christianity, and then of modern science. Psychoanalysis's "primacy of
the signifier" is only its most recent modification. Still, Lacan believes that
with the latter a decisive step has been taken. Where men traditionally
took the "logos" for something infinite and unlimited, it is now conceived
from the notion of the "signifier"—something radically finite. However
all-determining the signifiers may be, they do not coincide with reality
as such. The signifier is not able to touch real *being* as such. In contrast
to the presuppositions of Christianity and science, the autonomy of the
"logos" corresponds radically with its finitude, with the irrecuperable
impotence of realizing its aspirations with respect to the real. It remains
imprisoned in the "unreal" material it is made of, namely, its signifiers.
This doesn't prevent the desire "driving" this "logos" from remaining
thoroughly aimed at the real beyond the signifier. Here desire shows its
most dangerous aspect because, when it gives in to it, it becomes a mere
desire for death. A "logos" that could realize its own infinite aspirations
and reconcile the gap separating it from the real would without question
destroy itself because it would no longer desire. For psychoanalysis, it is
once more a question of detecting and paying attention to this limit of
"logos" and desire.

In the course of his seminar, Lacan already demonstrated how this
limit is nothing but the signifier itself, appearing as such in the phenomenon
of the beautiful. He alludes to this again in the sentence that immediately
follows the previously cited passage:

The limit involved, the limit that it is essential to situate if a
certain phenomenon is to emerge through reflection, is something
I have called the phenomenon of the beautiful, it is something
I have begun to define as the limit of the second death. (S7E:
260; S7F: 302)

On the following pages, Lacan reexamines this "limit of the second death." If he turns his attention exclusively to the way it is presented in Sade, it is because Sade enables him to reveal how this limit is denied—just as in the Christian and scientific traditions. Only afterwards will he focus on the figure of Antigone as an illustration of how one can acknowledge this limit affirmatively, which—as I will explain—is essential for an "ethics of psychoanalysis."

If Lacan approaches Sade's oeuvre as a work of art, it is because the "limit involved" emerges in the foreground in the figure of "the beautiful." But where, then, do we find beauty in the Sadean apotheosis of cruelty that holds everyone in its eternal death grip, making them suffer ad infinitum? For, according to the Sadean norm, it is not enough to simply kill the victim. This would only return the victim's mutilated body to the natural cycle of life and death, its decomposed matter incessantly reforming into new living beings.[40] The victim must therefore be given a "second death," a death that strikes beyond the limit of natural mortality. However, this "second death" fantasy presumes that the victim can be touched beyond his natural death, in other words, that he can endure more than normal agonies, that is, that he can go beyond this and even then keep on living. It is precisely this "perverse" logic that attributes a paradoxical beauty to the victim in the Sadean fantasy. Take, for example, Justine, the figure par excellence of what Sade calls "the misfortunes of virtue." Misused in the most inhuman ways, raped and tortured night after night, what do we see the following morning at breakfast? Precisely the victim's *untouched* beauty that seduces the libertine again. Despite the sadistic orgies of the night before, her beauty remains intact. It is as though the sadist can torture everything in her except her beauty. More precisely: only to the extent that she is perceived as absolute beauty can the sadist treat her so cruelly. Her beauty—that is, the fact that she functions purely as a signifier—is the condition of possibility for his sadism.

In such beauty, the sadistic fantasy thus runs up against its constitutive limit, a limit that according to Lacan is nothing other than the signifier itself. The sadist tries to strike his victim beyond her natural death but, in the same movement, must keep her alive, precisely in order to be able to do so. It is only because the victim functions purely as a signifier that such a perverse ruse is possible. The fact that she remains immune to whatever is done to her, that she can always with the same virginal blush on her cheeks reawaken the libertine's appetites, shows that she functions within the Sadean fantasy solely as a signifier. And by treating her like a signifier, the sadist tries, as it were, to force her back into the nothing—the "ex nihilo"—from which she originates. Of course, this can only be phantasmaticly occurring only in an imaginary scenario driven purely by the power of signifiers. This is why the sadist ascribes his victim an "indestructible support," a beauty surviving and resisting every violation. The victim's real existence is literally sacrificed to the status of a signifier—to beauty. A little further in the same passage, Lacan refers to the signifier as "the indestructible support" on which the sadistic fantasy rests:

> In the typical Sadean scenario, suffering doesn't lead the victim
> to the point where he is dismembered and destroyed. It seems
> rather that, in the phantasm,[41] the object of all the torture is
> to retain the capacity of being an indestructible support. (S7E:
> 261; S7F: 303)

So, Sade's oeuvre does indeed illustrate what Lacan means by "the function of the beautiful." Beyond the "function of the good," which is the first barrier on desire's path to the "thing" as Lacan put it, the function of the beautiful forms a second barrier. That the "beautiful" goes *beyond* the good is quite palpable in an oeuvre such as Sade's. Yet it is at the same time a barrier the sadist uses to protect himself from that deathly domain of the "thing" as presented in the victim's real pain. Worshiping his victim's unassailable beauty, the sadist denies the unbearable real at whose mercy the victim is, and imagines himself in a universe deprived of all lack, law, finitude or death. Violating every possible law (including the prohibitions against incest and murder), his phantasm is one of a limitless *jouissance*, albeit one that must disavow its failure each time by creating new victims or inventing new torture techniques. For the *sadist*, the victim's beauty functions as barrier that enables him to remain blind to anything that might point toward lack, law, death, and desire, in other words, toward the signifier and its deadly *Beyond*. For Sade's *readers*, on the other hand, this beauty functions as a barrier through which the horrible domain of the "thing" does indeed become visible. For us, it reveals beauty as a veil that covers an unbearable suffering but at which our desire nevertheless aims. One can also see beauty in Sade as "beginning of Terror we're still just able to bear" as Rainer Maria Rilke once called it.[42]

Lacan observes this intimate connection between beauty and pain not only in Sade's fantasies but in much of modern aesthetics as well, as for instance in Kant. In his *Critique of Judgment*, Kant defined the beautiful as the result of a pure, *reflexive* judgment of taste, that is, a judgment that says nothing about the object but speaks solely about the feeling this produces in the human faculty of cognition.[43] It tells of the feeling the intellectual capacities—and hence, so to speak, the autonomous "logos"—have of *themselves* while making an aesthetic judgment. The perceived object is never more than an occasion. Lacan sees a striking similarity in this with Sade. For in both Kantian and Sadean judgments of taste, the real object functions only in order to be "cut away" as it were. After evoking Kant's definition of beauty, Lacan asks his audience:

> I take it you see the analogy with the Sadean fantasm, since the object there is no more than the power to support a form of suffering, which is in itself nothing else but the signifier of a limit. Suffering is conceived of as a stasis which affirms that that which is cannot return to the void from which it emerged. (S7E: 261; S7F: 304)

By definition, Kant's judgment of beauty dispenses with the object. The object's "suffering" is its condition of possibility so to speak. An aesthetic judgment confirms that, once an object has been taken up in the realm of autonomous "logos," it can no longer return to where it came from, remaining trapped in this "logos." Once the "logos" has hauled something out of nothing—"ex nihilo,"—that same "logos" prohibits it from returning back to nothing. The real of the object remains forever behind in that "nothing," in that domain the ancient Greeks attributed to the gods and which has in fact been reduced to the pure limit of the "nothing" since Christianity. Only the fascinating beauty of this limit allows something of the real suffering that lies behind it to shimmer through.

Not without provocation, Lacan claims here that Kant's aesthetic judgment, as revealed in its Sadean structure, also applies to Christianity. What are the "good tidings" if not this "stasis which affirms that that which is cannot return to the void from which it emerged." Once it has been created out of nothing, the way back to that "nothing" becomes impossible. Once something has been saved by the Word, the way back to the real from which it came is forever cut off. All the real can do is shimmer in the fascinating beauty of the Word (the signifier) underneath which it wastes away. The Christian image par excellence of the Word (or, in Lacanian terms, of the "pure signifier") is the crucified Christ, says Lacan in the immediate conclusion to the above-cited passage:

> Here one encounters the limit that Christianity has erected in the place of all the other gods, a limit that takes the form of the exemplary image which attracts to itself all the threads or our desire, the image of the crucifixion. If we dare, not so much look it in the face—given that mystics have been staring at it for centuries, we can only hope that it has been observed closely—but speak about it directly, which is much more difficult, shall we say that what is involved there is something that we

might call the apotheosis of sadism? And by this I mean the divinization of everything that remains in this sphere, namely, of the limit in which a being remains in a state of suffering [. . .]. Need I go further and add that in connection with that image Christianity has been crucifying man in holiness for centuries? In holiness. (S7E: 261–262; S7F: 304)

In Christianity, the domain *beyond* the word is reduced to nothing, which is not simply nothing but the "limit" behind which the real is kept hidden. Lacan observes this even in the aesthetic image through which Christianity presents itself, the crucified Christ. That image expresses how the son of God has taken all sin, finitude, and death upon himself for the sake of universal salvation At least, this is what this image says *will* happen. However, it tells this by *solely* showing—in the glittering of its signifiers—pain, death, and finitude. So, in the same move, the image of the "good tidings" both shows and denies pain, sin, and death. The structure of this Christian disavowal is isomorphic to that of the Sadean hero, so Lacan argues. He even goes so far as to claim that this process surpasses the purely aesthetic and finds its counterpart in the way Christianity deals with man in reality. The Christian ideal of an "imitation of Christ" can assume such proportions that someone literally "sacrifices" himself out of pure devotion in an attempt to make himself equal to that "beautiful" image.

On the previous page, Lacan had already alluded how such a Sadean-ism functions in reality and had announced his theory of perversion in a nutshell (later to be set out in his tenth seminar [*Anxiety*, 1962/63] and in "Kant with Sade" [1963]).[44] Immediately following the passage where he described the beauty of the Sadean victim as its "indestructible sup-port," we read that the Sadean fantasy:

is indeed a fantasm whose analysis shows clearly that the subject separates out a double of himself who is made inaccessible to destruction, so as to make it support what, borrowing a term from the realm of aesthetics, one cannot help calling the play of pain. (S7E: 261; S7F: 303)[45]

In the Sadean fantasy, "the subject separates out a double of him-self," and projects this onto his victim. The stakes of this perverse process become clear once one realizes that the sadist projects his own lack, his own pain of being into the double (the other, in this case, the victim) in order to immediately deny its presence there as well. Thus, he both pretends to be without any lack himself while maintaining the illusion that his victim is unmarked by lack either. He literally carves his own lack into the victim's skin, branding it with death, suffering, and every possible sign of human finitude so that, once transferred onto the other, he can disavow it there too. In this way, the sadist tries to obtain proof through the other that he is himself without lack. *His* lack writhes in the other's pain, but this pain serves merely to prove that he, the sadist, enjoys it and can imagine himself above all pain. In this way, he creates the fantasy of a world without lack, a world filled with *jouissance* in which there is no lack and no law that can forbid him anything.

The perverse procedure Lacan focuses on here is not, however, limited to sadistic individuals who poke fun at the law. It applies just as much to anyone who demands a strict observance of the law. He, too, can deny the lack inherent to the law and project it onto others in order to deny it there. So can a lawmaker or politician project the lack inherent to his legal order onto the people and maintain that the reason there has to be a law at all is precisely because of *their* lack, of *their* failure to conform to the ideal. In this way totalitarian communism—to take an example Slavoj Žižek often came back to in his earlier work[46]—pretended that the falures of this kind of political and economic systems was caused by the way some (and virtually all) citizens fell short of "the great leap forwards," or sabotaged "the cultural revolution" so that the system was constantly obliged to go after its citizens, feeding the insatiable mouth of the Gulag. The moment a legal order disavows its own finitude through this kind of perverse logic, the consequences are incalculable, as the political history of the twentieth century illustrates abundantly, alas.

In Lacan's interpretation, Creon's position contains the seeds of such a disastrous perverse procedure. This is at least one of the reasons Lacan does not consider him the protagonist of the play.[47] Creon's reaction to Antigone's act illustrates his intention to reestablish the sovereignty of the law after a war between Thebe's leaders that could have destroyed the city. In itself, it is a noble intent except that Antigone's punishment shows how dubious and perverse (in the sense described above) his position is. For he does not summarily kill her, as his own law dictates, but imprisons her alive in a cave that will become her grave. He even gives her provisions so as to maintain the impression that it is not through his agency that she will die but rather because the gods, who she claims to support, refuse to save her. At the beginning of this chapter we cited this passage in Robert Fagles's translation. It is Creon's retort, right at the end of the third "episodion," just after Antigone is led away:

CREON:   I will take her down some wild, desolate path
         never trod by men, and wall her up alive
         in a rocky vault, and set out short rations,
         just the measure piety demands
         to keep the entire city free of defilement.

> There let her pray to the one god she worships:
> Death—who knows?—may just reprieve her from death.
> Or she may learn at last, better than ever,
> what a waste of breath it is to worship Death.
> (*Exit to the palace*)[48]

Clearly, Creon recoils from assuming the consequences of his own law. While he sentences Antigone to death, he refuses to take full responsibility for that death. At the crucial moment he thus refuses to accept that death and law have anything to do with each other. By literally leaving death to "the real" and pretending his legal order has nothing to do with it, Creon disavows the inherent lack, the structural finitude of this order. Lack, finitude and *hence* (from a Lacanian perspective) desire are affirmed rather than disavowed in the figure of Antigone. In her beauty radiates the "eros" or desire that underlies mankind and its world, its law included.

### 3.3. Catharsis . . .

This takes us back to the central thesis of Lacan's commentary on Antigone: the ethical meaning of the tragedy is to be found in the protagonist's radiant beauty. Yet how is this possible, since, in a sense, Antigone's beauty differs little from that of a Sadean victim? Like the victims in Sade, is she not just that "indestructible support" (S7E: 261; S7F: 303) onto which all the suffering of the world falls? In the phantasmatic space of the tragedy, she too situates herself beyond the first, natural death ("my life has long been dead") and is therefore touched by a "second death." In this sense, she is "between two deaths" (an expression that Lacan by his own admission appropriated from one of his listeners).[49] This is the precise place where the sadist puts his victim, as we can infer from what Lacan says in his first lesson on *Antigone*:

> How do we explain the dissipatory power of this central image [i.e., Antigone] relative to all others that suddenly seem to descend upon it and disappear? [. . .] It has to do with Antigone's beauty and with the place it occupies as intermediary between two fields that are symbolically differentiated. It is doubtless from this place that her splendour [éclat] derives [. . .]. I attempted to grasp it the first time by means of the second death imagined by Sade's heroes [. . .]. (S7E: 248; S7F: 290–291)

The purely symbolic "support" on which everything is "borne"—the signifier that represents her—shimmers through her suffering. This is where

Antigone's irresistible beauty stems from, says Lacan. More strongly, this inviolable beauty (i.e., this signifier) to which she is reduced is beautiful and attractive precisely because everything real about her has been repressed and crushed underneath this signifier. The real "that suffers from the signifier" (as Lacan formulates it[50]) glistens painfully through her image, although her beauty's function is to continue to keep this real at distance.

Yet while Antigone's beauty may be the same as the Sadean victim's, it functions differently. By worshipping the beauty of his tortured victim, the sadist indulges in the illusion that he has beaten all existential lack (the lack inherent in mortality, finitude, law and desire) and that now his entire existence is pure *jouissance*. Since Justine (in the novel of that name) functions solely as an absolute beauty, the Sadean hero can immediately disavow all the pain he has carved into her and, in so doing, imagine himself in a world no longer marked by lack, death, law, and desire.

If the tragedy of *Antigone* enables us to see a similar beauty, says Lacan, it is to confront us precisely with this very lack. In contrast to Sade, Sophocles' play makes us spontaneously identify not with the one causing Antigone's pain but with Antigone herself. We sympathize with her miserable fate and experience "pity and fear"—at least that is the way tragedy's effect on its audience has been described since Aristotle. More precisely, this effect involves a catharsis, a purification and purging of this type of feeling.[51] Like many psychoanalysts (think for instance of Breuer's cathartic method"; S7F 286–287), Lacan endorses this classical approach, albeit in a "decentered" way (as is the case with all the classic concepts he uses). Aristotle is correct when he claims that catharsis is a purification of our "*pathemata*," our feelings, affects, and passions. However, for Lacan, this catharsis brings us back not to our natural essence, but to our desire which is unnatural by definition, a desire that in a strict sense is not even our own and which decenters our presumed identity. Just prior to the previous citation, and referring to his previous seminar (*Desire and Its Interpretation*, 1958–59) Lacan claims:

> What in particular has been said about desire enables us to bring a new element to the understanding of the meaning of tragedy, above all by means of the exemplary approach suggested by the function of catharsis—there are no doubt more direct approaches. In effect, Antigone reveals to us the line of sight that defines desire [*Antigone* nous fait voir en effet le point de visée qui définit le désir]. (S7E: 247; S7F: 290)

According to the classical—that is, Aristotelian—theory of catharsis, Antigone has a purifying effect on the audience in the sense that she throws all of us back upon ourselves, upon our basic finitude. The play shows how dangerous it is for mortals to meddle with the dark world of the gods. Human beings cannot help but accept their limits and must protect themselves against their own arrogant "hubris." This is the ethical dimension of tragedy. To become happy—or, which for Aristotle amounts to the same thing, to foster self-realization—one must restrict his desires to the rule of the "mean" ('*mesótès*') and avoid extremities.[52]

But since desire is no longer grounded in being, nor is it automatically aiming at happiness, things are different, Lacan claims. In this case, catharsis does not bring us back to our natural happiness but confronts us with desire's extimate "line of sight," a line orientated toward our own death. Catharsis can longer correspond with a moral admonition not to drive our desire so far that it threatens our happiness. On the contrary, catharsis offers an X-ray of the hidden "structure" beneath our striving for happiness,[53] enabling us to see how our desire aims at a fatal "thing" beyond that happiness. It teaches us not so much that our desire must resist a tendency towards "hubris" but that this tendency comprises the very structure of our desire itself.

In the course of the play, Antigone shows us the path of desire in an almost didactical manner, Lacan says. After she manifestly takes the position of what Lacan called the subject ("My life has long been dead"), she pursues the path of desire step by step, including the transgression it contains. By choosing her maligned brother, she shows not only how the signifier, as the material "support" of the symbolic law, is simultaneously its limit, she also lets the *Beyond* of this limit to shine through, the domain of the "thing" desire aims at. This is what her desire aims at from the outset, and when she voluntarily ("autonomously") assumes her death sentence and, solemnly assisted by a long choral song ("*kommos*"), descends into her living grave, she unambiguously takes both the finite and transgressive nature of her desire upon herself. She assumes her desire in its most rigid form: as a desire for death.

Are we invited to imitate her example? This would be absurd, since it would be a direct exhortation to suicide. Is she then a negative example, an example of how one must not act? This moralizing interpretation also misses the point. For Lacan, the play's catharsis must purify us both in our tendency to pity Antigone and in our fear of being like her. The complex feeling she awakes in us, the fascination in which she holds us, is designed to give us a proper picture of our desire, including its finite and transgressive dimension. However, this picture cannot be lived as an example to follow. It presents an image of the hidden, repressed, unconscious structure of our desire, which, in order to able to function, must remain repressed and unconscious.

*Antigone*—the play and the way it functions in our culture—is not a moral example but a sublimation. It is an artistic product—a *"façonnement du signifiant"*—in which "an object is elevated to the status of a thing" (S7E: 112; 7F: 133). In Lacan's eyes, the play shows how, responding to her desire, Antigone comes to take the place of the "thing" so that, by identifying with this figure, our desire can take this same path. However, we do so not to take the place of the "thing" ourselves but to clarify how it is solely our "thing"—the object in relation to which we "are"—that is located in this place where we as subjects can never be.

The previous chapter indicated how vital it is that in sublimation, the place of the "thing" is occupied by the object, not the subject (6.5.2). For once we make a claim for ourselves there as subjects, we inevitably disavow our desire in the perverse, criminal way offered by Vailland's maffiosi or Sade's libertines. It is only when the object—and *only the object*—is claimed for the place of the "thing" and the subject explicitly kept at a distance that we can speak of sublimation. An artistic or cultural activity that can bring this off (courtly love, for example) sustains the radical openness of our desire and in this way appeals to the fundamentally open—because polymorph-perverse—structure of our most basic drive. Only then can we understand how, for Lacan, watching a tragic event can satisfy without "pathogenic" strategies such as repression or perversion.

### 3.4. ... and Image

In this lesson, Lacan expresses the "cathartic," "decentered" operation of tragedy in what is for him a more classical way. If tragedy confronts us with our desire "in its pure state," this implies it purifies us of the imaginary "demand" that is at work in us while watching the scene. Watching a tragedy decenters our imaginary—miscognizing, disavowing—relation to the desire we are and ensures that, if only in the fleeting moment of catharsis, we whole-heartedly affirm that desire. In short, Lacan interprets tragedy as a confirmation of his own, at that moment (1960) already classic thesis of the primacy of desire. The dimension of desire is more fundamental than the imaginary self-image through which we spontaneously suppose ourselves to be master of that desire. If, as the audience, we allow ourselves to be led by Antigone's power of attraction, we will be purified of the imaginary illusions that enable us to keep up appearances, so as finally to be confronted with the nakedness of our desire. Or, as he himself says:

> It is in connection to this power of attraction that we should
> look for the true sense, the true mystery, the true significance

of tragedy—in connection with the excitement involved, in connection with the emotions and, in particular, with the singular emotions that are fear and pity, since it is through their intervention, δι' ἐλέου καὶ φόβου [*di' eleou kai fobou*; Lacan quotes from Aristoteles's *Poetics* 1499b], through the intervention of pity and fear, that we are purged, purified of everything of that order. And that order, we can now immediately recognize, is properly speaking the order of the imaginary. And we are purged of it through the intervention of one image among others. And it is here that a question arises. How do we explain the dissipatory power of this central image [i.e., Antigone] relative to all others that suddenly seem to descend upon it and disappear? [. . .] It has to do with Antigone's beauty and with the place it occupies as intermediary between two fields that are symbolically differentiated. It is doubtless from this place that her splendour [éclat] derives [. . .]. (S7E: 247–248; S7F: 290)

The final sentences of this passage have already been cited. There, Antigone's beauty was said to have to do with the locus of her appearance, the site "between two deaths." In this phantasmatic place, she can only function as a signifier and her beauty confirms the explicitly symbolic status of her person. Only in this capacity does she fully confront us with the desire we are, and purify us of all imaginary (self-)images that miscognize this. And yet—as Lacan briefly but unmistakably admits here—Antigone functions as an image and, thus, imaginarily. She is "one image among many," an *image* that, while revealing the signifier and desire "in its pure state," nevertheless functions imaginarily. Rather than referring us to something else (the way a signifier does), it keeps us under the spell of what it displays. As soon as we show interest in Antigone, she clasps us in an imaginary embrace from which we can hardly escape. Her appearance thus functions as the "epiphany" of a "pure" and (therefore) explicitly *symbolic* desire, but it does so, Lacan explains, as an *imaginary* image. By saying this, Lacan makes a most remarkable claim, certainly as regards his theory up until now.

For only a few years back, he was still inveighing against Maurice Bouvet and other theorists of object relations, reproving them for failing to recognize the frequently imaginary dimension of this relation, and claiming that they ought to be able to distinguish this from the symbolic (see 1.2). For this reason, they remain blind to the true stakes of the analytic cure, which involves the switch the analysand undergoes from an imaginary to a symbolic subject position. "There where the imaginary ego was, the symbolic subject should be," Lacan interpreted Freud's famous saying ("Wo Es war, soll Ich werden"; see above: 1.3.2). Since then, the imaginary gained a negative connotation. Although still considered to be fundamental for subject constitution, its "raison d'être" was primarily to be overcome by the symbolic. Here, however, in his lesson on Antigone, his conception of it shifts and the imaginary is suddenly attributed a far more positive function.

It is now clear how Antigone defends her brother solely on the grounds that he is a signifier and, in this capacity, may not be reduced to "nothing" by Creon's law. To affirm this, she takes the inviolable position of the signifier but not in order to reincorporate her maligned brother into the laws of the symbolic order. On the contrary, it is precisely the structural lack of the law and the whole symbolic order that she aims to emphasize. However, as Lacan claims here, this would be impossible if she functioned solely as a pure signifier. She can expose the pure signifier she has indeed become (from which her radiant beauty stems) only as an image, as an imaginary figure that arrests the logic of the sliding signifiers at the moment this logic is about to complete its circle. There, a "Gestalt" stops the moving signifiers and shows a glimpse of what is beyond. A paralyzing fascinating image shows that no signifier is able to reconcile or to sublate (in the strict sense of "aufheben") the finitude or the lack of the subject's desire.

This revaluation of the imaginary can be understood as a sort of reply *avant la lettre* to Patrick Guyomard's Derridean-inspired critique. For Guyomard, Lacan falls into the trap of the contemporary *"Aufhebung,"* assuming a position reminiscent of Hegelian "absolute knowledge." As already indicated (see above: note 28), Guyomard claims one can find a metaphysical and idealistic moment in Lacan, certainly in the seminar we are commenting on. If the symbolic order literally lives off its lack, as Lacan claims, this order becomes a point of "pure" lack, a "pure loss": a loss so pure that there is no more loss at all and is therefore identical to pure gain (Guyomard, 1992: 26). In this sense, rather than a sign of finitude, lack becomes an almighty weapon capable of sublating all lack and finitude. The signifier and the unconscious, two concepts for explaining the finitude of human cognition, become instruments of what Hegel called "absolute knowledge."

It goes without saying that, from a psychoanalytical perspective, "absolute knowledge" is a pure fantasy.[54] If to emphasize this, Lacan now makes an appeal to the imaginary register, he is in fact grasping for a strategy that seems to fall even more easily into such absolute pretensions and to lead all the more directly to miscognizing finitude. It was precisely for its imaginary character that he had already critiqued the Hegelian dialectic, saying that although Hegel was right to place difference at the heart of consciousness and thought, nevertheless by conceiving it as—sublating—oppositions he remains caught in the impasses of the imaginary.[55] Yet it is precisely to counter this type of "*Aufhebung*" that Lacan now reaches for that very imaginary. How, then, can such an explicitly imaginary procedure prevent desire from attaining itself and, in so doing, undo the lack it stands for?

Was this not already the point where we arrived at when Lacan took measures, as it were, against the circular logic of his primacy of the signifier? In fact, when he was trying to determine the status of the ultimate object of desire at the end of his previous seminar (*Desire and Its Interpretation*), and was on the point of defining it as a pure signifier, he said he was forced to recognize it as real as well, precisely to maintain the radical openness of desire and avoid resolving it in the lack "itself." Recall the scene in *Hamlet* at Ophelia's funeral, a scene Lacan interprets as a "phallophany." The sight of Ophelia's dead body being mourned by Laertes broke the imaginary impasse in which Hamlet was imprisoned and opened up the dimension of lack for him and thus of desire. The object that reawakened the dimension of lack Lacan described as the phallus, the signifier as such (see above: 1.5.1). But in the lessons following his commentary on *Hamlet*, he felt inclined to emphasize the real status of that object, which in the following seminar (on ethics) became "*das Ding*." Although this "thing" is to be defined as exclusively real, it operates in an imaginary way, so Lacan concludes at the end of the ethics seminar. He seems to have made a strange move in his theory. In the final lesson of his sixth seminar, his intent was to emphasize the radical openness of desire as precisely as possible. And now, at the end of the seminar in which he had foregrounded the dimension of the real as never before, that same intent forces him into a revaluation of the imaginary.

## 3.5. Anamorphosis of Consciousness

However, none of this is as surprising as it seems, particularly if one remembers that the imaginary, here, refers primarily to the relation the subject can have with this the real "thing." If only because a symbolic relation with that "thing" is impossible by definition, an imaginary relation seems all that remains for Lacan. If he plays this card, he does so not without changing the content and the structure of that imaginary. It no longer involves a "simple" mirror reflection that immediately denies the other in whom I recognize "myself." The mirror *Antigone* holds up to us has a more complex structure. It holds me (imaginarily) fixated on a point where I expect to see myself as if it were the point where my desire is fulfilled. This point, however, remains absent in this mirror, which is why the latter stimulates (instead of fulfils) my desire. An ordinary mirror throws the reality it reflects back in the eye of the viewer, giving us the impression that what we see is just as real as the reality around us. But the kind of mirror we are talking about here maintains the reality to which it refers *behind* the mirror surface so that this image is literally only a passage to something that is not immediately visible. It is the sort of mirror reminiscent of René Magritte's famous painting *La reproduction interdite* (*The Forbidden Reproduction*) that depicts the back of a man looking at himself in a mirror. What he sees, however, is not his front, as one would expect, but his back. "A man who looks in the mirror" thus literally sees—but this is precisely why it is so surprising—"a man who looks in the mirror." In the same way, tragedy, which keeps us under the spell of Antigone's radiant beauty, carries us away from ordinary, recognizable reality. It takes us beyond the limits of the normal—beyond what Lacan, with Sophocles, calls "*atè*"—to a point that will never enter the picture but to which everything in that image refers.[56]

Hence, again, the importance of the anamorphic cylinder mirror Lacan exhibited to his audience one day. It is an excellent illustration of the structure of that new kind of imaginary image that comes to be central to his thinking. For, in such an anamorphosis, it is not so much my accidental, one-off glance that is caught (as with a flat mirror) but the entire "protocol of sight" I have passed through. The fact that, in order to get through the chaotic play of color, I must first find the right angle that allows me to recognize something, belongs to the strategy of the image itself and contributes to what I see. For the moment we recognize something in an anamorphosis, we observe not only an image looming up out of the chaos. We also realize that the representation is indeed only an image, the result of a fictive play between what, in themselves, are merely senseless scraps of color (or, if you wish, signifiers). In this way, the dimension of the signifier in itself appears. Such an anamorphosis enables us to see, however, how the image is clearly formed *behind* the mirror, in a space where, in contrast to a flat mirror, we immediately realize that there is absolutely nothing—certainly no reality that is the putative point of the image.

However, we now realize that this "nothing" cannot be thought away but rather forms the center of the entire image. This "nothing" is the image's real support, the "thing" in which it finds its ultimate ground. That "thing" itself never enters into the picture, although everything in the image points in this direction. It is in this sense, it can provide an image of my transgressive, "thing"-directed desire.

Lacan could in fact have found no better example to illustrate "the function of the beautiful." The image that rises up out of such an anamorphosis is not a classical, imaginary picture immediately denying its own lack of reality. Neither is it just a (symbolic) signifier that we thoughtlessly consume in the pleasure of looking and which immediately refers us to another image. In such an anamorphotic image, the "deceit" of the images we consume daily—including the self-image we receive from them—unmistakably comes to the surface and its fictive status (as a signifier) becomes visible *as such*.

Or, more precisely: *became* visible. In fact, at the moment when the epiphany of the fiction appears, it is, strictly speaking, already undone because what we see then is precisely an image reflected in the anamorphotic field. The anamorphotic protocol of seeing reveals how, at the moment of the "epiphany" of the beautiful itself, the viewer is unable to be its subject (bearer). The "function of the beautiful" is to bring the signifier as such to light and in this way grants us a glimpse of the beyond. However, when this happens, the subject of this experience of the beautiful is unable to be consciously present. It is first and foremost this paradox that Lacan's cylinder anamorphosis charts and it represents Lacan's answer to Guyomard's critique that he has fallen into the trap of Hegel's "absolute knowledge" and that the psychoanalytic theory of the unconscious has toppled over into a classical, "metaphysical" philosophy of consciousness.

The vision the anamorphosis forces us to see does in fact contain a moment of lucid consciousness, a moment of insight to which Lacan explicitly alludes. But what his unusual, "exemplary" anamorphosis (S7E: 272; S7F: 318) implies first of all is the fact that the subject can never be present in this lucid moment. All we can see is that everything *was* only a signifier. We can never consciously say that we *now* see and know that everything *is* just a signifier. When we stood before the anamorphosis and had not yet found the point from which the image can emerge, we saw nothing, "nothing" in the most banal sense of the word. Then we suddenly realize that every image emerges out of that "nothing." However, already in this very moment we no longer see that "nothing" but an image covering it up (i.e., the image in the tubular mirror). That image teaches us that we can never consciously be present at the epiphany of that "nothing," of that "ex nihilo" from which all signifiers—including all images—stem.

Now we can understand why the consciousness that becomes aware that everything is just a signifier can only have an imaginary image as its support. For at the moment of that insight itself, it is impossible for the subject to be present. Could it be present, it would indeed sublate the lack of the signifier and thereby turn the finiteness of the symbolic order into an infinitude. In other words, Guyomard's critique would be correct. At the moment the signifier signifies "itself"—that is, when desire finds "itself"—the subject of this lack and this desire are nevertheless absent and, then, both are borne (supported) by an imaginary image. In this way, the "selfhood" or identity of that self-knowledge or self-confrontation is also "decentered." Or, as Lacan puts it technically: a fully inclusive symbolic order or an absolute knowledge is a phantasm, an imaginary scenario that pictures the way the subject has disappeared from it.

The moment of desire's self-confrontation can thus only be reconstructed—*before* or *after* the event—and cherished as a phantasm, an imaginary figure in which the subject stages its own impossibility of being present with it (i.e., with its "full" figure). Only in an image deprived of its subject does something of the fact that everything is a signifier shimmer through, as well as of the real that yawns behind. But although without a subject, that imaginary image has an autonomous status and, so, fixes or saves the consciousness it contains. This is, according to Lacan, the function of the beautiful and, more specifically, of art. If a 2000-year-old play has something to say to us, this is because it is art, that is, a moment of impossible knowledge frozen in an imaginary figure. Only in the momentariness of a catharsis can an individual partially share in this knowledge. But he is unable to remain in this catharsis. He will always be dependent on the imaginary gem that is the beautiful and whose structure, as Lacan shows, is revealed in the cylinder anamorphosis.

For Lacan, Antigone's *ethical* dimension is to be found in the viewer's aesthetic moment of catharsis. It is clear from this that the moral good we strive for is merely a signifier that refers us to a domain where we cannot maintain ourselves as a subject: the domain of the "thing." In this sense, it is "good" that we cannot take our "good" for something absolute but must recognize it strictly as a signifier. Just as it is "good," too, that we realize that our pretension of wanting to materialize an absolute good can only give the opposite effect and result in a hell. It is, in other words, good to realize that "heaven does not exist but hell does." Sade's perversions are too often exceeded in reality for us to be in any doubt of this.

However, such awareness never becomes a "good" like any other. This is to say we cannot turn it into a rule to live by. Such a rule would mean precisely the miscognition of what this awareness is about, namely, that here—in *Antigone*, for example—precisely the finitude and the lack inherent in all rules is revealed. Such a scene shows us not what I ought or ought not to do; it shows us *what we are and do*. It shows us the map, the topology, the structure of our desire tout court, regardless of what we do. Thanks to the beautiful, we can peruse this map. More specifically, we can get a glimpse of that impossible domain of the "thing" around which the entire map (just like our desire) turns. Any conscious insight into this is, however, completely denied to us. All we can do is realize that we can never really be present to such an insight as a subject. We see this "truth" only as an external, separate thing frozen in a neutral and autonomous fantasy. The aesthetic experience of that truth ends—for

Lacan as for Aristotle—in a catharsis. In the final analysis, we become "purified" of the pretension that we can really be present at what we see there. We can never fully identify with the desire "itself" that emerges there, nor elevate it into a law. All Antigone can do is give us an *image* of ourselves as ethical subjects. This is precisely why she can never serve as an *example*.

The question remains, then, what might this mean in concrete ethical practice? What can we do with this moral insight if we cannot elevate it into a moral law or example? What role can it have in psychoanalysis which, in Lacan's own words, is a thoroughly ethical praxis, a commitment of one person to another where the express intent is that something "good" will take place? What does this mean, in other words, for what Lacan calls here an "ethics of psychoanalysis"? In the following chapter, a commentary on Lacan's final three lessons, we will look more closely at these questions.

# Chapter 9

# Ethics of Psychoanalysis

Combining the final three lessons of Lacan's *Ethics Seminar* under the heading "the tragic dimension of psychoanalytic experience" (S7E: 289; S7F: 355), Miller suggests that Lacan will apply the conclusions he draws from his commentary on *Antigone* to the concrete situation of the analytic cure. In themselves, these conclusions already concretize Lacan's general conception of the "ethics of psychoanalysis" as developed in the course of his seminar. If he were now to switch over to the particularity of the cure, this would be an excellent way to round off his theme and reach a general conclusion for the seminar.

Lacan may have had something like this in mind when he leaves off his *Antigone* commentary in his lesson of June 22, 1960, but in any event things turn out differently. Just as that commentary was left dangling, so his final lessons offer little in the way of the conclusions one would expect. All too often, the concluding remarks wander rapidly off into digressions about new, as yet unnamed departures, making the lines of his reasoning very difficult to follow at times. Moreover, many of the remarks can only be understood in the context of what Lacan will explain in his following seminar (*The Transference*, 1960–61). If he nonetheless explicitly tries to reach a general conclusion for his seminar, he is immediately obliged to state that it concerns only a number of "inconclusive" observations, which is why he will only offer, by his own admission, a sort of "mixed grill" (S7E: 311; S7F: 359). By the end of this lesson, all we get are a paltry three formulas that he explicitly presents as "paradoxes" (S7E: 321; S7F: 370).

Still, Lacan's unpredictable discourse does latch onto a well-defined line of thought whose direction can be found in a number of constants he continually comes back to in his series of closing remarks. His reference to the central importance of desire—certainly after what he develops in both this and the previous seminar—is practically a commonplace. In his previous seminar (*Desire and Its Interpretation*) he already emphasized the way he would take the primacy of desire—as psychoanalysis approaches it—as the point of departure for a new ethics. However, what is striking in the final lessons of his seventh seminar is how he devotes his attention primarily to *the desire of the analyst*. Where the desire of the analysand usually occupies the central place (he is, after all, the one whose desire has got him into the difficulties he is seeking help for in the cure), Lacan shifts the focus onto the analyst. If the specific implications of the "ethics of psychoanalysis" are felt anywhere, it is first in the analyst himself—more specifically, in the way desire also decenters his position in the analytic scene, as we will see (section 1).

A second train of thought in Lacan's concluding lessons focuses on the way the end of the psychoanalytic cure—that is, the confrontation with desire—must be described in negative terms (point 2). It is not the realization of a good or the recovery of happiness, as an ethics of (Aristotelian) common sense imagines. The seminar told us what it is *not*. The question now remains whether it can be described in positive terms at all. And if not (as we will see), it immediately raises the question of what this might mean for an ethics that is entirely directed toward a confrontation with desire. It is in the context of this question that Lacan reaches his more general conclusions about "the ethics of psychoanalysis."

## 1. The Analytic Toll

### 1.1. Paying . . .

Lacan already dwells on the position of the analyst in the first of the three "concluding" lessons. Referring to a lecture of two years earlier that, at the time of this seminar, had recently appeared ("The Direction of the Cure"; Lacan 2002: 215–270; 1966: 585–645), he claims that, during the analytic cure

> an analyst has to pay something if he is to play his role. [First,] he pays in words, in his interpretations. [Second,] he pays with his person to the extent that through the transference he is literally dispossessed. The whole current development of analysis involves the misrecognition of the analyst, but whatever he thinks of that and whatever panic reactions the analyst engages in through "the countertransference," he has no choice but to

go through it. [. . .] Finally, he has to pay with a judgment on
his action. (S7E: 291; S7F: 337)

The analytic scene is an intersubjective[1] event where the analyst has
an explicit task that Lacan accentuates in three separate ways: he must
interpret what the analysand says, he must bet with his *person* in the
analytic "game" (as one places a bet in any game of chance) and he must
pass *judgment*. In each case it is about a "payment," an engagement that
causes him to lose something. And it is up to the analyst, in the name
of an "ethics of psychoanalysis" to affirm this loss as clearly as possible
rather than to avoid it or turn it into a gain. Lacan clarifies on the same
page what it might mean to "pay with a judgment":

> Analysis is a judgment. It's required everywhere else, but if it
> seems scandalous to affirm it here, there is probably a reason.
> It is because, from a certain point of view, the analyst is fully
> aware that he cannot know what he is doing in psychoanaly-
> sis. Part of his action remains hidden even to him. (S7E: 291;
> S7F: 337)

The analyst must decisively intervene in the cure—he must pay for
his presence there with interventions, interpretations, words—while realizing in advance that he doesn't know precisely "what he is doing" there.
This is, so to speak, his inherently tragic condition. He is, first of all, not
there to make the analysand feel good and happy again, although this is
what she specifically demands. As analyst, he has learned that a demand
as such—that is, as an *imaginary* procedure—hides and denies that which
the analysand is really struggling with, namely her desire.[2] And, second,
although the analyst knows that her problem is her desire, he does not
know—and cannot know—himself what precisely this desire is, what is its
ultimate object. In this tragic condition he nevertheless has to pass judgment,
and for this he will have to pay—"with his person," as Lacan says.

## 1.2. . . . With His Person

This is an unavoidable toll underlying the phenomenon of transference,
that is, the inevitable libidinal bond that affects the analysand and analyst mutually. In the passage from "The Direction of the Cure" Lacan
paraphrases in the previous citation, he claims

> The analyst too must pay [. . .] with his person, in that, whoever
> he is, he lends it as a prop [support] for the singular phenomena

which the analysis discovered in transference. {Lacan, 2002: 216–217, modified translation; 1966: 587)

The analyst's person becomes the "prop" (the "support") of the transference. This means he becomes the point onto which the analysand projects the ultimate object of her desire. To this end, the analysand puts her entire imaginary box of tricks into play to try to seduce the analyst into pretending he can indeed give her that object. Should the analysand succeed, the analytic scene resembles a love situation and the "countertransference" will cause the analysis to fail. In that case, the analysand imagines her desire can be satisfied by the analyst, while the latter also feels satisfied because he seems to have helped her with her desire. Like in an amorous relation, both function as the completion of the other's desire, which is in fact nothing other than an (imaginary) miscognition of the specific (unfulfillable) dimension of the desire that drives them. In such situations, the confrontation with desire as such that the analyst aims for is farther away than ever. The analytic cure then overshoots its goal. By falling into the trap of the transference, the analyst has made any confrontation with desire impossible. It is no surprise, then, that everyone since Freud has warned about the dangers of such countertransference.[3]

As we already know from the first of the previously cited passages, Lacan turns against the term "countertransference" as such (S7E: 291; S7F: 337)—not against its content (he is the first to recognize the mutual libidinal bond, the desire, the analyst has toward his analysand). But he resists the common suppositions behind the term—as if the analyst could avoid his own libidinal bond, his own desire; as if a non-counter-transference could be possible. This is in absolute contradiction to the primacy of desire. In the final analysis, it is desire that masters us and not the other way around, even if one happens to call oneself a psychoanalyst. Desire is always involved in the analytic relation and "the desire of the analyst" is the primary concern of any analysis.

It is here that the toll demanded by the analytic scene comes most sharply into focus. In this scene, the analyst is reduced to nothing more than the support of the transference and in this capacity is constantly tempted to enter into the "countertransference." A classic device against this is to say that the analyst must have a strong, incorruptible personality. Through his own analysis, the analyst is supposed to have overcome the knotted tangle of his own desires, enabling him to be completely armed against the temptation of the desire of an other.[4] Lacan's criticism of the concept of countertransference is mainly a reaction against this moralizing. This is why, in his view, the analyst's position in the cure must be precisely one of "payment"—with his "person." He must let the transference "deprive" him of himself, of his "person." He must stop imagining he is the master of his own and the other's desire (including the countertransference) in order—like his analysand—to confront the desire that also masters him.

This is why he must be on his guard against relating to his analysand as a "subject." Instead, he must position himself explicitly where the analysand places him in the transference, and this is the place of an object, more precisely, the ultimate object of the analysand's desire, or—as Lacan puts it—of her "thing." Rather than occupying this place as a *subject*, and imagining that all his knowledge and expertise make him the master of the "thing" the analysand desires, he must realize that he has no access to the object the other desires. *If he must occupy the place of his analysand's "thing," it is precisely to leave the "person" that he is behind.* In this way, he keeps the place open, giving the analysand the chance to find her desire. So, a psychoanalytic cure cannot be considered an intersubjective event. The participants of that event never stand face to face with each other as two subjects but, in both cases, as a subject positing the *object* of their own desire in the other. It is up to the analyst not to "subjectify" the *object* whose place he occupies. This is the only way the analysand can confront the "thing" that keeps her desire open.

Lacan does not yet describe this dynamic in so many words in the final lesson of his seventh seminar. It is only in the following seminar, devoted not coincidentally to the theme of the "transference," that this will occur.[5] In that seminar too, Lacan will take several months to describe the tragic, impossible place the analyst inhabits and its impact on his task. Stationed in the place of the "thing" the analysand's desire seeks, he finds himself in a "nonplace," that is, a "place" that falls outside his analysand's symbolic system. Posited in that place, the analyst must avoid relating actively and directly to his analysand. If he does not avoid this, he risks playing along with the analysand's desire in a *perverse* way. The analysand's demand for help already indicates how she is in search of a law, a rule for life, a moral exhortation. It would not be unthinkable, then, for her to allow that law to be laid down by the analyst, a law that, once dictated from the locus of the "thing," inevitably generates the kind of evils we met in Sade's fantasies or that we saw in Vailland's novel *La loi*.

Lacan's claim that the analyst must "pay with his person" is thus an ethical claim that goes expressly against the analysand's inclination to allow the analyst to lay down the law for her. The "ethics of psychoanalysis" is first the ethics of the analyst, the ethics of someone who consciously inhabits a moral position from where he is continually asked to lay down the law, to say how one must live, what one must do, how one must act in order to possess the good and be happy. But the analyst's ethical engagement lies precisely in avoiding this and in keeping the moral authority he represents completely out of play. For standing in the place of authority, the analyst reduces himself to that unattainable "thing" that the analysand so hopelessly longs for, dispensing with all authority (including all moral and "personal" authority) so as thereby to keep that place open and enable the analysand to confront her desire.

If the analyst occupies the place of the "thing" as a subject (as a "person"), he gives the analysand the impression that the distance between her and the object with which she "is" an (object) relation has been bridged. But it is precisely the maintenance of this distance that enables her to confront her desire. Hence the explicit object-position of the analyst. The analyst tries to keep the analysand at a distance from the object in relation to which she "is," and therefore he assumes the position of that object, keeping that object empty, without any content. Only in this way can the analysand herself get on track as a *subject of that distance* or, what amounts to the same time, as a subject of desire.

### 1.3. *Bouvet*

Both here, at the end of his first "concluding" lesson, and at the beginning of the following, Lacan opposes himself once more to his unnamed contemporary, Maurice Bouvet. Bouvet, too, had attributed a central place to the idea of distance in his conceptualization of psychoanalysis. For him, "distance" is a variable quantity that, initially minimal (in the oral and anal phases), acquires the correct proportion with the definitive (genital) phase (see above chapter 1, point 2). In his eyes too, the libidinal being is fundamentally an object relation that can only gain its independence by distancing itself from the object with which it is a relation. For Bouvet, the cure entails a redoing of this process by the analyst, at first reducing the distance in relation to the object so as to reinstall it afterward.[6] And—final parallel with Lacanian theory—for Bouvet, too, the transference exists insofar as the analyst takes the place of the analysand's object. But it is precisely in making the "distance" variable in this situation that he lays himself open to Lacan's critique. First of all, at no moment is this distance to be reduced to zero, Lacan argues. For this would be the end of the object-*relation* and, hence, of the libidinal being. This distance is a structural given from the outset. However, in the libidinal being's development into a subject, this distance is *imaginarily* miscognized so as to later on take on the form of a desire borne by signifiers, thereby *symbolically* sealing the distance between the subject and object.

The miscognition of the imaginary and symbolic status of the object relation has far-reaching consequences. By allowing the distance between the analysand and the analyst to decrease to a minimum—by bringing them "closer to one another" in this way ("joiner," "*rapprocher*")—the analyst forces the analysand into a relation of total dependence. To get out of this, she risks of being forced into perverse or psychotic forms of acting out. At the end of the lesson of June 22, 1960, Lacan says:

> In that direction [as pointed out by Bouvet] the subject can achieve nothing but some form of psychosis or perversion, however mild its character, for the term "joiner" that is placed by the author at the center of the analytical dialectic does no more than reflect a desire of the analyst, whose nature the latter misperceives as a result of an inadequate theory of his position; it is the desire to draw closer to the point of being joined to the one who is in his charge. (S7E: 301; S7F: 348)

By trying to reduce the distance between himself and the analysand to zero, the analyst forces his analysand into an imaginary identification with him or, what amounts to the same thing in the transference situation described here, with the ultimate object of her desire. In other words, he forces her to appropriate the "thing," something she can do only through a criminal perverse "disavowal" (as, for example, the sadist) or through a "foreclosure" that lands her in psychosis. These dangers the analysand risks in her analysis are fully to be blamed, as Lacan morally reproaches Bouvet, on the fact that the analyst miscognizes his own desire. Bouvet refuses to recognize that the analysand's desire is beyond the reach of his own desire and, accordingly, that he can only exist as an analyst thanks to an affirmation of that very distance.

For Lacan, Bouvet misunderstands the *status* of the distance in play here. It is not the distance itself that varies, but the *imaginary*, and subsequently *symbolic* status that it acquires as the subject assumes a different position toward it. In this perspective, the *real* status of the object is also in play. As a subject (bearer) of signifiers, it is impossible for the libidinal being to cancel the distance separating it from the real object. It can only imaginarily miscognize that distance. If it is to recognize that distance—if, in other words, it is to affirm itself as "bearer" of that distance (i.e., as a subject of a desire)—it must explicitly declare its dependence on signifiers.

Lacan's point is that Bouvet miscognizes the analyst's "duty" to pay for his place in the cure "with his person." He remains blind to the fact that he does not sit face to face as a subject in relation to another subject. He thus assumes the place of his analysand's "thing" with all of its consequences. Since the analysand inevitably puts the analyst in the locus of his "thing," the latter must explicitly distance himself from his "person," his subjectivity, his professional and position as a moral master. Only in this way can he guarantee the space that gives the analysand the chance to encounter her desire. And this is precisely the aim of psychoanalysis. If "the ethics of psychoanalysis" answers to any criterion or norm, it is this.

Still, this is not the end of the story for desire as norm of an "ethics of psychoanalysis." This, at least, is what Lacan suggests in the final "concluding" lesson of his seminar. For not only does he make a number of concluding remarks here without really forming any definitive conclusion, these remarks themselves peter out into a number of unsolved paradoxes. This, finally, is all he can give his audience to take with them on vacation.

## 2. Measure without Measure

### 2.1. "Mè funai"

The beginning of Lacan's June 29 lesson clearly bears traces of his out-burst against Bouvet from the previous session. If he claims here that "the moral aim of psychoanalysis" is not to be sought in some kind of "psychological normalization" or in achieving a "mature" relation to the object, he has his familiar "target" Bouvet in mind for whom such a "normal" object relation is the result of a successful "genital phase" (S7E: 302; S7F: 349).[7] Normalization is not the aim of psychoanalysis, Lacan stresses. Neither is it the psychic comfort, moral comfort, or both that a cure may procure. And he adds that this must particularly be said when the analysand intends to become an analyst:

> When in conformity with Freudian experience one has articu-lated the dialectic of demand, need and desire, is it fitting to reduce the success of an analysis to a situation of individual comfort linked to that well-founded and legitimate function we might call the service of goods [le service des biens]? Private goods, family goods, domestic goods, other goods that solicit us, the goods of our trade or our profession, the goods of the city, etc. (S7E: 303; S7F: 350)

According to Lacan, the "success of an analysis" can only lie in a confrontation with desire. This comes down to a "decentering of the subject," a procedure during which every feeling of psychic and moral comfort is shaken up. For the analysand comes face to face with the fact that not only is her desire that of the Other, but furthermore that it stems from an object (the "thing") that escapes even the Other—being thus extra foreign to her—in order finally to accept how that absolute foreign "thing" is nonetheless her most intimate kernel. The confrontation with her "extimate" kernel thus brings the analysand back into the sphere of the radical, deadly helplessness that as libidinal being she stems from. This experience is inevitably coupled with anxiety, since it forces one to stand face to face with one's death—a death, we might note, that is worse than the "first," natural death and which, like Hamlet in his famous monologue, makes one fear that it is only after death that real hell begins.[8] As Lacan puts it at the beginning of his June 29 lesson, in a characteristically long and complicated sentence:

> As I believe I have shown here in the sphere I have outlined for you this year [the one of the "thing"], the function of desire must remain in a fundamental relationship to death. The question I ask is this: shouldn't the true termination of an analysis—and by that I mean the kind that prepares you to become an analyst—in the end confront the one who undergoes it with the reality of the human condition? It is precisely this, that in connection with anguish, Freud designated as the level at which its signal is produced, namely, *Hilflosigkeit* or distress, the state in which man is in that relationship to himself which is his own death—in the sense I have taught you to isolate this year—and can expect help from no one. (S7E: 303–304; S7F: 351)

The confrontation with desire brings the analysand into the vicinity of the "thing, that is, of the domain where her desire would be satisfied were it not that it is impossible to maintain herself there as a subject. In this sense, a confrontation with the "thing," the final, real ground of the desire we "are," is thus a confrontation with death as well as an appeal to assume our radical finitude. Such an appeal refers not to the fact that we must one day die but that our mortality is the ultimate *positive* condition of possibility for our existence tout court.

Here, by his own admission, Lacan comes very close to the Heideggerian idea of "Being-unto-Death." Heidegger, too, maintains that one's mortality is the positive condition of possibility for existence altogether.[9] My existence only has sense precisely because it is finite. I can only realize myself insofar as I am mortal. This Heideggerian idea easily resonates with the Lacanian "I am only insofar I will never be satisfied in my desire to be." Furthermore, both thinkers see anxiety as the affect par excellence (or, as Heidegger calls it, "*Befindlichkeit*") for arriving at a confrontation with finitude.[10] And finally, both equally emphasize that it involves an absolutely *singular* experience where—as Lacan says here—"one can expect help from no-one." To assume my death, my most proper project (in the sense Heidegger gives to the word "*Entwurf*"[11]) is something in which I am irreparably alone, just as I am radically alone in the confrontation with my desire and with the "thing" I seek. For the "thing" in which my desire finds its ultimate anchoring point lies outside the symbolic order and, at the moment I am confronted with it, I can no longer count on any communication or exchange that might represent some kind of assistance. This is why the analyst can take me only up to the moment of this experience but cannot *share* that moment *itself* with me.[12] I must go through this ultimate confrontation and its strange catharsis entirely alone.

For Lacan, the aim of analysis thus lies in the confrontation with finitude, mortality, desire—in short, with the lack that I "am." It clears away the imaginary cocoons that weighed down my demand for help, realizing in this way a catharsis that purifies my desires because it brings them back to their most "real" dimensions. One might imagine that any-one who goes through this process does in fact come out purified and capable of looking at life's pain in a calm, reconciled manner. Does the concrete moral goal of psychoanalysis lie in this? Does not the catharsis it generates have this kind of moral peace in mind, making the analysand meeker, kinder toward herself and her environment? Is this where the ultimate ethical value of psychoanalysis lies?

Lacan vigorously resists what was in his time this widespread con-clusion. While it may possibly turn out in such a way for a particular analysand, this can in no way be the general goal psychoanalysis should strive for. This would degrade its practice to a form of adjustment therapy and, as Lacan claims explicitly:

> [t]here's absolutely no reason why we should make ourselves
> the guarantors of the bourgeois dream. (S7E: 303; S7F: 350)

For Lacan, the moral aim of psychoanalysis is not to be found in the "service of the goods." Regardless of how equally "legitimate and well-founded" that service is (as he claims in one of the cited passages), no matter how crucial the role of desire is in this as well, the moral aim of psychoanalysis does not lie in the analysand's readjustment with the "order of the good." Its aim cannot be to generate a certain calm, steady, "wise" feeling of goodwill toward an existing system or toward existence tout court. With respect to this, Lacan often refers to Oedipus and, more specifically, to the utterly unreconciled position he still gives proof of at the moment of his final hour. In his final lesson, Lacan explicitly compares this attitude to the sense of goodwill evoked above:

> The goodness in question is so far from being confirmed in
> our experience that we start out from what is modestly called

the negative therapeutic reaction, something that at the more remarkable level of literary generality I last time called a malediction assumed or agreed to in the μή φῦναι [*mè funai*] of Oedipus. (S7E: 313; S7F: 361)

In his previous lesson (S7E: 305, 309; S7F: 353, 357), Lacan had already referred to *Oedipus at Colonus*, the Sophoclean tragedy that describes the final days of this tragic hero. Banned in his old age from Thebes, the old Oedipus arrives in Colonus near Athens and stops at the place, a holy wood, where it was said by the oracle he was to die. It is there his son Polyneices comes looking for him in order to get his blessing for his recently declared campaign against Thebes that is to drive his brother Eteocles from the throne. Rather than a steady, wise old man who has become reconciled with his death, Sophocles shows us an unreconciled Oedipus who is not yet too wretched to let fly against both his sons and lay a fatal curse on both—as well as on all of Thebes. Lacan links Oedipus' rancorous position with the choir's pronouncement in the third *choral* where the deplorable, tragic situation of man is described, resulting in the conclusion that it would be better for man had he not been born: μή φῦναι [*mè funai*].[13]

Lacan is less interested in the content of the complaint than in the idea that through the very fact of complaining man nevertheless gives proof of a stubborn, untamable desire. Face to face with death, Oedipus realizes that his entire existence has been one long drawn-out failure and that all he can do now is to accept his fate. The point is, Lacan stresses, that at that very moment, Oedipus nevertheless does not accept anything at all. Like Antigone, Oedipus continues to gratify us with an "éclat" of desire. Although he, too, realizes what a disastrous wreck his life has been, he is still capable of desiring and can still even prefer "not to have been born." So, rather than focusing on the rubble of existence, this tragedy focuses on the primacy of desire. Having failed in everything and dangling with both legs in death, Oedipus is still a lump of flaming desire. Here we see again how it is not from his nature that man lives, but out of the hard "polymorphous-perverse" negation of that nature. Even if one is literally nobody, one "is" also, still, a *desire* (for instance, to be no one).

According to Lacan, this "*mè funai*" aptly illustrates the position of the subject as the bearer of desire. Oedipus is no longer anyone apart from a desire not to have been. For Lacan, this shows how the "no one" that he is stems ultimately from a desire and this desire, in the final analysis, is borne by that "no one," that is, by the one who—to put it in Lacanese—exists only insofar as he is represented by signifiers. Here Lacan interprets this "*mè*" from "*mè funai*" in the same way as the French "*ne discordantiel*." At first sight, the "*ne*" is a meaningless insertion in sentences like "je crains qu'il ne vienne."[14] In this sense, the "*ne*" must remain untranslated. Hence it says not "I fear that he *won't* come" but "I fear that he comes." Still, according to Lacan who often appeals here to a study by Pichon on "The psychological signification of negation in French" (1928),[15] this "*ne*" is not entirely senseless. Lacan sees in this an indication of the structural place of the subject in the symbolic order. The "*ne*" refers directly to the subject, but only insofar as it is negatively present in the chain of signifiers, insofar, in other words, as it remains absent. This subject is in fact never present, in the full sense of the word, because the signifiers of this sentence only represent that subject, but never posit its presence as such. In this sense, the "*ne discordantiel*" constitutes a final sign of the fact that the libidinal being has radically alienated itself in the chain of signifiers. Like the "*ne discordantiel*," the "*mè*" from "*mè funai*"—as said a little farther on in the passage we have just cited—is "a negation, identical to the entry of the subject in the support of the signifier."[16]

The ethical aim of the analytic cure lies in giving the analysand the chance to confront this "*mè*," this impenetrable negation, this stubborn kernel of her desire that cannot be incorporated into the service of goods. Now it becomes clearer, too, why the aim of analysis cannot lie in the analysand's purified and reconciled position. Even if the analysand happens to reach such a position, rather than a moment of reconciliation, the actual confrontation with her desire is a moment of irrationally driven rebellion, easily recognizable in the frenzy of the old Oedipus.

This is true, too, for the specifically ethical dimension of the analysand's search for her desire. Lacan details this in connection with a discussion of an Ernest Jones article that examines the feelings of "fear, guilt and hate" that an analysand may experience towards moral authority (S7E: 306–310; S7F: 354–358). Of course, as Lacan argues in his commentary, the analysand does rediscover her desire through her manner of conforming with a code of morals, for her moral conscience ultimately stems from an internalization of the father figure represented here by the law. But as Freud showed in his essay, "Mourning and Melancholia," such an internalization is the underside of a hatred of and reproach to the internalized, mourned object (Freud SE14: 248; SA3: 202). A man, for instance, unconsciously hates his beloved dead wife that he mourns, precisely because it is clear now that she is unable to give him the "everything" she had promised. The melancholic's lifelong mourning is at the same time a reproach to the Other for having revealed its lack.

While desire, as Lacan analyzes it here, similarly realizes itself in the law, it preserves a structural hatred of the law. Precisely because it attempts to bring the analysand to that level where she upholds her desire against the law, the "ethics of psychoanalysis" is not an ethics of a superego. This is why, at the end of this lesson—albeit with slightly too heavy an emphasis—Lacan claims that "the internalization of the [moral] law [ . . . ] has nothing to do with the law" (S7E: 310; S7F: 358). Of course, ethical susceptibility results from an internalization of the symbolic law (from which the superego stems), but it is not limited to that. Desire does not restrict itself to the domain of the law but aims at what lies beyond the law, where one is confronted with the pure but impossible (because real) dimension of desire. A confrontation with this "real" dimension of desire is thus something an "ethics of psychoanalysis" must also give the analysand a chance to do.

## 2.2. Do not "cede on your desire"

A little farther in the "*mè funai*" passage we cited, Lacan talks about what an ethical judgment must lead to, namely, a moral action. He interprets this, too, from out of the primacy of desire, saying:

> [. . .] it is because we know better than those who went before how to recognize the nature of desire, which is at the heart of this experience, that a reconsideration of ethics is possible, that a form of ethical judgment is possible, of a kind that gives this question the force of a Last Judgment: Have you acted in conformity with the desire that is in you? This is not an easy question to sustain. I, in fact, claim that it has never been posed with that purity elsewhere, and that it can only be posed in the analytical context. (S7E: 314; S7F: 362)

"Have you acted in conformity with the desire that is in you?" Justly, Miller makes this question the subtitle of Lacan's final lesson (S7E: 311; S7F: 359), if only because with this question Lacan formulates the sole ethical criterion that he ascribes any weight to in the psychoanalytic cure. To this he immediately adds how difficult this criterion is to sustain ("*soutenir*").

Why is this? Because it asks for a "*Last* Judgment": so Lacan answers referring to a term from the Christian *Apocalypse*. To judge desire, one must evaluate the result and determine whether or not it has been realized. However, as psychoanalysis has discovered, desire by definition never reaches its realization. It never arrives at the ultimate point (the "thing") it seeks, but infinitely defers it. Judging desire should therefore proceed from that *infinite* point and in this sense can only be a Last Judgment. It is as in the Christian myth, where every existent judgment is held in reserve against a final judgment, pronounced by the Infinite (God) at the end of time. We moderns, however, are definitely finite; nonetheless our desire is able to step over its limits and stand face to face to what in this seminar Lacan calls the "thing." Such a confrontation does not sublate desire's finitude but highlights it. For it is a confrontation with the deadly nullity of what lies beyond finitude's limit, a nullity that nevertheless coincides with the "extimate" kernel of our identity. It is a confrontation with the absolute and "nonsublatable" singularity of our desire. Judging desire in this way delivers no "good" through which the subject can adjust to the symbolic order. All it does is follow desire's path until it passes beyond the symbolic and enters the domain "between-two-deaths," the deadly terrain where we saw Antigone take up her position.

In this context, another formulation of the question that is "not easy to sustain" must be interpreted with care, namely, where Lacan claims that

> from an analytical point of view, the only thing of which one can be guilty is of having given ground relative to one's desire [d'avoir cédé sur son désir]. (S7E: 319; S7F: 368)

This passage is often misquoted as if it were an actual imperative and the phrase *"ne pas céder sur son désir"* ("don't give ground relative to your desire") is often cited as if it were a statement taken directly from Lacan's text. It is, however, nowhere literally there. It is true that Lacan talks about "having given ground relative to one's desire" as something of which the analysand can be guilty, but nowhere does he explicitly formulate this thought as an injunction. Hence anyone who cites "do not cede on your desire" or "do not give way to your desire" as the new ethical ground-rule Lacan proposes as an alternative to the old ethics has ventured seriously far from the Lacanian text.[17] Even where it is cited correctly, it is still often interpreted in this sense, as Simon Critchley does, for example, when he speaks of it as the "categorical imperative of Freud's Copernican revolution."[18]

In any event, with his reference to "giving way on your desire," Lacan does not have in mind a moral law that enables me to test my action and then adjust it to ensure I remain in line with my desire. This reference is valid solely in the specific situation of an analytic cure whose goal it is to direct the analyst's and analysand's attention to desire. Such a reference is necessary precisely because in the normal order of things desire as such cannot but be repressed and ignored.[19] Its intention is not to require that the analysand realize this desire in her personal life. She is still in search of that desire. So, all that this reference does is stimulate the analyst and analysand to pay attention to everything that refers to desire. One must try to discover where she "has ceded on her desire."

By focusing on these moments in her narrative, she increases the chance of coming upon the traces of her desire as such.

Is desire, then, the actual "measure" for human action and, in this sense, for ethics? Of course, man acts according to the measure of desire, but we should realize it is an "immeasurable, infinite measure," as Lacan emphasizes once again when comparing its difference to Kant's categorical imperative.

> Our experience gives rise to a reversal [with regard to Kantian ethics] that locates in the center an incommensurable measure, an infinite measure, that is called desire [une mesure incommensurable, une mesure infinie, qui s'appelle le désir]. (S7E: 316; S7F: 364)

It is a measure we cannot use in our daily life but serves only within the analytic context to help track down the excessiveness the analysand's desire is after and where, in search of "herself," she descries the ultimate, real "thing" that, escaping the measure of her self-preservation, is nevertheless her most intimate kernel. As we read in Lacan's analysis of *Antigone*, this "measureless measure" of desire does not function as an example for us to follow but as an image in which we see ourselves insofar as we escape our own grasp so as to be confronted with the desire that we "are."

## 2.3. "The Paradoxes of Ethics"

An ethics that "decenters" the existing moral measure (the "service of goods," in Lacan's terms) through reference to this other "immeasurable measure" can only leave a mass of paradoxes in its wake. But to expect Lacan to lay these out and reveal their underlying logic is to be disappointed. At the most, he limits himself to three "propositions" that circle around a single paradox. At the end of this lesson, he neatly summarizes these as follows:

> I have, therefore, articulated three propositions. First, the only thing one can be guilty of is giving ground relative to one's desire. Second, the definition of a hero: someone who may be betrayed with impunity. This [i.e., to be a hero] is something that not everyone can achieve; it constitutes the difference between an ordinary man and a hero, and it is, therefore, more mysterious than one might think. For the ordinary man, the betrayal that almost always occurs sends him back to the service

of goods, but with the proviso that he will never again find that factor which restores a sense of direction to that service. The third proposition tells that the field of the service of goods of course exists, and that there is no question of denying that. But turning things around, I propose the following: There is no other good than that which may serve to pay the price for access to desire. [. . .]. (Modified translation[20])

Two of these three propositions are still to be clarified. Lacan's second proposition tells us that "the hero may be betrayed with impunity." The "hero" he is referring to here and in the previous lessons are figures such Antigone and Oedipus who illustrate what it means for someone to be confronted with the final, real ground of their desire. "Betrayal" refers to the fact that, through their own or another's doing, their desire can be betrayed, that is, it can voluntarily or involuntarily be given up. When this happens to a hero, it remains unpunished in the sense that his or her desire is unaffected. Lacan gives the example of Philoctetes, the protagonist of another Sophoclean play. On the way to Troy, this Greek king is bitten by a holy snake that leaves a wound that casts such an intolerable smell that he is left behind on an island. In itself this was already a betrayal of his desire (to gain fame on Troy's battlefield). When, for the sake of his magic bow, he is secretly taken against his wishes to Troy his desire is betrayed a second time (he swore never to fight for the Greeks again). Yet despite this betrayal, he keeps his untouchable desire. A "hero doesn't need to be heroic to be a hero," says Lacan in connection with the "poor type" Philoctetes. It is only the "éclat" of his desire that makes him a hero.[21]

Here we see the difference between a hero and the non-heroes we all are. Once betrayed in our desire—and in some kind of way, we have all betrayed our and the other's desire—this affects our desire in the sense that we hold fast to the domain of the good(s) and let that take precedence over our desire. As Lacan already explained, the domain of the good forms a deceptive barrier that deters us from the domain where the ultimate real dimension of our desire would become visible. In this sense, deceived by the "service of the good," we have lost our desire's real orientation.

The first two "propositions" can be summarized as follows: from a psychoanalytic perspective (i.e., the cure), all that matters is whether we are guilty at the level of our desire—or, in other words, whether or not we have "betrayed" it. And—second proposition—this is indeed what we have done, resulting in the fact that, being no "heroes," we have lost sight of our desire's aim. Deceived by the "function of the good," we need the "function of the beautiful" to steer us back toward our desire's real orientation. In other words, we have to look to the image of the tragic hero, not to follow his example but—through the aesthetic catharsis that this image achieves—to gain access to the deception of the good or, what amounts to the same thing, the fundamental and tragic dimension of the desire that we "are." Building on the second, the third proposition draws a specific conclusion from this: in order to gain access to desire, a toll must be paid, which can only be obtained from the domain of the good (or goods).

To understand the last proposition correctly, one must realize how it presupposes the very turn taken by Lacan's theory in the seventh seminar. Where, in the previous seminars, desire was regarded as an exclusively symbolic affair situated at the level of signifiers, here desire is explicitly highlighted in its real dimension. Our desire, as he claims in the rest of the sentence we just cited, must be defined as "the metonymy of our being" (S7E: 321; S7F: 371). In those previous seminars, we read how, from a libidinal perspective, we exist not as real but as linguistic creatures whose "being" (thanks to the signifiers of language) is interminably, "metonymically" displaced. In this way, the real being beneath the chain of signifiers is maintained and we realize our integral being as a desire that is borne by signifiers (or, what amounts to the same thing, as a desire *of the Other*). But here, at the end of the seventh seminar, Lacan must correct this definition of desire as a "metonymy of our being":

> The channel in which desire is located is not simply that of the modulation of the signifying chain, but that which flows beneath it as well; that is, properly speaking, what we are as well as what we are not, our being and our non-being—that which is signified in an act passes from one signifier of the chain to another beneath all the significations. (S7E: 321–322; S7F: 371)

Desire is situated in what flows *beneath* the chain of signifiers as well, in our brute real being that the signifying chain dislodges (and which in this sense is forced back into "nonbeing"). Any confrontation with the desire that one "is" (the aim of the analytic cure) must, in the final analysis, confront this real dimension of desire, a confrontation that is impossible without the toll Lacan refers to in the "third proposition." The real dimension of desire—desire insofar as it does not deceive us with seducing us from one good or another—must be sought beyond the good, which is why we must relinquish the good for it. In the "absolute choice" of desire (S7E: 240; S7F: 281)—a choice that is made at the end of the cure—the subject must choose the "evil" of *jouissance*. For it is this *jouissance* that the libidinal being must have given up to gain access

to the symbolic order in which it can realize itself as desire. Referring
to the "discontent" of civilization (read, the discontent of the libidinal
being that must realize itself in the symbolic order), Lacan says a few
sentences later:

> Sublimate as much as you like; you will have to pay for it
> with something. And this something is called *jouissance*. (S7E:
> 322; S7F: 371)

Here we confront again the basic thesis on which Lacan's *Ethics
Seminar* is built, namely, the distinction between the good and *enjoyment*.
To gain access to the symbolic order—to become a desire at all—the
libidinal being must abandon its *jouissance*. Only then will it be able to
feel "good" and realize itself as a moral being. But once it has become
the bearer of a desire, if that same libidinal being is to confront its desire
as such, it must refind its connection with that domain in which *jouissance* lies. Seen from the order of the good, this *jouissance* can only be
described as evil, so that access to the domain of *jouissance* comes only
at the cost of the good. The toll one must pay for this must necessarily
be such a "good": this is Lacan's "third proposition."

With this idea, Lacan gives us a total paradox. For the good and
*jouissance* are mutually incompatible, so that words such as toll and
"payment" are not appropriate, or must at least be understood with an
explicitly "tragic" connotation. The fact that I must pay with the good in
order to gain access to desire in its most real dimension does not mean
I can *buy* that access *off*. In that domain of the "thing," an uneconomic
logic governs that responds only to enjoyment, to death drive and to
waste. I cannot capitalize on the loss of the sacrificed good so as to *gain
jouissance* from it. In this sense, this loss can only be regarded as a tragic, hateful and irrecuperable loss. When, beyond the limit of the good, I
enter enjoyment, I have literally lost myself as well. In enjoyment, I lose
myself insofar as I disappear as a subject—as the bearer of the desire I
am—and the drive economy from which I stem is supported only by the
imaginary scenario of my phantasm.

Nevertheless, Lacan provides for the possibility of access to that
domain of *jouissance* where I do not simply disappear as a subject but can
still more or less be present. Precisely for ethical reasons, one must pursue
desire beyond the good so as to track down its real dimension. There one
confronts the space in which singular enjoyment is situated and where one
can no longer hold fast to any "good." But if one wants ethically to make
use of that confrontation—along with the toll it requires—one may not
yield to this *jouissance*, otherwise the confrontation becomes impossible
if only because at that moment there is no more subject. The whole of

Lacan's "ethics of psychoanalysis" is based on the paradoxical possibility that one can consciously confront oneself with the domain in which one usually disappears, namely, the domain of the "thing," of *jouissance*. Only such a conscious confrontation with the unconscious lets us experience what is at the most fundamental level purely "to be desire."

Because of this paradoxical requirement, Lacanian ethics necessarily must be supported by an explicit aesthetic, that is, the "function of the beautiful."[22] The beautiful ensures that, at the point of disappearing into *jouissance*, one is still able to protect oneself against that domain. And it is this aesthetically solidified distance that enables consciousness of what is usually kept unconscious. It is in this way that the "immeasurable measure" of desire, which escapes consciousness in principle, can still get through to us somewhere.

Why must this immeasurable measure get through to us? Precisely because it is immeasurable. In the final analysis, the desire we stem from responds not to the self-preservation principle but to the death principle. Desire has lost its natural ground and must henceforth be approached as the polymorphous-perversion of that nature. This implies that the drive or the desire that drives it no longer coincide with that nature. Regardless of how unconscious the drive or desire may be, it is precisely because of the death principle (to which they both ultimately respond) that one must be conscious of it and that desire and drive must become the object of insight and knowledge.

When, at the end of the final lesson, Lacan ventures a small "word of conclusion," it is not coincidental that it concerns precisely the relation between desire and knowledge. Today's constellation does not yet permit a "science of desire" (S7E: 324; S7F: 373), he claims, because science—including the human sciences—has fully integrated itself into the "service of goods" and thus by definition cannot reach the most radical, real dimension of desire. But this does not stop desire from doing the job, and doing it in the very heart of science. As analyzed previously, precisely by denying all desire and lack, science is no less unconsciously led by desire. More strongly, for Lacan, science is the only place where desire can indulge itself unlimitedly and give the "immeasurable measure" to which it unconsciously listens a proper hearing. But it is at the same time also the place par excellence where desire can change tack and, in a way that is more real than we like, go beyond the limits of the good. In this case, the danger that even its subject will disappear in a "real" way is not merely hypothetical. Here Lacan's reference to Robert Oppenheimer, the inventor of the nuclear bomb, is unmistakable (S7E: 325; S7F: 374). Any science—and any culture in general—that denies desire runs the risk of becoming the victim of that "immeasurable measure." This is why a science that takes this immeasurable measure that is desire as its object cannot help but appear. For Lacan, this is the historical place of Freudian psychoanalysis, while at the same time it illustrates its ethical engagement. Precisely because of the excess of the unconscious desire that drives us and the dangers that accompany it, a knowledge must be created that brings this into the picture.

Lacan's seminar on the *Ethics of Psychoanalysis* is an attempt to give form to this knowledge. But at the same time, it shows up the weakness of such knowledge because it is forced to assign it an exclusively aesthetic status. Only the "function of the beautiful" can give us insight into that impenetrable desire that lies beyond our self-preservation. It is no surprise that a knowledge built on this insight simultaneously averts what it pretends to know. It offers a paralyzing image that forbids us from taking it as an example, and through its anamorphic structure confronts us with the impossibility of being present at that which we see.

# Epilogue

Freudianism is in brief nothing but a perpetual allusion to the fecundity of eroticism in ethics. (S7E: 152; S7F: 182)

One might object that the title of this book, *Ethics and Eros*, does not really do justice to its topic. Although eros is not absent from Lacan's *Ethics Seminar*, it still seems a little tendentious to bring all of its topics and issues under this title. Doesn't the term "eros" seem a bit too insignificant in the course of the seminar? Lacan himself says that psychoanalysis's contribution to our modern ethics cannot be sought in some kind of new, psychoanalytically inspired erotics. Recall an earlier cited passage (in 2.3) from his very first lesson where he talked about psychoanalysis' impotence when it comes to providing new content for our modern ethical code. In the same context, he also admitted that, despite its recognition of the prominent role of love and sexuality, psychoanalysis still seems unable to create—or even contribute to—a new erotic culture:

> Analysis has brought a very important change of perspective on love by placing it in the center of ethical experience; it has also brought an original note, which was certainly different from the way in which love had previously been viewed by the *moralistes* and the philosophers in the economy of inter-human relations. Why then has analysis not gone further in the direction of the investigation of what should properly be called an erotics? This is something that deserves reflection. (S7E: 8–9; S7F: 17)

Why, as Lacan wonders in the same lesson, must we in fairness continue to speak of "the limitations, or [even] the non-existence of a [psycho]analytic erotics"?[1] Although Lacan thereby explicitly brings up the erotic in this question, considering it worthy of reflection, this does not lessen the fact that nowhere in his subsequent lessons does he explicitly address it. So, it does not seem exaggerated to claim that the erotic is a mere marginal theme in his *Ethics Seminar*.

And yet on closer examination it is just the other way around. Lacan's seminar can in fact be interpreted as one long drawn-out reflection on the erotic and its impact on ethics. The reason psychoanalysis has neither developed a new general ethics nor provided its own contribution to a modern moral code, is the reason, too, that it has generated no new kind of erotics. All this is not only to be blamed on the way psychoanalysis grants "love" a place "in the centre of ethical experience," as Lacan suggests in the above quotation. It lies primarily in the fact that it has interpreted love as "eros" in the strictest sense of the word. It is precisely its erotic interpretation of the love that lies at the basis of our post-Christian, humanistic ethics that has forced psychoanalysis to critically investigate this ethic. It is this "erotic investigation" that finally has obliged it if not to overturn, then at least to "decenter," the formal structure of ethics altogether. To demonstrate this, let us briefly look again at a number of the main ideas from the seventh seminar.

The fact that love lies at the heart of ethics is not an invention or discovery of psychoanalysis. It is an historical "acquisition" for which we, in our post-Christian culture, have Christianity to thank. It is from there that we get the idea that the good we strive for has to do with the love we feel for our fellow man. This love, according to Christianity, lies at the basis of our entire reality. The ancients' self-knowledge always had maintained that the good we strive for was founded in reality. What Christianity added was that, in its turn, this reality was founded in an infinite heavenly love. Everything that is, is "made," created: and the motive for this creation is called love. Christianization made us think that the ultimate way for man to relate ethically to the world was through love. Only through love can man find the way to extricate himself from the quagmire of death and despair he has found himself in since the fall.[2] Hence the Christian moral demand that we must love our neighbor as ourselves. The fact that Christianity's role as the central bearer of culture is over does not prevent our basic trust in man and world from still being fully imbued with that belief in the power of love.

Psychoanalysis is indisputably embedded in this tradition, albeit with one far-reaching difference: it interprets love in a strictly erotic way. In its eyes, the love that inhabits our ethical self-understanding must not be thought through the paradigm of Christian *agape* but through ancient *eros*.[3] The latter does not stem from an all-powerful heavenly love that makes everything turn out all right, but from a frivolous playful Eros that throws everything incessantly into confusion. For psychoanalysis, the ideal of love that is still maintained by our most advanced ethics stems from this blind ancient god, the one for whom no altars are built and to whom it made no sense to dedicate sacrifices.[4]

Freud's idea of the polymorph perverse, purely pleasure-directed drive is only the modern translation of this blind, playful god of antiquity. For Freud, the pleasure that "drives" us comes down to such a playful "perversion" of our biological life-functions. We do not so much live life as *play* with life. However, we do so not from the position of an autonomous "soul" (psyche, anima) as the tradition in all kinds of variations maintains, but from an unreal fantasized point that Lacan calls the "subject," and which, as the bearer of our whole (symbolic) drive economy, is itself without any (real) ground.

To explain the ethical implications of erotically-interpreted love, Lacan highlights its ancient origins in his seventh seminar. The ethical law, as Christianity maintained, recognized a Beyond, a *Jenseits* where the law no longer counts because its promises have been fulfilled. This fulfilment is what Paul—and with him the entire Christian and post-Christian tradition—called love. For psychoanalysis, too, love goes beyond the law but rather than ending in fulfilment, it ends in a fearless and by definition "criminal" transgression of the law. The *jouissance* the subject obtains there is situated *beyond* the good and necessarily comes at the cost of that good, as Lacan emphasized in his final lesson. It is situated in the forbidden domain of the "thing." It is this domain of the "real" that Lacan explicitly associates with the ancient gods. The impact of the real on our pleasure life is that of a criss-crossing of fateful frivolous gods who, in contrast to the monotheistic God, do not envelop us in an immortal Sense but interminably and definitively throw us back to our mortality.

Thus for psychoanalysis too, the love that drives us remains aimed at a *Beyond* but in so doing closely resembles the frivolity of an ancient *eros* because it merely "plays" with the law and its beyond. The obedience to the law is secretly motivated by the possibility to transgress the law. The pleasure the drive animal responds to thus not only "plays" with the biological functions but also with the laws and rules that are necessarily (in the sense of life's necessities) enforced on it. However, the transgressive game with the law is in fact no more than a "game" that ends nowhere and delivers nothing. For, experienced symbolically, *jouissance* implies the phantasmatic disappearance of the subject, which in real terms is completely impossible because it can only coincide with literal death.

If something binds us to that domain of the "thing," it is that frivolous erotic game. To conceive Lacan's theory of the relation of the "thing" as an "attachment" (see the beginning of chapter 1) would, from a Lacanian perspective, only be meaningful if one accentuates the "erotic" frivolous relation that such an attachment still allows.

The ethical aim of psychoanalysis consists in tracking down this frivolous, polymorphous-perverse "erotic" game that binds us (given the fact that we *are* a relation) to our object, and to affirm it as such. But precisely because it concerns an erotic game, it is impossible to establish a *general* rule—an ethics—for reaching this goal. For this, the domain around which the transgressive game of Eros turns is too singular an affair. As Sade showed us in a highly caricatured but nevertheless clear way, anyone who lays down the law for others from that point risks falling into a criminal perversion.

Because psychoanalysis is unable to create an alternative ethical law, it also cannot really offer a critique, in the normal Platonic sense of the word, of existing ethics. It cannot, in other words, regard ordinary ethics as a lie that is revealed by its own truth. All it can do is "decenter" this ethics and show how its center does not lie in the good it promises but in the evil it warns us against yet which it nevertheless secretly aims. With this idea of a simultaneously attractive and repulsive "thing," Lacan formulates in his seventh seminar the impenetrable, polymorph perverse "erotic" foundation of the "love" that enables us to live. However, he must conclude that any insight into this structure cannot become the content of a normal ethical demand. It is precisely in this that psychoanalysis must recognize the finitude of its ethical impact.

Yet a culture such as ours that constantly threatens to fall prey to its infinite pretensions needs this insight. And although it cannot be articulated as a law, such an insight can become the object of a sublimating cultural expression. It is not by chance that Lacan refers to an erotic culture such as courtly love to illustrate the possibilities and the scope of sublimation. There, the transgressive (polymorphous-perverse "erotic") game with the law can simultaneously become the object of a "playful" set of instructions that enables us to play with our finitude in a satisfying way and (what amounts to the same thing) confront our desire. The way man is able to consciously get around that unconscious "eros" or that repressed desire is thus of primary ethical importance for Lacan. It is a function that, by his own account, belongs to the beautiful par excellence. Regardless of how fascinated Lacan himself is by aesthetical sublimation, he still says in the same breath that the ethical practice of psychoanalysis is unable to make an example of it. For this, he is too well aware that no sublimation can calculate the effect of its "ethical decentering" in its own practice, without falling into precisely the criminal perversion it is trying to combat.

In this sense, psychoanalysis must realize that, in the final analysis, it remains just as blind as the "eros" to which it gives the central place in ethics. The paradox of psychoanalysis—Lacanian theory included—lies in focusing on this blind spot while at the same time affirming that by doing so it has not reconciled or "sublated" this blindness. It is not by chance that Lacan's seventh seminar ends with a difficult reflection on precisely the status of the analyst's "knowledge" and of psychoanalysis tout court. Nor is it coincidental that at the beginning of his eighth seminar, Lacan reaches for a figure who stands at the cradle of what we have for centuries called "knowledge," namely, Socrates who claims to have no knowledge of anything, except of eros.[5]

# Notes

## Introduction

1. S7E: Jacques Lacan (1992), *The Ethics of Psychoanalysis 1959–1960—The Seminar of Jacques Lacan, Edited by Jacques-Alain Miller, Book VII*, translated with notes by Dennis Porter, London and New York: Routledge. S7F: Jacques Lacan (1986), *Le séminaire, Livre VII, L'éthique de la psychanalyse*, texte établi par Jacques-Alain Miller, Paris: Les éditions du Seuil.

2. Unfortunately, in the English translation Lacan's word play with the verb "trouver" (to find) gets lost. The analysand "comes to seek you out" ("celui qui vient nous *trouver*") "in order to feel good" and "to be in harmony with himself" ("pour se *trouver* bien," "pour se *trouver* d'accord avec lui-même"). But the thing we, analysts, "find in the margin" ("ce que nous *trouvons* pourtant en marge"), is what the analysand has repressed: her desire.

3. The conceptual distinction between *symbolic* and *imaginary* will be explained in later chapters. Yet, one comment can already be made in advance. Lacan uses the term "symbolic" in two senses. It refers first of all (as in Lévi-Strauss where the term comes from) to the fact that we approach reality, not as a "real" (in the "essentialist" sense of the word) but as a *symbolic* universe, that is, as a set of signifiers. In this sense we *always* live in a symbolic universe. Second, *symbolic* also names one of the ways a subject constitutes itself within the (symbolic) universe of signifiers. For, in that universe, its constitution can be either imaginary or symbolic. So, in an imaginary subject-constitution, the subject relates to the symbolic order in an imaginary way. This is what happens in the case of "Demand" (French term: *Demande*), which relates to the world in an imaginary way. For a more elaborate explanation, see further on: 1.3.1–2. In his fifth seminar (*Les formations de l'inconscient*, 1957–1958), Lacan had already exhaustively treated the difference between imaginary demand and symbolic desire. See, for instance, his lesson of December 4, 1957 (S5F: 86–92). See also his eighth seminar (*Le transfert*, 1960–1961): S8F: 240–247.

4. This is not without consequences regarding the "healing" expected from the psychoanalytic cure. Lacan provocatively describes the analyst's desire as a "non-desire to heal." The end of an analysis is not to be described in term of "healing" but in terms of "confronting desire." In his lesson of May 11, 1960, he claims: "that one might be paradoxical or trenchant and designate our desire as a non-desire to cure. Such a phrase is meaningful only insofar as it constitutes a warning against the common approaches to the good that offer themselves with a seeming naturalness, against the benevolent fraud of wanting-to-do-one's-best-for-the-subject." But in that case what do you want to cure the subject of? There is no doubt that this is central to our [psychoanalytic] experience, to our approach, to our inspiration—wanting to cure him from the illusions that keep him on the path of his desire" (S7E: 219; S7F: 258).

5. As already mentioned, the patient's problems are basically "ethical" in the sense that they concern his (feeling) good and his demand for the good and well-being.

# Chapter 1

1. (Our translation). "La psychanalyse n'est ni une Weltanschauung, ni une philosophie qui prétend donner la clé de l'univers. Elle est commandée par une visée particulière, qui est historiquement définie par l'élaboration de la notion de sujet" (S9F: 74).

2. The link between "*das Ding*" and the idea of "attachment" is characteristic of the reception of Lacan's *Ethics Seminar* in the Dutch-speaking part of Europe. See, for instance, Moyaert, 1994: 152–153 and passim; Vanden Berghe, 1994: 174.

3. See, for instance, Fairbairn's article "A Revised Psychopathology of the Psychoses and the Psychoneuroses" (1941), where he makes a conceptual distinction between the object relation and the libidinal relation ("It must always be borne in mind, however, that it is not the libidinal attitude which determines the object-relationship, but the object-relationship which determines the libidinal attitude," in Buckley, 1986: 77).

4. In lesson 17 of his first seminar, Lacan critiques Balint's theory of the child's primordial object relation to the mother. He locates Balint's theory between "the classical, Viennese conception" that emphasizes the libidinal reaction of the child ("its sensations [. . .] on the plan of stimulus-response" and its "auto-erotism"), on the one hand, and the theory of Melanie Klein that emphasizes the object relation, on the other. Obviously, Lacan opts for a position in between, defending the primacy of object relations, yet not without making an appeal to reconsider, from this viewpoint, the libidinal (in this case, the auto-erotic) aspect of the event: "[. . .] it is clear that Balint and those who follow him are on the track of a truth. Who can seriously deny, if he has observed a baby of fifteen to twenty days at the breast, that it takes an interest in specific objects? So, the traditional idea that the original vicissitude of the libido is auto-erotism has to be interpreted. It is certain that it has some value [. . .]" (S1E: 211; S1F: 237; for the terms quoted here, see S1E: 210–211; S1F: 236). This kind of libidinal

relation, Lacan continues, must be approached beginning from its "polymorphous-perverse" character: "If analysis has made any positive discovery about libidinal development, it is that the child is a pervert, even a polymorphous pervert" (S1E: 214; S1F: 239).

5. The three other components Freud distinguishes in the drive, as "Instincts and Their Vicissitudes" tells us, are the pressure ("*Drang*"), the aim ("*Ziel*"), and the source ("*Quelle*"); see Freud, SE14: 122; SA3: 85.

6. See Karl Abraham's famous article "Versuch einer Entwickelungsgeschichte der Libido auf Grund der Psychoanalyse seelischer Störungen" (Abraham, 1924; 1979: 418–501).

7. Recall, for instance, the case study of a psychotic child who became famous as "Dick": "The Importance of Symbol-Formation in the Development of the Ego" (see Klein, 1947: 263–278; Grosskurt, 1986: 185–188).

8. See, for instance, "Instincts and Their Vicissitudes," where the object is described as "the thing in regard to which or through which the instinct is able to achieve its aim. It is what is most variable about an instinct and is not originally connected with it, but becomes assigned to it only in consequence of being peculiarly fitted to make satisfaction possible" (Freud, SE14: 122; SA3: 85). See also Diaktine, 1989: 1037, and Grigg, 1990: 41: "the object is in no way adapted or adequate to the subject's desire and instinctual maturation."

9. An important step in this evolution is the work of Michael Balint. See his influential article, "Early Developmental States of the Ego" (in Balint, 1952).

10. Lacan fulminates against this kind of (so-called) psychoanalysis, for instance, at the end of the first part of his famous "Discours de Rome" (Lacan, 2002: 53–54; 1981d: 25; 1966: 263).

11. At the end of *Drei Abhandlungen zur Sexualtheorie*, Freud speaks of a "inverse relation holding between civilization and the free development of sexuality" (Freud, SE7: 242; SA5: 144).

12. Alfred Zenoni speaks in this sense of "denaturation" ("dénaturation") or of the "perversion of the instinct" ("perversion de l'instinct") (Zenoni, 1993: 98). According to Freud, all "unnatural" perversions that Richard von Kraft-Ebing describes in his well-known *Psychopathia sexualis* are in fact ways in which all normal human beings live their nature. Refering to Kraft-Ebing, Freud claims in his case study about Dora: "When, therefore, any one has *become* a gross and manifest pervert, it would be more correct to say that he has *remained* one, for he exhibits a certain stage of *inhibited development*" (Freud, SE7: 50; SA6: 125; Freud's italics).

13. In his *Three Essays on Sexual Theory*, "sucking" ("das Lutschen") is Freud's first example to illustrate "the expression of infantile sexuality" (Freud, SE7: 179; SA5: 87). The polymorphous-perverse structure of the drive is also the content of Freud's "pansexualism." This is not to say that all of human life is oriented toward genital sexuality, but only that all life functions are essentially characterized by the kind of polymorph-perverse structure described above. For a detailed explanation of this psychoanalytic axiom and of the way it developed in Freud's oeuvre, see Jean Laplanche, *Vie et mort en psychanalyse* (Laplanche, 1970; on the basic structure of sexuality, see p. 33; 1990: 18). See also Laplanche & Pontalis, 1968; 1985). Lacan will remain faithful to this psychoanalytic axiom until the end of his days. In his twenty-third seminar, for example (Le sinthome,

1975/76), Lacan emphasizes how "all sexuality is persverse, if we follow what Freud says. He [Freud] never was able to consider sexuality than as perverse. And this is why I investigate what I call the fertility of psychoanalysis. [. . .] after all [. . .] perversion is the essence of man." (My own translation; Lesson of 11.05.1976; Lacan, 1997, 171–172; see also Miller's edition of the text: Lacan, 2005a: 153).

14. Augustine develops this thesis in book XIV of his *De civitate Dei* (Augustine, 1948: 254–273). The erection as the sin of "insurrection" is treated in chapter 23 and 24 (ibid. p. 269–271. Lacan focuses on the Augustinian connotation of pleasure as sin—as "convoitise" and "luxure"—at the beginning of his lesson of May 13, 1959 (Lacan, 1996a: 394–395). See also Lacan, 2002: 245; 1989: 284; 1966: 620), where he interprets "*Wunsch*" as "concupiscentia" (Latin for sinful desire).

15. In this sense, the object relation follows the "principe d'inadéquation," as Serge Leclaire defines the basic principle of the psychic apparatus (Leclaire, 1987: 56–57).

16. Maurice Bouvet (1911–1960) was not only Lacan's major "target" right from the beginning in the fourth seminar (see S4F: 13 among others) on, precisely, "The Object Relation." The final seven lessons of the fifth seminar were also extensively dedicated to articles by him. His "Variations of the type of cure" (1955; see Lacan, 1966: 323–362) was a direct reaction to Bouvet's article "Cure-type" in the Encyclopédie medico-chirurgicale of 1954 (in Bouvet, 1976; 9–96). It is striking that Lacan rarely if ever mentions Bouvet by name (as, for example, in SF5: 387) and the reader thus runs the risk of simply not noticing him, (aided by the refusal of the editor of Lacan's text to insert a clarifying footnote). This is also true of the texts Lacan himself wrote. In the index of the *Écrits*, Bouvet simply does not appear, although Lacan is frequently engaged with him. In "The direction of the cure," he deals extensively with his theories without once naming him (Lacan, 1966: 405–409). But when Lacan ventures "la débilité de la théorie dont un auteur systematise sa technique" (the debility of the theory with which an author systematizes his technique), the "author" in question is certainly Maurice Bouvet. For a summary of the relation between Lacan and Bouvet, see Roudinesco, 1986: 280–287; 1990: 268–278. Why Lacan sets himself so strikingly against Bouvet is perhaps because he wanted to spare the English representatives of this theory who he seriously admired in other ways. This is at least the reason Elisabeth Roudinesco and Michel Plot offer in their *Dictionary of Psychoanalysis*. Lacan had too much admiration for the Ango-Saxon analysts who belonged to the Object-Relations school—Michael Balint, Ronald Fairbairn, Donald Winnicott—to focus on them in his critique (Roudinesco and Plon, 1997: 739).

17. "La clinique psychanalytique: la relation d'objet," an article from 1956 and appearing in Bouvet, 1972: 161–225.

18. "The pre-genitals [prégénitaux] are persons with a weak ego, more or less according to their belonging to the group of the orals [oraux] or the anals [anaux] [. . .]. The stability, the coherence of [their] ego depends strongly on the persistence of the objectal relations with a significant object. The loss of these relations, or of their object (which is synonymous, since here, the object only exists insofar it relates to the subject) seriously disturbs the activity of the ego. [. . .]

The genitals (les génitaux), on the contrary, have an ego that is not dependent on having a significant object in order to be able to function [. . .]" (Bouvet, 1972: 169; my own translation). Lacan reads and comments the entire passage in the first session of his fourth seminar, *La relation d'objet* (S4F: 20–21).

19. Bouvet, 1972: 268. The transition from the pregenital (where the ego still needs the support of oral and anal objects which function as a kind of "Moi auxiliaire") to the genital phase (where the "Moi" operates independently from the object), is apparently a "natural" phenomenon: he characterizes genitalization as "maturation" (Bouvet, 1972: 178; the quoted terms in the next sentence are all from p. 179).

20. From "Findings, Ideas, Problems" ("Ergebnisse, Ideen, Probleme"), in: Freud, *Gesammelte Werke XVII*, p. 150 (own translation). In "La direction de la cure," Lacan evoking the Kleinian theory, writes: "but above all he is these objects" (Lacan, 2002: 240; 1966: 614, Lacan's italics).

21. Jacques Lacan, "The Mirror Stage as Formative of the Function of the I" (Lacan, 2002: 3–9; 1989: 1–8; 1966: 93–100).

22. "To miscognize" refers to the Lacanian concept of "miscognition," the English translation of "méconnaissance" (see Muller & Richardson, 31, 36). Fink uses the word "misrecognize" and "misrecognition" (Lacan, 2002, 360).

23. Further on, I discuss this typically imaginary "miscognition" ("méconnaissance") (see below I.3.4).

24. Paul-Laurent Assoun emphasizes this as the line of thought Lacan has followed from the very beginning of his œuvre: "If Lacan's 'operation' starts (chrono)logically from the concept of a specular subjectivity, the viewpoint of the 'object' imposes itself in the course of the trajectory: in the beginning as correlate of the mirror experience—i.e., what the child meets as the object's imaginary anchoring—at the end as 'object a' " (Assoun, 1997, 658, my translation, MdK; see also Bernard Vandermersch's essay "Objet a" in Chemama, 1995: 218–219). At the end of his seminar on transference, Jean Laplanche criticizes the soundless metamorphosis the "a" undergoes in the course of Lacan's oeuvre (imaginary "a," big "A," object "a"). Yet the key to understanding this metamorphosis is I think to be found in Lacan's focus on the object relation problem. In the different stages of his thirty-year-long seminar project, the object is characterized in different ways (respectively imaginary, symbolic, and real). See Laplanche, 1998, V: 301.

25. Sometimes, Lacan refers to the subject with the specifically Aristotelian term "hypokeimenon": "Knowledge [. . .] as unconscious [. . .] seems to imply a supposition [. . .], which is ourselves, the subject, ὑποκείμενον [hupokeimenon]; all this means is that [. . .] we "suppose" that something named the speaking being [. . .] exists. Which is a pleonasm, since there is only being because of speaking; if there were not the word being, there would be no being at all." (Le séminaire *Les non-dupes errent*, Lesson of 15.01.1974; Lacan, 1981b: 64; my translation). In Lacan, see also S17F: 12; 23. See also Nobus, 1996: 168; Nasio, 1987: 54). Similarly, Philippe Julien names "hypokeimenon" the imaginairy mirror image Lacan talks about in the thirties and forties (Julien, 1990: 194).

26. Raspe, 2003. The paradoxical structure of the Lacanian subject can also be illustrated by the comic figure, Felix the Cat. One recalls the well-known scene in which Felix runs headfirst down a small mountain path and doesn't notice how,

in a bend, he goes off the road. Undisturbed, he runs farther until he notices he is running above the abyss, with no ground under his feet. At that moment, he stops and, from this very place, quickly jumps back onto the mountain path and runs farther as if nothing has happened. This fictional "point" from where, hanging above the abyss, he makes a jump is what Lacanian theory calls the "subject." Using its typical (polymorphously) perverted logic, the libidinal being occupies a "point" in which its basically incoherent and groundless pleasure economy nonetheless acts as if this is its unifying ground. "Subject" names this kind of fictive point. For a further, non-Lacanian elaboration of the Felix the Cat figure, see: De Kesel, 1996b: 122–123.

27. The unconscious concerns the subject, that is, the place from where man relates to the world (including himself): this is one of Lacan's basic intuitions. About one of his obsessional patients he says, for instance: "he does not know which place he occupies, and this is unconscious in him. [. . .] He realizes that the game is not played where he is, [. . .] which does not imply he knows where he sees all this from" (S4F: 27; my translation). For an elaboration of this "from where" as characterizing the subject, see: De Kesel, 1998b.

28. "Die andere Schauplatz," is an expression Freud borrowed from Fechner; Freud, SE5: 536; SA2: 72, 512.

29. At least the Hegel as read by Kojève and—following the latter—Sartre, that is, with a very strong emphasis on the anthropological problematic. See, for instance, Borch-Jacobsen, 1991.

30. See Lacan's 1948 essay "Aggressiveness in Psychoanalysis" (Lacan, 2002: 10–30; 1989: 9–32; 1966: 101–124).

31. An influence plainly recognized by Lacan. One illustration: at the beginning of his reply to a lecture by Lévi-Strauss for the *Société Française de Philosophie* (May 26, 1956), Lacan says: "I want one to know that, when I come to hear Claude Lévi-Strauss, it is always in order to be instructed" (Lévi-Strauss, 1956: 114). For a more general elaboration of Lévi-Strauss' influence on Lacan, see for instance Georgin, 1983.

32. Manfred Frank 1984: 372.

33. Although never named as such, Freud's oeuvre is full of "linguistic" analyses as found, for instance, in the *Interpretation of Dreams*, *Psychopathology of Everyday Life*, his book on jokes, and the great case studies. Yet he never claims the theoretical primacy of a "linguistic" approach. For that, Freud believes too much that psychoanalysis will someday be translated into neurological terms, physiological terms, or both. Lacan, on the contrary, never shared that belief. From the very beginning of his oeuvre, he regarded the cause of unconscious processes and symptoms could be interpreted entirely psychically (see, for instance, a lecture from 1946 in which he explicitly argues that claim: "Propos sur la causalité psychique"; Lacan, 1966: 151–193).

34. Bouvet, 1972: 290; see also: 266.

35. See Freud's "Lecture" 31 (Freud, SE22: 80, SA1: 516). For Lacan's interpretation that there where the imaginary "*Moi*" was, the symbolic "*Je*" has to be, see, for instance, his well-known comment in "La chose freudienne." There, he subtly replaces the word "*ce*" (translating the German "*Es*") by the similar-sounding French reflexive pronoun "*se*": "Là où c'était, peut-on dire, là

où s'était, voudrions-nous faire qu'on entendit, c'est mon devoir que je [i.e., the subject of the symbolic] vienne à être" (Lacan, 2002: 121; 1966: 417–418); English translation by Sheridan: " 'There were it was,' I would like to be understood, 'it is my duty that I should come to being" (Lacan, 1989: 142).

36. The first version of this "move" is to be found in Lacan's 1953 text "Le symbolique, l'imaginaire et le réel" (Lacan, 1982).

37. Note that the drive-induced lack, which is a central notion in Lacanian theory, does not concern the drive itself or its principle (pleasure), but the fact that absolutely nothing in its environment is compatible with what the pleasure principle requires. It is precisely for that reason that the libidinal being coincides with an object relation, that is, a tense *pleasure* relation toward an object that nonetheless is *in*capable of definitely fulfilling the pleasure demands and that, for that reason, remains a relation.

38. This is indicated by the Lacanian "matheme" *s(A)* ["signifié de l'Autre," "signified of the Other"]. It names the topological point of reference for the Ego on the "graphe du désir"; it is the point where the signifiers, coming from the Other, form a *"Message,"* a *"signifié."* The ego constitutes itself as that Message, as the signified of those (as such nonsensical) signifiers.

39. Note that here the term "subject" refers to Lacan's imaginary "subject" theory, that is to say, to what he defines as the Ego. Yet Lacan will reserve the term "subject" for the "symbolic subject," that is, for the subject as "bearer" of signifiers. What is described above is precisely the transition from an imaginary to a symbolic "bearer" ("subject") of the object relation defining the human libidinal being.

40. Lacan quotes the question *"Che vuoi?"* ("What do you want?") from *Le diable amoureux* (1772), a novel by Jacques Cazotte [Cazotte, 1992]. Ironically calling up the devil, the main character suddenly becomes terrified, not only when the devil does indeed appear, but particularly when the monster at once asks the question (in Italian): *"Che vuoi?"* Throughout the story, the main character will chase after his own devilish phantasm, looking for what he wants from that (devilish) Other who, from that very moment, determines his life. In a sense, this story is paradigmatic, according to Lacan, for the way in which man struggles with himself as with the "Other" he is. Lacan introduces this *"Che vuoi?"* in his fourth seminar, *La relation d'objet* (S4F: 169; see also Lacan, 2002: 300; 1989: 346–347; 1966: 814–815) and maintains that concept throughout his entire oeuvre.

41. Or, according to Lacan's well-known formula, "le désir de l'homme est le désir de l'Autre" (see for instance Lacan, 2002: 300; 1989: 346–347; 1966: 814–815). The infant will no longer be able to "miscognize" the lack in the Other; all it can do is long for the filling in of that lack. The unlimited field of signifiers offers very adequate "support" for this procedure since the desired object is permanently displaced from one signifier to another. In this way, the object will never cease to be a lack at the same time. It is in this sense that Lacan interprets the Freudian *Verdrängung* (repression), which he distinguishes from the imaginary "miscognition." The imaginary ego *miscognizes* the lack it rests upon, the symbolic subject *represses* it.

42. In Lacan's conceptual apparatus, castration and phallus refer to one another: the phallus is by definition a castrated one and the body from which it

is castrated is never a real, but always an imaginary body. This is why, from a Lacanian perspective, male and female are strictly symbolic entities. Lacan's "phallocentrism" concerns the strictly symbolic phallus and not that which, biologically, makes a part of the population to be male. See for instance the chapter "Reading the Phallus" in Gallop, 1985: 133–156.

43. One should not forget that Lacan himself denies any parallel with Bouvet. When discussing him, Lacan always characterizes the concept of "distance" as worthless for thinking the relation with the object, because it promotes an exclusively imaginary approach to the problem. See for instance Lacan, 2002: 235 (1966: 608): "I myself suggested to this author [Bouvet, once again unnamed], at a time we used to discuss things, that if one confines oneself to an imaginary relation between objects there remains nothing but the dimension of distance to order it. [. . .] To make distance the sole dimension in which the neurotic's relations with the object are played out generates insurmountable contradictions." Only at the end of the seventh seminar will Lacan return to the problem of the "distance" toward the object. But even then, Lacan does not thematize the (admittedly superficial) parallel between his theory of desire and distance and that of Maurice Bouvet.

44. In this sense, the male genital zone is only sexuated when marked by a "distance"—which is to say in this case: when it is instilled with libidinal fear of castration.

45. This scenario—this "phantasm"—is an imaginary entity, but is to be distinguished from the imaginary "Gestalt," the "image" that gives a "ground" (a "subjectum") to the libidinal being during the mirror stage. The "phantasm" is what remains from that mirror image in the next stage, that is, once the subject is constituted in a symbolic way. It is the imaginarily "congealed" scenario of a few signifiers picturing the subject's symbolic castration, that is, the burial of the subject beneath the signifiers—a subject which from that moment only exists insofar as it is represented by these signifiers. Within the slippery universe of signifiers, this (imaginarily) congealed story—that "phantasm"—gives the symbolic subject (i.e., the subject as being the bearer, not of an image, but of signifiers) an imaginary consistency.

46. Freud, "Ein Kind wird geschlagen" (Beitrag zur Erkenntnis der Entstehung sexueller Perversionen) (Freud, SE17: 179–204; SA7: 229–254). Lacan comments on Freud's essay in the lessons of February 12, 1958 (S5F: 233–243) and January 7, 1959 (Lacan, 1996a: 140–142). He returns to it again in the lesson of June 10, 1959 (Lacan 1996a: 482–484).

47. See Lacan's lesson of May 21, 1958 (SV: 408–409), January 28, 1959 (Lacan, 1996a: 191), May 27, 1959 (Lacan 1996a: 438).

48. In his lesson of May 20, 1959, Lacan defines the "phantasm" as follows: "There emerges something what we call *a* insofar it is the object of desire [. . .] insofar as this object comes into play in a complex which we call the phantasm, the phantasm as such; this is to say insofar as this object is the support around which, at the moment where the subject fades away facing the absence of the signifier that responds to his place at the level of the Other, [the subject] finds its support in that object" (Lacan 1996a: 416; my translation). The letter "a" indicates the object of desire as it functions in Lacan's "matheme" of the phantasm: $ \diamond a.

49. "Arriver à savoir exactement ce qu'a perdu l'avare à qui on a volé son trésor; on apprendrait beaucoup" (Weil, 1948: 26; 1987: 21). Lacan quotes this passage for the first time in the lesson of December 10, 1958 (Lacan, 1996a: 100). April 8, he returns to that passage (Lacan, 1996a: 333; Ornicar?, 25 [1982]: 36). He quotes the aphorism once again in the next lesson, April 15 (Lacan, 1996a: 342; Ornicar? 26/27 [1982]: 11) and in that of May 13, 1959 (Lacan 1996a: 410). For a general overview of Simone Weil's oeuvre from a Lacanian perspective, see Fabian Fajnwaks's essay "Simone Weil: un amour sans objet" (Fajnwaks, 1998). It is remarkable however that Fajnwaks does not refer to the just cited passages from the sixth seminar, even if these are the only ones in his oeuvre where Lacan explicitly discusses Weil. See also Wajcman, 1999: 32.

50. Lacan, 1996a: 100; my translation. Two years later, in his eighth seminar (on transference), Lacan recalls this passage (S8F: 164). In his book Collection, Gérard Wajcman also comments on this Renoir film (Wajcman, 1999: 10, 36–37).

51. A quote from "Les deux versions de l'imaginaire," one of the "Annexes" of L'espace littéraire (Blanchot 1982: 356; 1989: 261–262).

52. "For the good which we can neither picture nor define is a void for us. But a void that is fuller than all fullnesses. If we get as far as this we shall come through all right for God fills the void" (Weil, 1987: 13; 1948: 15).

53. See Weil's first aphorism about the miser: "But when God has become as full of significance as the treasure is for the miser, we have to tell ourselves insistently that he does not exist. We must experience the fact that we love him, even if he does not exist. It is he who, though the operation of the dark night, withdraws himself in order not to be loved like the treasure is by the miser" (Weil, 1987: 15; 1948: 18).

54. Weil analyzes the riches of the miser as a weak imitation of the (ethical) good, which he can no longer deal with in a free way (see Weil, 1987; 46 [1948: 59]: "The miser's treasure is the shadow of an imitation of what is good").

55. See for instance Weil, 1987: 110 [1948: 141]: "Sin is nothing else but the failure to recognize human wretchedness. [. . .] The story of Christ is the experimental proof that human wretchedness is irreducible, that it is as great in the absolutely sinless man as in the sinner. But in him who is without sin it is enlightened. . . ."

56. In this sense, what is at issue in Lacan's Hamlet comment is the object relation. On March 18, 1959, he once again fulminates against the current object relations theories of his time, stating explicitly: "This is what it is about, and as regards Hamlet, nobody ever mentioned the object relation" (see Lacan, 1996a: 312; see also Ornicar? 25 [1982]: 25). The latter reference to Ornicar? concerns Jacques-Alain Miller's editing of Lacan's lessons on Hamlet from his sixth seminar (Le désir et son interprétation, lesson of March 4, 11, 18–April 8, 15, 22, 29, 1959). Because of the irresponsibly inferior quality of this edition, I cite exclusively from the (within the Lacanian field) very reliable, but unpublished version, "edited" (only for his members) by the Association lacanienne (former Association freudienne).

57. See for instance the lesson of March 11, 1959: "What distinguishes the tragedy of Hamlet is essentially that it is the tragedy of desire" (Lacan 1996a: 271; Ornicar? 24 [1981]: 18). Note that here Lacan uses the term "désir" in

the strictly "technical" meaning he has given to this concept (distinguishing it from "Besoin" and "Demande"). His close reading of *Hamlet* (over seven lessons, from March 4 through April 29, 1959)—is an elaboration of his concept of desire. For a more extensive comment, see the chapter "Le deuil selon Lacan interprète d'Hamlet" in: Jean Allouch, *Érotique du deuil au temps de la mort sèche* (Allouch, 1995: 195–276).

58. According to Lacan, this marks the difference with the Oedipus myth. Oedipus faces the lack in the symbolic order (i.e., the death of the father with whom, as his killer, he is bound precisely by death) only after executing his fatal act. Hamlet, on the contrary, faces this lack from the outset; he knows from the very beginning that the symbolic order (i.e., the father) falls short and that, despite this, he must be bound to that order by means of a crime (see the lesson of April 29, 1959: Lacan 1996a: 375 e.v.; *Ornicar?* 26/27 [1983]: 33; see also Zupančič, 2000: 173–174.) For its implications for a theory of modernity, see De Kesel, 2000.

59. Again and again, he urges his mother to immediately break up with her new lover/husband, but the moment she is about to do so, he completely changes position and allows her complete freedom with regard to her desire. The idea that his mother would neglect her desire *as such* is, for Hamlet, apparently worse than whatever "bad object" he must tolerate with her. See *Hamlet*, III, 4, v. 180–196: "QUEEN: What shall I do? / HAMLET: Not this [i.e., to renounce her new husband], by no means, that I bid you do: / Let the bloat king tempt you again to bed; / pinch wanton on your cheek; call you his mouse." Lacan analyzes this passage on March 18, 1959 (Lacan, 1996a: 307–311; *Ornicar?* 25 [1982]: 20–22).

60. See the lesson of April 29 (Lacan 1996a: 386–390; *Ornicar?* 26/27 [1983]: 41–44) and May 13, 1959 (Lacan 1996a: 405).

61. Hamlet V, 1, v. 290–292.

62. "[. . .] cette sorte de bataille furieuse au fond d'une tombe sur lequel j'ai déjà insisté; cette désignation comme d'une pointe de la fonction de l'objet comme n'étant ici reconquis qu'au prix du deuil et de la mort" (Lacan, 1996a: 352: *Ornicar?* 26/27 [1983]: 18–19).

63. This is how he constitutes himself as a "castrated," "split" (i.e., symbolic) subject. Only as split subject is Hamlet able to regard Ophelia again as the object of his desire. (See among others: Allouch, 1995: 254.)

64. It is impossible to go into these last lessons of Lacan's sixth seminar in detail here (*Le désir et son interprétation*, 1958–59), where, hesitating, he tries to distance himself from his exclusively "phallic" (i.e., symbolic) interpretation of Hamlet's phantasm so as to put an increasing emphasis on the real character of the object-pole of desire.

65. The term "objet (petit) a" refers to the *a* of Lacan's definition of phantasm, for which since his fifth seminar he uses the matheme $ \lozenge a $ [to be read as "S barré poinçon a": the barred, split subject ($) insofar it relates ($\lozenge$) to the object of desire (*a*)]. In his sixth seminar, the expression "objet *a* (du désir)" slowly begins to operate as a more or less standard term (see for instance the lesson of December 17, 1958; Lacan, 1996a: 119). As a specific concept, "objet petit a" only emerges in his seventh and eighth seminar after Lacan had conceived this "*objet a du désir*" as "*das Ding*" and as "*agalma*" respectively. According

to Jean Allouch, the term became a concept when Lacan extracted all imaginary connotations from the object. In the second chapter of his *La psychanalyse: une érotologie de passage*, he shows how Lacan treated this "*objet a*" both as imaginary and as real for a year, causing a lot of ambiguity in his theory. Only a strictly "mathematical" formulation enabled him to cut the knot, more exactly, according to Jean Allouch, during his tenth seminar—*L'angoisse* (Anxiety)—in the lesson of January 9, 1963 (Allouch, 1998: 31–42).

66. "But what is important to maintain is the opposition from which this exchange operates, that is, the group $ vis-à-vis *a* [formula of the fantasm: $ ◊ a], of a subject which is certainly imaginary but in a most radical way, in the sense that it is the mere subject of the disconnection, or the spoken cut [la coupure parlée] insofar as the cut is the basic scansion on which the word is built [en tant que la coupure est la scansion essentielle où s'édifie la parole]. The group, I say, of the subject with a signifier which is what? Which is nothing else than the signifier of being, to which the subject is confronted insofar as being is itself marked by the signifier" (Lacan, 1996a: 534; my translation).

67. "C'est-à-dire que le a, l'objet du désir, dans sa nature est un résidu, un reste. Il est le résidu que laisse l'être auquel le sujet parlant est confronté comme tel [. . .]. Et c'est par là que l'objet rejoint le réel" (Lacan, 1996a: 534; my translation).

68. Or, as Bernard Baas puts it in his book, *De la chose à l'objet*: "thinking man as desire is thinking his most basic 'experience' as 'openness' " (Baas, 1998: 24).

69. "L'objet comme tel, l'objet a, si vous voulez, du graphe, [. . .] c'est quelque chose d'ouvert [. . .]." (Lacan 1996a: 533).

70. "Ce désir du sujet, en tant que désir du désir [de l'Autre], il ouvre sur la coupure, sur l'être pur, ici manifesté sous la forme de manque." And about the "ouverture sur la coupure" he adds: "without which we cannot think the situation of desire" (Lacan 1996a: 541; my translation).

71. Lacan, 1996a: 542.

72. "C'est de l'ouverture [qu'il s'agit], c'est de la béance de quelque chose de radicalement nouveau qu'introduit toute coupure de la parole" (Lacan 1996a: 542).

73. "Je veux plus ou moins m'arrêter à ce qui a été à cette endroit la position des philosophes, parce que je crois qu'elle a été très exemplaire du point où se situe pour nous le problème [i.e., the problem of desire]. J'ai pris soin de vous écrire là-haut ces trois [*sic*!] termes, pleasure-seeking, object-seeking. En tant qu'elles [i.e., the positions "philosophers" take in that matter] recherchent le plaisir, en tant qu'elles recherchent l'objet, c'est bien ainsi que depuis toujours s'est posée la question pour la réflexion et pour la morale j'entends la morale théorique, la morale qui s'énonce en préceptes et en règles, en opérations de philosophes, tout spécialement dit-t-on, d'éthiciens" (Lacan 1996a: 14–15). The displaced emphasis in Fairbairn's theory (as well as in most object relations theories) from pleasure ("pleasure-seeking") to the object ("object-seeking") introduces a new conceptual hierarchy: the principle of object attachment prevails over the pleasure principle, a primacy that for Fairbairn defines the object relation tout court. It is via this displaced accent that classical moral paradigms return in the psychoanalytic

theory of desire. Again, desire is defined as based in (a "natural" link to) its object, which is the classical ontological base of ethics: the good I seek is founded in the ontological ground of reality; or, what amounts to the same thing, the pleasure that makes me desire is based in reality as such. Lacan has always vehemently reacted against the object relations theories of his time, precisely because of the classical ethical claims they presuppose. This is why, in his "object relations theory," there is no place for a hegemony of the object attachment over the pleasure principle. His intention, on the contrary, is to develop his object relations theory proceeding from the primacy of the (polymorph perverse, "open") pleasure principle.

# Chapter 2

1. See above chapter 1, point 3.2, note 35. In his introduction to the volume edited with Hans-Dieter Gondek: *Ethik und Psychoanalyse*, Peter Widmer, too, immediately refers to this Freudian imperative to characterize the ethical dimension of psychoanalysis: "This intention to bring up the truth of the subject [Wahres vom Subjekt zur Sprache zu bringen] is an ethical dimension which is inherent to psychoanalysis. *Wo Es war, soll Ich werden*" (Gondek & Widmer, 1994: 10; my translation). In his later seminars, too, Lacan maintains the same thesis, for instance in the eleventh seminar, *The Four Fundamental Concepts of Psychoanalysis*, where he states: "The status of the unconscious [. . .] is ethical. In his thirst for truth, Freud says, *Whatever it is, I must go there*, because, somewhere, the unconscious reveals itself" (S11E: 33; S11F: 34; Miller's italics).

2. Compare, for instance, what Freud writes in *Civilisation and Its Discontents*: "For the more virtuous a man is, the more severe and distrustful is its behaviour, so that ultimately it is precisely those people who have carried saintliness furthest who reproach themselves with the worst sinfulness" (Freud, SE21: 126; SA9: 252).

3. In his first lesson, Lacan remarks how, in the title of his seminar, he did not choose the word "ethics" rather than "moral" by accident: "In speaking of the ethics of psychoanalysis, I chose a word which to my mind was no accident. I might have said 'morality' instead. If I say 'ethics,' you will soon see why. It is not because I take pleasure in using a term that is less common" (S7E: 2; S7F: 10). However, nowhere in the seminar does he explain his preference for "ethics" over "morality" and nor does he even hold onto this conceptual distinction. He may possibly have intended to reserve "morality" for the law of the superego and "ethics" for what goes beyond that kind of law.

4. See for instance Bollack, 1999: 76. For a more general overview of how Antigone has been used as ethical reference since German Idealism, see George Steiner's *Antigones* (Steiner, 1986).

5. To cite one passage from the first session of his *Ethics Seminar*: "Moral experience as such, that is to say, the reference to sanctions, puts man in a certain relation to his own action that concerns not only an articulated law but also a direction, a trajectory, in a word, a good that he appeals to, thereby engendering an ideal of conduct. All that, too, properly speaking constitutes the dimension of ethics and is situated beyond the notion of a command, beyond what offers itself with a sense of obligation" (S7E: 3; S7F: 11).

6. Lacan refers to Angelo Hesnard (1886–1969; one of the prominent French psychoanalysts of the first generation) at the beginning of his first lesson (S7E: 2; S7F: 10). His book, "*L'univers morbide de la faute*," deals with the ethical conclusion to be drawn from analytical praxis (Hesnard, 1949). Lacan shares the antimoralist intention of Hesnard's "scientific" approach of ethics, but completely disagrees with the author's optimistic conclusions (see, for instance, Hesnard, 1949: 453) elaborated in his later publications (see *Morale sans péché*; Hesnard, 1954).

7. I discuss this quote extensively in the final chapter (see under: chapter 9, point 2.2).

8. This is how Lacan explicitly defines eroticism. As he says in one of the next lessons (December 23, 1959): "We will have to explore that which, over the centuries, human beings have succeeded in elaborating that transgresses the Law, puts them in a relationship to desire that transgresses interdiction, and introduces an erotics that is above morality" (S7E: 84; S7F: 101).

9. The entire passage runs: "No doubt something should remain open relative to the place we currently occupy in the development of erotics and to the treatment to be given, not simply to the one individual or other, but to civilization and its discontents. Perhaps we should give up the hope of any genuine innovation in the field of ethics—and to a certain extent one might say that a sign of this is to be found in the fact that in spite of all our theoretical progress, we haven't even been able to create a single new perversion" (S7E: 14–15; S7F: 24). Throughout his entire oeuvre Lacan has regretted this. See for instance the passage from *Le sinthome* I already referred to (chapter I, note 13: "[...] all human sexuality is perverse, if we follow what Freud says [...] and this is what I investigate in what I will call the fertility of psychoanalysis. You heard me very often claim that psychoanalysis did not even invent a new perversion. It is sad. If perversion is man's essence, what an infertility in that practice!" (Lacan, 2005: 153; my translation; see also: 1977: 8).

10. Lacan has changed his opinion. Two years before, he claimed "if we owe psychoanalysis a progress, it is precisely on the level of what is to be named by its name: eroticism" (S4F: 374; my translation).

11. Aside from its ethical context, this idea is not new to Lacan. Already in his 1948 lecture, "The mirror stage," he ends with the following sentence: "In the recourse of subject to subject that we reserve, psychoanalysis may accompany the patient to the ecstatic limit of the '*Thou art that*,' in which is revealed to him the cipher of his mortal destiny, but it is not in our mere power as practitioners to bring him to that point where the real journey begins" (Lacan 1989: 8, 1966: 100). See also Guyomard, 1998: 33; Allouch, 1998: 150.

## Chapter 3

1. Alexandre Koyré develops this idea in a number of his books. See for instance Koyré, 1973: 211.

2. Steven Shapin cites a passage in Newton where he explicitly abandons the pretension to be able to think the "inward substances" of things: "In bodies," Newton wrote, "we see only their figures and their colours, we hear only

the sounds, we touch only their outward surfaces, we smell only the smells, and taste the savours; but their inward substances are not to be known either by our senses, or by any reflex act of our minds" (Shapin, 1998: 157). However, God as the Creator is not absent in Newton's physics. On the contrary, he remains an indispensable point of reference and an ultimate guarantee (see Le Gaufey, 1994: 38–53).

3. Since Kant's *Critique of Pure Reason*, the "thing itself" ("*das Ding an Sich*") has become definitely unknowable. Henceforth, so Kant concludes, science can no longer pretend to be based in the things themselves, in the real.

4. In his seventh seminar, Lacan refers only occasionally to this thesis (S7E: 75 ff., 122, 313; S7F: 91 ff., 147, 361) because he had already done so several times in his previous seminars. In the fourth seminar, for instance, he discusses the concept of gravity, which Newton never mentions as "metaphysical" but always as "mathematical force"—as Koyré affirms, for instance, in an article of the early fifties ("Science et portée de la synthèse newtonienne"; Koyré, 1968: 36). The discovery of gravity and its laws, Lacan concludes, is not due to mere observation, but to observation done from mathematical construction—or, in Lacan's term, from constructions of signifiers (see S4F: 429).

5. The definition of the subject as the "bearer" of signifiers (referring to the desire of the Other) is, in this perspective, indeed a "subversion" of the (classical, Cartesian) subject. See, for instance, the lesson of March 5, 1958, where he states: "What is revealed by the phenomenon of human desire, is the basic subduction, if not to say the perversion by the signifier: this is the sense of what I try to make clear: desire's relation to the signifier" (S5F: 251; my translation).

6. "Theory of Fictions" is a compilation of Bentham's texts on fictions edited by Charles Kay Ogden (Ogden, 1932). I refer here to the well-annotated bi-lingual edition by Gérard Michaut (Bentham, 1996). For the definition of "real entities," see Bentham 1996: 44; for "fictitious entities": 49; for "fabulous entities": 58. For the list of "ethical fictitious entities" (compiled by George Bentham, nephew of the philosopher) (see *o.c.*, p. 334). For a similar exposition of "Entities real and fictitious," see Bentham's *Of Ontology* (Bentham, 1997: 80–89). A more elaborated exposition of Lacan's reading of Bentham is found in Soubbotnik, 1992.

7. " '*Fictitious*' means 'fictif' but, as I have already explained to you, in the sense that every truth has the structure of fiction. [. . .] The fictitious is not, in effect, in its essence that which deceives, but is precisely what I call the symbolic" (S7E:12; S7F: 21–22).

8. Bentham's interpretation of language differs profoundly from Lacan's, if only because of Bentham's idea that language should be seen as an instrument (i.e., as a *sign*) and not as a *signifier*. "Language is the sign of thought, an instrument for the communication of thought from one mind to another [. . .] of the thought which is in the mind of him by whom the discourse is uttered" (Bentham, 1996: 164).

9. "C'est dans cette dialectique du rapport du langage avec le réel que s'instaure l'effort de Bentham pour situer quelque part ce réel bien, ce plaisir en l'occasion, dont nous verrons qu'il l'articule d'une façon tout à fait différente de la fonction que lui donne Aristote. Et je dirai que c'est à l'intérieur de cet accent mis sur cette opposition entre la fiction et la réalité que vient se placer le mouve-

ment de bascule de l'expérience freudienne" (Lacan 1959/60, lesson of 18.11.59, p. 12; 1999: 24; my translation).

10. "L'effort de Bentham s'instaure dans cette dialectique du rapport du langage avec le réel pour situer le bien—le plaisir en l'occasion, dont nous verrons qu'il l'articule d'une façon tout à fait différent d'Aristote—*du côté du réel*" (S7F: 21–22; my italics).

11. According to Lacan, one should consider utilitarianism not only as "far from being made up the pure and simple platitude one imagines" (S7E: 12; S7F: 21). It is also "quite right" ("tout à fait raison"; S7E: 187; S7F: 220). In the next seminar (*Le transfert*, 1960–61), he says that "the ethics named utilitarian is the most founded; there is no other" (S7FI: 285; my translation). The reason why, for Lacan, utilitarianism is "right" is due not only to its affirmation of the signifier ("*fiction*") as such, but also to the fact that Bentham is perfectly able to disprove the criticism that reproaches it as an egotistic ethics. See below VI.3.1.

12. In his third lesson, Lacan asks why, in the "interval" he only zeroes in on Aristotle and Bentham. His answer is that Aristotle is responsible for the topic of pleasure in western ethics. Utilitarianism is "significant for the new direction with culminated in Freud" (S7E: 36; S7F: 46).

13. Lacan had already discussed this idea in the first lesson of his previous seminar (*Desire and Its Interpretation, 1958–59*): "But with regard to desire, you will see to what extent Aristotle himself must recognize [. . .] that ἐπιθυμία (*épithumia*), desires, go easily beyond a certain limit which is precisely the one of mastery and of the ego [and enter] in a domain of what he calls bestiality. These desires are banned from the proper field of man, insofar man is indentified with the reality of the master; they are something like perversions" (lesson of 12.12.1958; Lacan, 1996a: 15–16; my translation). Aristotle discusses "bestiality" (θηριότμς, *thèriotès*) in book VII of his *Ethica Nicomachea* (1148b15–1149a24; VII, v; Aristotle, 1994: 401–405).

14. In Aristotle, "striving" or "desire" (ὄρεξις, *orexis*) is defined as the tension that characterizes a being insofar it has not yet completely realized its (ontological) aim. This is why, rather than the faculty of knowledge, desire is the "motor" of the soul (see: *De anima* 433a21).

15. *Nicomachean Ethics* VII, v.1 (1148b18): "Besides those things however which are naturally pleasant [. . .], there are other things, not naturally pleasant, which become pleasant either as a result of arrested development or from habit, or in some cases owing to natural depravity." (Aristotle, 1994: 401). The given illustrations make clear it concerns "bestialities": "I mean bestial characters, like the creature in woman's form that is said to rip up pregnant females and devour their offspring, or certain savage tribes on the coasts of the Black Sea, who are alleged to delight in raw meat or in human flesh, and others among whom each in turn provides a child for the common banquet [. . .] All these various morbid dispositions in themselves do not fall within the limits of Vice [and, thus, of ethics as such] [. . .]." (1148b20–24; Aristotle, 1994: 401–403).

16. Lacan refers to the Aristotle's play on words with the Greek terms "ethos" (ἔθος) and "èthos" (ἦθος). The human character (ἦθος, "èthos"; i.e., habit), must conform to an "ethos" (ἔθος), "that is, to an order that from the point of view of Aristotle's logic has to be brought together in a Sovereign Good"

(S7E: 22; S7F: 31; see also S7E: 10; S7F: 19; Lacan, 1984: 11). Ethics in the sense of rule or law—"ethos" (ἔθος)—is based on the habits, on a settled attitude and character—"èthos" (ἤθος)—that, by means of repetition (both words stem from the Greek word for repetition), have been approved as good or, even, that lead to the Supreme Good, that is, to the ultimate fulfillment of being.

17. Lacan turns against Hegel's definition of the "master" as the dialectical antagonist of the "slave." Like his entire dialectics, this definition, too, reveals how Hegel is locked up in a dual, that is, imaginary logic and how he "miscognizes" the irremovable third factor, that is, the Other or the symbolic order. This is why the ancient "master" must first of all be considered a member of a "society of masters" (S7E: 23; S7F: 32), that is, as part of a *symbolic* system in which the "master" identifies with an ideal mediated by a symbolic code. Aristotelian ethics offered him a moral code appropriate to his symbolic position. The highest form of "mastership"—or, as Aristotle says, "αυταρκεια" ("*autarkeia*")—did not consist in having power over slaves, but in the development of the highest virtue (capacity), which for Aristotle is thinking (*Ethica Nicomachea*, X, 7 [1177ab; Aristotle, 1994: 612–614]; Lacan refers to this passage in S7E: 22; S7F: 31). In his book *Lacan, lecteur d'Aristote*, Christophe Cathelineau even suggests that Aristotle's theory of master-ethics is an attempt to develop a valuable, humane legitimization for slavery (Cathelineau, 1998: 111, 114). Yet Lacan agrees with Hegel that the idea of the "master" has been historically superseded. After the (modern) break with the real, such an ancient ideal of an ontologically based masterdom has become simply impossible. Utilitarianism offered an answer to the "radical decline of the function of the master." A passage already cited makes the connection: "At the beginning of the nineteenth century, there was the utilitarian conversion or revision. We can define the moment—one that was no doubt fully conditioned historically—in terms of a radical decline of the function of the master, a function that obviously governs all of Aristotle's thought and determines its persistence over the centuries. It is in Hegel that we find expressed an extreme devalorization of the master, since Hegel turns him into the great dupe, the magnificent cuckold of historical development, given that the virtue of progress passes by way of the vanquished, which is to say, of the slave, and his work" (S7E: 11; S7F: 21). At the end of his seminar, Lacan takes up again this idea (S7E: 292; S7F: 339).

18. This is the way, for instance in his second lesson, that Lacan puts Aristotle and Freud in opposition to one another. "Pleasure in Aristotle is an activity that is compared to the bloom given off by youthful activity—it is, if you like, radiance. In addition, it is also the sign of the blossoming of an action, in the literal sense of ἐνεργεια,' a word that expresses the true praxis as that which includes its own end. [...] But let us consider the case of the man who questions us directly, of Freud. What cannot fail to strike us right away is that his pleasure principle is an inertia principle [...] It is essentially a matter of everything that results from a fundamental tendency to discharge in which a given quantity is destined to be expended. That is the point of view from which the functioning of the pleasure principle is first articulated" (S7E: 27; S7F: 36–37).

19. So, in the wake of Georges Canguilhem, one can speak of a kind of "Copernican revolution" in the paradigm of how one thinks life. In his book *La formation du concept de réflexe aux XVII⁰ et XVIII⁰ siècles* Canguilhem describes

step by step the way in which the point where life is situated moves from the *kernel* to the periphery, a move explicitly described as a "de-centering"—"décentration du centre" (Canguilhem, 1955: 128).

20. The *Entwurf* is a (posthumously published) neurophyisological sketch of the psychic apparatus as Freud conceived it in 1895. It is inspired by his old professor Sigmund Exner (who wrote *Entwurf zu einer physiologischen Erklärung der psychischen Erscheinungen*, 1894) and was an addition to one of his letters to Wilhelm Fliess, with whom for more than a decade he had an intense correspondence. In one of these letters, he names the *Entwurf* "a psychology for neurologists"; Freud, 1986: 129). The originally untitled text is first published in 1950 as "Entwurf einer Psychologie" as an appendix to the partial edition of his letters to Fliess (Freud, 1975: 297–384) and later included under the same title in the *Gesammelte Werke* (Freud, 1987: 373–477). For a comment about the problematic place of this text within Freudian psychoanalysis, see among others Frank Sulloway, *Freud, biologist of the mind* (Sulloway, 1979: 113–131).

21. Jean Laplanche comments several times in his oeuvre on Freud's description of the "psychic apparatus," including its inconsistencies and paradoxes (at times he discovers the absurd character ["délibérément absurde"] of the system; Laplanche, 1998 I: 177). Yet it is not so much a matter of discussing the validity of the scheme (at several points Freud, too, is full of doubt and at one point he calls the entire system "fiction" [Freud, SE5: 598; SA2: 568]), as of discussing its logical lines and their suppositions. As Laplanche points out, Freud's (speculative) conceptualization of the "psychic apparatus" considers life as a "secondary" phenomenon, making things more complicated since the apparatus, against its own principle, now has to accumulate (instead of to discharge) energy. See, for instance, in *The New Foundations of Psychoanalysis*: "[T]his mechanism predates the biological; the biological simply makes it more complicated. Freud now refers to the intervention of the 'exigencies of life' (the *Not des Lebens*) which, in some unexplained fashion, intervenes like a veritable Deus ex machina, forcing the apparatus to economize on energy, whereas its sole purpose was originally to accumulate energy" (Laplanche, 1989: 38–39. 1994: 42; Laplanche's italics).

22. In chapter VI of *Civilisation and Its Discontents*, Freud gives a nice summary of the increasing stress he has put on the conflictual working of libidinal life (see Freud, SE21: 117–122; SA9: 245–249). See also Laplanche's excellent long comment in *Life and Death in Psychoanalysis* (Laplanche, 1990).

23. For the "*Not des Lebens*" ("vital needs"), see among others the seventh chapter in *The Interpretation of Dreams* (Freud, SE5: 565; SA2: 538) or the *Entwurf* of 1895 (Freud, SE1: 279, 301, 303).

24. Lacan refers explicitly to this in his lessons on Freud's *Entwurf*: "An important part of the P system [system in the psychic apparatus responsible for the content—the representations—of the unconscious] is, in fact, constituted of raw Q quantities [Q is the general quantity term for energy] from the outside which are transformed into quantities [. . .]" (S7E: 40; S7F: 51).

25. See the crucial passage in the fourth chapter of *Beyond the Pleasure Principle*, where Freud must conclude that the "first drive" the animate organism has ever shown is "to return to the inanimate state" (Freud, SE18: 38; SA3: 248).

26. Freud, SE18: 35; SA3: 245.

27. Freud, SE18: 36; SA3: 246.

28. "*It seems, then, that an instinct is an urge inherent in organic life to restore an earlier state of things* which the living entity has been obliged to abandon under the pressure of external disturbing forces; that is, it is a kind of organic elasticity, or, to put it another way, the expression of the inertia inherent to organic life (Freud, SE18: 36; SA3: 246; Freud's italics). Note here again that Freud's claim supposes life as coming primordially from the outside, that is, from the stimuli exciting the organism.

29. In his conceptualization of the energy concept, Freud is partly tributary to Breuer who supposes a kind of reservoir full of "energy" stemming from "intracerebral tonic excitation" enabling the organism to react to stimuli. The origin of this energy is, according also to Breuer, not only internal but also "external excitations" (Laplanche & Pontalis, 1988: 171).

30. In *Beyond the Pleasure Principle*, Freud explains the cell wall hardening of a unicellular organism as follows: "This little fragment of living substance is suspended in the middle of an external world charged with the most powerful energies; and it would be killed by the stimulation emanating from these if it were not provided with a protective shield against stimuli. It acquires the shield in this way: its outermost surface ceases to have the structure proper to living matter, becomes to some degree inorganic and thenceforward functions as a special envelope or membrane resistant to stimuli. In consequence, the energies of the external world are able to pass into the next underlying layers, which have remained living, with only a fragment of their original intensity; [. . .] *Protection against* stimuli is an almost more important function for the living organism than *reception of* stimuli" (Freud, SE 18: 27; SA3: 237; Freud's italics; see also Laplanche, 1998 I: 186–187).

31. "My analysis continues and remains my chief interest. Everything is still obscure, even the problems, but there is a comfortable feeling in it that one has only to reach into one's storerooms to take out what is needed at a particular time. The most disagreeable part of it is the moods, which often completely hides reality [Stimmungen, die einem die Wirklichkeit oft ganz verdecken]" (Freud, 1985: 276; 1986: 298). Lacan refers to that passage in S7E: 26 (S7F: 35).

32. See also S7E: 35; S7F: 45 (quoted below); S7E: 37–38; S7F: 48 ("if we are following so closely the development of Freud's meta-psychology this year, it is in order to uncover the traces of a theory that reflects an ethical thought. [. . .] If we always return to Freud, it is because he started out with an initial, central intuition, which is ethical in kind."); S7E: 72; S7F: 88 ("[ethical] good is already pointed out [. . .] as the significant result of a signifying composition that is called up at the unconscious level"). Also later, he retakes that idea (see o.a. S11E: 33, 40; S11F: 34, 40).

33. For the primary and secondary processes, see for instance Freud's exposé in *The Interpretation of Dreams* (Freud, SE5: 601 ff.; SA2: 571 ff.).

34. See the title J.-A. Miller gave to Lacan's third lesson: "Rereading the *Entwurf*" (S7E: 35; VII: 45).

35. After having criticized the reading of Freud's *Entwurf* as a mere illustration of "mechanist ideas [idéaux mécanistes] of Helmholz and Brücke," Lacan declares that, if there is a need to compare this text to some other one, the best

choice one can make is Aristotle's *Ethica Nicomachea*: "Isn't the functioning of the apparatus that supports the reality principle strangely similar to what one finds in Aristotle?" (S7E: 29; S7F: 38).

36. "How can a man fail in self-restraint when believing correctly that what he does is wrong?" (Aristotle, *Nicomachean Ethics*: 1145b22; Aristotle, 1994: 379). For few pages (until 1147b18), Aristotle discusses this problem. In S7E: 29 (S7F: 39; already anounced in S7E:22; S7F: 31) Lacan discusses only one of Aristotle's arguments, more precisely the one connecting the problem to desire, which Aristotle names here the "natural cause" ("φυσικῶς" [*fusikoos*])—that is why Lacan speaks about a "solution" that is "physical" [S7E: 29; S7F: 39]). See *Nicomachean Ethics* 1147a23–1147b6; Aristotle 1994: 391–393. For a general comment on this passage, see Kenny, 1979: 158–161.

37. Thus, Plato in (for instance) *Protagoras* 352bc–358bc.

38. The passage is unclear for many reasons: first of all Lacan is unclear, omitting several elements in the presentation of Aristotle's argumentation. And, second, the official edition has modified Lacan's words even more confusingly. Compare the passage in the official edition (S7F: 39, first paragraph) with the (more original) "pirate" edition: Lacan, 1999: 44).

39. Aristotle, *Nicomachean Ethics* 1147a24–b5 (Aristotle, 1994: 391–393).

40. See also Micheli-Rechtman, 1992: 92.

41. A few lines after his evocation of the "aporia" in Aristotle's *Nicomachean Ethics*, Lacan says: "If Freud returns to the logical and syllogistic articulations, which have always been used by ethical philosophers in their field, it is in order to give them a very different meaning" (S7E: 30; S7F: 39).

42. The stimuli must find a way not only through the system with permeable "neurons" (the φ system,) but first and foremost through the system with impermeable neurons (the ψ system), Freud writes in his *Entwurf*. It is in this latter layer that the facilitations—"Bahnungen"—leave traces that support the (memory-)representations. The two "main theses" of Freud's *"sketch"* of the psychic apparatus suppose its energy to be entirely quantifiable (Freud, SE1: 295–296) and that "the nervous system consists of distinct and similar constructed neurones, which have contact with one another through the medium of a foreign substance" (Freud, SE1: 298). The φ system stands for neurones "which serve for perception, the ψ system for neurones which are "the vehicles of memory and so probably of psychical processes in general." And a few lines further: *"Memory is represented by the facilitations existing between the ψ neurones"* (Freud, SE1: 300; Freud's italics).

43. For the "specific action" ("spezifische Aktion"), see Freud, SE1: 297, 318, 366, 369, 383, 386.

44. See for instance in the last chapter of *The Interpretation of Dreams* (Freud, SE5: 536 ff.;
SA2: 513 ff.). See also his letter to Fliess of December 6, 1896 (Freud, 1985: 207ff.).

45. Lacan uses this expression several times. In his fourth lesson, for instance, he states: "the chain that extends from the most archaic unconscious to the articulate form of speech in a subject, all that takes place between *Wahrnehmung* und

*Bewusstsein*, between glove and hand, so to speak. [entre cuir et chair]" (S7E: 51; S7F: 64). See also S7E: 61; S7F: 75; S11E: 45, 56; S11F: 46, 55; Lacan, 1984: 17; 1996b: 98, 411.

46. Freud, SE5: 565; SA2: 538. One could call this kind of immediate discharge a "non-specific" act, contrary to the reaction on endogenous stimuli (such as hunger) which require a "specific act."

47. Because of the unconscious character of the "orthos logos" operating here, the latter must be "ironically highlighted by inverted commas," as Lacan explains. This kind of "logos" cannot claim universal pretensions as did the one Aristotle had in mind: "the ὀρθος λόγος that concerns us here are not simple major premises [ce ne sont justement pas des propositions universelles], [. . .] they concern the discourse that is employed on the level of the pleasure principle. It is in relation to this ὀρθος, ironically highlighted by inverted commas, that the reality principle has to guide the subject in order for him to complete a possible action" (S7E: 30; S7F: 39–40).

48. The passage at the end of Freud's "Formulations on the Two Principles of Mental Functioning" cannot be misunderstood: "The strangest characteristics of unconscious (repressed) processes [. . .] is due to the their entire disregard of reality-testing; they equate reality of thought with external actuality, and wishes with their fulfilment—with the event—just as happens automatically under the dominance of the ancient pleasure principle" (Freud, SE12: 225; SA3: 23).

49. This is the metapsychological reason why, according to Lacan, the unconscious presents itself as language. See also Micheli-Rechtman, 1992: 93:

50. This is what Freud, in his famous letter to Fliess of December 6, 1896 defines as a system of "*Niederschriften*" (Freud, 1985: 207). In the first (partial) edition of Freud's letters to Fliess, this letter was numbered as "letter 52" (Freud, 1975: 151–156). Under this tile, the letter occupies a special—and famous—place in the reception of Freud. See also S7E: 50; S7F: 63.

51. "Nicely" is intended euphemistically here. Not only is the scheme far from transparent and clear, the scheme of the official edition (S7E: 34; S7F: 44) differs from the two other versions of the same scheme: that in Lacan's own *Compte rendu* of his *Ethics Seminar* (Lacan, 1984: 16) and the one he puts on the blackboard during one of the lessons of his ninth seminar (*L'identification*; Lacan, 1996b: 97; lesson of 10.01.62). An analysis of the very dense passages in which each of the three version appears, as well as of their mutual differences (displacements?), would go beyond the limits of our reading of Lacan's *Ethics Seminar*, requiring a separate detailed study.

52. The last sentence ("Je vous propose pour l'instant d'y mettre un point d'interrogation") is not translated in the English edition, making the passage even more obscure.

53. These words are omitted in the English edition; compare with the French edition: "S'il y a quelque chose qui s'appelle son bien et son bonheur, il n'y a rien à attendre pour delà ni du microcosme, c'est-à-dire de lui-même, ni du macrocosme."

54. Compare for instance what Freud writes in *Civilization and Its Discontents*: "As we see, what decides the purpose of life is simply the programme of the pleasure principle. This principle dominates the operation of the mental apparatus

from the start. There can be no doubt about its efficacy, and yet its programme is at loggerheads with the whole world, with the macrocosm as much as with the microcosm. There is no possibility at all of its being carried through; all the regulations of the universe run counter to it. One feels inclined to say that the intention that man should be 'happy' is not included in the plan of 'Creation' " (Freud, SE21: 76; SA9: 208).

## Chapter 4

1. Erik Porge and Peter Widmer have observed how one already finds the term in his essay on aphasia (for Porge, see a discussion edited in "Lettres de l'Ecole freudienne," nr.18, 1976, p. 158; for Widmer, see Gondek & Widmer, 1994: 11). The passage from the aphasia article is edited as an appendix ("Words and Things") with *The Unconscious* (Freud, SE14: 209–215; SA3: 168–173). The term *"Ding"* appears once again in "Negation" (*Die Verneinung*), although it is hardly defensible that the single expression "vorgestelten Dinges," "something of which there is presentation" (Freud, SE19: 237; SA3: 375) suffices in order to make the notion into a concept. It is Lacan who explicitly links the passage from "Negation" with the one from the *Entwurf* to suggest an affiliation at the level of content, that is, between the problem of judgment, on the one hand, and that of the object, on the other. Only by means of this connection does the notion acquire the weight Lacan gives it.

2. Freud explains how the psychic apparatus has to *judge* the compatibility between *wished* and *perceived* "aggregates of neurones," and gives the example of a *"wishful cathexis"* containing "neurone $a$ + neurone $b$" and a "perceptual cathexis" composed with "neurone $a$ and neurone $c$." The judgement process must make a distinction between the identical "neurone a" and the varying "neurones b and c." This, however, is an unconscious process, and so Freuds adds: "it [language] will call neurone $a$ the *thing* and neurone $b$ its activity or attribute, in short, its *predicate*" (Freud, SE1: 328; Freud's italics).

3. Freud, SE1: 331; Freud's italics. See also further in the third part of the *Entwurf* where he once more describes how these "complexes [of neurones] [. . .] are dissected into an unassimilable component (the thing) and one known to the ego from its own experience (attribute, activity)—what we call *understanding* (Freud, SE1: 366; Freud's italics). On p. 383 he discusses this once more.

4. "Representations" as the basic element with which the psychic apparatus operates is a notion Freud took from the first generation of "scientific" psychologists, among others Herbart (1776–1841). For a more elaborate discussion of this notion in Freud, see for instance Le Gaufey, 1997: 192–198.

5. Hence one does not need to interpret the "cry" as referring to the mother's orgasmic cries at the moment of sexual enjoyment, as François Peraldi claims (Peraldi, 1987: 312–313). With this idea, he tries to explain Freud's description of the one with whom the child has a symbiotic relation as "alien." According to Lacan, it is the speaking aspect of the mother that makes her alien for the child (see my comments on *Che vuoi?* in the first chapter). It is in the symbolic order (i.e., the realm of signifiers) that the infant will be forced to be *alienated*.

6. Perhaps Lacan confuses a passage from the *Entwurf* with the one he is about to quote from "Negation" where the origin of the inside and outside worlds is related to the structure of judgment. In this way, as Freud writes, "what is bad, what is alien to the ego [das dem Ich Fremde], and what is external are, to begin with, identical" (Freud, SE19: 237; SA3: 374).

7. Throughout his entire oeuvre, Freud holds onto this idea. Still in the *Abriss der Psychoanalyse* (1940), he says: "Reality will always remain 'unknowable' " (Freud, SE23: 196).

8. For the passage in "Negation," which Lacan cites correctly here, see, Freud, SE19: 237–238; SA3: 375.

9. In the same context of the cited passage, Lacan stresses once again: "In the end, in the absence of something which hallucinates it in the form of a system of references, a world of perception cannot be organized in a valid way, cannot be constituted in a human way. The world of perception is represented by Freud as dependent on that fundamental hallucination without which there would be no attention available" (S7E: 51–53; S7: 66).

10. "Moreover, since it is a matter of finding it again, we might just as well characterize this object as a lost object. But although it is essentially a question of finding it again, the object indeed has never been lost" (S7E: 58; S7: 72).

11. Referring to that passage from the *Entwurf*, Bruce Fink in *The Lacanian Subject* writes: "As is often the case, however, Lacan's 'lost object' goes far beyond anything «found» in Freud's work. Examined in context, Freud never claims that objects are inexorably or irremediably lost, or that the 'rediscovery' or 'refinding' of an object implies an object that is always already lost" (Fink, 1995: 93).

12. According to Lacan himself, the emphasis that since the seventh seminar he put on the real does not affect the primacy of the signifier. On the contrary, until his last seminars he keeps on stressing that Freud's principal and single discovery is the primacy of language. In a lecture in Louvain, Belgium, October 13, 1972, he once more repeats how the basic hypothesis of psychoanalysis (and of any kind of scientific approach of human subjectivity) is that the human being equals a speaking being: "the speaking being [. . .] is a pleonasm, isn't it? It is because he is speaking that he is being, for only in language there is being. [. . .] You have to proceed from this. Even when he is on a lost island, he lives in language and in a way his least ideas come from there; it is a mistake to believe that, if language did not exist, he would think; he does not think with language, it is language that thinks" (Lacan, 1981c: 6–7, my own translation). Two years later, in Seminar XXI (*Les non-dupes errent*, 1973–1974), he repeats his emphasis on language in quite similar words: "[. . .] speaking being. Which is a pleonasm, because there is only being because there is speaking; if words were not there, there would be no being at all." (Lesson of January 15, 1974; Lacan, 1981b: 64; my own translation). Lacan's emphasis on the real (here, in Seminar VII, on the Thing) must be approached from his claim concerning the primacy of the signifier. Precisely to think the cut made in the real by language (and, thus, by desire), he is obliged to develop the notion of the real in a nuanced way. No wonder, then, that in his early work, one can find traces of what later will be defined as the "*das Ding*" or "the real." See, for instance, the passage from his famous "Discours de Rome": "To say that this mortal meaning reveals in speech a centre exterior to

language is more than a metaphor; it manifests a structure" (Lacan, 1989: 115, 1966: 320). In this "exterior centre," Lacan, in his *Ethics Seminar*, will locate "*das Ding,*" which for that reason he will describe as an "extimité" (S7E: 139; S7F: 167). See also farther on in this chapter: 2.1.

13. In this sense, Slavoj Žižek can write that the "real [. . .] is inherent to the symbolic." It "is the internal stumbling block on account of which the symbolic system can never 'become itself,' achieve its self-identity" (Žižek, 1997: 217).

14. For an overview of Lacan's topological schemes, see among others: Granon-Lafont, 1985; Darmon, 1990 and Gilson, 1994.

15. Only from the ninth seminar onward (*L'identification, 1961/62*) will Lacan trace out his "cartography" of the libidinal economy by means of strictly topological figures—"topological" in the technical sense of the word, that is, referring to geometrical figures which are not defined as classic, Euclidian ones. With Möbius, Félix Klein, and Poincaré, this kind of topological geometry makes a real breakthrough in the beginning of the twentieth century. It is a geometry of surfaces defined as figures that do not change when one modifies their shape without breaking the coherence of the surface. For instance, the surface of a bike tire (a torus) can be described regardless of what shape it occupies in space (full with air, without air, stretched, folded back). Other figures in the topology Lacan refers to are the Möbius strip, the cross-cap, and the Klein bottle. Lacan uses them to locate such concepts as subject, Other, object a, and phallus within the libidinal economy.

16. S7E: 139 (S7F: 167): "this intimate exteriority or 'extimacy,' that is the Thing." See also S7E: 101 (S7F: 122): "What is involved is that excluded interior, which in the terminology of the *Entwurf*, is thus excluded in the interior."

17. To put in a more nuanced fashion, one can say that Lacanian psychoanalysis is the "subjective" counterpart of the revolution which, with Einstein, has been accomplished on the "objective" level by Newtonian physics. In his remarkable book *L'éviction de l'origine*, Guy Le Gaufey show how Newton still supposes a voluntaristic God (a "Lord") as the ultimate guarantor for his system, whereas Einstein's relativity theory develops a physical model that can do without such a guarantor. Le Gaufey remarks a similar distinction in the step Lacan makes beyond Freud. In Freud, the oedipal structure proper to the psychic life is still referred to a real father (whose most definitive shape is the leader of the primitive horde as described in *Totem und Taboo* [1912/13]), whereas Lacan's structuralist interpretation can do without such a reference to a real origin (Le Gaufey, 1994).

18. In this sense, Erik Porge can claim that the "thing" is in a way the subject itself: "La Chose, c'est le sujet" (Porge, 1976: 164). Somewhere in his fourteenth seminar, Lacan calls the subject "*chosique*" (les van 22.02.1967). The real "*hypokeimenon*" ("*subjectum,*" bearer) of the object relation (the libidinal being coincides with) is indeed the "thing." But the libidinal being does not live on the level of the real, but on the one of the imaginary and the symbolic. Only this way, it operates as a "subject of desire," that is, as a subject *tout court*. On the level of the mere drive, it is the "thing" that gives that drive its ontological dimension, so Lacan states at the end of his eleventh lesson: "the *Trieb* can in no way be limited to a psychological notion. It is an absolutely fundamental ontological notion, [. . .]" (S7E: 127; S7F: 152).

19. In Lacanian theory, the original trauma refers to the radical incompatibility between pleasure and the real world, that is to say, between the requirements of pleasure, and pleasure's inability to find something in the real world that directly satisfies its requirements. The libidinal being will only be able to *in*directly gain pleasure from reality. This is why the libidinal economy will always remain affected by that incompatibility (i.e., the original trauma). This is to say that there will never be a fully adequate way of satisfying an organism's pleasure requirements; pleasure will always be more or less excessive or deficient. In "*Manuskript K*," an appendix with the letter to Wilhelm Fliess of January 1, 1896, Freud discusses the defense neuroses and gives for the first time a more developed analysis of hysteria, obsessional neurosis and paranoia, as three forms of defense against the original trauma. Hysteria, Freud writes, is a matter of "too much unpleasure"; obsessional neurosis is a matter of too much pleasure (concerning paranoia, Freud is still unsure) (Freud, 1985: 162–169; see also André, 1995: 84).

20. Lacan explicitly connects Freud's early notion of *das Ding* with his late concept of death drive. See, for instance, S7E: (S7F: 124): "the field of *das Ding* is rediscovered at the end [in Freud's oeuvre], and [. . .] Freud suggest [it] there [as] that which in life might prefer death."

21. This is one more indication why Lacan's emphasis on the real doesn't affect the primacy of the signifier. It is because of the lethal gravitation exercised by the real that the libidinal economy is forced to seek refuge in the autonomously operating symbolic universe of signifiers.

22. The reference to the subject is crucial in defining the death drive. Not every inclination to aggression and destruction expresses the death drive. This is the case only where *self*-preservation is jeopardized. This is why the death principle is something other than a "violence fondamentale," as the French psychoanalyst Jean Bergeret claims, referring to the "fundamental violence" of the young child's instinct to survive. The latter concept should replace the old Freudian one, he claims (see Bergeret, 1994; I cite from Verbruggen, 1999: 92). However, Bergeret's new concept cuts away the most provocative aspect of the Freudian death drive, that is, the inherent *auto*-destructive tendency of the drive. Bergeret presumes the drive's violence to be in the end a good violence. What Lacan's concept of *das Ding* tries to conceptualize is, precisely, the radically evil (because self-destructive) tendency haunting the drive. This is one of the main reasons why psychoanalysis cannot simply adhere to an "ethics of the good."

23. For Heidegger's criticism of modern technics, see for instance what he writes about this in "Wozu Dichter?" from 1946 (Heidegger, 1980: 286) or at the beginning of his essay "Das Ding" (1949), where he interprets the nuclear threat as a consequence of man's already centuries old increasing inability to respect the right distance towards the (nevertheless close) "things" (Heidegger, 1990: 158).

24. During a press conference in Rome (October 29, 1974), Lacan evokes another illustration, biotechnics, which will be able to cultivate bacteria so immune they can destroy all other life they encounter—the end life as such. It is this infinite capacity of man that must be interpreted as what Freud calls the death drive: (Lacan, 1975c: 11; 2005b: 75–76).

25. See also S7E: 211 (S7F: 250): "The death drive is to be situated in the historical domain") and Vaysse, 1999: 457 (where the author refers to that pas-

sage in Lacan). The idea is not new to Lacan. See for instance a passage in the fourth seminar (*La relation d'objet, 1956/57*): "Man's relations to the signifier in its totality are more precisely connected to the possibility of the abolition of all that has been lived. (S4F: 48; my own translation).

26. Although the definition of sublimation is a difficult point, almost everyone agrees that it is "the only remedy without repression against the unsatisfiable condition of the drive" (Vergote, 1997: 37). In the *Three Essays on Sexuality*, Freud describes "repression" and "sublimation" as two different procedures (Freud, SE7: 237–239; SA5: 140–141) and in *Instincts and their Vicissitudes,* they are two of the four different vicissitudes (Freud, SE14: 126; SA3: 90). See also *Civilization and Its Discontents*, where "sublimation" (*"Sublimierung"*) is put in opposition to "renunciation of instinct" (*"Triebverzicht"*) and considered one of the forms of "repression" (Freud, SE21:97; SA9: 227). This does not prevent Lacan, in one passage, from talking about sublimation as repression: "In the same way that in art there is a *Verdrängung,* a repression of the Thing, and in religion there is probably a *Verschiebung* or displacement, it is strictly speaking Verwerfung that is involved in the discourse of science" (S7E: 131; S7F: 157).

27. See farther, in chapter 7, section 2.

## Chapter 5

1. On the cover of the *Écrits*, Lacan suggests that his own psychoanalytic theory is still an integral part of this Enlightenment project. As he puts it unmistakably in the first sentence: "One should have read this volume, and at length, in order to notice that here, a long—and always the same—debate is continued, a debate, outdated as it may seem, to be recognized as the one of the Enlightenment" (Lacan, 1966; my translation). For the relation between psychoanalysis and the (specifically Kantian) Enlightenment, see for instance Whitebook, 1996: 119 e.v.

2. Kant, 1996: 46; 1974 Bd. VII: 140 (original pagination: A: 54). Lacan cites this formulation in S7E: 76; (S7F: 93).

3. Already on the first page of Kant's preface to the *Critique of Practical Reason*, we read that "the reality of the concept of freedom is proved by an apodictic law of practical reason" (Kant, 1996: 14; 1974 Bd. VII: 107; original pagination: A: 4).

4. Kant does indeed allow the subject to be approached in its quality of "*Ding an sich.*" He makes a distinction between the subject insofar as one can consider it "phenomenally" (*"als Erscheinung,"* that is, as object of scientific reason subjected to temporally determined, naturally causal—and, thus, unfree—laws) and the subject insofar as it is to be thought as the *"Ding an sich,"* that is, as freedom: "But the very same subject being on the other side conscious of himself as a thing in itself, considers his existence also *in so far as it is not subject to time* conditions, and regards himself as only determinable by laws which he gives himself through reason [this is to say through rational freedom]" (Kant, 1996: 120;1974 Bd. VII: 223; original pagination A: 175–176; Kant's italics; see also Philonenko, 1993 II: 135). A few lines earlier in the same passage, Kant more generally states that freedom can only be "saved" by maintaining a strong difference between the

phenomenal and the noumenal. However, when we limit "natural causality" to (time determined) phenomena, it is possible to extract the "things themselves" from time—and thus from natural causality—and to "save" freedom: "Consequently, if we would still save it [i.e., freedom], no other way remains but to consider that the existence of a thing, so far as it is determinable in time, and therefore its causality, according to the law of physical necessity, belong to *appearance*, and to attribute *freedom to the same being as a thing in itself*" (Kant, 1996: 117;1974 Bd. VII: 220; original pagination A: 171; Kant's italics).

5. Lacan will interpret one of Kant's lines of thought in such a "Kantian" way that, in the end, he will find himself far beyond the limits of the Kantian system. This occurs often in Lacan. By putting so much emphasis on just one of the author's ideas, he deconstructs the inner logic of the cited work, enabling something new to come to light. Philippe Lacoue-Labarthe and Jean-Luc Nancy characterize this procedure as a "déplacement" or a "détournement." In *The Title of the Letter*, they analyze the "strategy" behind this kind of reading (Lacoue-Labarthe & Nancy, 1992: 88 ff.; 1990: 117 ff.).

6. This is not to say that the "thing" is the single link between Lacan and Kant. If I limit myself to that one "thing," it is because of Lacan's exclusive emphasis on it in his Ethics Seminar. For an overview of the lines connecting Lacan and Kant, see Bernard Baas's essay "Le désir pur" (which gives an explicitly Kantian reading of Lacanian theory; Baas, 1992: 22–82), or the fifth chapter of Jean-Marie Vaysse, *L'inconscient des modernes* (Vaysse, 1999: 175–226).

7. In the next sentences, Lacan eulogizes this book, praising it for its extraordinary "humour" and for the passages in the text where "the abyss of the comic suddenly opens up before you."

8. "Pathological" is used here in the strictly Kantian sense: as what affects man and, thus, makes us dependent, unfree. Desires, sorrow, passion (also the most noble ones) are "pathological" in the sense that they affect and move people. The only thing that is not pathological is the free moral law, the categorical imperative, precisely because it overcomes these phenomenal affects and, therefore, claims noumenal universality. (See for instance Kant, 1996: 48, 95; 1974 Bd. VII: 143, 194; original pagination A: 58, 133.)

9. On Kant's distinction between "das Wohl" en "das Gute" (and their "negatives," respectively, "das Übel" en "das Böse") in the *Critique of Practical Reason*, see Kant, 1996: 78–79; 1974 Bd. VII: 177 (original pagination: A: 105–106).

10. This is how Lacan defines the death drive in his early seminars. In his second seminar, for instance, he says that the function of the symbolic is already discernible in Freud's *Interpretation of Dreams*, although it is only with *Beyond the Pleasure Principle*—thus with the introduction of the death drive—that he understood that the real implications of his earlier energetic theory of the psyche were in the symbolic. In that seminar Lacan states: "It took him another twenty years of a life which was already quite advanced at the time of this discovery, to be able to look back to his premises and to try to recover what it means in terms of energy. That is what required him to produce the new elaboration of the beyond of the pleasure principle and of the death instinct" (S2E: 76;S2F: 97;

for the relation between the symbolic and the death drive, see also S3E: 215; S3F: 244; S4F: 48, 50).

11. Within "general Reason" ("Vernunft"), Kant distinguishes *(pure) Reason* (*[reine] Vernunft*), *Understanding [Verstand]*, and *Perception [Anschauung]*). Knowledge must be built up from perception; these result in judgments (made by the understanding), which are combined with one another by means of concepts delivered by pure reason. Knowledge based *solely* on the concepts of pure reason is nothing but "transcendental illusionary appearance" and is, thus, to be criticized; which is, as is well known, what Kant's *Critique of Pure Reason* is about.

12. See the capter on "Transcendental Illusion," Kant, 1965: 297–300; 1974 Bd. III: 308–311; original pagination *B*: 350–355. Note that these ideas cannot simply be banned since it is in reason's very nature to imagine them. In that sense, "here we have to do with a *natural* and inevitable *illusion*, which rests on subjectve principles" (Kant, 1965: 300; original pagination *B*: 354; Kant's italics).

13. "Logik des Scheins," "logic of appearance," or "logic of illusion": this is how Kant names it when, in the *Critique of Pure Reason*, he introduces the concept of "transcendental illusion" (Kant, 1965: 297; 1974 Bd. III: 308; original pagination: *B*: 350).

14. Whether or not the highest concepts of reason (*Vernunft*)—the world, the I, and God—are really existing things as such is irrelevant for scientific knowledge because the latter operates within the limits of the phenomenal world, which according to Kant coincide with the limits of *understanding* (as distinguished from *pure Reason—"reine Venunft"*).

15. As Rogozinski indicates, this is the first thing Kant emphasizes in his preface to the *Critique of Practical Reason*: "it has no need to criticize the *pure faculty* of [practical] reason in order to see whether reason in making such a claim does not presumptuously *overstep* itself (as is the case with the speculative reason). For if, as pure reason, it is actually practical [wenn sie, als reine Vernunft, wirklich praktisch ist], it proves its own reality and that of its concepts by fact [durch die Tat], and all disputation against the possibility of its being real is futile" (Kant, 1996: 13; 1974 Bd. VII: 107; original pagination: *A*: 3). Rogozinski concludes: "The Critique of pure practical reason will never be written. It will only be matter of '*proving that the pure practical reason exists*'; this 'proof,' assured by the 'fact' of the Law, makes all critique superfluous, all investigation of its conditions of possibility and of legitimacy. [. . .] Rejected by definition is the possibility of a *practical illusion*, i.e., an illusion *inner* to the *pure practical reason* similar in this to the transcendental appearance analysed in the first *Critique*. [. . .] The second *Critique* is only a 'critique' in a restricted sense, as a critique of *impure* practical reason" (Rogozinski, 1999: 47–48; Rogozinski's italics; my translation).

16. In Freud, the term indicates the "*Vorstellung*" which is not only a memory trace, but is also explicitly linked to the drive (another name for the same is "*Triebsrepresentanz*"; see Freud, SE14: 148, 177; SA3: 109–110, 136; see also Laplanche & Pontalis, 1988: 200; Le Gaufey, 1997: 203). Lacan translates the term as "representative of the representation" ("représentant de la représenta-tion," S7E: 102; S7F: 122). It indicates what makes diverse representations into a group, a unity of representations/signifiers, as Lacan for instance states in S7E:

61 (S7F: 75–76): "[it] turns *Vorstellung* into an associative and combinatory element. In that way the world of *Vorstellung* is already organized according to the possibilities of the signifier as such." So, Lacan can only see the term as a confirmation of his own concept of the symbolic by giving another meaning to it than Freud does.

17. For Melanie Klein, the child constitutes its libidinal economy as an object relation with the mother figure. The baby introjects the "good objects" in that figure and represses the "bad" ones (Klein, 1947: 284–297; Grosskurt, 1986: 216–217).

18. There cannot be any doubt that Lacan is referring to *La Loi* (1957), and not to *La fête* (1960), as the English translation mistakenly indicates in the "Bibliography" (S7E: 330). On the date Lacan refers to the Vailland novel—December 23, 1959—*La fête* was not yet published.

19. "The Law is played throughout southern Italy. [. . .] The winner, the chief, who dictated the law, has the right to speak and not to speak, to interrogate and to reply in the place of the interrogated, to praise and to blame, to insult, to insinuate, to revile, to slander and to cast a slur on people's honour; the losers who have to bow to the law, are bound to submit without sound or movement. Such is the fundamental rule of the game of the Law" (Vailland, 1985: 36–37).

20. And the text continues: "The ὀρθος λογος of the unconscious at this level—as Freud indicates clearly in the *Entwurf* in relation to hysteria—is expressed as πρῶτον ψεῦδος, the first lie." In the last sentence, Lacan refers to a passage in the second (more clinical) chapter of Freud's *Entwurf* (Freud, SE1: 352–356), where Freud describes a case in which the patient's traumatic experience becomes traumatic only afterward, "*nachträglich.*" It is only by means of signifiers that an experience can be experienced, so to speak. This makes every experience into something profoundly "pseudo," that is, into what, with Aristotle, we can call "*proton pseudos*" (Aristoteles, *Prior Analytica* II, XVIII, 16–17). The same structure goes more generally for the "thing," which originates in the original trauma by which the (pleasure) experience is immediately divided between representation (which we unconsciously experience) and the "thing" (that is beyond any experience). In that sense, the "thing" is an irrevocably "*nachträglich*"—and thus deceitful—object of experience.

21. See the epigraph of this chapter.

22. Patrick Valas, who quotes this passage in his book *Les dimensions de la jouissance*, concludes that Lacan regards his concept of *jouissance* as "his most important contribution to Freudianism" (Valas, 1998: 56).

## Chapter 6

1. Lacan, 2002: 305; 1966: 819.

2. Lacan incidentally indicates this at the beginning of his sixth seminar (*Le désir et son interprétation*, 1958/59). About *jouissance*, he says: "The juridical phenomenology has traces of it: they say one has the enjoyment of a good [on dit qu'on a la jouissance d'un bien]" (lesson of December 17, 1958; Lacan 1996a: 122; my translation). See also: Braunstein, 1992: 14; Valas, 1998: 10–11, 44. The

medieval Dutch term "ghebruken" ("to use"), used by fourteenth century medieval mystics (to whom Lacan often refers) to describe the enjoyment of the unification with God, can be considered as having object-relational connotations.

3. See, for instance, the lesson of June 10, 1959: "The neurotic gains access to the phantasm; he gains access to it at certain exquisite moments in which his desire is satisfied" (Lacan, 1996a: 474; my translation).

4. In this lesson of his fifth seminar (*Les formations de l'inconscient*, 1957/58), Lacan announces that he will discuss "*jouissance*" as desire's "opposite" (S5F: 252), but he does not arrive at a strict formulation or definition. He only vaguely indicates the direction a concept of *jouissance* might possibly take by means of a few references to literature (a fragment from *If It Die (Si le grain ne meurt)* by André Gide, *The School for Wives (L'école des femmes)* by Molière, *The Balcony (Le balcon)* by Jean Genet).

5. Genitalization is the last phase in the development of the libidinal being on its way to becoming the subject of desire. The core element in this phase is the phallus since it makes the imaginary Ego (bearer of the Demand) a symbolic subject (of desire). As already mentioned (chapter 1, section 3.4), it is not the male genital that gives the phallus its signification; it is merely the signifier that gives the genital its signification. This is the central thesis of what Lacan calls symbolic castration: what gives the genital zone its sexual dimension (i.e., what is responsible for the highest pleasure investment) is not found in that zone itself, but in its reference to what lacks in the (imaginary) other and must be ascribed to a merely symbolic Other (i.e., to the field of signifiers). This is to say that the Other is "castrated," and the "phallus" is the term for what irrevocably lacks in the Other.

6. "[. . .] comedy manifests, by way of a kind of inner necessity, the relation of the subject to his own signified, as the result, the fruit of the signifier relation. [. . .] the appearance of that signified [is] called the phallus" (S5F: 262; my translation).

7. This is why only a comedy can stage the drama of a miser, Lacan explains in that same lesson about *jouissance*, referring explicitly to *The Miser (L'avare)* by Molière. There it becomes clear how a miser is more preoccupied with the outside rather than the contents of his treasure chest. Even when the contents of the chest have been secretly stolen, he continues to cherish his chest as a something more precious than his own life. When it, too, is taken away from him, he cries out "my chest! my beloved chest!" and the audience laughs because, indeed, for a long time, he had merely been cherishing a chest, an empty cover (see S5F: 261, where Lacan typifies this cry as "le cri comique par excellence"). That which he prohibited everyone from enjoying (including himself) appears in the end to be literally a thing of nothing. In following (sixth) seminar, where he cites Simone Weil's aphorism about the miser (see above chapter 1, section 3.5), Lacan suggests that only a comedy can interpret this figure (see the lesson of December 12, 1958; Lacan, 1996b: 101).

8. The reference to Paul's Letter to the Romans (Rom. 7:13: ". . . sin by the commandment might become exceeding sinful") is discussed later on in this chapter.

9. See also S7E: 195 (S7F: 229), where he talks about "*jouissance* of transgression."

10. Lacan translates verses 7 through 11 from Rom. 7, not "paragraph 7," as he mistakenly says. In 1 Cor. 15:56, Paul summarizes the same thesis again: "The sting of death is sin, and the power of sin is the law."

11. Here we encounter the second "change" Lacan effects in Paul's text. Where Paul writes that by means of the Law, sin brings death (Rom. 7:11), Lacan says that "the Thing [. . .] made me desire death [m'a fait désir de mort]." For Paul, death is a phenomenon which is historical and, thus, can be overcome; for Lacan, it is a structural principle, constitutive of human desire.

12. See the fourth chapter of *Totem and Taboo* (Freud, SE13: 100–161; SA9: 387–444; for the reference to Darwin, see: Freud, SE13: 125–126; SA9: 410).

13. See for instance what Lacan says about it in *Television*: "That's what myth is, the attempt to give an epic form to what is operative through the structure" (Lacan, 1990: 30; 1974: 51).

14. Even the most extreme libertine, who supposes himself to be beyond any law, comes up against the law in the end. We will discuss this idea further on in the comment on Lacan's reading of the Sadean libertine.

15. Lacan already refers to it in his first lesson (see the passage from SE: 7, cited here in II.1).

16. Or as one can conclude with Michel Lapeyre: "One knows well that prohibiting something does not prevent one from desiring it. But psychoanalysis goes further: desire is conditioned by the very position of what is prohibited. It is not because what is prohibited attracts, but because there is a radical relation of crime and fault to the law" (Lapeyre, 1997: 26; my translation).

17. At any rate, Lacan himself refers explicitly to his Ethics Seminar as the place where he introduced *jouissance* as a concept in his theory. In his fourteenth seminar, *La logique du phantasme* (1966/67), he says: "it is neither here at this moment nor for the first time that I introduce the term into what I call enjoyment, I mean I did it long ago, namely in my seminar on ethics" (lesson of May 30, 1967; Lacan 1966/67: 274; see also Valas, 1998: 10, 44, 48).

18. If moral reason had the laws of the phenomenal world at its disposal, it would be able to make the Supreme Good real. Or, as Kant writes in a passage Lacan probably has in mind here: "For the moral law, in fact, transfers us ideally into a system [in eine Natur] in which pure reason, if it were accompanied with adequate physical power, would produce the *summum bonum*, and it determines our will to give the sensible world the form of a system of rational beings" (Kant, 1996: 60–61; 1974 Bd. VII: 157; original pagination: A 76).

19. Bataille, "Sade" (in *Literature and Evil* from 1957; Bataille, 2001: 103–129; 1979: 239–258); Klossowski, *Sade My Neighbor* (Klossowski, 1991; 1947); Blanchot, "Sade's Reason" (in *Lautréamont and Sade*; Blanchot, 2004: 7–41; 1949: 15–49); Adorno and Horkheimer, "Juliette or Enlightenment and Morality" (in *Dialectic of Enlightenment*; Adorno and Horkheimer, 1972: 120–167). See also Baas, 1992: 35–36. See also the third chapter of: Marcel Hénaff, *Sade: The Invention of the Libertine Body* (Hénaff, 1999: 84–103; 1978: 97–118).

20. Sade, 1991: 296–339. For the French text, see: Sade, 1976: 187–257.

21. Sade, 1991: 340; 1976: 253.

22. Lacan refers explicitly to Blanchot's work on Sade (Blanchot, 2004; 1949). He recommends this book to his audience as "material to put in our file

[about Sade]" (S7E: 201; S7F: 236), and he confesses he is "continuously citing him" (S7F: 236, omitted in the English translation: S7E: 200). As to the fact that the sadist also enjoys his own pain, Blanchot writes: "All the great libertines, who live only for pleasure, are great only because they have obliterated within them every capacity of pleasure. [. . .] [T]hey have become unfeeling: they expect to find pleasure in their insensitivity, in their rejected sensitivity. [. . .] insensitivity makes the entire being tremble, says Sade; 'the soul transforms into a form of apathy which is soon metamorphosed into pleasures a thousand times more divine than the ones that pander into their weaknesses' " (Blanchot, 2004: 38; 1984: 45).

23. In the context of the just cited passage in Kant, "nature" is literally defined as "the existence of things under laws" (Kant, 1989: 60; 1974 Bd. VII: 156; original pagination: A 74).

24. Lacan cites Kant literally; see Kant, 1989: 93; 1974 Bd. VII: 192–193; original pagination: A 129.

25. Blanchot cites the example of a female libertine who says to a male sadist: "I love your ferocity [. . .], [p]romise me that one day I too will be your victim; since the age of fifteen, my mind has been obsessed with the idea of perishing as the victim of the cruel passions of libertinage" (cited in Blanchot, 2004: 21). I discuss the issue of sadism and perversion later on (see: chapter 7, section 5.1–2).

26. Thus three years later, in his essay *Kant avec Sade*, where he elaborates this thesis from his seventh seminar, he literally says, "we show that it [*Philosophy in the Boudoir*] [. . .] gives the truth of the *Critique* [*of Practical Reason*]" (Lacan, 1989b: 55; 1966: 765–766).

27. See Žižek, 1997: 229, among others.

28. See also S7E: 199; S7F: 234. For the thesis of libertinism as an historical failure, see Reichler, 1987.

29. More precisely, nature complies with the laws of crime, Sade argues. These laws are only crimes from our perspective, not from nature's own perspective. One of the main characters in *Philosophy in the Boudoir*, for instance, says: "Destruction being one of the chief laws of Nature, nothing that destroys can be criminal [. . .] murder is no destruction; he who commits it does but alter forms, he gives back to Nature the elements whereof the hand of this skilled artisan instantly re-creates other beings: now, as creation cannot but afford delight to him by whom they are wrought, the murderer thus prepares for Nature a pleasure most agreeable [. . .] 'This our pride prompts us to elevate murder into crime' " (Sade, 1991: 237–238; 1976: 107–108).

30. Lacan refers to the last episode of the fourth part; see: Sade, 1968: 765–798; 1987 IX: 165–199. Klossowski discusses this "*System of Nature* that the Pope expounds at length to Juliette" in his book *Sade My Neighbor* (Klossowski, 1991: 84–90; 1947: 75–83). See also: Vereecken, 1988).

31. Sade, 1968: 366–376; 1987 VIII: 420–430 (Lacan refers to this passage in S7E: 197; S7F: 232; see also S17F: 75; Lacan, 1989b: 64; 1966: 776). The term "Being Supreme in Wickedness" is not literally found in Sade. Lacan borrows it from Klossowski's *Sade My Neighbor* (Klossowski, 1991: 75, 86, 90–91, 101; 1947: 61, 78, 84–85, 102).

32. Lacan quotes literally from Sade (Sade, 1968: 772; 1987 IX: 172–173).

33. In this lesson, the term "second death" is used for the first time and will henceforth be used as a concept. In the previous lesson he still had spoken about the "second destruction that Sade was talking about the other day" (S7E: 232; S7F: 272). There is an obvious link with the concept of death drive. At the end of *Civilization and Its Discontents,* Freud defines the death drive as a destruction drive, that is, destruction that strikes nature in its "power to create, to multiply life" (Freud, SE21: 12; SA9: 248).

34. One can illustrate this with Sade's fantasy about his own death. In his "Testament" of January 30, 1806, he expresses the wish to be buried without leaving any trace. "Once the grave has been covered over, the ground should be sprinkled with acorns so that all traces of the grave shall disappear from the face of the earth as quickly as I shall expect all memory of me should fade out of the minds of all men but those very few who in their goodness have loved me until these last moments of my existence (and memory of whom I carry with me to the very end) (Sade, 2005: 313); see also: Lely, 1967: 351–352; Pauvert, 1993: 376). In other words, this fantasy shows how Sade wants to be erased as signifier. Lacan refers to this fantasy in S7E: 202; S7F: 238.

35. It is in this sense Lacan resolves the contradiction he raises in S7E: 202 (S7F: 238): "we see emerge in him [Sade] in the distance the idea of eternal punishment. I will come back to this point, because it amounts to a strange contradiction in a writer who wants nothing of himself to survive, who doesn't even want any part of the site of his tomb to remain accessible to men, but wants it instead to be covered with bracken."

36. "La philosophie doit tout dire," are Juliette's last words in Sade's novel of the same name, thus formulating a final, concluding word for the entire book (Sade, 1987 IX: 582). This, at least, is how it is often interpreted in the critical tradition. See among others Hénaff, 1977: 29; 1978: 65–95.

37. Remember the famous passage from the *Critique of Practical Reason*: "*Duty!* Thou sublime and mighty name . . ." (Kant, 1989: 108; 1974 Bd. VII: 209; original pagination: A 154).

38. At least this is how Lacan quotes him: see S7E: 292 (S7F: 338; see also S7E: 303; S7F: 350; Lacan, 2002: 240 ff.; 1966: 614 ff., 785, 866). In Saint-Just we read that "happiness has become a new idea in Europe" ("Le bonheur est une idée neuve en Europe!"; Saint-Just, 1957: 150; 1984: 715). Together with Robespierre, Saint-Just belonged to the first government in history (namely 'Committee of Public Safety') who explicitly made "social happiness" a primary political issue. The first article of the *Constitution* from 1793, written by Saint-Just, said: "The aim of society is the common happiness" (quoted in: Soboul, 1982: 398, my translation).

39. In the last sentence (between quotation marks), Lacan is citing himself from his 1951 lecture, "Psychanalyse, dialectique" (unedited; see Roudinesco, 1993: 635). Lacan had already discussed this quote in the previous seminar (lesson from June 3, 1957; Lacan, 1996a: 455–456).

40. Aristotelian ethics is indeed embedded in the social structure of that time, which was divided into free men and slaves. Only free men could become "masters" of their passions and desires, an exercise in mastery that ended in

intellectual contemplation of the truth: see the last chapter of the *Nicomachean Ethics*. This kind of elitist moral exercise was impossible without the sacrifices of others, that is, slaves (see Cathelineau, 1998: 110).

41. See, for instance, S7E: 198 (S7F: 233): "it is from this fellow as such that the misrecognitions which define me as a self are born"; or S7E: 186 (S7FI: 219): "It is the nature of the good to be altruistic."

42. Freud, SE21: 109; SA9: 238.

43. In *Civilization and Its Discontents*, Freud is trying to understand why it is that civilization, living off sexual energy, is nevertheless hostile to sexuality "But we are unable to understand what the necessity is which forces civilization along this path and which causes its antagonism to sexuality. There must be some disturbing factor which we have not yet discovered" (Freud, SE21: 109). A few lines further, Freud discusses the command of neighbourly love and puts forward his raw and realistic view of humans, concluding that it is this "inclination to aggression" that forces civilization into such a high expenditure [of energy]" (Freud, SE21: 112). Thus, sexuality must be repressed ultimately because of the death drive hidden in it. The death drive is legible both in human aggression and in jouissance.

44. Lacan goes into the issue of "the domain of the good" more extensively in his seventeenth lecture that Miller titles "The function of the good" (S7E: 218–230; S7F: 257–270). Lacan considers this "domain of the good" (also to be read as the "domain of the goods," that is, of "commodities") as a economical field in which the laws of the pleasure principle apply. Within this symbolic, man is granted a certain contentment and happiness. This, however, is not the ground of ethics, since it is oriented toward *jouissance* and is hanted by death drive. Like the idea of the symbolic as such, its application within the economic field (a field of exchanging goods), is also borrowed directly from Lévi-Strauss. See for instance his essay "Les mathématiques de l'homme" (Lévi-Strauss, 1956: 527).

45. Martinus of Tours (316?–397) was the son of a Roman magistrate and officer in the army. In Amiens (France), he cuts his cloak in two in order to share it with a beggar. That night, Christ appears to him, dressed in half of his cloak, an experience which makes Martin into a convinced Christian. He founds a monastery in Ligugé and becomes bishop of Tours in 371.

46. See, for instance, Miller, 2000: 15.

47. The clarity of this passage does not prevent some authors from arguing away the "scandalon" of Lacan's interpretation. For instance, Michaël Turnheim stresses that the naked beggar "perhaps" begs for something else. He connects this with the idea that neighborly love always presupposes something accidental, an unforeseen encounter stressing the singularity of the person involved. This is perhaps possible, but the idea that Lacan is saying the beggar is asking Martin to respect his singularity at the moment Martin is going to kill him, is obviously a misreading. Turnheim writes, "The term 'jouissance' does not only designate the object of the subject's will, but also the singularity he will face in an encounter—*both possibilities are true at the same time*. The question is not if Saint Martin dares to kill the beggar, but if he should be able to kill him *respecting his singularity*" (Turnheim, 1998: 2; italics at the end are mine).

48. This is at least the reproach one can hear behind the final words of the hunger artist when, abandoned by everyone, he says: "Forgive me [. . .] I always wanted you admired my fasting" (Kafka, 1995: 277). I thank Lieven Jonckheere for bringing this parallel between Kafka and Lacan to my attention.

49. Think for instance of the well-known scene in *The Trial*, where Joseph K. discovers that the so-called law books the judges have before them during the trials are in fact dirty erotic novels (Kafka, 1980: 68). Slavoj Žižek discusses this passage in *For they know not what they do* (Žižek, 1991b: 237–238).

50. Angela da Foligno was an Italian mystic from the thirteenth century. Lacan refers to a passage from the *Liber visionum et instructionum*: "On Maundy Thursday, I suggested my companion to go out and find Christ: 'Let us go,' I told her, 'to the hospital and perhaps we will be able to find. [. . .] And after we had distributed all that we had, we washed the feet of the women and the hands of the men, and especially those of one of the lepers which were festering and in an advanced stage of decomposition. Then we drank the very water with which we had washed him. And the drink was so sweet that, all the way home, we tasted its sweetness and it was as if we had received the Holy Communion. As a small scale of the leper's sores was stuck in my throat, I tried to swallow it. My conscience would not let me spit it out, just as if I had received the Holly Communion. I really did not want to spit it out but simply detach it from my throat" (Angela of Foligno 1993: 162–163; see also Lachance, 1995: 104–105; for a general introduction to Angela da Foligno, see Lachance, 1990). The anecdote from the life of Marie Alacoque (A*l*acoque and not A*ll*acoque, as both Miller, the French editor, and Porter, the English translator, write), a mystic from the seventeenth century and known for her devotion to the Holy Hart, is to be found in Alacoque, 1945: 86: "I was so overdelicate that the slightest dirtiness horrified me. His [God's] reproach was so hard that, once when I wanted to clean the vomit of a sick woman, I could not but do it with my tongue and eat it [. . .]" (my translation). Notice that Lacan changes the oral "vomit" into the anal "excrements." For a similar case of charity (the case of "Juette," twelfth century), see Duby, 1997.

51. Christianity is the religion that emphasizes the Son (Christ). In this sense, it reveals the crime that lies at the basis of civilization, which is the murder of the Father by the sons, as described in *Totem und Taboo* (1912–1913). Christianity, in which the expiatory sacrifice has a crucial role, is to be interpreted as an almost open confession of guilt on the part of the sons. From this perspective, one can say that, in Christ, the originally repressed guilt is put forward in an almost unconcealed way. Hence the central role of Christianity in Freud who devotes his final major reflection to it in *Moses and Monotheism* (1939) (see among others, Freud, SE23: 87–88; SA3: 535–536). Lacan refers to Freud's "strange Christocentrism" in S7E: 177 (S7F: 207).

52. S7E: 22; S7F: 30. This is why the ethics of psychoanalysis is only "preliminary" (S7E: 22; S7F: 30), leading the analysand to a point where she is alone in what she has to do, that is, assume the desire she is. I discussed this above in chapter 2, section 3.

53. Kant, 1996: 44–46; 1989: 139–140 (original pagination: A 53–54). See also Julien, 1995: 87–92; Zupančič, 1995: 68–73; 2000: 53–54.

54. "[T]he subject will envisage accepting his own death in the name of the so-called categorical imperative" (S7E: 189; S7F: 222).

55. Because of the opacity and the difficulty of the passage, I cite also the French text: "Et si par hasard je changeais un peu l'exemple? Parlons d'un vrai témoignage, du cas de conscience qui se pose si je suis mis en demeure de dénoncer mon prochain, mon frère, pour des activités qui portent atteinte à la sûreté de l'État? Cette question est bien de nature à déporter l'accent mis sur la règle universelle. Et moi, qui suis pour l'instant en train de témoigner devant vous qu'il n'y a de loi du bien que dans le mal et par le mal, dois-je porter ce témoignage? Cette Loi fait de la jouissance de mon prochain le point pivot autour duquel oscille, à l'occasion de ce témoignage, le sens de mon devoir. Dois-je aller vers mon devoir de vérité en tant qu'il préserve la place authentique de ma jouissance, même s'il reste vide? Ou dois-je me résigner à ce mensonge, qui, en me faisant substituer à toute force le bien au principe de ma jouissance, me commande de souffler alternativement le chaud et le froid?—soit que je recule à trahir mon prochain pour épargner mon semblable, soit que je m'abrite derrière mon semblable pour renoncer à ma propre jouissance."

## Chapter 7

1. Miller's edition omits Lacan's explicit reference to the Greek word 'νοῦς' (*nous*, reason) (Lacan, 1999: 132; 1959/60, lesson of 23.12.1959, p. 13). I discuss this a few lines further.

2. Also in his next lesson, he has the same Greek text in front of him (S7E: 96; S7F: 115).

3. Rom. 7:25: "So then with the mind [νοΐ, *noï*] I myself serve the law of God; but with the flesh [σαρκί, *sarki*] the law of sin [νομοι ἁμαρτίας; *nomoi hamartias*]." Saint Paul makes this distinction already in verse 23: "[. . .] but I see another law in my members, warring against the law of my mind [τῷ νόμῳ τοῦ νοός, *tooi nomooi tou noös*]."

4. In what follows, Lacan refers to the diverse eroticisms that have appeared in culture. The "game" eros plays with the law is a striking illustration of how law and transgression can be compatible with one another. Lacan examines one of these eroticisms, namely courtly love. When Lacan mentions religion together with eroticism, it is not without provocation. Here, religion is introduced, not as a kind of "reason" (νοῦς, *nous*) that has overcome the perfidious game of law and transgression, as Saint Paul supposes, but as a cultural shape in which that very game is ongoing. In its religious—in this case Christian—shape, too, reason does not overcome the anomalies of sin (despite what it itself claims); in fact, (Christian and other) religion maintains and cultivates the dubious—sinful—relation between law and transgression. Like erotics, religion also illustrates the possibility of consciously relating to our transgressive desire. A victim of what Kant called "Schwärmerei," religion focuses attention on transgression, since it is supposed to establish a positive relation to what is beyond the limits of the law (Kant's *das Ding an sich*, Lacan's "thing"). As Lacan says in the passage cited above: religion installs a "relation to *das Ding* somewhere beyond the law."

5. The last addition, "notre dame" (which can be spelled with capitals) also alludes to the religious transformation of the courtly love ideal into the cult of Notre Dame, which stems from the twelfth century as well. On the moralizing character of this Christian appropriation of courtly love, see De Kesel, 1998a: 180, note 15.

6. For a more elaborated comment on all passages where Freud discusses sublimation, see Antoine Vergote's book on this topic (Vergote, 1997); unfortunately, Vergote leaves the Lacanian concept of sublimation almost completely without comment.

7. This is Freud's definition of sublimation from his case study on "Dora" (Freud, SE7: 50; SA6: 125; see also Green, 1993: 291), later confirmed in *Three Essays on Sexuality* (Freud, SE7: 178; SA5: 85–86), as well in his essay "Leonardo da Vinci and a Memory of His Childhood," where one finds the most elaborated discussion of this issue (Freud, SE11: 63–137; SA10: 91–159).

8. See for instance in *Instincts and Their Vicissitudes* (Freud, SE14; 126; SA3: 90). See also "On Narcissism: An Introduction" (Freud, SE14: 94–95; SA3: 62).

9. In "On Narcissism," Freud defines the change of object as "idealizing," while sublimation is defined as a modification of the drive itself (Freud, SE14: 94–95; SA3: 61). There is one passage in Freud where sublimation is explicitly defined as a change, not only of the aim of drive, but also of its object. In Lecture 32 of the *New Introductory Lectures on Psychoanalysis* (1933), he writes: "A certain kind of modification of the aim and change of the object, in which our social valuation is taken into account, is described by us as 'sublimation' " (Freud, SE22: 97; SA1: 530; Freud's italics).

10. As, for instance, in *The Ego and the Id*. There he explains how the Ego detaches the object-libido from the object, how it changes this into narcissistic libido and relates it to itself in order to point it now at a different aim: "Indeed, the question arises [. . .] whether all sublimation does not take place through the mediation of the ego, which begins by changing sexual object-libido into narcissistic libido and then, perhaps, goes on to give it another aim" (Freud, SE19: 30; SA3: 298). The term "desexualized libido," which he uses in this context, is a contradiction in terms since libido is by definition sexual. The contradiction increases when one notes that in *The Ego and the Id*, Freud makes the desexualized libido a part of Eros, while Eros inherits precisely what previously was called sexual (object-)drive (Freud, SE19: 45–46; SA3: 312.

11. A few lines following our next citation, Lacan calls this principle literally "the single universal and dominant *Primat*" (S7E: 91; S7F: 110).

12. "Satisfaction" is something that occurs at the level of the drive and is therefore not to be treated as *jouissance*, which names satisfaction at the level of the subject. So, sublimation is not to be confused with enjoyment, because in sublimation, the subject does not fade away into its phantasm. Nevertheless, it is still a satisfaction insofar as it gains pleasure at the level of the drive. It is in this sense Lacan uses the term in the quotation that follows.

13. In the sentences preceding the fragment just cited, Lacan mistakenly says he is referring to a passage in *Three Essay on Sexuality*. He is in fact referring to a passage in Lecture 22 of Freud's *Introductory Lectures on Psychoanalysis*

(which he had cited before, see S7E: 91; S7F: 109–110; see Freud, SE16: 345; SA1: 339) and to the end of Lecture 23 (Freud, SE16: 375–377; SA1: 365–366). There, Freud does indeed emphasize the social dimension of the sublimated object and so illustrates his "compensation theory." This theory is absent from the four passages in the *Three Essays on Sexuality* where sublimation is mentioned (Freud, SE7: 156, 178, 206, 238–239; SA5: 66, 85–86, 111, 140–141).

14. Lacan calls it "a trap into which thought, with its penchant for facility, would love to leap, merely by constructing a simple opposition and a simple reconciliation between the individual and the collectivity" (S7E: 94; S7F: 113). He also talks about this compensation theory in SE7: 107; 144–145; S7F: 128–129, 173.

15. Farther down, Lacan writes: "[For Freud,] it doesn't seem to be a problem that the collectivity might find satisfaction there where the individual happens to need to change his batteries or his rifle from one shoulder to the other; where, moreover, it would be a matter of an individual satisfaction that is taken for granted, all by itself. Yet we were told at the beginning how problematic the satisfaction of the libido is" (S7E: 94: S7F: 113).

16. "*Reaktionsbildung*" (S7E: 95; S7F: 113–114). Lacan refers to the "Summary" at the end of the *Three Essays*: "A sub-species of sublimation is to be found in suppression by reaction-formation [*Reaktionsbildung*]" (Freud, SE7: 238; SA5: 141; Freud's italics). The inconsistency of Freud's theory of sublimation becomes obvious when one compares this passage with the footnote he adds in 1915 where he makes a sharp distinction between sublimation and reaction formation: "in general it is possible to distinguish the concepts of sublimation and reaction-formation from each other as two different processes" (Freud, SE7: 178; SA5: 86).

17. In his essay on narcissism, Freud revises his theory of the ego. The ego is no longer seen as a function of the conservative ego-drive, but of the all-hazarding sexual *object drive*. The formation of the Ego is thus no longer considered the result of the conservative side of the drive economy, but of the side that takes risks in order to conquer objects. The libidinal being has to conquer its ego as an object, which is an ongoing process because it lies forever *before* him. This new theory of the ego enables Freud a few years later to rearrange his entire theory and frame it not on the basis of the triad "unconscious, preconscious and conscious," (i.e., the "first topography"), but on the basis of "ego, superego, and id" ("second topography"). It is only in the context of the second topography and of the narcissistic theory of the ego that the various kinds of object relations theory are possible, including Lacan's own version of it. If sublimation is a positive detour of the originally sexual drive, it must thought as a vicissitude of the object drive. It must be thought not from the paradigm of the conservative ego drive, but from the risky object drive orienting the libidinal being toward the outside world. Sublimation zeroes in on its relation to its ideal, that is, to that impossible object it aims at.

18. See Freud, SE14: 94; SA3: 61.

19. The distinction between the (imaginary) "*ideal ego*" ("*Moi Idéal*") and the (symbolic) "*ego ideal*" ("*Idéal du Moi*"), is a distinction that only Lacan makes. He usually elaborates it in reference to his theory of the mirror stage (see, for

instance, Lacan 1966: 671–675). Unlike what Lacan states, Freud does not make any conceptual distinction between "*Ideal-Ich*" and "*Ich-Ideal*."

20. In his lesson of January 27, 1960, Lacan discusses an essay by Melanie Klein where she comments on a case study by Karin Michaëlis about a patient suffering from a melancholic depression. This patient, a woman, became depressed after she had given back a borrowed painting that she really admired. The only remedy against that loss was to make a similar painting herself, a "sublimation" that really helped her. In the analysis, Michaëlis notes the association between the painting and the patient's mother, which is why this case offered itself perfectly for a Kleinian analysis. For a (Lacanian) analysis of Klein's study, see the essay by Catherine Millot, "La sublimation, création ou réparation?" (Millot, 1982; see also Muller, 1987: 320–321; Palomera, 1995: 116–118). For Lacan's analysis, see S7E: 115–117; S7F: 140–142; for Melanie Klein's essay, see Klein, 1947: 227–235.

21. Lacan also gives this suggestion at the end of his (double) lecture in Brussels (March 9 and 10, 1960), in which he summarizes the main topics of his Ethics Seminar (Lacan, 1992b: 20; 2005b: 63). See further S7E: 212, S7F: 251, where he characterizes the death drive as a "creationist sublimation."

22. A few lines after the previous quotation with the formula of sublimation, Lacan says that this requires an illustration. ("The definition I gave you doesn't close the debate, first, because I must confirm and illustrate it for you [. . .]"; S7E: 113; S7F: 134). This illustration is courtly love.

23. See for instance S7E: 125 (S7F: 150): "This is why I have chosen the history of the *Minne* as the point of departure"; S7F: 131 (S7F: 157) where he qualifies courtly love as the "paradigm" of sublimation; S7E: 136 (S7F: 163): "This is why in raising the problems of the relationship of art to sublimation, I will begin with courtly love"; S7E: 214 (S7F: 253): "and this is why the first example I gave you was taken from courtly love." Even where he states that the problem of sublimation cannot be reduced to the "man/woman relation" (and, in this sense, to courtly love), he nevertheless claims explicitly: "I believe on the contrary that to start out from this example is essential in order to arrive at a general formula [of sublimation]" (S7E: 129; S7F: 154).

24. In his monumental study, *L'érotique des troubadours*, René Nelli describes how "around 1120, noble men imagined to subject themselves to their lady-friends as vassals to their lieges" (Nelli, 1963: 90; my translation). The lord's subjection to the lady as well as the fascination for love's desire as such are at the origin of courtly love (Nelli, 1963: 86).

25. To illustrate this, Lacan mentions the brutal escapades of a certain Pierre d'Aragon who "stole" a man's wife because of her rich inheritance; after having been badly treated, she was forced to seek refuge with the pope (S7E: 147; S7F: 176).

26. Lacan turns against the idea of a collective unconscious which he sees as a useless and misleading concept because everyone's unconscious is always that of the Other, that is, of the limitless field of signifiers out of which a culture comes into being.

27. The term "courtly love" ("*amour courtois*") is of recent date. It was first named by French philologist Gaston Paris around 1880 (Rey-Flaud, 1983: 7).

28. Almost all historical facts concerning the courtly love of the *Langue d'Oc* are controversial. It is, for instance, not certain whether the decline of the Aquitainian courtly culture was caused exclusively by the crusade against the Cathars (the thesis criticized by Henri-Irénée Marou; see Marrou, 1971: 13). Lacan's claim that it takes its departure already in the *beginning* of the eleventh century is probably not correct (S7E: 145; S7F: 174). Generally its origin is supposed to coincide with the first "troubadour," Guilhem IX van Poitiers, count of Aquitaine (1071–1127; Lacan gives an impression of his *"vida"*—before his career as poet he was "a formidable brigand" ("un fort redoutable bandit"; S7E: 148; S7F: 177). The end of the courtly culture in Aquitaine is sited around 1250 when the last Occitan poet, Montanhagol, died.

29. A typical example is the poet Folquet de Marseille, who for years courted—in vain—the woman of his lord (*Sire Barral, seigneur de Marseille*). When she died, thus his *"vida,"* "he, together with his wife and his two sons, entered in a Cistercian monastery. He became abbot of a rich abbey in the *Provence* named Toronet. Later they made him bishop of Toulouse" (Egan, 1985: 78–81; our translation). Marrou confirms the historical reliability of this *"vida"* (Marrou, 1971: 34).

30. If he could only simply have a glimpse of his Dame undressing: many courtly poems tell us this was a real "obsession" for the courtly lover (Lazar, 1964: 58–59).

31. The sexual act as such had a negative valence in the courtly code. René Nelli writes somewhere: "No matter how one interprets it, it is a fact that the amorous service [. . .] was meant to manage desire and to postpone as long as possible the "act," which was considered incompatible with love" (Nelli, 1963: 182; my translation).

32. For a elaborated explanation of the " '*asag*' (or love test)," so typical in courtly love, see Nelli, 1963: 199–209 and Rey-Flaud, 1983: 28–32. That it sometimes took a rather indecent shape is proven by the "scatological" *asag* that Bernard de Cornil received from his lady. She asked Cornil to do credit to his name and to "blow her horn" ("cornar"; "corn" is "horn"). She was asking him to blow her horn, where she blows her own horn in the scatological sense of the word. The troubadour refused, the "courtly case" informs, but was severely criticized by others for this. Reading a poem by Arnaut Daniel (which is part of the "courtly case") Lacan goes extensively into this case, if only to show that sublimation does not necessarily imply desexualization (S7E: 161–164; S7F: 191–194). For a comment on the entire "case," see Nelli, 1977: 79–95. For a more elaborate comment on Arnaut Daniel's poem, see De Kesel, 1998a: 173–183.

33. For a detailed study of "the eroticism of Guilhem IX," see the second chapter of Nelli's *L'érotique des troubadours* (Nelli, 1963: 79–104).

34. See for instance the seventh chapter of Book Two, where Andreas Capellanus reviews a number of cases and their "love judgements" ("De variis iudiciis amoris," Capellanus, 1982: 250–271). It is one of the main sources for Stendhal's *De l'amour* from 1822 (Stendhal, 1959: 336–346). Lacan mentions both authors as well as the phenomenon of the "love court" in SE7: 145–146 (S7F: 174–175).

35. On the next page as well, courtly love is described as "an artificial and cunning organization of the signifier" (S7E: 152; S7F: 181).

36. In the French, official edition, "à cette époque" is omitted (see Lacan, 1959/60, lesson of 10.02.1959, p. 12; 1999: 225).

37. In order to do this, one must investigate the complex history of the way in which the Church has contested courtly love while nevertheless assuming it, not without removing its erotic character. Precisely the courtly ideal of love was a good weapon for the Church to keep the institution of marriage away from the hands of feudal leaders. By controlling the way those leaders maintained their possessions (marriage), the Church tried to enforce its control over the feudal (political) order as such.

38. Lacan refers to Denis de Rougemont's *L'amour et l'occident*, 1939, reedited with some modifications in 1956. It is most probably this version Lacan has "re-read," as he says in S7E: 123; S7F: 148). It was precisely the chapter on the twelfth century that Rougemont had "profoundly" ("à peu près en entier") rewritten, so he said in the introduction of 1956 (Rougemont, 1975: 10; this introduction is not included in the English translation: Rougemont, 1983).

39. S7E: 119, 120, 121, 122, 125; S7F: 144, 145, 146, 147, 150.

40. Several times Lacan mentions the connection between the primacy of the signifier and the creationist myth, which has ruled our culture since the emergence of monotheism (where God's word creates everything out of nothing—*ex nihilo* (see for instance S7E: 119ff., 225, 260–261; S7F: 144 ff., 265, 303).

41. S7E: 118, 125, 134, 143; S7F: 142, 150, 161, 172

42. Lacan characterizes her in this context once as an "absolute object" (S7E:214; S7F: 253).

43. See, for instance, S7E: 121; S7F: 146: "the fashioning of the signifier and the introduction of a gap or a hole in the real is identical."

44. Lacan refers to Heidegger's lecture from 1949, "*Das Ding*," where he develops the idea by means of a reflection about the jar. The jar is essentially not an object made by a sovereign subject (as modernity has thought since Descartes), but stems from a "*Seinsgeschick*." With this term he refers to being as an occurrence, as a happening that can never be reduced to a closed totality (as is supposed in the classical metaphysics' idea of Substance). This is why the being of the jar must be located in its emptiness, in its void (Heidegger, 1990: 161). Without going into Lacan's "forced" interpretation of Heidegger, one can at least say that he organizes his subversive reading of Heidegger from the viewpoint of his "primacy of the signifier." That the jar should be thought as a "fashioning of the signifier," is something Heidegger would never say.

45. See the quote from S7E: 84 (S7F: 102), at the end of chapter 7, section 1 above, where he makes the little word play with "Dame" en "dam" ("damage," "doom").

46. Lacan discusses this in S7E: 130; S7F: 155 (in fact this is a retake on a previous analysis from S7E: 53–54; S7F: 67). I cited from this passage in chapter 4, section 2.2. Lacan borrows the parallel between "healthy" and "sick" drive constellations from "*Manuscript K*," an addition to Freud's letter to Fliess of January 1, 1896 (see above: chapter 4, note 26). For a short comment on this parallel, see Ansaldi, 1998: 57–61.

47. In his lesson of February 3, 1960, he characterizes "courtly love" explicitly as "an example of sublimation in art" (S7E: 131; S7F: 157).

48. "All art is characterized by a certain mode of organization around this emptiness" (S7E: 130; S7F: 155).

49. Omitted by Miller in the official edition; see Lacan, 1959/60, lesson of 03.02.1960; 1999: 199.

50. In this sense, for Lacan, "*l'Unglauben*" (unbelief) underlying science is not so much the opposite of belief as a certain (negative) form of belief (S7E: 130; S7F: 155–156).

51. Here, a mere greeting—which is a confirmation that his desire has been recognized—was enough to send him into ecstasies. According to the courtly code, such a greeting is as such already "the supreme gift" or, as Lacan interprets it, "the sign of the Other as such" (S7E: 152; S7F: 182).

52. For the Aristotelian idea of the "first lie" ("πρῶτον ψεῦδος," "proton pseudos") as well as for how Freud and Lacan use this concept, see above: chapter 5, note 22.

53. There, he literally says that his lecture is a "pré-leçon," preparing his next seminar (Lacan, 1996a: 542; see above: chapter 1, note 75).

54. Our translation of the passage in Lacan, 1996a: 538–539: "Ce qui se présente dans la société comme culture [. . .] est quelque chose qui instaure un mouvement, une dialectique, laissant ouverte la même béance à l'intérieur de laquelle nous essayons de situer la fonction du désir. C'est en ce sens que nous pouvons qualifier ce qui se produit comme perversion, comme étant le reflet, la protestation au niveau du sujet logique de ce que le sujet subit au niveau de l'identification, en tant que l'identification est le rapport qui ordonne, qui instaure les normes de la stabilisation sociale [. . .]."

55. Our translation of Lacan, 1996a: 539: "De sorte que nous pourrions dire que quelque chose s'instaure comme un circuit tournant entre ce que nous pourrions appeler conformisme [. . .] [et] la perversion pour autant qu'elle représente [. . .] tout ce qui dans la conformisation se présente comme protestation dans la dimension à proprement parler du désir en tant qu'il est rapport du sujet à son être—c'est ici cette fameuse sublimation dont nous commencerons peut-être à parler l'année prochaine. Car à la vérité c'est bien là la notion la plus extrême, la plus justificatrice de tout ce que je suis en train d'avancer devant vous [. . .]." Lacan retakes that issue in the eighth seminar (*Le transfert*, 1960–61) and, there, he refers explicitly to the last lesson of his sixth seminar; see S8F: 43).

56. Here, in this sentence, even Porter's translation does not follow the officially edited French text, which at this point is incorrect and misses the point about "culture" Lacan wants to make here. Our translation modifies Porter's. In the stenograph we read: "Disons que nous le mettrons sous le registre du culturel, et que son rapport justement avec la société, à savoir ce que la société peut bien y trouver de satisfaisant est justement ce qui maintenant est mis par nous en question" (Lacan, 1959/60, lesson of 20.01.1960; Lacan, 1999: 163).

57. Lacan *first* comments on a passage from Kant's second *Critique* (Kant, 1996: 45; 1989: 139–140; in original pagination A: 53–54) in his lesson of January 20, 1960. I now go into this lesson. Lacan comments on this passage a *second*

time at the end of his lesson, March 23, which I commented on in the previous chapter (chapter 6, section 4).

58. Porter's translation "weight of reality" is wrong here. It should read "weight of reason."

59. Lacan's new concept of "perversion" is very close to what is commonly called perversion: crime, corruption, deceit, and so on. Previously—see, for instance, the last lesson of his sixth seminar—"perversion" refers conceptually to the polymorphous perverse nature of the libidinal animal.

60. See also what follows after the last quotation: "Sublimation and perversion are both a certain relationship of desire that attracts our attention to the possibility of formulation, in the form of a question, a different criterion of another, or even of the same, morality, that takes its direction from that which is to be found on the level of *das Ding*; it is the register that makes the subject hesitate when he is on the point of bearing false witness against *das Ding*, that is to say, the place of desire, whether it be perverse or sublimated" (S7E: 109–110; S7F: 131).

61. A passage in Michel de Montaigne's *Essays* says that the most profound foundation of laws is "mystical," which is to say that they cannot be rationally legitimized (Montaigne, 2003: 1216), an idea that Blaise Pascal takes up in his *Pensées* (Lafuna numeration 30, Brunchvicg numeration 294; Pascal, 1995: 24). Both passages are the basic points of reference for a long philosophical reflection on the idea of a "mystical," illegitimate foundation of the law that continues to this day. See, for instance, Walter Benjamin's "Critique of Violence" (Benjamin, 1986: 277–300) and Jacques Derrida's *Force of Law* (Derrida, 1990). With the appearance of Freud's *Totem and Taboo* and its myth of the primitive horde leader, psychoanalytic theory participates in this debate.

62. Only when his theory of the "thing" forms an integral part of his theory of the phantasm—this is to say when the notion of the "thing" is integrated as "object a"—does he succeed with a more elaborate theory of perversion. This can be found in the (almost unreadable, but famous) essay "*Kant avec Sade*" (1962) and, more clearly, in his tenth seminar (*L'angoisse*, 1962–63). See, for instance, Piera Aulagnier's lesson in this seminar (lesson of 27.02.1963; Lacan, 1996c: 184–194). Little by little, "perversion" will become one of the three major psychic structures (besides neuroses and psychoses) in Lacanian theory. Here, too, the work of Piera Aulagnier is decisive, especially her article "La perversion comme structure" (Aulagnier-Spairani, 1967).

63. S7E: 216; S7F: 255–256. See also above: VI.3.2.

64. "The reference the subject makes to some other seems quite absurd, when we [analysts] see that he [    ] continually refers to the other as to someone who lives harmoniously and who in any case is happier, doesn't ask any questions and sleeps soundly in his bed" (S7E: 237, modified translation; S7F: 278).

65. In his lesson of May 18, 1960, he talks about the "paradox of desire—in the sense that the goods obscure it" (S7E: 230, modified translation; S7F: 271).

66. "That in this sense, when one aims for the center of moral experience, the beautiful is closer to evil than to the good, shouldn't, I hope, surprise you very much. As we have long said in French: 'Better is the enemy of the good' " (S7E: 217; S7F: 256).

67. Regarding what lies beyond the barrier separating us from the "thing," Lacan says: "Don't forget that if we know there is a barrier and that there is a beyond, we know nothing about what lies beyond" (S7E: 232; S7F: 272). And about the unconscious in general, he says in the same lesson: "In its own cycle the unconscious now appears to us as the field of a non-knowledge, even though it is locatable as such" (S7E: 236–237; S7F: 277).

## Chapter 8

1. S7E: 268, 281, 298; S7F: 311, 327, 345, S8F: 450.

2. Sophocles, 1984: 101.

3. Verses 773–784; Sophocles, 1984: 100–101.

4. Sophocles 2002: 79.

5. With respect to the latter term, in his lessons on *Antigone*, Lacan refers a few times to Plato's *Phaedrus* (S7E: 257, 259, 268; S7F: 299, 301–302, 311), where love is described as a "madness of beauty." Plato expressively explains there how the pederastic lover catches the desire (*himeros*) which, literally and substantially, flows from the beloved boy. ("Wherefore as she [i.e., the soul] gazes upon the boy's beauty, she admits a flood of particles streaming therefrom—that is why we speak of the 'flood of passion [Himeros]'—whereby she is warmed and fostered" [251c; Plato, 1978: 497–498]). When Lacan describes Antigone as "himeros enargès," he always also has that plastic image from the Phaedrus in mind.

6. Thus the influential definition given by Aristotle for whom the function of tragedy is to bring about a "catharsis" in the audience, that is, a purification of both affects (Aristoteles, 1995: 47–49; Poetics 49b26 ff). In his first lesson on *Antigone*, Lacan goes into the Aristotelian theory of catharsis in some detail, if only because this is the background against which psychoanalysis began with its "cathartic" method for curing psychical diseases (S7E: 244–246; 7F: 286–289).

7. For Aristotle, a tragedy requires six features: "plot, character, diction, thought, spectacle, and lyric poetry." Yet, his emphasis—as well as that of the entire tradition—is on the "plot": "The most important of these things is the structure of events, because tragedy is mimesis not of persons, but of action and life" (Aristotle, 1995: 51; Poetics 1450a7–16).

8. This is what Martha Nussbaum, for example, says in *The Fragility of Goodness* (Nussbaum, 1986: 64). See also Vernant, 1972: 34–35. The erotic character of Antigone's appearance is thus entirely to be put down to Lacan's own inventiveness.

9. For a good overview, see Steiner, 1986.

10. The lesson of June 15 is also about *Antigone*, but is actually Pierre Kaufmann's exposition on the Kantian sublime. (For reasons which cannot be justified, the text of this lecture is not part of the official edition of Lacan's seminar; you can find it in Lacan, 1959/60, lesson of 15.06.1960, pp. 3–18 and Lacan, 1999: 456–473). In this context, the Kantian reference is very interesting and one should expect a reaction by Lacan. Lacan, however, says nothing about it, although he considers Kaufman's exposition to be the final word on *Antigone*, since he drops the theme in the next session (see S7E: 287; S7F: 333; see also

Balmès, 1999: 200 note 3). At the end of that session (S7E: 310; S7F: 348) he refers a final time to the Kantian idea of the sublime, even suggesting a link with sublimation, but again leaves the theme untouched.

11. S7E: 135–136, 139–142; S7F: 162–163; 167–170. Lacan borrowed the anamorphosis from Prévert, he says at S7E: 135 (S7F: 162): "It belongs to the collector I have already referred to," a collector you find in S7E: 114 (S7F: 136). For an illustration of the anamorphotic version of Rubens's *Crucifixion*, see Milman, 1992: 100–101, Leeman, 1976: 139 (fig. 130) or Baltrušaitis, 1977; 1996: 189, fig. 98. Jurgis Baltrušaitis is one of Lacan's sources on the anamorphosis. He refers to the first version of Baltrušaitis's book he mentions here, which appeared in 1955 (Olivier Perrin, Paris) titled *Anamorphoses ou perspectives curieuses* (S7E: 140; S7F: 169).

12. This is how Miller titles one of those lessons (S7E: 257; S7F: 299).

13. At the moment Lacan begins his commentary on *Antigone*, he clearly says that it is "with a view to finding something other than a lesson in morality" (S7E: 249; S7F: 292).

14. Verses 72–73; 555; Sophocles, 2002: 11; 55. In the last conversation, Antigone had told Creon: "I knew that I would die, of course, even if you have made no proclamation. But if I die before my time, I account that a gain" (v. 460–462; Sophocles 2002: 45). And she even challenges Creon to kill her at once ("Then why do you delay?"; v. 499; Sophocles 2002: 49). A few lines farther, Creon objects that the brother enemy of the city (Polyneices who led a coalition of seven cities waging war against his own town, Thebes) cannot receive the honor of a funeral that the brother defender of the city had received. But, again, Antigone replies: "The dead body will not bear witness to that" (v. 515; Sophocles 2002: 51).

15. Sophocles 2002: 55.

16. "[. . .] she appears as the victim at the center of the anamorphic cylinder of the tragedy" (S7E: 282; S7F: 328).

17. "Not smitten by wasting maladies nor paid the wages of the sword, of your own will [αὐτόνομος, '*autonomos*'] you alone of mortals while yet alive descend to Hades" (v. 818–822; Sophocles, 2002: 81).

18. See for instance the famous passage about Antigone in the *Phenomenology of Spirit* (Hegel, 1997: 261 ff.; 284 ff).

19. Just before he waged war against Thebes to dethrone his brother Eteocles, Polyneices came to Colonos to ask his father's blessing for this project. Instead, Oedipus lays a curse upon his two sons. It is at this moment Polyneices says to Antigone: "My sisters, daughters of this man, since you hear my father pronounce this cruel curse, do not you at least, I beg you if my father's curses are fulfilled and you somehow return home, do not you dishonour me, but place me in my tomb with funeral rites" (v. 1405–1410; Sophocles, 2002: 561).

20. Lacan mentions this repeatedly from his early seminars onward (S2E: 87, 103; S2F: 109, 128; S3E: 6, 20, 21–22, 48, 55; S3F: 14, 29, 31, 59–60, 67; see also S7E: 278; S7F: 324; S8F: 229–230, 234). Indeed, the analyst's interpretation cannot be defined as *understanding* his patient. If he believes otherwise, he already is caught up in the *imaginary* tricks involved in the analysand's *demand*. Instead of understanding, the analyst perpetually has to analyze the ways his own

and the patient's subject-positions move under the influence of desire's vicissitudes. Moreover, during the cure, the analyst has to intervene in the moments when neither he nor his patient know, that is, when the analysand's discourse gets stuck and, for instance, she makes a slip. Finally, by definition the unconscious resists an exhaustive conscious understanding.

21. "In virtue of what law do I say this? If my husband had died, I could have had another, and a child by another man, if I had lost the first, but with my mother and my father in Hades below, I could never have another brother. Such was the law for whose sake I did you [Polynices] special honour [. . .]" (v. 908–912; Sophocles, 2002: 87–89).

22. In S7E: 254–255 (S7F: 297–298) Lacan examines Goethe's interpretation. Lacan refers to a passage in Goethe's conversations with Johann Peter Eckermann, more specifically, Eckermann's notes from March 28, 1827 (Eckermann, 1986: 544).

23. Just before he introduced his cylindrical anamorphosis, Lacan had shown that almost all protagonists in Sophocles' tragedies are "marked by a stance of the-race-is-run [à bout de course] and have entered a kind of 'limit situation.' " (S7E: 272; S7F: 317–318).

24. Although, in his *La jouissance du tragique*, Patrick Guyomard cites the passage where Lacan refers to his subject theory, he omits it in his comment and translates "autonomos" as "voluntary," in the clearly voluntarist sense of the word, albeit adjusted in the Kantian sense. His main argument is Lacan's frequent reference to Kant's moral *Critique*. See Guyomard, 1992: 43–44, note 12: "If one considers [on the one hand] Lacan's many references to the *Critique of Practical Reason*, with its central questions concerning purity and autonomy, and that, on the other hand, Antigone *wants* what she desires, the best translation of *autonomos* would be *voluntarily*" (author's italics; my translation). Guyomard interprets the conflict at stake in *Antigone* as a conflict between two laws (i.e., the incestuous family law in conflict with the public law represented by Creon), and so misses the crucial point that *Antigone* only illustrates the lack and finitude of Creon's law (and of the symbolic order in general).

25. For a good overview of the way *Antigone* is interpreted as rebel in the last two centuries, see Steiner, 1986.

26. This is the same for the passage in S7E: 279 (S7F: 325). There, too, he links the "break" and the "ex nihilo" where Antigone remains with her "autonomos" character: "This break is manifested at every moment in the fact that language punctuates everything that occurs in the movement of life. Αὐτόνομος, [*autonomos*] is the word the Chorus uses to situate Antigone."

27. "The adjective 'pure,' which is found frequently in Lacan to qualify what he has in mind here (i.e., in the Ethics Seminar), undoubtedly designates a 'desire at the limit,' as an affect of the mere structure." (Hatzfeld, 1992: 40; my translation).

28. This is Guyomard's claim. Although desire stems from an ontological lack, the fact that it turns this lack into an operational, symbolic one enables desire to "sublate" all lack (in the Hegelian sense of the word "*Aufhebung*"). Precisely where desire becomes nothing but loss, it no longer has anything to lose. Where it becomes *pure* loss (as with Antigone), it should find itself as pure omnipotence. "Pure desire" becomes a "power of pure loss, [power] because it should be loss

of nothing" (Guyomard, 1992: 26; my translation). Although Guyomard's book requires a longer and more in depth analysis than is possible here, I can state that a correct understanding of Lacan's theory of the subject (as the very locus where the libidinal economy "takes place," occurs) would have forced Guyomard to other conclusions. In a situation as Antigone's, desire seems to make full circle; however, the "locus" (the "platform," the "bearer," the "subject") of where this occurs is not located in a point where desire reaches its full identity, but in a pleasure animal that splits that very identity. At the point where desire reaches its full identity, its subject is destroyed. Lacan defines this point as the "thing," the new central concept in his Ethics Seminar. From this perspective, it is striking that Guyomard's study, which deals exclusively with that seminar, alludes only once to this concept, and even then without further explanation (Guyomard, 1992: 102 note 37). I discuss Guyomard further on in section 3.4.

29. In the official edition we read "the good for all." "For all" is Miller's addition. See Lacan, 1959/60, lesson of 01.06.1960; 1999: 417: "Son erreur de jugement [. . .] est justement [. . .] pour lui Créon de vouloir faire de ce bien la loi sans limites, la loi souveraine, la loi qui déborde, qui dépasse une certaine limite, qu'il ne s'aperçoit pas qu'il franchit cette fameuse limite [. . .]."

30. The word "vouloir" (to want) is omitted in the official edition ("Le bien en saurait vouloir régner. . . .") (Lacan, 1959/60, lesson of 01.06.1960; Lacan, 1999: 418).

31. See also S8F: 68, where the gods are called "a manifestation of the real." See also S8F: 93, 103, 148, 171, 191–193, 447.

32. "Οὐ γάρ τί μοι Ζεύς ἦν ὁ κηρύξας τάδε" (v. 450): thus the sentence in the bilingual edition by Robert Pignarre that Lacan refers to. Pignarre also does not translate the word "me" [μόι] and interprets the sentence in the sense criticized by Lacan: "Oui, car ce n'est pas Zeus qui les [Creon's laws] a proclamés" (Sophocles, 1947: 105). Robert Fagles's translation, in contrast, translates the word, although the sentence is still ambiguous: "It wasn't Zeus, not the least, / who made this proclamation—not to me" (Sophocles 1984: 82).

33. "The ordinary reading is: 'It was not Zeus who issued this decree' or 'who proclaimed this edict to me.' A third reading seems to hover on the far edge of grammatical possibility. If we treat the article as wholly indefinite or as ambiguous, it would be conceivable to construe Antigone as saying that "neither Zeus nor the goddess of Justice enthroned among the nether powers (Δικη) have commanded *this*"—i.e. her disobedience, her two-fold attempt to bury Polyneices! The impulse, the deed would be entirely Antigone's own and *autonomous* in just the sense in which this epithet is used about her in the play. This reading for radical ambiguity, for subconscious or rhetorically masked paradoxicality, is, we must presume, foreign to the passage in its Sophoclean tenor" (Steiner, 1986: 92–93; Steiner's italics).

32. In *La faute tragique*, Suzanne Saïd counts nine: the verses: 4, 185, 533, 584, 614, 624, 862, 1097–1260 (Saïd, 1978: 119 note 178). One can also add verse 625 (where the term is also mentioned). So we have ten.

33. Lacan indicates the specific verses: "Lines 611–614 and 620–625 have to do with the Chorus's statement on the limit that is 'Atè,' and it is around this that what Antigone wants is played out" (S7E: 270; S7F: 315).

34. In the choir's same hymn, the expression "ἐκτὸς ἄτας [ektos atas]" is used in verse 614: "For present, future and past this law shall suffice: to none among mortals shall great wealth come without disaster [ἐκτὸς ἄτας]" (Sophocles, 2002: 61). Literally, that no great happiness will come once one has passed [ἐκτὸς] the *atè*.

35. At the end of the play, Creon appears on the scene with his son Haemon's corpse (who committed suicide after having seen the hanged corpse of his beloved and future bride Antigone). Then, the chorus says: "Here comes the king himself, bearing in his arm an all too clear reminder; if we may say so, his ruin came not from others, but from his own error [ἁμαρτών, hamartoon]." (v. 1256–1260; Sophocles, 2002: 119).

36. See for instance *Poetics* 53a (Aristotle, 1995: 70). Lacan refers to Aristotle in this context in: S7E: 277; S7F: 323.

37. God's act of creation consists in speaking, thus the first lines of Genesis: "God *said*: 'Let there be light,' and there *was* light!" (Gen. 1:3; my italics).

38. The well-known beginning of the gospel of Saint John emphasizes both the primacy of the Word and the certainty that this very Word will deliver us from all evil since Adam's fall. "In the beginning was the Word [ὁ λόγος, *ho logos*] and the Word was with God and the Word was fully God. [. . .] Now, the Word has become flesh [σάρξ, *sarx*] [namely in Christ] and took up residence. We saw his glory [. . .]. For we have all received from his fullness one gracious gift after another" (John 1:1, 14, 16).

39. For the relation between Christian monotheism and modern science, see for instance Alexandre Kojève's contribution to a book in honor of Alexandre Koyré (two authors Lacan has read in great detail): "L'origine chrétienne de la science moderne" (Kojève, 1964).

40. This is to say that Sade has in mind a radically unbound nature, a nature so free that she is free even from her own laws. It is for this reason he wants to reduce his victim to "nothing," a "nothing" as radical as the "ex nihilo" from which God created the universe and into which Sade wants that universe to be pushed back. Sade's fantasy, too, supposes "creationism," albeit without any religious veil. The "nihil" that civilization rests on is not the godly "nihil" from which the Creator let emerge the universe, but the "nihil" where only Crime reigns. Each libertine act thus mirrors this Crime and is therefore never satisfied by a "first," natural and regenerative death of his victim. It is all matter of giving him a *second* death. What must be destroyed in the victim is his capacity to return to the circle of life and death.

41. "[D]ans le fantasme," which is included here in the translation, is omitted in the official edition (see Lacan 1959/60, lesson of 01.06.1960; 1999: 420).

42. See the first lines of the *Duino Elegies* by Rainer Maria Rilke (Rilke 1977: 25).

43. This is one of the basic points in Kant's analysis of the judgment of taste. As already indicated in his first paragraph of the *Critique of Judgment*, this kind of judgment "denotes nothing in the object, but is a feeling of which the Subject has of itself and of the manner in which it is affected by the representation" (Kant, 1992: 42; 1974 Bd. X: 115; in the original edition: *A*: 4). In the next paragraph, Kant draws the conclusion that the aesthetic judgment is completely

indifferent with regard to its object: "One must not be in the least prepossessed in favour of the real existence of the thing, but must preserve complete indifference in this respect, in order to play the part of judge in matters of taste" (Kant, 1992: 43; 1974 Bd. X: 117; in the original edition: *A*: 6–7). This requirement of indifference and apathy is to be found in Sade as well.

44. See for instance Lacan's seminar on Anxiety, especially the lecture given by Piera Aulagnier (lesson of 27.02.1963; Lacan, 1996c: 184–194). For *Kant avec Sade*, see: Lacan 1966: 765–790.

45. The beginning of the quotation—"Effectivement, c'est bien un fantasme, où . . . ," is omitted in the official edition (see: Lacan 1959/60, lesson of 01.06.1960; 1999: 420).

46. Žižek, 1988: 211–212; 1989: 142–149; 1991a: 108–109; 1996: 143–144.

47. While the "thesis" of the play is Antigone, Creon is the "antithesis," Lacan states in S7E: 314 (S7F: 362). Lacan is not the first and only commentator to refuse Creon the role of protagonist. It is characteristic of an age-old tradition extending from antiquity. Martha Nussbaum cites Demosthenes who qualifies Creon's role as "tritagonist." Nussbaum draws the conclusion "that the view that Creon is the 'hero' of the tragedy was not supported by ancient performance practice" (Nussbaum, 1986: 439 note 27).

48. Verses 773–784; Sophocles, 1984: 100–101.

49. S7F: 369; S7E: 320. He takes up this idea again a few times in the eighth seminar (*The Transference*, 1960–61; (S8F: 5, 60, 102, 120, 126, 154, 158, 322–323). Note also the title Jacques-Alain Miller gives to the third and final lesson on *Antigone* (June 8, 1960): "Antigone between two deaths" ("Antigone dans l'entre-deux-morts"; S7E: 270; S7F: 315).

50. In his lesson of January 27, 1960, he defines the "thing" as "that which in the real suffers from the signifier" ("ce qui du réel [. . .] pâtit du signifiant"; S7E: 125; S7F: 150; see also S7E: 134; S7F: 161).

51. See Aristotle, *Poetics* 1449b–1450a (Aristoteles, 1995: 45–51). Lacan mentions (S7E: 245; S7F: 287) that the Aristotelian idea of tragedy as catharsis is not without difficulties, if only because we have only a part of Aristotle's text. Aristotle takes up the idea of catharsis again in the *Politica* (1341b), but this does not fill the gap.

52. Aristotle, *Nicomachean Ethics* II, vi, 15–16 (1107a ff.); Aristotle 1994: 95 ff.

53. Lacan was quite clear about this already in the lesson in which he announced his commentary on *Antigone*: "I will continue our enquiry next time with relation to a document [i.e., Sophocles, *Antigone*]. It's not exactly a new document. Down through the centuries longwinded commentators have cut their teeth and sharpened their nails on it. This text appeared in the field where the morality of happiness was theorized and it gives us its underlying structure. It is there that its underlying structure is the most visible, there where it appears on the surface" (S7E: 240; S7F: 281).

54. Lacan's analysis of modern science as the "foreclosure" of the "thing" is compatible with this (see above chapter 7, section 4.1 and the there quoted passage from S7E: 131; S7F: 157).

55. See for instance what he says about Hegel in his first seminar: "[His] point of departure, being imaginary, is hence mythical" (SE1: 223; SF1: 248). He criticizes Hegel's interpretation of the ancient slave society. The difference between masters and slaves is not due to a struggle for mutual recognition (as Kojève claims), but is based on rules and laws that mediate this struggle from the very beginning. See also Lacan's discussion with Jean Hyppolite in the second seminar (S2E: 70–72; S2F: 90–92).

56. For Lacan, it is not by accident that, as spectators, we are not direct witnesses of what happens in Antigone's "grave" once she is definitely beyond the "atè." This also goes for the two other tragedies to which he refers, *Hamlet* and *Oedipus at Colonos*. In S7E: 269 (S7F: 312) he evokes what happens in Antigone's grave: "Haemon kisses her (Antigone, who has just hanged herself) and emits a final groans, but we do not know what happened in the sepulcher any more than that we know what goes on when Hamlet goes into the sepulcher. Antigone has after all walled in at the limit of *atè*, and one is justified in wondering at which moment Haemon entered the tomb. As when the actors turn their faces away from the spot where Oedipus disappears, we don't know what happened in Antigone's tomb."

# Chapter 9

1. At first sight at least, analysis is an intersubjective event. A little later on (1.2) it will become apparent how the paradigms of the object relation are valid here as well, and the relation between the analyst and analysand must be thought as that between the subject and (his desired) object.

2. All things considered, it is thus a logical step when, immediately after the cited passage, Lacan dwells again on the impotence of psychoanalysis to offer the analysand the happiness she demands. Space constraints prevent a detailed look at Lacan's long "detour" here with its Kantian references and enlargements (S7E: 292–300; S7F: 338–346).

3. See among others Freud's essay "Future Prospects of Psycho-Analytic Therapy" (1910) where he uses the term "counter-transference" for the first time (Freud, SE9: 144; Freud, SA11: 126)

4. Many of the psychoanalysts in the fifties were responsible for this interpretation and are the target of Lacan's critique here. See, for example, Paula Heimann (Lacan discusses her article "On Counter-Transference" in S8F: 223–228) and Margaret Little (see Lacan, 1996c: 158–163). For a short discussion of Lacan's relation to the countertransference see Assoun, 1997: 502–503.

5. Lacan will approach the situation of the transference in connection with a long analysis of Plato's *Symposium* (S8F: 29–195). He not only shows how dangerously close the analytic cure comes to a love relationship, but also finds a figure in it who illustrates the position of the analyst in an exemplary manner: Socrates. The high point of his analysis forms a reading of the last part of the Symposium where a drunk Alcibiades storms into the banquet hall and gives his famous speech about his ex-lover Socrates (212c–223d). In it, Alcibiades reveals that Socrates' irresistible erotic attractiveness does not lie in his external beauty (for he wasn't a beauty at all) but in his "agalmata," in "the little images inside

[him]" (216e; Plato, 1978: 568). According to Lacan, he evokes avant la lettre Lacan's own theory of *das Ding*. What one desires in Socrates is a "thing" that escapes the normal symbolic order and lies behind the radiance of the signifier. But Socrates shows himself a true analyst, says Lacan, by fully agreeing with Alcibiades' explanation of the "agalmata" except with the fact that these are *his* (i.e., of Socrates). Actually, replies Socrates to the eulogy from his former lover, you mean the "agalmata" of Agathon, our guest and my new lover, and you want to sow your whole discourse between him and me (paraphrase of 222cd; Plato, 1978: 573). Socrates thus agrees he stands on the place of the agalmata, but he refuses to fall into Alcibiades' trap. He refuses, that is, to appropriate this place as a subject and to act as if it were *his* "thing." It is in this sense that he "pays with his person" in the transference situation with Alcibiades. See S8F: 163–195 (lesson X and XI).

6. "The distance varies at each moment of the analysis, but generally, as the analysis progresses, that distance tends to shorten and become zero; this is what I call 'joiner' (the culminating point of transferential neurosis)" (Bouvet, 1972: 267; my translation). It is against this idea of "joiner" ("*rapprocher*") that Lacan turns at the end of his lesson of 22 June, 1960 (S7E: 301; S7F: 348).

7. Recall the (morally loaded) distinction he makes between the two types of object relation, "the pregenitals" and "the genitals." See Bouvet, 1972: 169. See also above chapter 1, section 2.

8. As Hamlet says a few lines after the famous "To be or not to be": "To die, to sleep; / To sleep: perchance to dream: ay, there's the rub; / For in that sleep of death what dreams may come / When we have shuffled off this mortal coil, / Must give us pause. [. . .] who would fardels bear, / To grunt and sweat under a weary life, / But that the dread of something after death, / The undiscover'd country from whose bourn / No traveller returns, puzzles the will / And makes us rather bear those ills we have / Than fly to others that we know not of?" (*Hamlet* III, 1, v. 64–68, 76–82; Shakespeare, 1978: 958–959).

9. Here in this final lesson Lacan refers a couple of times explicitly to Heidegger's "*Existential*" (see *Being and Time*, §49–§53); see among others S7E: 309; 313; 320; S7F: 357, 361, 369.

10. See *Being and Time*, §40.

11. For Heidegger, man is not *first* a being that *subsequently* "projects" his life. Rather, man coincides with that "project" ("*Entwurf*"): he *is* his "*Entwurf*," he is the anticipation of a "himself" that lies primordially in the future (see *Being and Time*, §31, §41).

12. If the "moral act" for psychoanalysis lies in assuming one's desire, the analysand can only assist the analysand up to that moment. The analyst can only take the analysand to the door; he cannot go through the door with her. Lacan already states this explicitly in one of the first lessons of his Ethics Seminar (S7E: 21; S7F: 30), see above chapter 2, section 3).

13. After praising death as the best thing that can happen to man (because it delivers him from all suffering), the choir rectifies itself: "Not to be born is best / when all is reckoned in" (v. 1224–1225; Sophocles, 1984: 358). Already in his second seminar, Lacan connects Oedipus's attitude in the hour of his death with the "mè funai" of the choir: "What does the theme of *Oedipus at Colonos*

amount to? The chorus says—*Say what you will, the greatest boon is not to be; / But, life begun, soonest to end is best,* . . . And Oedipus calls down the most extreme maledictions upon posterity and the city for which he was a burnt offering—read the maledictions addressed to his son, Polynices" (S2E: 230; S2F: 269; Miller's italics; see also S2E: 233; S2F: 272).

14. It is an example Lacan often uses; see S7E: 64; 305–306; S7F: 79, 353, S8F: 354, Lacan, 1966: 663.

15. This article later appeared in the first volume of Eduard Pichon's and Jacques Damourette's study of French grammar (Damourette & Pichon, 1930).

16. "[. . .] that μή [mè], the negation that is identical to the entrance of the subject supported by the signifier" (S7E: 313). In the French edition we read: "[. . .] ce μή [mè], la négation identique à l'entrée du sujet, sur le support du signifiant" (S7F: 361–362). Misleadingly and incorrectly, Miller puts a comma between "sujet sur" and "le support" (see Lacan, 1959–60, lesson of 06.06.1960; 1999: 506).

17. Jean Ansaldi, for example, calls "do not cede on your desire" (cited in fact in this erroneous way) a "maxim" (Ansaldi, 1998: 100; see also 7 and 13). Those who cite it correctly are exceptions to the rule, as for example Johan and Tim Schokker in their book *Extimity* where they write "Important, at the very least, is that Lacan never expressed 'do not cede on your desire' in such a way" (Schokker & Schokker, 2000: 131; my translation).

18. This is how he formulates it in his essay, "Das Ding: Lacan and Levinas": "[ . . . ] at the end of Seminar VII, Lacan writes that from a psychoanalytical point of view, 'the only thing one can be guilty of is giving way on one's desire.' Such is the categorical imperative of Freud's Copernican revolution—do not give way on your desire" (Critchley, 1999: 202).

19. Lacan gives a striking sociopolitical characterization of repression: "What is Alexander's proclamation when he arrived in Persepolis or Hitler's when he arrived in Paris? The preamble isn't important: 'I have come to liberate you from this or that.' The essential point is: 'Carry on working. Work must go on.' Which of course means: "Let it be clear to everyone that this is on no account the moment to express the least surge of desire" (S7E: 315; S7F: 363; Miller's italics).

20. I include here the official French edited version as well. Due to its imprecision, some commentary is necessary: "Je vous ai donc articulé trois propositions. La seule chose dont on puisse être coupable, c'est d'avoir cédé sur son désir. Deuxièmement, la définition du héros—c'est celui qui peut impunément être trahi. [In the official edition, we read now "Troisièmement . . ." This is an incorrect addition by Miller. What follows in Lacan's text is an explanation of the second proposition. Later on, Lacan announces explicitly his "third proposition," but in conformity with his own incorrect editing, Miller changes this in "quatrième proposition." My translation here is closer to the stenotype version.] Ceci n'est point à la portée de tout le monde, et c'est la différence entre l'homme du commun et le héros, plus mystérieuse donc qu'on ne le croit. Pour l'homme du commun, la trahison, qui se produit presque toujours, a pour condition qu'il ne retrouvera jamais ce qui l'oriente vraiment dans ce service. [From here, I follow the stenotype version in its entirety] La troisième proposition est celle-ci,

c'est qu'en fin de compte, les biens, naturellement, ça existe, leur champ et leur domaine, il ne s'agit pas de les nier, mais que renversant la perspective, je vous propose ceci, il n'y a pas d'autre bien que ce qui peut servir à payer le prix pour l'accès au désir [. . .]" (S7E: 321; S7F: 370–371; Lacan 1959/60, lesson of 06.07.1960; 1999: 516).

21. "Take the example of *Philoctetes*, where you will learn other aspects of the question, that is to say, that a hero doesn't have to be heroic to be a hero. Philoctetes isn't much of a man" (S7E: 320; S7F: 369).

22. Philippe Lacoue-Labarthe coins the term "*esthéthique*" for this blending of ethics and aesthetics (Lacoue-Labarthe, 1991: 31).

# Epilogue

1. A couple of lines above, Lacan says: "Do I need to say, a propos what I call the limitations or the inexistence of the erotic analysis [. . .]" ("Ai-je besoin de dire, qu'à propos de ce que j'appelle les limitations ou la non-existence [de l'] érotique analytique [. . .]"). This sentence fragment is missing from the official edition (Lacan, 1959/1960, lesson of November 18, 1959; 1999: 19).

2. Think of the famous hymn to love in Saint Paul's *First Letter to the Corinthians*, chapter 13.

3. "*Agape*" is the word Paul (and the Christian tradition following him) uses for love, by which a de-eroticized love is in fact meant. In connection with this, Lacan refers a number of times in his following seminar to Andres Nygren's influential study from 1953 *Agape and Eros* (S8F: 25, 164; Nygren, 1982).

4. This, at least, is how Eros is characterized in the Euripidean tragedy *Hyppolytos* (v. 538–541, Euripides 1995: 176). In this tragedy it is claimed that there is no point in trying to propitiate this god with sacrifices because he shoots his famous arrows *blindly*.

5. See Plato's *Symposium* where Socrates claims "that love is the one thing in the world I understand" (177d), a claim that he must take back a little later (198d) and admit "what a fool I'd been [. . .] to claim a special knowledge about the subject" (see Plato 1978: 532; 550).

# Abbreviations

SA1–SA11 Freud, S. (1969–1975), *Studienausgabe*, Bd. I—X + Ergänzungs-band, Frankfurt am Main, S. Fischer Verlag.

SE1–SE24 Freud, S. (1953–1961), *The Standard Edition of the Complete Psychological Works of Sigmund Freud*, Translated under the General Editorship of J. Strachey, Vols. I–XXIV, London: The Hogarth Press and the Institute of Psycho-Analysis.

S1F Lacan, J. (1975a), *Le séminaire, Livre I, Les écrits techniques de Freud: 1953–1954*, texte établi par J.-A. Miller, Paris, Seuil.

S2E Lacan, J. (1988), *The Seminar of Jacques Lacan, Book II, The Ego in Freud's Theory and in the Technique of Psychoanalysis, 1954–1955*, edited by J.-A. Miller, translated by S. Tomaselli, with notes by J. Forrester, New York and London, W. W. Norton & Company.

S2F Lacan, J. (1978), *Le moi dans la théorie de Freud et dans la technique psychoanalytique*, texte établi par J.-A. Miller, Paris, Seuil.

S3F Lacan, J. (1981), *Le séminaire, Livre III, Les psychoses: 1955–1956*, texte établi par J.-A. Miller, Paris, Seuil.

S4F Lacan, J. (1994), *Le séminaire, Livre IV, La relation d'objet: 1956–1957*, texte établi par J.-A. Miller, Paris, Seuil.

S5F Lacan, J. (1998), *Le séminaire, Livre V, Les formations de l'inconscient: 1957–1958*, texte établi par J.-A. Miller, Paris, Seuil.

S6F        Lacan, J. (1996), *Le séminaire, Livre VI, Le désir et son interprétation: 1958–1959*, Paris, Publication hors commerce de l'Association Freudienne Internationale.

S7E        Lacan, J. (1992), *The Ethics of Psychoanalysis, 1959–1960,The Seminar of Jacques Lacan*, edited Jacques-Alain Miller, translated with notes by Dennis Porter, London: Routledge.

S7F        Lacan, J. (1986), *Le séminaire, Livre VII, L'éthique de la psychanalyse: 1959–1960*, texte établi par J.-A. Miller, Paris, Seuil.

S8E        Lacan, J. (s.d.), *The seminar of Jacques Lacan: Transference, 1960–1961, Book VIII*, translated by Cormac Gallagher from unedited French manuscripts.

S8F        Lacan, J. (2001 [1991]), *Le séminaire, Livre VIII, Le transfert: 1960–1961*, texte établi par J.-A. Miller, Paris, Seuil.

S11E       Lacan, J. (1981), *The Four Fundamental Concepts of Psyco-Analysis*, Edited by J.-A. Miller, translated by A. Sharidan, Norton Paperback, New York and London, W. W. Norton & Company.

S11F       Lacan, J. (1973), *Le séminaire, Livre XI, Les quatre concepts fondamentaux de la psychanalyse: 1964*, texte établi par J.-A. Miller, Paris, Seuil.

S17F       Lacan, J. (1991b), *Le séminaire, Livre XVII, L'envers de la psychanalyse: 1969–1970*, texte établi par J.-A. Miller, Paris, Seuil.

S20F       Lacan, J. (1975b), *Le séminaire, Livre XX, Encore: 1972–1973*, texte établi par J.-A. Miller, Paris, Seuil.

# Bibliography

Abraham, K. (1924), *Versuch einer Entwicklungsgeschichte des Libido auf Grund des Psychoanalyse seelischer Störungen*, Leipzig & Wien & Zürich, Internationaler Psychoanalytischer Verlag.

Abraham, K. (1979), *Selected Papers*, translated by D. Bryan and A. Strachey, introduction by E. Jones, London: Maresfield Reprint.

Adorno, T. W. and Horkheimer, M. (1972), *Dialectic of Enlightenment*, translated by J. Cumming, New York: The Seabury Press.

Alacoque, M. (1945), *Vie de Sainte Marguarite-Marie Alacoque, Écrite par elle-même*, Paris, J. de Gigord.

Allouch, J. (1995), *Érotique du deuil au temps de la mort sèche*, Paris: Les Éditions E.P.E.L.

Allouch, J. (1998), *La psychanalyse: une érotologie de passage*, Paris: Les Éditions E.P.E.L.

André, S. (1995 [1986]), *Que veut une femme?* Paris: Seuil.

Angela of Foligno (1993), *Complete works*, translation and introduction by P. Lachance, Mahwah, NJ: Paulist Press.

Ansaldi, J. (1998), *Lire Lacan: L'éthique de la psychanalyse, Le Séminaire VII*, Nîmes: Éditions du Champ social.

Aristotle, (1994), *Nicomachean Ethics,* with an English translation by H. Rackham, Loeb Classic Library, Cambridge, MA and London: Harvard University Press.

Aristotle, (1995), *Poetics*, edited and translated by S. Halliwell; Longinus, *On the Sublime*, translated by D. Russel; Demetrius, *On Style*, translated by D. C. Innes, Loeb Classical Library, Cambridge, MA: Harvard University Press.

Assoun, P.-L. (1976), *Freud, la philosophie et les philosophes*, Paris: Presses Universitaires de France.

Assoun, P.-L. (1997), *Psychanalyse*, Paris: Presses Universitaires de France.

Augustine, A. (1948), *Basic Writings of Saint Augustine*, edited, with an introduction and notes by W. J. Oates, Vol. II, New York: Random House.

Aulangier-Spairani, P. (1967), "La perversion comme structure," in: *L'inconscient* 2: 11–41.

Baas, B. (1992), *Le désir pur. Parcours philosophiques dans les parages de J. Lacan*, Leuven: Peeters.

Baas, B. (1998), *De la chose à l'objet. Jacques Lacan et la traversée de la phénoménologie*, Leuven: Peeters.

Balint, M. (1952), *Primary Love and Psychoanalytic Technique*, London: The Hogarth Press.

Balmès, F. (1999), *Ce que Lacan dit de l'être*, Paris: Presses Universitaires de France.

Baltrušaitis, J. (1977), *Anamorphotic Art*, translation by W. J. Strachan, Cambridge: Chadwyck-Healey.

Baltrušaitis, J. (1996 [1984]), *Anamorphoses ou Thaumaturgus opticus. Les perspectives dépravées II*, Paris: Flammarion.

Bataille, G. (1979), *Oeuvres Complètes IX*, Paris: Gallimard.

Bataille, G. (2001), *Literature and Evil*, translated by A. Hamilton, London: Marion Boyars Publishers.

Benjamin, W. (1986), *Reflections: Essays, Aphorisms, Autobiographical Writings*, edited and with an introduction by P. Demetz, New York: Schocken Books.

Bentham, J. (1996), *Théorie des Fictions*, texte anglais et français, traduction, introduction et notes par Gérard Michaut, Paris: Éditions de l'Association Freudienne Internationale.

Bentham, J. (1997), *De l'ontologie et autres textes sur les fictions*, éditon bilingue, Paris: Seuil.

Bergeret, J. (1994), *La violence et la vie*, Paris: Payot.

Blanchot, M. (1982 [1955]), *L'espace littéraire*, Paris: Gallimard.

Blanchot, M. (1984 [1949]), *Lautréamont et Sade*, Paris: Les Éditions de Minuit.

Blanchot, M. (1989), *The Space of Literature*, translation, with an introduction, by Ann Smock, Lincoln: University of Nebraska Press.

Blanchot, M. (2004), *Lautréamont and Sade*, translated by S. and K. Kendall, Stanford: Standford University Press.

Bollack, J. (1999), *La mort d'Antigone. La tragédie de Créon*, Paris: Presses Universitaires de France.

Borch-Jacobsen, M. (1991), *Lacan: The Absolute Master*, translated by D. Brick, Stanford: Stanford University Press.

Bouvet, M. (1972 [1967]), *Oeuvres psychanalytiques I: La relation d'objet*, Paris: Payot.

Bouvet, M. (1976 [1967]), *Oeuvres psychanalytiques II: Résistance, Transfert*, Paris: Payot.

Braunstein, N. (1992), *La jouissance. Un concept lacanien*, Paris: Point Hors Ligne.

Buckley, P. (Ed.) (1986), *Essential Papers on Object-relations*, New York and London: New York University Press.

Cambien, J. (1997), "Qu'advient-il d'Hamlet en psychanalyse?" in: *La Psychanalyse* 11: 93–109.

Canguilhem, G. (1955), *La formation du concept de réflexe aux XVII^e et XVIII^e siècles*, Paris: Presses Universitaires de France.

Capellanus, A. (1982), *On Love*, vertaling door P. G. Walsch, London: Duckworth.

Castanet, H. (s.d.), *Regard et perversion à partir des 'Lois de l'hospitalité' de Pierre Klossowski*, Nice: Z'éditions.

Cathelineau, C. (1998), *Lacan, lecteur d'Aristote. Politique, métaphysique, logique*, Paris: Éditions de l'Association Freudienne Internationale.

Cazotte, J. (1992), *The Devil in Love*, New York: Hippocrene Books.

Chemama, R. (Réd.) (1995), *Dictionnaire de la psychanalyse*, Paris: Larousse.

Critchley, S. (1999), *Ethics, Politics, Subjectivity*, London and New York: Verso.

Damourette J. and Pichon E. (1930), *Des mots à la pensée. Essai de grammaire de la langue française, tome I*, Paris: d'Artrey.

Darmon, M. (1990), *Essais de topologie lacanienne*, Paris: Édition de l'Association Freudienne.

De Kesel, M. (1998), *Wij, modernen: Essays over subject and moderniteit*, Leuven: Peeters.

De Kesel, M. (2000), "Als spoken spreken / When Ghosts speak," in: Myriam Van Imschoot & Rudi Laermans (red.), *Ghost. The Journal #3 of Highway 101 Project by Meg Stuart and Damaged Goods*, Brussel: Damaged Goods, pp. 47–51; 115–119.

Deleuze, G. (1990), *Pourparlers*, Paris: Les Éditions de Minuit.

Derrida, J. (1990), *Force of Law. The Mystical Foundation of Authority*, translation by M. Quaintance, New York: Cardozo Law Review Ed. Office New York.

De Rougemont, D. (1975), *L'amour et l'occident*, Paris: Union Générale d'Éditions.

De Rougemont, D. (1983), *Love in the Western World*, Princeton: Princeton University Press.

Diaktine, R. (1989), "Introduction à une discussion sur le concept d'objet en psychanalyse," in: *Revue française de psychanalyse* 53/4: 1037–1043.

Dosse, F. (1991), *Histoire du structuralisme I: Le champ du signe 1946–1966*, Paris, Éditions La Découverte.

Duby, G. (1997), *Women of the Twelfth Century*, Cambridge: Polity Press and Chicago: University of Chicago Press.

Eckermann, J. P. (1986), *Gespräche mit Goethe in den lezten Jahren seines Lebens*. Herausgeben von J. Schlaffer, München, Carl Hanser Verlag.

Egan, M. (1985), *Les vies des Troubadours*, Paris: Union Générale d'Éditions.

E.L.P. [École Lacanienne de Psychanalyse] (1991), *'Le Transfert' dans tous ses errata*, Paris: Les Éditions E.P.E.L.

Euripides (1995), *Children of Heracles, Hippolytus, Andromache, Hecuba*, edited and translated by David Kovacs, Cambridge, Mass. and London: Harvard University Press.

Fajnwaks, F. (1998), "Simone Weil: un amour sans objet," in: *La Cause freudienne* 40: 117–124.

Fink, B. (1995), *The Lacanian Subject. Between Language and Jouissance*, Princeton: Princeton University Press.

Frank, M. (1989), *What Is Neo-Structuralism?* Minneaplis: University of Minnesota Press.

Freud, S. (1975 [1962, 1950]), *Aus den Anfängen der Psychoanalyse 1887–1902: Briefe an Wilhelm Fliess*, Frankfurt am Main: Fischer Verlag.

Freud, S. (1969–1975), *Studienausgabe*, Bd. I–XII, Frankfurt am Main: Fischer Verlag.

Freud, S. (1953–1961), The Standard Edition of the Complete Psychological Works of Sigmund Freud, translated under the General Editorship of J. Strachey, Vols. I—XXIV, London: Hogarth Press and the Institute of Psycho-Analysis.

Freud, S. (1985), *The Complete Letters of Sigmund Freud to Wilhelm Fliess 1887–1904*, translated by J. Moussaieff Masson, Cambridge, Mass. and London: The Belknap Press of Harvard University Press.

Freud, S. (1986), *Briefe an Wilhelm Fliess 1887–1904*, Frankfurt am Main: Fischer Verlag.

Freud, S. (1987), *Gesammelte Werke, Nachtragsband*, Frankfurt am Main, Fischer Verlag.

Gallop, J. (1985), *Reading Lacan*, Ithaca and London: Cornell University Press.

Georgin, R. (1983), *De Lévi-Strauss à Lacan*, Paris: Cistre.

Gilson, J.-P. (1994), *La topologie de Lacan. Une articulation de la cure psychanalytique*, Montréal: Les Éditions Balzac.

Gondek, H.-D. and Widmer, P. (Eds.) (1994), *Ethik und Psychoanalyse: Vom kategorischen Imperativ zum Gesetz des Begehrens: Kant und Lacan*, Frankfurt am Main: Fischer Taschenbuch Verlag.

Granon-Lafont, J. (1985), *La topologie ordinaire de Jacques Lacan*, Paris: Point Hors Ligne.

Green, J. (1993), *Le travail du négatif*, Paris: Minuit.

Grigg, R. (1990), "Lacan on object-relations" in: *Analysis* 2: 39–49.

Grosskurth, P. (1986), *Melanie Klein, Her World and Her Work*, Northvale, NJ and London: Jason Aronson.

Guyomard, P. (1992), *La jouissance du tragique: Antigone, Lacan et le désir de l'analyste*, Paris: Aubier.

Guyomard, P. (1998), *Le désir d'éthique*, Paris: Aubier.

Halsema, A. (1998), *Dialectiek van de seksuele differentie. De filosofie van Luce Irigaray*, Amsterdam: Boom.

Hatzfeld, M. (1992), "Variations sur le thème tragique dans *L'ethique de la psychanalyse*," in: *Littoral* 36: 39–63.

Hegel, G. W. F. (1977), *Phenomenology of the Spirit*, translation by A. V. Miller, foreword by J. N. Findlay, Oxford: Oxford University Press.

Heidegger, M. (1954), *Vorträge und Aufsätze*, Pfullingen, Neske.

Heidegger, M. (1980 [1950]), *Holzwege*, Frankfurt am Main: Vittorio Klostermann.

Heidegger, M. (1990 [1954]), *Vorträge und Aufsätze*, Pfullingen: Neske.

Hénaff, M. (1977), "Tout dire ou l'encyclopédie de l'excès," in *Obliques* 12/13: 29–37.

Hénaff, M. (1978), *Sade: L'invention du corps libertin*, Paris: Presses Universitaires de France.

Hénaff, M. (1999), *Sade: The Invention of the Libertine Body*, translated by X. Callahan, Minneapolis: University of Minnesota Press.

Hesnard, A. (1949), *L'univers morbide de la faute*, Paris: Presses Universitaires de France.

Hesnard, A. (1954), *Morale sans péché*, Paris: Presses Universitaires de France.

Jones, E. (1929), "Fear, Guilt and Hate," in: *The International Journal of Psycho-Analysis* X, 4: 383–397.

Julien, P. (1990 [1985]), *Le retour à Freud de Jacques Lacan: L'application au miroir*, Paris: Les Éditions E.P.E.L.

Kafka, F. (1995 [1971]), *Complete Stories*, edited by Nahum N. Glatzer; with a foreword by John Updike, New York: Schocken Books.

Kafka, F. (1980 [1977]), *The Trial*, translation by D. Scott and C. Waller, introduction by J. P. Stern, London: Penn Books.

Kant, I. (1992 [1952]), *The Critique of Judgment*, translation J. Creed Meredith, Oxford: Claredon.

Kant, I. (1974), *Werkausgabe, Bd. I–XII*. Herausgegeben von W. Weischedel, Frankfurt am Main: Suhrkamp.

Kant, I. (1996), *Critique of Practical Reason*, translated by T. K. Abbott, New York: Prometheus Books.

Kant, I. (1965[1929]), *Critique of Pure Reason*, translation by N. Kemp Smith, New York: St. Martin's Press.

Kenny, A. (1979), *Aristotle's theory of the will*, New Haven: Yale University Press.

Klein, M. (1947), *Contributions to psycho-analysis*, London: Hogarth Press.

Klossowski, P. (1947), *Sade mon prochain*, Paris: Seuil.

Klossowski, P. (1991), *Sade My Neigbor*, translated by A. Lingis, Evanston: Northwestern University Press.

Kojève, A. (1964): "L'origine chrétienne de la science moderne," in: Collectif, *Mélanges Alexandre Koyré. L'aventure de l'esprit II*, Paris: Hermann.

Koyré, A. (1973 [1966]), *Études d'histoire de la pensée scientifique*, Paris: Gallimard.

Koyré, A. (1968), *Newtonian Studies*, Chicago: University of Chicago Press.

Koyré, A. (1968), *Études newtoniennes*, Paris: Gallimard.

Kusnierek, M. (1989), "A propos d'Hamlet," in: *Quarto* 35: 15–18.

Lacan, J. (1959/60), *Le séminaire, Livre VII, L'éthique de la psychanalyse: 1959–1960*, version signed with M.A.–M.M., unedited.

Lacan, J. (1966), *Écrits*, Paris: Seuil.

Lacan, J. (1973), *Le séminaire, Livre XI, Les quatre concepts fondamentaux de la psychanalyse: 1964*, texte établi par J.-A. Miller, Paris: Seuil.

Lacan, J, (1974), *Télévision*, Paris: Seuil.

Lacan, J. (1975a), *Le séminaire, Livre I, Les écrits techniques de Freud: 1953–1954*, texte établi par J.-A. Miller, Paris: Seuil.

Lacan, J. (1975b), *Le séminaire, Livre XX, Encore: 1972–1973*, texte établi par J.-A. Miller, Paris: Seuil.

Lacan, J. (1975c), "Conférence de presse du Dr. Lacan," in: *Lettres de l'École freudienne* 16: 6–26.

Lacan, J. (1977), "Le sinthôme. Séminaire du 11 mai 1976," in: *Ornicar?* 11 (1977): 3–9.

Lacan, J. (1981), *Le séminaire, Livre III, Les psychoses: 1955–56*, texte établi par J.-A. Miller, Paris: Seuil.

Lacan, J. (1981b), *Les non-dupes errent: 1973–1974*. Notes intégrales prises au Séminaire les deuxième et troisième mardis de chaque mois à la Faculté de Droit par un groupe d'élèves, onuitgegeven.

Lacan, J. (1981c), "Jacques Lacan à Louvain, le 13 octobre 1972," in: *Quarto* 3: 6–20.

Lacan, J. (1981d), *The Language of the self. The function of Language in Psychoanalysis*, translated, with notes and comments by A. Wilden, Baltimore and London: Johns Hopkins University Press.

Lacan, J. (1981e), *The Four Fundamental Concepts of Psyco-Analysis*, Edited by J.-A. Miller, translated by A. Sharidan, Norton Paperback, New York and London: W. W. Norton & Company.

Lacan, J. (1982), "Le symbolique, l'imaginaire et le réel," in *Bulletin de l'Association freudienne* 1: 4–13.

Lacan, J. (1984), "Compte rendu avec interpolations du Séminaire de l'Éthique," in: *Ornicar?* 28: 7–18.

Lacan, J. (1986), *Le séminaire, Livre VII, L'éthique de la psychanalyse: 1959–1960*, texte établi par J.-A. Miller, Paris: Seuil.

Lacan, J. (1988), *The Seminar of Jacques Lacan, Book II, The Ego in Freud's Theory and in the Technique of Psychoanalysis, 1954–1955*, edited by J.-A. Miller, translated by S. Tomaselli, with notes by J. Forrester, New York and London: W. W. Norton & Company.

Lacan, J. (1989 [1977]), *Écrits: a selection*, translated by A. Sheridan, with a foreword by M. Bowie, London and New York: Routledge.

Lacan, J. (1989b), "Kant with Sade," translated by J. B. Swenson, Jr. in: *October* 51 (winter 1989): 55–104.

Lacan, J. (1990), *Television*, translated by D. Hollier, R. Krauss, and A. Michelson, New York and London: W. W. Norton and Company.

Lacan, J. (1991), *Le séminaire, Livre XVII, L'envers de la psychanalyse: 1969–1970*, texte établi par J.-A. Miller, Paris: Seuil.

Lacan, J. (1992), *The Ethics of Psychoanalysis 1959–1960. The Seminar of Jacques Lacan, Book VII*, translated with notes by Dennis Porter, London and New York: Routledge / W. W. Norton & Company.

Lacan, J. (1992b), "Conférences à Bruxelles," in: *Quarto* 50: 7–20.

Lacan, J. (1993), *The Seminar of Jacques Lacan, Book III, The Psychoses 1955–1956*, edited by J.-A. Miller, translated by R. Grigg, New York and London: W. W. Norton & Company.

Lacan, J. (1994), *Le séminaire, Livre IV, La relation d'objet: 1956–1957*, texte établi par J.-A. Miller, Paris: Seuil.

Lacan, J. (1996a), *Le séminaire, Livre VI, Le désir et son interprétation: 1958–1959*, Paris: Publication hors commerce de *l'Association Freudienne Internationale*.

Lacan, J. (1996b), *Le séminaire, Livre IX, L'identification: 1961–1962*, Paris: Publication hors commerce de *l'Association Freudienne Internationale*.

Lacan, J. (1996c), *Le séminaire, Livre X, L'angoisse: 1962–1963*, Paris: Publication hors commerce de *l'Association Freudienne Internationale*.

Lacan, J. (1998), *Le séminaire, Livre V, Les formations de l'inconscient: 1957–1958*, texte établi par J.-A. Miller, Paris: Seuil.

Lacan, J. (1998), *The Four Fundamental Concepts of Psychoanalysis: Book XI of the Seminar of Jacques Lacan*, New York and London: W. W. Norton & Company.

Lacan, J. (1999), *Le séminaire, Livre VII, L'éthique de la psychanalyse: 1959–1960*, Paris: Publication hors commerce de l'*Association Freudienne Internationale*.

Lacan, J. (2001a), *Le séminaire, Livre VIII, Le transfert: 1960–1961*, texte établi par J.-A. Miller, Paris: Seuil.

Lacan, J. (2002), *Ecrits. A Selection*, Translated by B. Fink, in collaboration with H. Fink and R. Grigg, New York and London: W. W. Norton & Company.

Lacan, J. (2005), *Le séminaire. Livre XXIII, Le sinthome.*, texte établi par J.-A. Miller, Paris: Seuil.

Lacan, J. (2005b), *Triomphe de la religion*, précédé de *Discours aux catholiques*, Paris: Seuil.

Lachance, P. (Réd.) (1995), *Le livre d'Angela de Foligno, d'après les textes originaux*, traduit par J.-F. Godet, présenté par P. Lachanche avec la collaboration de T. Matura, Grenoble: Jérôme Millon.

Lachance, P. (1990). *The Mystical Journey of Angela of Foligno*, Toronto: Peregrina.

Lacoue-Labarthe, P. (1991), "De l'éthique: à propos d'Antigone," in: N. Avtonomova, et al., *Lacan avec les philosophes*, Paris: Albin Michel.

Lacoue-Labarthe, P. and Nancy, J.-L. (1990 [1973]), *Le titre de la lettre. Une lecture de Lacan*, Paris: Galilée.

Lacoue-Labarthe, P. and Nancy, J.-L. (1992), *The Title of the Letter. A Reading of Lacan*, Albany: State University of New York Press.

Landman, P. (1987), "A propos de l'Entwurf," in: *Bulletin de la Convention Psychanalytique* 13: 89–105.

Lapeyre, M. (1997), *Au-delà du complexe d'Oedipe*, Paris: Anthropos & Economica.

Laplanche, J. (1970), *Vie et mort en psychanalyse*, suivi de *Dérivations des entités psychanalytiques*, Collection Champs Flammarion, Paris: Flammarion.

Laplanche, J. (1990), *Life and Death in Psychoanalysis*, translated by J. Mehlman, Baltimore: Johns Hopkins University Press.

Laplanche, J. (1994 [1987]), *Nouveaux fondements pour la psychanalyse*, Collection Quadrige, Paris: Presses Universitaires de France.

Laplanche, J. (1989), *The New Foundations of Psychoanalysis*, translation by D. Macey, Oxford: Basil Backwell.

Laplanche, J. (1992), *La révolution copernicienne inachevée. Travaux 1967–1992*, Paris: Aubier.

Laplanche, J. (1998 [1980–1987]), *Problématiques I–V*, Collection Quadrige, Paris: Presses Universitaires de France.

Laplanche, J. and Pontalis, J.-B. (1967), *Vocabulaire de la psychanalyse*, Paris: Presses Universitaires de France.

Laplanche, J. and Pontalis, J.-B. (1985), *Fantasme originaire. Fantasme des origines. Origines du fantasme*, Paris: Hachette.

Laplanche, J. and Pontalis, J.-B. (1968), "Fantasy and the Origins of Sexuality, Part 1," in: *The International Journal of Psychoanalysis*, 49 (1968): 1–18.

Laplanche J. and Pontalis J.-B. (1988 [1973]), *The Language of Psychoanalysis*, translated by D. Nicholson-Smith, London: Karnak.

Lazar, M. (1964), *Amour Courtois et* Fin'Amor *dans la littérature du XIIIe siècle*, Paris: Klincksieck.

Leclaire, S. (1972), "L'objet a dans la cure," in: *Lettres de l'École freudienne* 9: 422–450.

Leclaire, S. (1987), "La fonction éthique de la psychanalyse," in: J. Zafiropoulos, *Aspects du malaise dans la civilisation*, Paris: Navarin.

Le Gaufey, G. (1975), "Que la psychanalyse n'est pas un idéalisme," in: *Lettres de l'École freudienne*, 16: 55–64.

Le Gaufey, G. (1994), *L'éviction de l'origine*, Paris: Les Éditions E.P.E.L.

Le Gaufey, G. (1997), *Le lasso imaginaire. Une étude traversière de l'unité imaginaire*, Paris: Les Éditions E.P.E.L.

Lely, G. (1967), *Sade. Études sur sa vie et sur son oeuvre*, Paris: Gallimard.

Lévi-Strauss, C. (1956a), "Sur les rapports entre la mythologie et le rituel," in: *Bulletin de la Société Française de Philosophie*, t. XLVIII, 1956.

Lévi-Strauss, C. (1956b), "Les mathématiques de l'homme," in: *Esprit* 24, 10: 525–538.

Marrou, H.-I. (1971), *Les troubadours*, Paris: Seuil.

Micheli-Rechtman, V. (1992), "Aristote et la question du réel dans l'éthique," in: *Littoral* 36: 83–95.

Miller, J.-A. (1981), "La topologie dans l'ensemble de l'enseignement de Lacan," in: *Quarto* 2: 13–29.

Miller, J.-A. (1982–83), *Séminaire 1982–83: Du symptôme au fantasme et retour*, onuitgegeven typoscript.

Miller, J.-A. (2000), "L'apologue de «saint Martin et son manteau," in: *Mental* 7: 7–25.

Millot, C. (1982), "La sublimation, création ou réparation?" *Ornicar?* 25: 70–74.

Milman, M. (1992 [1982]), *Le trompe-l'oeil. Les illusions de la réalité*, Genève, Skira.

Montaigne, M. de (2003), *The Complete Essays*, translated by A. Screech, London: Penguin Books.

Moyaert, P. (1994), *Ethiek en sublimatie*, Nijmegen: SUN.

Muller, J. P. and Richardson W. J., *Lacan and Language: A Reader's Guide to Écrits*, New York: International Universities Press.

Muller, J. (1987), "Lacan's view of sublimation," in: *The American Journal of Psychoanalysis* 4/4: 315–323.

Nasio, J.-D. (1987), *Les Yeux de Laure. Transfert, objet a et topologie dans la théorie de J. Lacan*, Collection Champs Flammarion, Paris: Flammarion.

Nelli, R. (1963), *L'érotique des troubadours*, Toulouse: Privat.

Nelli, R. (1977), *Écrivains anticonformistes du moyen-âge occitan. 1. La Femme et l'Amour*, Paris: Phébus.

Nobus, D. (1996), "Het subject als wezenloos fundament. Omtrent Lacans verwerping van de subjectieve autonomie," in: J. Doormael (red.), *Ik & het verhaal*, Hasselt: W&A.

Nussbaum, C. M. (1986), *The Fragility of Goodness: Luck and Ethics in Greek Tragedy and Philosophy*, Cambridge: Cambridge University Press.

Nygren, A. (1982 [1953]), *Agape and Eros*, London: SPCK.

Ogden, C. K. (1932), *Theory of Fictions*, London and New York: Kegan Paul, Trench, Tubner & Co & Brace & Co.

Palomera, V. (1995), "*Das Ding* and sublimation," in: *Analysis* 6: 115–119.

Pascal, B. (1995), *Pensées and Other Writings*, translation by H. Levy, Oxford / New York: Oxford University Press.

Pauvert, J.-J. (1990), *Sade Vivant: 'Cet écrivain à jamais célèbre 1793–1814*, Paris: Robert Laffont.

Philonenko, A. (1993), *L'oeuvre de Kant. La philosophie critique I & II*, Paris: Vrin.

Peraldi, F. (1987), "The Thing for Freud and the Freudian Thing," in: *The American Journal of Psychoanalysis* 47/4: 309–314.

Plato, (1978 [1963]), *The Collected Dialogues of Plato Including the Letters*, Edited by E. Hamilton and H. Cairns, Princeton: Princeton University Press.

Porge, E. (1976), "Sur la chose," in: *Lettres de l'école freudienne* 18: 158–165.

Porge, E. (1989), *Se compter trois. Le temps logique de Lacan*, Toulouse, Érès.

Rajchman, J. (1991), *Truth and Eros. Foucault, Lacan and the Question of Ethics*, New York and London: Routledge.

Raffoul, F. (1998), "Lacan and the event of the subject," in: H. J. Silverman, *Cultural Semiosis: Tracing the Signifier*, New York and London: Routledge.

Raspe, R. E. (2003), *The Surprising Adventures of Baron Munchausen*, Rockville: Wildside Press.

Reichler, C. (1987), *L'âge libertin*, Paris: Les Éditions de Minuit.

Rey-Flaud, H. (1983), *La névrose courtoise*, Paris: Navarin.

Rilke, R. M. (1977 [1939]), *Duino Elegies,* translation, introduction, and comment by J. B. Leishman and S. Spender, London: Chatto and Windus.

Rogozinski, J. (1999), *Le don de la loi. Kant et l'énigme de l'éthique*, Paris: Presses Universitaires de France.

Roudinesco, E. (1986), *La bataille de cent ans. Histoire de la psychanalyse en France. 2 (1925–1985)*, Paris: Seuil.

Roudinesco, E. (1990), *Jacques Lacan and Co: a History of Psychoanalysis in France 1925–1985*, Chicago: University of Chicago Press.

Roudinesco, E. (1993), *Jacques Lacan. Esquisse d'une vie, histoire d'un système de pensée*, Paris: Fayard.

Roudinesco, E. (1997), *Jacques Lacan*, translated by B. Bray, New York: Comumbia University Press.

Roudinesco, E. and Plon, M. (1997), *Dictionnaire de la psychanalyse*, Paris: Fayard.

Sade, D. (1968), *Juliette*, translated by A. Wainhouse, New York: Grove Press.

Sade, D. (1976), *La Philosophie dans le boudoir ou Les Instituteurs immoraux*, Paris: Gallimard.

Sade, D. (1987), *Oeuvres Complètes I–XV*, mise en place par A. Lebrun et J. J. Pauvert, Paris: Pauvert.

Sade, D. (1991), *Three complete Novels: Justine, Philosophy in the Bedroom, Egénie de Franval, and Other Writings*, London: Arrow Books.

Sade, D. (2005), *The Complete Marquis de Sade*, translation by P. J. Gilette, Los Angeles: Holloway.

Saïd, S. (1978), *La faute tragique*, Paris: Français Maspero.

Saint-Just, L. A. (1957), *Discours et rapports*, Introduction et notes par A. Soboul, Paris: Éditions sociales.

Saint-Just, L. A. (1984), *Oeuvres complètes*, Paris: Lebovici.

Schokker, J. and Schokker, T. (2000), *Extimiteit. Jacques Lacans terugkeer naar Freud*, Amsterdam: Boom.

Shakespeare, W. (1978), *The Complete Words of William Shakespeare*, edited with a glossary by W. J. Craig, London: Henry Prodes.

Shapin, S. (1998), *The Scientific Revolution*, Chicago: University of Chicago Press.

Shapin, S. (1998), *La révolution scientifique*, Paris: Flammarion.

Sjöholm, c. (1998), "The Atè of Antigone; Lacan, Heidegger and Sexual Difference," in: *New Formations* 35: 122–133.

Soboul, A. (1982), *La civilisation et la Révolution Française. II. La Révolution Française*, Paris: Arthaud.

Sophocle, (1947), *Théatre de Sophocle*. Traduction nouvelle avec texte, introduction et notes par Robert Pignarre, tome deuxième, Paris: Garnier.

Sophocles, (1884 [1982]), *The Three Theban Plays: Antigone, Oedipus the King, Oedipus at Colonos*, translated by R. Fagles, introduction and notes by B. Knox, New York and London: Penguin Books.

Sophocles, (2002 [1994]), *Sophocles*, edited and translated by H. Lloyd-Jones, Loeb Classical Library 21, Cambridge. Mass.: Harvard University Press.

Soubbotnik, M. A. (1992), "Le tissu de la fiction: approche de Bentham," in: *Littoral* 36: 65–81.

Stendhal (1959), *De l'amour*, Paris: Armand Colin.

Steiner, G. (1986[1984]), *Antigones. The Antigone Myth in Western Literature, Art and Thought*, Oxford: Oxford University Press.

Sulloway, F. J. (1979), *Freud, Biologist of the Mind. Beyond the Psychoanalytic Legend*, London: Burnett Books.

Turnheim, M. (1998), "L'amour du prochain," in: *La lettre mensuelle de l'École de la cause freudienne*, décembre 1998: 1–8.

Vailland, R. (1972 [1957]), *La loi*, Paris: Gallimard.

Vailland, R. (1985), *The Law: A Novel*, translation by P. Wiles, preface by J. Keates, London: Eland Books.

Valas, P. (1998), *Les dimensions de la jouissance. Du mythe de la pulsion à la dérive de la jouissance*, Paris: Éditions Érès.

Vanden Berghe, P. (1994), "Lacan lecteur de Simmel: une étrange alliance," in: S. Lofts and P. Moyaert, *La pensée de Jacques Lacan: Questions historiques—Problèmes théoriques*, Leuven & Louvain and Paris: Peeters & Éditions de l'Institut Supérieure de Philosophie.

Vaysse, J.-M. (1999), *L'inconscient des modernes. Essai sur l'origine métaphysique de la psychanalyse*, Paris: Gallimard.

Verbruggen, G. (1999), "Van doodsdrift naar violence fondamentale," in: *Tijdschrift voor Psychoanalyse* 5/2: 89–101.

Vereecken, C. (1988), "Lectures de Sade," in *Ornicar?* 47: 105–111.

Vergote, A. (1988), *Guilt and Desire*, Yale University Press.

Vergote, A. (1997), *La psychanalyse à l'épreuve de la sublimation*, Paris: les éditions du Cerf.

Vernant, J.-P. (1972), "Tensions et ambiguïtés dans la tragedie," in: J.-P. Vernant and P. Vidal-Naquet, *Mythe et tragédie en Grèce ancienne*, Paris: Éditions de la découverte.

Wajcman, G. (1999), *Collection, suivi de L'avarice*, Caen: Nous.

Walsch, J. (1963), *Aristotle's Conception of Moral Weakness*, New York: Columbia University Press.

Weil, S. (1948), *La pesanteur et la Grâce*, Paris: Plon.

Weil, S. (1987), *Gravity and Grace*, translated by G. Thibon, London: Routledge.

Whitebook, J. (1996 [1995]), *Perversion and Utopia. A Study in Psychoanalysis and Critical Theory*, Cambridge, Mass. and London: The MIT Press.

Zenoni, A. (1993), "La biologie de la psychanalyse," in: *Quarto* 52: 93–99.

Žižek, S. (1988), *Le plus sublime des hystériques: Hegel passe*, Paris: Point Hors Ligne.

Žižek, S. (1989), *The Sublime Object of Ideology*, London and New York: Verso.

Žižek, S. (1991a), *Looking Awry: An Introduction to Jacques Lacan through Popular Culture*, Cambridge, Mass. and London: The MIT Press.

Žižek, S. (1991b), *For They Know Not What They Do. Enjoyment as a Political Factor*, London and New York: Verso.

Žižek, S. (1997), *The Plague of Fantasies*, London and New York: Verso.

Zupančič, A. (1995), *Die Ethik des Realen. Kant, Lacan*, Wien: Turia and Kant.

Zupančič, A. (2000), *Ethics of the Real. Kant, Lacan*, London and New York: Verso.

# Index